The Land and the Loom

The Land and the Loom

PEASANTS AND PROFIT

IN NORTHERN FRANCE

1680–1800   **LIANA VARDI**

DUKE UNIVERSITY PRESS   1993   Durham and London

For Jon

© 1993 Duke University Press
All rights reserved
Printed in the United States of America
on acid-free paper ∞
Library of Congress Cataloging-in-Publication Data
appear on the last printed page of this book.

Contents

Tables and Figures

Tables

Figures

Preface

People outside the profession, and even inside, periodically ask me how I came to work on rural industry. With the passage of time, they have probably become more curious, rather than less, and that reflects the change in direction of historical studies, away from economic history. My original interest in French economic development grew out of the debates on the nature of the bourgeois revolution. It seemed natural, then, that one way to answer that question would be to examine the economic legislation of the Constituent Assembly, and I proceeded to write a masters thesis, under the direction of George Rudé, on the abolition of the guilds. While working on the guild system, I became interested in its counterpart, that is, unregulated production, and especially in trying to understand how this alternate system functioned—something that the secondary literature available at the time did not really explain to my satisfaction. Franklin Mendels had recently enunciated his theory of proto-industrialization, and while it provided a framework for discussing the problem of rural industry, it still remained vague about the actual mechanisms and organization of this sector and about its effects on village society. I was not especially interested in the demographic aspects that seemed pivotal to most students of proto-industry at the time, and so did not place my work within the context of "proto-industrialization" as such. My perspective was that of the village. I wanted to know how industry came to the countryside, how it affected the peasant economy, and what role the villagers played in the system. And so my dissertation focused on a microanalysis of a particular place, tracing developments over time and following individual careers. It also looked at the peasants' connections with the outside world and at the broader economic forces that affected them.

Because my questions tended to be technical, that is, concerned with understanding "how things worked," I let a vision of the peasant world emerge, one where peasants were actively involved in shaping their own lives. This challenged other approaches to the peasantry so that my work placed itself within the ongoing debate about the nature of peasant society. What began, then, as an interest in the Old Regime economy turned into an inquiry into rural society, and a statement about its dynamism and its importance to economic development.

This book argues the economic vitality of the countryside. It looks at the ways in which peasants responded to the opportunities offered by a growing market economy in a particular region of France, Cambrésis, and within it, a specific village, Montigny. Peasant options and peasant actions only make sense through a detailed examination of the local context. But, if the local context explains specific developments in northern France, such as the peasants' involvement in the linen trade, the approach and general arguments extend beyond the specific example and apply to the rest of France and to peasants in general. I view peasants not merely as victims of circumstances and of more powerful groups in society, but as people actively involved in the economy of their times.

In the process of thinking out these issues and of reworking the dissertation into a book, I have benefited from the help, suggestions, and support of numerous people. Pierre Boulle directed the thesis at McGill University, and Franklin Mendels, who did so much to stimulate interest in rural industry, was the external reader for the dissertation. I would like to thank as well Robert Forster, George Grantham, and Steven Kaplan, early readers of the work, and especially John Merriman for his enthusiastic response to Montigny and his unflagging interest in its fate. My thanks also to Daniel Hickey, Philip Hoffman, Gilles Postel-Vinay, Donald Sutherland, and David Troyansky, who commented on various portions, Christopher Johnson for his strong endorsement, and other readers for the press for their suggestions. Part of the Introduction first appeared in the *Proceedings of the Western Society for French History,* vol. 17 (1990), and I am grateful to the editors for permission to reprint it. It has been a pleasure dealing with Lawrence Malley and his staff—Pam Morrison, Bob Mirandon, and Cherie Westmoreland.

The Social Sciences and Humanities Research Council of Canada and the Quebec Ministry of Education provided funding for the research; the staff of the Archives départementales du Nord, and especially Henri Guy, were gracious and helpful; and I remain grateful, as always, to those people associated with the years of research and writing: Luce Abélès, Gail Bossenga, Véronique Demars, Pierre and Solange Deyon, Mike Fitzsimmons, Philippe Guignet, Jean Pierre Hirsch, Stuart Juzda, Françoise Levioux, Judith Miller, Robert Muchembled, Michael Sibalis, and my children, Nicolas and Elise, who have lived with this project all of their lives. The book, in its present form, owes much to the stimulating discussions I had with Jonathan Dewald. I am indebted to him, in more ways than I can express, for his encouragement and support, and for the joy he brings into my life.

Conversion Table

Area

one mencaudée = 35.46 ares or .3546 hectare
The mencaudée contained four boitelées, sixteen pintes, and 100 verges.

Capacity

pinte =   3.46 litres
boisseau = 13.85 litres
mencaud = 55.12 litres
rasière = 83.13 litres
rasière of wheat = 70.11 litres

Currency

A florin divided into 20 patars, each patar containing 25 doubles.
A livre divided into 20 sous, each sou containing 12 deniers.
The florin was worth 1.20 livres, or 25 sous.

Figure 1. Map of France

Introduction

This is a book about peasants, about a village, about a region. It seeks to understand how these people acted, the nature of their goals and ambitions, the constraints under which they labored. Literature has not always been kind to the peasants, even when it does not fall into Balzacian excesses. Consider the opening of George Eliot's novel of village life, *Silas Marner*.

> To the peasants of old times, the world outside their own direct experience was a region of vagueness and mystery: to their untravelled thought a state of wandering was a conception as dim as the winter life of the swallows that came back with the spring; and even a settler, if he came from distant parts, hardly ever ceased to be viewed with a remnant of distrust . . . especially if he had any reputation for knowledge, or showed any skill in handicraft. All cleverness, whether in the rapid use of that difficult instrument the tongue, or in some other art unfamiliar to villagers, was in itself suspicious: honest folk, born and bred in a visible manner, were mostly not over-wise or clever—at least, not beyond such a matter as knowing the signs of the weather; and the process by which rapidity and dexterity of any kind were acquired was so wholly hidden, that they partook of the nature of conjuring.[1]

Such misapprehensions have not totally disappeared, for we remain the heirs of a complicated relationship to the peasants, one that viewed them either as the repositories of pristine innocence and virtue, or else as the manifestations of all that was nasty, brutish, and at best dull. Twentieth-century social scientists have not disdained such contrasts, and Robert Redfield compared the sober, hardworking, God-fearing peasants of northern Europe with those southern Italians for whom work was hateful, unending drudgery.[2] Is the choice still between Bergman and Fellini?

What were the peasants really like? The question involves more than simple curiosity, for preconceptions about the peasantry underlie so much of the work on rural economies. Since 1900, historians have devoted studies to the peasantry that have relied increasingly on theoretical paradigms borrowed from anthropology, economics, and sociology. These approaches, this book will suggest, continue to exhibit traits manifested in Eliot's literary vision. Despite generations of fine research, we continue to see the early modern peasants as suspicious of the outside world and committed to age-old routines. In these pages an alternative vision of the peasantry is suggested, one that emphasizes their adaptation to economic change and that integrates them within the rest of society.

The most famous and still most influential examination of the French peasantry remains Marc Bloch's *Les Caractères originaux de l'histoire rurale française,* published in 1931.[3] Bloch brought to the peasantry the legacy of geographical and legal perspectives that emphasized the constraints of terrain and institutions. His argument went as follows. The basic features of the French countryside devolved from a mixture of geographical and historical circumstances. He distinguished between three zones: the long-furlonged northern open fields, the irregularly patterned, square-shape fields of the south, and the enclosed Western *bocage.* These reflected the nature of the soil—heavy, light, and marshy, respectively—as well as what he termed different "civilizations." By different, he meant that natural factors, accidents of terrain, period, and extent of land clearance, and especially the search for grazing grounds stimulated a collectivist mentality in the north while allowing for greater individualism in the south and west.[4] The northern plains adopted a system of triennial rotation of crops on the village's arable (with peasants owning plots in each of the sections), together with animal pasture on the fallow (for lack of available space). These required both uniformity and the cooperation of the villagers. Developed out of necessity and refined through practice, this arrangement then solidified into rigid requirements supported by custom and legal codes. Bloch alternated between descriptions of agricultural methods and judgments about human behavior. His peasants had needs, embodied in their communal organization (or lack thereof), which in turn shaped their consciousness to such an extent that they rejected innovation. The failure of the Physiocrats and of the Revolution to change traditional outlooks and break this collective mentality demonstrated the resilience of these deep-rooted modes of "civilization."

Bloch attributed French agricultural backwardness to the weakness of large-scale agriculture and the strength of village communities. He took England as his model and the northern open fields as the natural cradle of progress. For though he gave Norman individualism and growing specialization or the more varied husbandry of the south their due, still the traditionalism of the corn belt cast its shadow over France. "The full story of man's liberation from fallow farming . . . has yet to be written."[5] Bloch's emphasis on the linkage and immutability of practices and outlooks minimizes the historical process. The early modern peasant acted no differently from his forebears, except in the new challenges he met. The patterns conditioned by geography and reinforced by time were still recognizable in Bloch's own day. "In some regions, especially of long-furlong fields, which happen to be among the most fertile, the ancient lay-out of the fields has scarcely altered and dictates the continuation of agrarian habits for which it was originally designed."[6]

This determinism has not gone unchallenged and has found at least one answer in the recently published work of Jean Meuvret, who argued that whatever constraints existed were pragmatic rather than inherently fixed and that agricultural stagnation in the period he studied, the seventeenth century, might better be attributed to ill-organized markets.[7]

Nonetheless, Bloch's central theme—the interplay between natural and social factors—has been the mainstay of *Annales* historiography. A series of studies of the early modern French peasantry informed by this methodology appeared in the 1960s and 1970s. These studies asked very broad questions about French agricultural performance and ascribed its limitations to climate, prices, and demographic instability, as well as antiquated husbandry and routine. With slight variations (climate is the obvious exception), these factors repeatedly came into play, imposing a ceiling on production. Malthusianism replaced communalism as an explanatory framework, and it served the same purposes as Bloch's work did: aligning the forces of progress against those of tradition, and with the same constancy. Historical events were played out against basic structural limitations.

The relationship between peasant mentality and agricultural productivity remained a persistent theme of this literature, even when not its explicit focus. When such historians as Pierre Goubert and Emmanuel Le Roy Ladurie asked why France was backward, they answered that its peasantry was tradition-bound. They expressed this position clearly in popular textbooks: "These millions of country people were securely rooted in their way of life through their small social cells (the household family or *domus*) and through their mental or to be more precise, spiritual structures: religion bound them to the country of the dead and to hope in a supra-terrestrial salvation of which Christianity, with a strong admixture of folklore, provided the main outlines."[8] Goubert put it even more strongly: "They preserved all the fears, panics, brutality, and submission in a kind of obscure mental recess."[9] Rebelliousness was mitigated by "a kind of stupefaction caused by a non-existent, even positively damaging cultural life, [which would] more often result in the listless acceptance of dull, fitful mediocrity."[10] Thus, dragging this ball and chain, French agriculture could advance only fitfully in cyclical rises followed by rapid decline. Population growth upset the ecological equilibrium, stretching resources to the point where dearth and epidemic took their toll and restored a more advantageous balance. The real breakthrough came in the eighteenth century with the retreat of plague and famine and under the dynamic leadership of large seigneurial farms.

French Marxist historiography has shared a large number of these assumptions. Although Marx himself mistrusted the peasantry, whom he viewed as reactionary, Marxist students of French rural society have attempted to liberate peasants from such stigmas. For them, the peasant was more sinned against than sinning. He not only bore the burden of feudal exactions, but he suffered other encroachments on his livelihood. Seigneurs trying to secure their incomes—for profit or profligacy—monopolized local resources such as forests and commons with the connivance of the state. As the wheat trade grew more profitable and agriculture became more commercialized, the peasant became the victim of a three-pronged attack: from seigneurs, from royal finances, and from capitalist incursions into the countryside.[11] Such outside intrusions clashed with his vision of the world. The peasant participated in a moral economy with its own set of expectations and particular logic.

Georges Lefebvre was especially influential in showing that peasants had specific interests that diverged from those of other social groups.[12] Marxist historians did not claim that the rural community was idyllic, but that need and entitlement were considered more important than property rights.[13] The peasants aspired to self-sufficiency and felt they were entitled to this basic livelihood. Taken a step further, this argument came to mean that peasants mistrusted profit and accumulation. Consonant with this view, the peasants fought a separate battle during the Revolution to realize their particular aims. This interpretation of a peasant phase of the Revolution, put forward by Lefebvre, has become a commonplace.[14]

Both Annalistes and Marxists thus take as their starting point peasant yearning for autonomy, self-sufficiency, and land. If definitions of the peasantry are often subsumed within descriptions of rural society, it is because it is understood that a peasant is in fact defined by the amount of land available to him. This assumption arises in part from the historical records themselves, which rank the peasantry according to legal/feudal categories or taxable units based primarily on property. A peasant who at one time had been either free or enserfed would now be classed according to the amount and quality of the land at his disposal. His place in the pyramid depended on his degree of self-sufficiency. In the French context this generally meant separating the ploughmen, or *laboureurs,* from the smaller tenants or landowners whose holdings hovered near or below economic viability.[15] Beneath, there followed a throng of landless or near-landless unfortunates: a rural proletariat of day laborers, cottage workers, vagrants, and beggars.

Historians have generally presumed that the categories that their documents employed reflected real levels of economic dependence and independence. The less land the peasants had, the more they relied on supplementary sources of income, the more fragile and more marginal their position. They were peasants, in fact, because they had the right aspirations: they wanted *more* land. And they rarely got it. For the irony of such definitions is that one finds so few "pure" peasants in Western Europe, and this was true from the Middle Ages on. M. M. Postan defined the peasant as "an occupying owner or tenant of a small holding capable, but only just capable of providing his family with a 'subsistence income,'" and went on to say that in the thirteenth century "the great mass of smallholders" fell below that level.[16] The same pattern recurs century after century. Rural society is divided into a hierarchy of yeomen, rich farmers, or laboureurs, followed by the "real" peasantry—that group of subsistence farmers, shrinking or expanding accordion-like depending on the time or region but never exceeding half of the population, always on the brink of pauperization—and then by a "vast majority" of property-less wage earners. In seventeenth-century France one-half to nine-tenths of rural households could not survive without supplementary incomes.[17] In the eighteenth century, with the rise in population and continued fragmentation of landholdings, 85 percent of the peasants of the Nord, for example, could not live off their land and needed to work as laborers for others. Where then the peasantry? Should one conclude that such statistics imply "the end of the peasantry, since the essence of peasant society is that the basic form of productive labour within it is that of the peasant family living on its own holdings"?[18] One need not throw out the baby with the bathwater, as Alan Macfarlane did for England, and deny that France had a peasantry just because it does not fit the standard definitions.[19] Rather, the parameters need to be reshaped to take in the realities of rural life, the fact that the countryside consisted of people who divided their time between agrarian occupations and other pursuits.[20]

A similar emphasis therefore marks all of these approaches. Peasant society is treated as a separate entity where all aspects connect: agriculture, social structure, and mentality. What is more, peasants form the major stumbling blocks to progress, even if unwittingly. Their demands are so minimal and self-contained that they operate outside the sphere of broader economic forces. They have their own outlook, goals, roles, and expectations, though they may be drawn into the market and necessary contacts with the politico-juridical apparatus that surrounds them. The dominant image remains that of a holistic if part-society—a world within a world. "The peasant stands, as it were, at the center of a series of concentric circles, each circle marked by specialists with whom he shares less and less experience, with whom he entertains fewer and fewer common understandings."[21] Peasants enter outside relationships only reluctantly and in a subservient position.[22] "Their economic, social, political, and cultural dependence was total and as a rule they could hope for no improvement."[23] The peasant ideal remains rooted in community, land, and the survival of the household. "The family farm operates as the major unit of peasant property, production, consumption, welfare, social reproduction, identity, prestige, sociability and welfare."[24]

These last citations do not come from historians but from the anthropologist Eric Wolf and the sociologist Theodor Shanin. They demonstrate the degree of overlap between current anthropological and sociological models and the long-standing assumptions of French historiography. Wolf and Shanin adopted formulations that combined a leftist perspective with the findings of the Russian economist A. V. Chayanov, whose theory of the peasant economy centered on the use of household labor.[25] Shanin's popular sociological *Reader* contains a standard definition of the peasantry. It first appeared in 1971 and reemerged, unchanged, in the revised edition of 1987. Shanin listed the four elements that gave the peasants a separate identity:

1. The peasant family farm as the basic unit of multidimensional social organization.
2. Land husbandry as the main means of livelihood directly providing the major part of the consumption needs.
3. Specific traditional culture related to the way of life of small communities.
4. The underdog position—the domination of peasantry by outsiders.[26]

There is nothing here that would either shock or surprise the Marxists or Annalistes. In fact, this is their working definition. Both give primacy to material factors and long-term movements, to the basic agricultural unit and to a traditional mentality. Though change eventually comes to the countryside (and they might disagree on its origins), they would accept this fundamentally static definition of rural society. For the four features outlined by Shanin, or the ones espoused by Wolf, are meant to fit all or most peasant societies with minor tinkering to incorporate specific instances. We are told that reality is more complex, but that the scholar must examine specific examples within the framework of the general model.[27]

Emphasis on the specificity of peasant societies derives partly from a concern to grant peasants their own identity. It also devolves from a belief that peasants' economic motives differ from those of more modern economic actors. Economic anthropologists thus separate primitive, peasant, and industrial economies, even if they do not necessarily agree that these represent various stages of development.[28] For Raymond Firth, peasant economies are not the same as industrial economies, but they share similar characteristics with differing emphases. Karl Polanyi and George Dalton express a more radical view when they argue that the categories used by economists derive from and apply solely to market economies and have little or nothing to do with societies organized under other guiding principles. Markets do exist in nonindustrial economies, but their role is peripheral. The supraeconomic elements in exchange weigh more heavily than simple profit maximization. Motivations are different. "Economic man" is not a universal phenomenon but a late eighteenth-century invention suited only to the economy for which he was conceived.

For anthropologists like Firth, the interesting questions are how societies allocate resources and organize exchange, what options they have, and what kind of social organization this entails. Polanyi's and Dalton's belief that capitalism brought unmitigated disaster lends a golden glow to primitive and peasant societies where more humane relations are presumed to obtain. There, the market principle does not dictate actions. Commodity exchange is ruled as much by gift-giving and redistribution of goods by the powers-that-be. Peasants may resort to markets, of course, but they disdain a "market culture." To understand the economic organization of a society, one must therefore begin by understanding its culture, for the culture will determine how it treats production and exchange. Anthropologists may still be interested in social and economic organization, but one of the dominant trends today, and one that has taken hold of the historical imagination, is the primacy accorded to culture in the explanation of societies—and culture defined primarily as a system of symbols and meanings.[29]

Marshall Sahlins exemplifies this position. Though he shares Polanyi's vision of a fundamental difference between peasant and capitalist societies, his focus has moved to isolating the cultural mechanisms that allow one set of structures to evolve into another. This interest has led him to explore the historical accidents that shake the existing order.[30] Part of his concern is to bridge the gap between anthropology and history and redress the former's tendency to favor structure over event and permanence over change. But Sahlins deals less with historical description than with the symbolic apprehension of reality. He looks for links between economy, polity, society, and culture and sees the last as joining all the strands. Societies are embodied in their cultures, and culture is the expression of an internal coherence whose signs and symbols need to be decoded. Historical changes then become primarily changes in *meaning,* which in turn affect structures and social organization.

The task of the anthropologist (and that of the historian in tow) then is to interpret the cultures he examines, to make sense of a coherent but alien perspective. For the anthropologist, this interlocking system of meaning can be observed in even the smallest of units, the village community. Here, Clifford Geertz and his "thick descriptions" offer tempting models for the historian trying to breathe life into microhistory.[31] The village is treated as a microcosm whose essence is embodied in cultural codes. Links with the outside can be important, but what is significant occurs within the village. For this reason, cultural anthropology, despite its stimulating insights, can provide only a partial guide for the historian trying to understand rural society. Preoccupation with the internal dynamics of the village obscures the wider societal context. The focus on cultural norms underplays other aspects of peasant experience. In fundamentals, I am arguing, the new anthropology does not diverge from the old social history. Categories used by Bloch under the term civilization reappear in Wolf, Shanin, and the new cultural anthropology. All emphasize the rigidity of peasant structures, the isolation of peasant culture, and above all the very close linkages among all aspects of peasant society.

At the other end of the spectrum, the network of exchanges that connect the village to the outer world has been the principal concern of students of rural industry. Over the past twenty years this literature has sought to understand how cottage industry came to be implanted in certain regions, how it affected the peasants that it touched, and how "proto-industrialization" relates to the Industrial Revolution as a whole.[32] Since proto-industry is defined as manufacture for export carried out in the countryside (unlike occasional cottage production for local needs), it quite naturally involves the world beyond the village.

Studies of proto-industry, then, focus on two issues: the economics of trade, and the social consequences of trade for its participants. In both cases, old views of the peasants remain surprisingly present. The rural artisan is no longer physically bounded by the village, but he remains a prisoner either of a traditional mentality or of economic forces he cannot control. Essentially, he is merely the lowest element in a process that involves producers, suppliers, and merchants. Rural participation in the trade is viewed in simple terms: the producers are either "independent" artisans who sell their product to urban merchants, or they are "dependent" on suppliers. Whatever the case, they rarely do more; the motors of economic activity are elsewhere, in the cities. Those few villagers who are involved in marketing activities, as middlemen, are generally viewed as belonging to the farming elite or as having a separate status within the village.[33] Some historians have gone even further and argued the villagers' fundamental inaptitude for the entrepreneurial role. They underline the peasants' preference for leisure over profits and their rootedness in traditional cultural patterns.[34] Thus, Hans Medick speaks of workers turning "to the traditional leisure time rituals in which 'plebeian culture' found its expression. Rising money incomes and a decreasing inclination toward work resulted in an increased dynamic of socio-cultural reproduction," leading to expenditures that could only seem irrational within a bourgeois calculus.[35]

The peasants did not engage in entrepreneurial activities, then, for two reasons: there was no room for them in a system essentially controlled by big merchants, and their traditional outlook was not suited to such capitalist pursuits. The same arguments figure in explanations of the spread of rural industry and its consequences. Rural industry emerged, it is typically argued, in response to poverty and the need to find supplementary incomes. Participation in artisanal production provided only a temporary solution to these difficulties, however, because peasants misconstrued and misused it. They approached production in traditional terms, as a means of preserving their old way of life. They saw their earnings as offering them a way to stay in the village and hold on to a parcel of their inheritance. Wages, however, showed them that they could survive without land, and they began, instead, to define their status in terms of consumption. This encouraged overexpenditure and subsequent impoverishment; their dependence on wages led to early marriage and rapid population growth, upsetting traditional balances between people and land. Indeed, villagers might deliberately seek large families, for in their situation labor would determine economic success.[36]

For there are, apparently, only clear-cut winners and losers in this process. The peasants had to acquire another, alien mentality to succeed in business. Most could not because they remained locked in a noncapitalist and even anticapitalist outlook, an outlook averse to risk-taking.[37] Yet they did not preserve their old world either, a number of historians contend, because industrial work and its wages increasingly removed them from peasant values and especially from attachment to the land. Paul Bois in his study of the West clearly differentiates textile workers from the rest of the peasantry: "their occupation, their lifestyle, their interests, their connections set them apart from the true peasantry."[38] Myron Gutmann also emphasizes the difference between rural artisans and "the peasants among whom they lived. . . . They performed different work and had a different attitude toward the land."[39] Hans Medick takes this further and suggests that artisanal work involved new dangers that widened the gap between rural workers and peasants: "coffee, tea, and alcohol became necessary stimulants as the conditions of production deteriorated and work became more degrading," while at the same time "sensuality and sexuality could develop much more freely in the peer group socialization of rural artisans than was possible in a community of peasant proprietors."[40] More than work and property, then, separated the peasant from the rural artisan. The differences extended to all aspects of life. Peasants and rural artisans had nothing left in common. Jerome Blum puts this argument in dramatic terms: "In districts where a large proportion of the population earned their living from rural industry, severe tensions developed between these people and those who depended primarily upon agriculture. The industrial peasants had little or no reason to concern themselves with the problems and operations of communal agriculture, or with the preservation of the village communal organization and its communal agricultural resources."[41] In fact, historians have always found it difficult to deal with residents of the countryside who relied on nonagricultural income.[42] Georges Lefebvre devoted only ten pages to rural industry in his massive study of the peasants of the Nord, although textile production occupied as many as two-thirds of households in some parts of the department.

Ultimately, studies of proto-industrialization have offered a bleak view of rural society. Rural industry failed to integrate villagers within the capitalist order because, although they learned how to function within it, their role remained passive. They became detached from agrarian concerns without fully adopting bourgeois values. Capitalism did not offer rural producers new alternatives in the way that it did for other members of society.[43] Rural producers had no way of making the system work for them since it was serving other interests, and their involvement brought them only hardship: it impoverished them and it destroyed their traditional culture.

This study examines a village—Montigny, on the northern plains of Cambrésis—in which industry came to play an important role during the eighteenth century, and in certain respects its experiences confirm the version of events that historians of proto-industrialization have developed. The peasants and rural artisans did "lose" in the end, with the specialization that accompanied the Industrial Revolution. Some zones industrialized and others deindustrialized, and in the process rural industry fell under the strict control of the towns. Even during rural industry's eighteenth-century heyday, numerous peasants failed to profit from it.

But in important ways Montigny's eighteenth-century history suggests an entirely different reading of the impact of rural industry—and of village society more generally. In the eighteenth century, and in some measure even in the nineteenth, the system of rural industry allowed for active participation by the rural population.[44] Peasant entrepreneurship existed and without it rural industry could not have flourished the way it did. Indeed, one could even argue that it is in the eighteenth-century countryside that one encounters entrepreneurship in its purest, most unregulated form.

This implies that rural producers were not afraid to take risks, were not afraid of investments, and were open to new ideas. This does not mean that they based everything on "rational" calculations. There were areas in which tradition remained an important guide and treasured security. Human activity is not always coherent. There is no necessary connection between religious practices, however superstitious, and cropping methods, between enjoying a beer at the pub and a leisure preference that neglects any form of profit. The early modern peasantry demonstrates how easily different impulses can coincide and how life can be compartmentalized. For the village is not a microcosm. It is but a way station in a series of exchanges and complex relationships. Montigny's peasants saw farther than the farm gates and the village boundaries. Their connections to the world beyond were dynamic, born out of a mixture of necessity and response to opportunity. Given that only a minority could live off the land, the remainder had to search for alternate sources of income. It is important to remember that this was the case from the Middle Ages on. The peasant economy was perforce a complex economy. Whatever the ideal, and it may well have been autonomy (which is not the same as autarky), peasants were willing to take risks in order to attain it. In the eighteenth century in particular, rural industry offered them chances for economic improvement, and they responded by taking chances.

The argument in this book is that peasants did not merely contend with the outside world; they actively sought such contacts and inserted themselves within far-flung networks. They saw no antithesis between a world ruled by tradition and another governed by profit-making and competition. They partook of both and used both. When peasant attitudes to the land are examined, this mixture of "old" and "new" will become evident. Peasants clung to their acquired rights and familial claims on leaseholds because they provided a safeguard. At the same time, they speculated with their own property, buying, selling, and mortgaging it to raise funds for craft-related activities. This did not "unpeasant" them.

In the region I examined, weavers remained actively involved with the rural community. This relationship was the more important to them because cottage industry operated in a context of risk-taking and competitiveness that recognized few allegiances. The organization of trade in the second half of the eighteenth century encouraged country weavers to market cloth and to act as independent suppliers to urban wholesale merchants who handled foreign sales. Credit mechanisms allowed a growing number of weavers to expand their activities and enter the trade, and this climate of opportunity reduced their community of interests. Since expansion had its limits, the success of one venture implied the failure of another. Trade and industry in the eighteenth-century countryside became an experiment in unfettered capitalism. The weavers only recognized mutual affinities once the system collapsed in the late 1780s and competition presented more of a threat than an opportunity. The series of prerevolutionary bankruptcies brought a call for controls over the scale of individual enterprises that recalled urban guild regulations.

Since cottage industry and rural trade did not evoke corporate feelings and the community did not meddle in industrial production, weavers and merchant-weavers relied on older associations. Some of these associations were personal, and villagers still expected kin support, even for industrial ventures. Most importantly, all local residents—be they weavers, merchants, artisans, or subsistence farmers—remained members of the rural community. The village in the eighteenth century continued to function as an agrarian unit, one that envisaged itself in relation to the land and that upheld and protected agrarian rights. The village regulated the harvest, hired herders, defended communal rights, oversaw all local property transactions, and allocated taxation primarily on the basis of landownership. The weavers shared all of these concerns. Even when the bulk of their income came from textile production, they did not sever their ties to the land. They lived and worked in the countryside in an atmosphere still commanded by the agricultural cycle. Most of them owned land, but even those with hardly any property still took part in the harvest or expected to glean or to keep a pig or a cow.[45]

Peasants who traded or wove thus did not cease to be peasants. Definitions of the peasantry must be sufficiently flexible to allow for supplementary or even alternate forms of income if they are to apply to more than a minority of rural dwellers. Otherwise, we might indeed have to conclude that the peasantry had ceased to exist in Europe by the late Middle Ages. It seems more sensible to keep the nomenclature and argue that peasants lived complex lives that involved more than tilling their plots of land. Once we look at peasants this way, they no longer appear as such a distinct group, with so separate an outlook. Some of their activities may be different, but this need not imply a completely different mentality.

Eighteenth-century Cambrésis combined a dynamic linen industry with a prosperous agriculture. Both remained sufficiently traditional, however, to be representative of Old Regime France. The region thus offers an exceptional vantage point for examining interactions between industry and agriculture and for understanding the place of both within village life. The village of Montigny is small enough that it had to deposit its parish records in the departmental archives in Lille, yet the materials on this village proved surprisingly rich. I uncovered hundreds of bundles of litigation. Fiscal, notarial, and parish records allowed me to reconstruct the patterns of life and of work both in Montigny and in the surrounding villages. The intendancy of Flanders and Hainaut left behind sufficiently detailed records to move out from the village into the province. This study, therefore, incorporates a variety of approaches. It is statistical in parts and alternates between assessments of the broader arena and a detailed analysis of a particular case. It moves from discussions of structures to a more direct, narrative account of individual experiences gleaned primarily from judicial records. Whether through statistical or narrative approaches, my purpose remains to understand how individuals reacted to new circumstances, how they used the system around them, and how they moved beyond it.

The work is divided into three parts. The first deals with the particular setting of Montigny, the village, its inhabitants, its institutions. The second part examines the agrarian setting. It outlines the pattern of landownership over the eighteenth century, how land was viewed and used. It examines agricultural productivity and argues for improvements over the eighteenth century and follows the vagaries of the farming establishment. The group of middling farmers, in particular, underwent a major transformation as the independent farmer of the early eighteenth century turned to weaving, while an opposite movement prompted successful weavers in the latter part of the century to invest in land and eventually become farmers themselves. What might appear to be a stable element in the agrarian hierarchy was in fact largely overhauled.

The third part deals with weaving itself. It describes the nature of the industry and the organization of rural trade. It accompanies the weaver and rural merchant to the urban counters where they sold their wares. In the first half of the eighteenth century weavers sold their cloth directly to urban merchants, but by midcentury they relied increasingly on rural intermediaries. Middlemen came to play a crucial role in the organization of the trade after the Seven Years War when both urban merchants and rural producers saw them as useful buffers who shouldered most of the risks. This conjunction of events and outlooks, combined with the spread of credit in the countryside, allowed rural middlemen to create independent businesses and to rise to an enviable level of affluence and power. Many weavers attempted to emulate them. For a while, easy credit and a boom mentality held out golden prospects, which were crushed by a series of bankruptcies in the late 1780s. Rural merchants who had treated land as a useful mortgageable asset began to view farming as a safe alternative and gradually withdrew from the linen trade. When the Revolution provided them with a chance to acquire more land, many merchants definitively abandoned their commercial pursuits and became full-time farmers. The Revolution thus re-created an agrarian hierarchy and renewed the village's agrarian vocation. Rural industry persisted in the nineteenth century, but it provided steadily declining wages and no longer offered the road to riches. Such opportunities were once again confined to the cities.

I

THE

SETTING

❖ ❖ ❖

1

The Human Context

The village of Montigny is located in the southeastern part of the old province of Cambrésis, in what is now the district of Cambrai in the department of the Nord. It lies south of the road linking Cambrai to Le Cateau[1] and burrows down from the plain that encompasses its farmland to a low-lying square where the church, town hall, and single remaining café can be found. Few of the eighteenth-century structures still stand, and newly erected bungalows replace the old weaver cottages. Yet a few cottages still exist as partial witnesses to the past. The weavers' cellars with the large windows have been bricked up and additions superimposed to increase the living space and provide modern amenities. The last eighteenth-century barn was pulled down the day I first visited the village.

Montigny nowadays is reached by means of local roads, *vicinales,* which jut from the more important *départementales,* linking Valenciennes to Saint-Quentin and those crossing the neighboring Clary, Ligny, Bertry, and Caudry (fig. 2). In fact, in some stretches Montigny now appears as a residential extension of its more prosperous neighbors such as Clary or Caudry, which since the middle of the nineteenth century grew from village to populous town through the development of an important tulle industry. Montigny in the last quarter of the twentieth century presents itself as a small, retiring village where the present population of 650 just surpasses that of 1789 and where the inhabitants, aside from those working in its one textile factory and the few still tilling the land, earn a living elsewhere.

Two centuries ago, though of modest proportions in a province of a hundred villages, Montigny's position was not insignificant. Connected to Cambrai through its seigneur, the Chapter of the Metropolitan Church, and commercially both to Saint-Quentin to the south and to Valenciennes to the north, pleading a case before the Conseil d'Etat in Paris, Montigny in the eighteenth century gives the image of a busy community linked to the outside world.[2]

While contemporary descriptions of Cambrai and its region do not abound, some echoes both flattering and disparaging guide our impressions. A seventeenth-century chronicler marvels at local virtues: "The

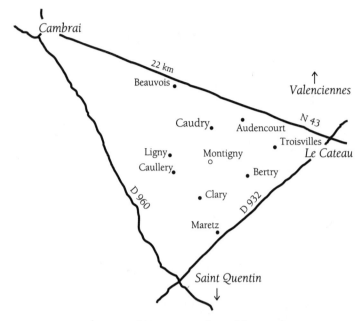

Figure 2. Recent Map of Montigny and Neighboring Towns

men reared in this town [Cambrai] are usually of good height, handsome and fair, tough and hardy. Their courage is no less strong than their bodies. They are a friendly and pleasant people, highly industrious and much given to trading but especially adept at manual work, and mechanics. . . ."[3] His description of the countryside is simply arcadian.

> The plain is filled with crops, hillsides once covered with vines and pastures produce excellent fare, the forests abound with deer, boar, hares, and other game; the rivers and ponds nurture good fish and numerous wild birds; the gardens yield excellent fruit for the table; the sheep are covered with very fine wool which the inhabitants sell far and wide; horses are of a fine quality, and can even be used in battle, as if the martial character which shines forth from the Cambrésiens, had somehow spread to their animals. The delicious water springs, close one to the other, give the residents and travellers both pleasure and needed relief. Moreover, the earth has made special efforts to endow it, by producing flax, which the inhabitants then fashion into cloths finer than spiders' webs, and which are known to every nation under the name of *Cambrics*.[4]

The justification for such a lengthy quotation is that it is unlikely that such enthusiasm will be encountered again. For if Cambrésis belonged to

Figure 3. Map of Cambrésis, 1675 *Photo Populu, Archives départementales du Nord, Plans Cambrai.*

the prosperous wheat belt north of Paris, it was not as flourishing as its Flemish neighbor, while its southeastern portion, which concerns us here, was downright poor (fig. 3). It was of course Flanders that impressed the English agronomist Arthur Young. He mused on the contrast between the old Burgundian kingdom and the French province and attributed its backwardness both to the fallow system and an overdependence on a single crop: wheat.[5]

Less interested in agriculture and more concerned about his creature comforts, another Englishman, Charles Burney, was dismayed by the city of Cambrai.[6] While Young had described the streets as "broad, handsome, well-paved and lighted,"[7] Burney added a proviso: "In general the churches of the [Flemish] towns are superb and magnificent, and the people and houses poor and dirty. At Cambray one of the most pleasantly situated of all I passed thro', this is true to a supreme degree, the houses and people being so dirty as to strike the inhabitants of the neighbouring towns with wonder."[8] Similar sentiments would be voiced over and over in the next century as administrators and social reformers stressed the link between living conditions and health hazards, both in town and country.

The insalubrity of life is at the core of the reports submitted to the Napoleonic prefect Christophe Dieudonné who was preparing a statistical compendium on the department.[9] Observations made around 1800 were echoed in later surveys, and that of 1859 provides as good a recapitulation as any.

> The cause of ill-health can be traced to the filth of the inhabitants who pile refuse around their houses or on the public roads, to the cesspools and ponds which are never cleaned out, and the proximity of the cemetery, located in the heart of the parish. The workers' houses lie close together, the floor is below-ground, the windows small, the beds gathered in a single room often contain a number of persons of both sexes. This promiscuity, which is so very improper, impairs the children's health and explains the incidence of scrofulous diseases and epidemics.[10]

Medical surveys furnish further insights. Humidity and poor nutrition were seen as contributing to the people's poor health along with the more visible aspects such as dirt and inadequate housing.

While the diet was generally sufficient—white bread (*froment*), vegetables, fresh meat, and beer—the poor were ill-fed, ill-clothed, lived in damp cellars or mud huts, and were prey to "the evils of drink."[11] One doctor stressed the need for warm clothing and asked that the price of wool cloth be reduced.[12]

If the cold killed the old and infirm, as elsewhere, heat in the spring and summer brought a range of contagious diseases, fevers, colics, and dysenteries.[13] The weather itself was inclement. "The department of the Nord has a cold and humid climate: winters last six to seven months, and are rainy rather than dry; one cannot really say that there is any spring, and sometimes hardly any summer, or at least not in any sustained way: the winds bring on sudden shifts from hot to cold and vice versa; therefore a prudent man owns no summer clothes, and never closes off his fireplace."[14] Inadequately protected from the elements in houses whose tiny asymetrical openings were boarded with pressed paper (*papier fort*), the rural household centered on the hearth. The walls were blackened with smoke. Wood, straw, and stems provided fuel, and the

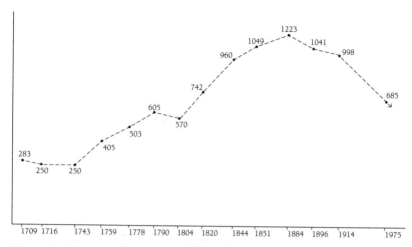

Figure 4. Montigny's Population, 1709–1975 *Source:* C suppl. 524, C20869, L1341-2, M473/7; Duthoit, *Montigny-en-Cambrésis,* p. 66; Lottin, *La Désunion du couple,* p. 19.

young and aged were sent to rummage for faggots of deadwood and leaves at the risk of capture from vigilant forest guards.[15]

Despite what appear to have been appalling conditions, Cambrésis at the end of the Ancien Régime was one of the most densely populated areas of France, supporting ninety to one hundred inhabitants per square kilometer in 1778. Of the eighty-eight villages fully within the provincial boundaries, thirteen counted more than one thousand inhabitants and thirty-three between five hundred and a thousand, with the average per household at 4.2.[16] Montigny's population of 503 in that same year stood just under the average of 550 for the province.[17] The villages surrounding it, except for Audencourt with a mere 137 and Caullery with 391, considerably surpassed it. Troisvilles numbered 771, Ligny 934, and Bertry 994, while Clary's total of 1,028 was double that of Montigny and nearly twice the provincial average. Since the greater part of Caudry belonged to the province of Hainaut, it was left out of the contemporary survey.

By the 1740s the population hovered between 250 and 300, and in the 1770s it was around 500.[18] In 1790 Montigny's population had reached 605, while military levies made it drop to 600 in 1796 and 570 by 1804.[19] The threat of further hostilities, however, provided the incentive for hastily contracted marriages and sent Montigny's population on an upward spiral broken only in the late nineteenth century (fig. 4).[20]

Table 1. Population Growth in Three Cambrésis Villages, 1716–1820

	Montigny		Ligny		Troisvilles	
Year	*Population*	*Base*	*Population*	*Base*	*Population*	*Base*
1716*	250	100	500	100	450	100
1743	250	100	505	101	455	101
1778	503	201	934	187	771	171
1790	605	242	1,124	225	1,119	249
1805	570	228	1,095	219	1,160	258
1820	742	297	1,391	278	—	—

*Information in Lottin, *La Désunion du couple*, pp. 19–20, on the number of communicants to which a conservative ratio of 25 percent of noncommunicants was added, based on the estimate of 1778.
Source: C21043, C21170, C20869, L6980; Dieudonné, *Statistique*, III, tables, M473/7.

Other villages paralleled Montigny's population growth (table 1). The most striking expansion occurred some time between 1743 and 1778.[21] If improvements in agricultural yields influenced this process, coupled with a slight drop in mortality rates, the significant factors were a recovery in both industry and commerce and a shift toward secondary income. In some ways, life was clearly better during the eighteenth century.

Life expectancy, however, changed little. Some 40 to 50 percent of the population continued to die before the age of ten, and a third of these failed to reach their first year.[22] More males than females died in childhood and early manhood. The proportion was reversed after the age of thirty-five and steadied in old age. In the last half of the eighteenth century a man who survived beyond the age of twenty could expect to live until he was fifty-three. The average for women was slightly higher, fifty-seven.

Changing marriage patterns, not changing life expectancy, caused population growth. The average age at first marriage dropped by only one year between 1740 and 1820 (with the exception of 1813 when eighteen young men married in the hopes of evading military service).[23] Yet this continuity hides significant changes (table 2). Before the 1780s those who married under the age of majority, set at twenty-five, generally received handsome dowries or else were full orphans or half orphans who had come into their inheritances (table 3). Of those who married young after 1800, their parents were more likely still to be alive (table 4). What is more, many came to the altar burdened with illegitimate children or a pregnant bride.[24] By the end of the Ancien Régime, couples did not

Table 2. Average Age at First Marriage in Montigny (under 45 years old)

Period	Brides			Grooms		
	All	*Weavers*	*Others*	*All*	*Weavers*	*Others*
1740–50	26.9	26.0	28.5	28.6	28.0	28.6
1751–60	26.8	26.8	26.8	27.6	27.9	27.0
1761–70	27.6	28.7	26.5	27.7	26.5	29.0
1771–80	25.6	24.7	26.6	27.4	27.0	27.9
1781–90	26.0	26.5	24.4	27.7	28.0	25.9
1791–1800	26.3	26.4	26.0	26.8	26.5	27.5
1801–10	25.6	25.8	25.2	25.6	26.4	22.6
1811–22*	25.7	25.0	27.2	27.2	26.0	30.2
1813	22.6	21.9	24.0	25.9	24.9	27.8

*Excluding 1813.
Source: J857.

expect to set up households on the basis of their landed inheritance and therefore did not wait until their parents' deaths. A fundamental change in familial expectations had taken place. Land ceased to determine family choices.

The protracted recessions and crises of the seventeenth century served to keep the population down. At the same time, previous to the introduction of textile manufacture, late marriage, emigration, and celibacy provided options for families with insufficient land. Even in the eighteenth century, offspring continued to settle in nearby villages, while a small minority emigrated outside the province, thereby turning "expatriez."[25]

Parish registers, marriage contracts, and land sales that required the assent of all co-owners permit a partial reconstitution of the migration pattern of Montigny spouses. Weddings were traditionally celebrated in the bride's village, and although the law demanded that a record be kept

Table 3. Marriages of Couples Aged Twenty-five or Under

Period	Number of unions	Percentage of unions	Number pregnant	Percentage of marriages	Number with illegitimate children
1740–80	32	31	6	19	1
1781–1800	26	25	10	39	—
1801–22	46	44	14	30	3

Table 4. Percentage of Marriages of People Under Twenty-Five with Parents Still Alive

	All			Weavers		
Period	Number	Percentage of young	Number pregnant	Number	Percentage of young	Number pregnant
1740–80	18	35	4	11	31	3
1781–1800	10	20	4	6	17	2
1801–22	23	45	7	18	51	6

in both localities, this was rarely done. Montigny's parish registers survive only from 1740, and so earlier data were assembled from the sources mentioned above, although they provide an incomplete picture. The readiest information concerns wives, for they either married in the village (even if they subsequently left it) or, in the case of "immigrant" brides, appeared in a multiplicity of other records. The growth of population and earlier marriage gave endogamy a boost in the prerevolutionary period (table 5).

While emigration provided one solution to insufficient prospects, remaining single might have been a voluntary or involuntary alternative. While members of the Henninot, Delacourt, Boursier, or Taine families tended to leave, celibacy was encouraged in some wealthier or rising families. The weaver Pierre Allart had two sons, only one of whom, Michel, took a wife, while Jacob stayed single. Marianne Leclercq, widow of Pierre Boursier, built up a small linen business coupled with a steady purchase of land. Only two of her six surviving children married. She lived to the ripe old age of ninety, and her children lived nearly as long. The unmarried died at the ages of sixty-six, eighty-three, eighty-eight, and ninety-one. One of them, Pierre Ignace Boursier, who became mayor during the Revolution, had a modest capital of 3,050 livres in 1796, by which time he had become a farmer.[26] The cloth merchant Philippe Cauchy likewise did not marry, and neither did the weaver Pierre Philippe Renard, who died at the age of sixty-five in 1773. Unmarried weavers and spinners appear in a dozen families—members of a generation born in the first decades of the century.

Most of the villagers, however, married, especially after 1750, and only a minority remained childless. Very few took religious orders, most likely because it required a pension beyond the means of the family. There were two such vocations in the wealthier Allart household. Marie

Table 5. Origin of Spouses in Montigny Unions, 1675–1822

Period	Number of unions	Both spouses local (%)	Immigrants (%)			Emigrants (%)		
			Groom	Bride	Both	Groom	Bride	Both
pre-1700	68	49	4	24	—	6	18	—
1700–1724	75	49	8	19	—	12	11	—
1725–49	102	42	15	20	2	10	11	1
1750–74	120	41	18	12	1	5	24	—
1775–89	95	41	22	17	—	8	11	—
1790–95	51	35	26	12	—	10	16	2
1796–1822	155	55	14	12	5	5	8	3
Entire period	666	46	15	16	2	7	14	1

Reine Allart, sister of the merchants Michel and Jacob, took the veil, while Michel's son (Jean Pierre) in turn entered the community of the Carmes Chaussés in Valenciennes. The pattern was repeated in Montigny's premier merchant family where Marie Catherine Lantier's son, Jean Michel Malesieux, became a member of the abbey of Cantimpré.[27] The advent of a secondary occupation, weaving, reduced the incidence of forced migration or enforced bachelorhood without putting a stop to the endemic and natural movement of men.

Although historians have often viewed the eighteenth century as progressively disastrous for the peasantry, culminating in a massive agrarian crisis, this does not appear to have been the case in Montigny.[28] Quite the contrary, the eighteenth century brought with it new opportunities and buoyancy. The standard of living improved. People lived better in late eighteenth-century Montigny than they had either fifty or a hundred years earlier.

Montigny in the age of Louis XIV had already witnessed changes, evidenced, for one, by the list of names in sixteenth-century documents that no longer appear a century later.[29] The crises of the late Renaissance and early Bourbon period lie beyond the confines of this study. Suffice it to emphasize that the semipastoral society of the late seventeenth century, where textile production was already making inroads, was no paradise lost and serves merely as a basis of comparison for further transformations.

Victim of the fiscal demands of a warring monarch and the ravages of armies on the move, Montigny like other villages faced the new century depleted and exhausted, its farmers and small landowners ruined or indebted.[30] Yet what is most striking about the early eighteenth-century village is the predominance of agriculture. The households divided between farmers and farm laborers, with only a few artisans and weavers. Sheep, horses, cattle, and barnyard animals were numerous; there were bitter struggles over the use of the commons. Parents often shared accommodations with at least one married offspring who had access to the cellar, fireplace, and vegetable garden.[31] The youngest child generally inherited the house, by a *droit de maîneté,* although property in this region was otherwise partible and divided equally among all children.

What the nineteenth century decried on moral or hygienic grounds only incited comment in cases of unwanted pregnancies: "One time, when he was in Crinon's house, Crinon's wife asked Gaspard, their shepherd . . . if he had not slept with the plaintiff, his sister-in-law, and he answered that once when he had come home, he had found his sister-in-law sleeping with his wife, and had made her move, and that the plaintiff then went to sleep at the bottom of the bed with his son who is nine or ten years old, and that Crinon's wife then asked him whether he had had any naughty thoughts, and he answered no."[32] Servants and youths commonly slept in the barn: "The witness further states that Jean Lenglet told him that Jean Michel Bans, resident of Montigny, had robbed him of a gold louis worth fifteen crowns and a coin of forty patars when they lay side by side."[33] Lenglet recalled more precisely that he was then "in the barn which they usually call the sheep barn."[34] It was when visiting her in the cow shed where she was fast asleep that Jean Delbar seduced his sister's servant.[35]

Family holdings would be subdivided to accommodate an expanding population dependent on textiles and less ready to emigrate.[36] One child stayed under the paternal roof, and others received materials to erect new homes. While in 1690 one widow ceded the kitchen (*la maison*) as living quarters for her married son, other arrangements became more common.[37] The parents agreed to build a new structure or to expand the existing one, something like "two rooms fifteen feet deep each, with an adjoining barn ten feet deep built out of cob, and delivered with roof and cover, oven, window frame, window, and locks" within a year's time.[38]

These houses had some sort of attic, as the expression "une place hault et bas" would suggest, and of course more and more commonly half-basements to fit two or more looms. Most houses were tiny: a kitchen, one or two rooms, and a barn. Farmers' younger sons who turned to

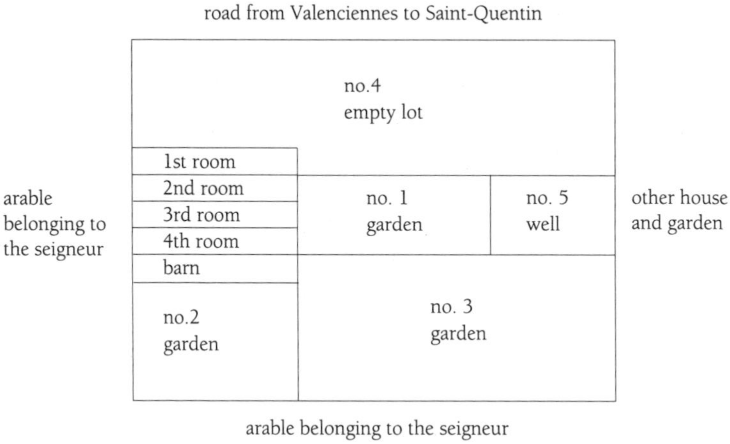

road from Valenciennes to Saint-Quentin

		no.4 empty lot		
arable belonging to the seigneur	1st room / 2nd room / 3rd room / 4th room	no. 1 garden	no. 5 well	other house and garden
	barn			
	no.2 garden	no. 3 garden		

arable belonging to the seigneur

Figure 5. Plan of a Peasant House, 1764 *Courtesy of Archives départementales du Nord.*

weaving and settled independently could expect somewhat larger homes, with one or two extra rooms.[39]

Descriptions are usually brief with few elaborations beyond size and access to, or provision of, a fireplace, oven, courtyard, chicken coop, or cow shed. A more detailed plan of a Troisvilles house and garden is attached to a 1764 marriage contract (fig. 5).[40] A similar document yields further details concerning house construction.[41]

[The parents] . . . promise to erect . . . two rooms measuring sixteen feet square each or smaller ones should the couple so wish it, as well as an adjoining barn of the same length but . . . measuring twelve feet the other way . . . all of which will be made of *muré* [cob], except for the spot where the cellar used to be, which will serve as partition. There will be a double fireplace made completely from bricks between the two rooms. The roof will be covered with straw, and as for the wood, the father and mother will provide whatever kind they wish, as well as a window in each room, so that the entire dwelling will be built in the customary manner and be ready, with the key on the door, within the coming year except for the window panes . . . for which the newlyweds will have to pay.

There were few frivolities. A young couple setting up house received only a medley of kitchen utensils, a bed, and, more rarely, bits of furniture: a cupboard or a chest.[42] In the course of the eighteenth century, weavers' utensils, looms, and yarn replaced earlier gifts of cow or lamb as the villagers came to depend on industry and had fewer agricultural resources.

Such a spare existence demanded mutual support. Its presence in the form of female solidarity emerges from the case of the unfortunate who drowned herself after killing her six-day-old illegitimate son.[43] The greater part of the evidence has unfortunately vanished, but the little that remains gives a most vivid account of life in the early eighteenth century and underlines areas of mutual dependency.

Marguerite Allart, who was present at the birth, relates that the victim, Marguerite Leducq, "did not seem too distressed by her misfortune, and that it was true that the midwife and several others had helped to console her by explaining that the child would keep her company."[44] Torn between the urge to describe Leducq's melancholy state and yet the need to distance themselves from what was considered a crime, most witnesses tried to shift the emphasis to the support and advice they provided. Marguerite Allart urged her to sell some trees as she seemed so concerned by her financial plight, and this cheered Leducq no end. The same witness also sent some milk along for the baby. Another woman testified that on the day of the suicide she had sat by Leducq's bedside and had done the household chores and taken care of the child, while "a girl . . . breastfed the infant."[45] She also took the baby "to be nursed by the women in the neighbourhood . . . and then, having been called to work in the fields, she told Leducq that she was going but that she would be back that evening." The testimony of a forty-five-year-old neighbor, Catherine Leducq, is so colorful that it merits full quotation. It underlines the mutual aid and conviviality in the village, within a backdrop of daily occupations.

> Marguerite Leducq, whom she knew intimately, walked into her house, looked for her in the kitchen, and then came into the room where the witness was sifting flour. She seemed dreamy, pensive, and very distressed, and her listlessness made the witness cry when she first saw her and a little while later she said to her, "here you are," Leducq took a step back, let her arms drop, and said the following: "what will become of me, we are two lost souls." The witness told her, "what are you talking about, how dare you say that, are you lacking something, does your baby need anything?" Leducq replied "I do have some boiled milk and some plain milk, but what will become of me tomorrow." The witness answered her: "God will provide, you will have enough, and if your baby needs anything, I will give it to you." At that moment Leducq warned her that there was a calf in her kitchen chewing on a piece of fine linen (*trufet*) lying on the

warping frame, and the witness ran off to chase it away and yelled at her children for not keeping an eye on the animal. During that time Leducq remained in the kitchen, then left without saying a word. The witness went back to her room to finish her sifting, and then went out to the garden to pick some herbs for the soup, prepared to light the fire, and set off to the square in Ligny known as Le Quesnoy. She called out to her daughter to have a look at the cow which was supposed to be in a nearby meadow, she rushed like a bullet shot by Leducq's house, heard the baby cry but did not think of going in . . . she fetched water from the well . . . and had a chat with the people gathered in the vicinity . . . and scolded one of her nieces . . . for running about all over the place without taking care of her mother who had been ill for some time.

It was later, when she returned with her husband to the well for more water, that the body was discovered in the three-foot gulley, head wrapped in an apron.

Though little survives to apprise us of the details, it is easy to imagine that such helping relations were widespread among neighbors. Jeanne Marguerite Faré of Montigny, for example, bid an elderly woman to look in on her child while she attended mass and left her the key to her house.[46] While the attitude toward children, spouses, and kin cannot be addressed at this time, it appears that loyalty if not affection could be counted on—though no one was loath to use force or call on the law to redress any slights.[47]

Quarrels repeatedly demonstrate how one could count both on kinship ties and loyalty to employers. The servant would rush to the aid of his master in the same way that a relative would answer the call of blood.[48] Parents could be relied on to stand up for their children,[49] and family relations and friends had no trouble testifying to the well-known virtue of girls who had got pregnant, prey to false promises of wedlock.

Cleavages and solidarities operated on multiple levels. Some were village-wide, while others rested on particular bonds. When Alexandre Leclercq of Saint-Vaast had a fight with François Demoulin of Saint-Hilaire, he alerted the whole community by shouting, "Help, Saint-Vaast!"[50] A report from Selvigny shows that neighbors were expected to rally.[51]

The incident took place around nine or ten in the evening when Beauchemin, two of his brothers-in-law and his father-in-law were drinking in his establishment. Beauchemin asked for a refill but he refused because it was getting late: after his refusal the above-mentioned tried to hit him, and one of his brothers-in-law even grabbed him by the collar, so that he ran

out of his house shouting "help, help," and that all he had meant by that
was to get the support of his neighbors in kicking Beauchemin out.

There were other bonds forged by age, profession, and mutual interest. The evidence is once more strongest for the earlier part of the century.
In this period the community ostracized two of the village's youths
suspected of theft. "Rumor has it that Antoine Delacourt and Nicolas
Langlet are under suspicion; the witness also knows that the single men
from Montigny refused to take Delacourt and Lenglet's money for their
brotherhood of Saint Nicolas because of the nasty rumors that were
circulating against them."[52] Yet the same witness declared that he had
spent the evening of the feast of St. John the Baptist drinking with them,
along with "a number of other young men" (*plusieurs autres de la jeunesse*).
Such single men feasted together and visited the neighboring fairs. Jean
Michel Lantier was attacked in a Caullery tavern while on his way home
drunk from the local *ducasse,* while other young men forwent vespers
and wasted money "in several saint-day celebrations in the neighboring
villages."[53]

Not all of their pastimes were harmless. They might on the one hand
chat up the spinsters, but also steal ham and beer or mock Protestant
rituals.[54] The only other trace of the traditional activities associated with
such youths comes in the Chapter's records, which mention the prosecution "of the young men of Montigny for having demanded that Joseph
Desains pay them *la bienvenue,* and for trying to throw him down a
hole."[55]

While each village had such confraternities, it is more surprising to
discover the existence of craft associations in the countryside. One such
example comes from Selvigny, two villages southwest of Montigny.[56] "He
remembers it was St. Crispin day because the cobblers were making
merry in his establishment, though he could not say whether it was a
Monday or Saturday, but he does recall that the cobblers were making
merry and that his daughter, the widow of a cobbler, was there with
them." The support that farmers evoked to sustain their particular grievances demonstrate their consciousness of common interests. Antoine
Crinon, one of the local farmers, called on the *censiers* of Montigny,
Caudry, Bertry, and Selvigny in his defense against the priest Mathias
Prouveur who complained that he had gathered his crop before the tithe
could be levied.[57] Similarly, when two other labours were accused by
a later curé of feeding green oats to their horses (once more without
paying the tithe), they gathered a multitude of affidavits from nearby

Clary, Caudry, Bertry, Maretz, Caullery, and Ligny, as well as from their own village of Montigny, establishing this as the local custom.[58] Again, in a struggle with Montigny's new clerk, the widow of the previous one obtained certificates supporting her cause from the clerks of the villages of Clary, Béthencourt, Cagnoncle, Haucourt, Walincourt, and Serain.[59]

Although much of communal life and communal bonds revolved around the church, we are given few insights into religious attitudes. The curé of nearby Walincourt reflected that the local population possessed a simple faith, at best, which made them easy prey to Protestant propaganda.[60] No Protestant lived in Montigny in the eighteenth century despite the growing number of converts in villages such as Caudry and Ligny. The Montignaciens, for their part, manifested both a public and private piety, which suggests that they attended mass not merely to congregate socially but to partake in the service.[61] The growing number of parishioners demanded an enlargement of the existing church structure in the 1740s.

Yet the people had no special respect for the priest, and clashes were frequent, at least until the curé gave up collecting the tithe. One incumbent fought with a local farmer not only metaphorically in court but with a club on the open road.[62] The curé was reputed to be a violent man who regularly mistreated his parishioners. During a holy procession he struck one of the villagers, and in the middle of the Christmas mass of 1714 "slapped his clerk in front of the assembled parish."[63]

Religion appears to have played no part in the peasants' relations with their seigneur, the Metropolitan Chapter, and invoked but a handful of vocations. It centered on the whole on the church and the curé, and in Montigny up to the middle of the century, the priests were more concerned with terrestrial matters than with eternal salvation.

Eighteenth-century Montigny was a rapidly growing village, and this growth was permitted by the advent of textile weaving. The possibilities offered by weaving broke down certain traditional restraints, allowing young couples to set up households without landed property. Yet other traditional attachments remained very strong. Whether their activities took them to the fields or kept them in their cellars, villagers continued to share mutual concerns and congregated daily in the village square or gathered in the tavern or the church. Solidarity revolved around the *terroir* and agrarian bonds. While textile production would engender greater individualism and fewer controls, economic necessity and sociability would nevertheless keep such traditional patterns alive.

2

The Institutional Setting

All French villages during the Old Regime functioned within institutional and fiscal systems that extended beyond their boundaries, but this was particularly true of Montigny. Its seigneurs, the Chapter of the Cambrai cathedral—one of the richest and most powerful churches in France— were located in the city of Cambrai and channeled resources and monies, judicial and administrative decisions to the town.[1] This concentration of power shaped village life and economic development in several ways. For all of their power, Montigny's absentee lords exerted less pressure on the village than seigneurs who depended primarily on one or two localities. Relations with the Chapter were erratic, the weight of lordship rather light. The Chapter's power required of villages direct contact with the urban world.[2] Finally, though seigneurial dues were insignificant, the church's domination of land meant that little was available for purchase.

The village was situated in a province dominated by the church. Forty percent of the regional soil belonged to ecclesiastics, and most local power was concentrated in their hands. This reflected the fact that Cambrésis was not only a bishopric, but until 1677 had been an independent principality, ruled by the bishop. In the division that followed Charlemagne's reign, Cambrai and its hinterland joined what would later become the Holy Roman Empire. Emperor Henry II granted the bishop full powers over city and county in 1007, but the prelate owed fealty to the emperor and sat as a member of the imperial Diet until the seventeenth century. Cambrésis did not always succeed in retaining its independence and at various points became the protectorate of the counts of Flanders, the Burgundian dukes, and the English, French, and Spanish crowns. Elevated to an archdiocese in 1559, Cambrai fell to Spain in 1559 before its conquest by Louix XIV, who entered the city on Easter Monday in 1677 and incorporated it into the French state with the status of a Province Reputed Foreign.[3]

The archbishop had traditionally shared his powers with other bodies. Sole ruler over Le Cateau and its dependencies, he administered Cambrai with a fourteen-member municipal council. Since the sixteenth century, Estates composed of the representatives of the clergy, the nobility, and the city aldermen advised in government of the province.[4] These Estates met annually to negotiate and establish taxation rates and

Figure 6.   The Estates of Cambrésis, Seventeenth Century   *Photo Populu,*
Archives départementales du Nord, Plans Cambrai.

in two separate groups to oversee daily affairs: one, the *états de Cambrai,*
in charge of urban, and the other, the *états du Cambrésis,* of rural matters
(fig. 6). They survived until the Revolution.

A medley of bodies dispensed judicial functions in the city, but the
most important remained the ecclesiastical tribunal (*officialité*), which
besides its religious jurisdiction heard civil suits in the province. Famed
for its probity and speedy judgments, the officialité handled much of the
region's litigation and was a favorite with the inhabitants of Montigny.
After the French conquest, all cases judged by these courts could be
appealed before the Parlement of Flanders, which after several moves
finally settled in Douai.[5] Communities and individuals could also seek
justice from the intendant or the monarch sitting in his council.

While lay authorities (municipal and imperial) contested and reduced
the bishop's and then the archbishop's authority, the French regime

added two sets of permanent officials. The first was administrative, centering on the intendant of Flanders, installed in Lille, and seconded by a number of bureaucratic assistants, the *subdélégués*, located in smaller provincial centers. The central government also added its own military governors to the existing military hierarchy. After 1754 Cambrésis was administered by the newly created intendancy of Hainaut, centered in Valenciennes. Powerful relations at court enabled the then archbishop (a member of the powerful Choiseul family and brother of the first minister) to strengthen his position, and in 1766 and 1773 royal decrees curbed some municipal independence.[6]

Other religious institutions besides the Cathedral Chapter also enjoyed property in Montigny. These were the abbeys of Cantimpré and Prémy of Cambrai as well as the nearby abbey of Honnecourt, which received the tithe and named the priest; the abbey of Saint-André at Le Cateau (1025), which collected dues on several small fiefs; and the Guillemains of the abbey of Notre-Dame of Walincourt (1255), who controlled a small portion of land.[7] The wealthy abbey of Anchin, established in 1079 in Pecquencourt near Douai, owned the large farms of Le Troncquoy, situated north of Montigny.[8]

Montigny's situation was typical of the region, for religious bodies held extensive property in Cambrésis. The Metropolitan Chapter owned twenty-one seigneuries scattered east and west of Cambrai (with only Caullery and Montigny located in the less fertile southeast) as well as enclaves within the city.[9] The Chapter raised 500,000 livres a year from this land. By comparison, the archbishop's revenues amounted to 400,000 livres, while their properties yielded the Chapters of Saint-Géry and Sainte-Croix 100,000 livres each.[10] The Chapter was extraordinarily wealthy. Only the very richest lay seigneurs had incomes that exceeded 50,000 livres. Political power accompanied this extraordinary concentration of economic power. As seigneurs, each of these bodies exercised feudal justice over their villages and ruled over the personnel within their own walls. The Chapter possessed diverse attributes. It had its own law courts, prison, and administrative apparatus.[11] Twenty Cambrésis villages came under its jurisdiction, as did "several other fiefs whose names we do not know" (Montigny fell in this category), all of which could appeal its rulings to the Parlement of Flanders.[12]

In Montigny these duties were met by an overseer, or *bailli*, named by the Chapter to administer several dependencies. He resided in Cambrai and occasionally deputized a magistrate to investigate some major crime.

In day-to-day affairs the village's most important farmer acted as the seigneur's local representative and served as mayor. Both Moyse Crinon and his son, Charles, who occupied the Chapter's farm for half a century between 1715 and 1765, held this post. Their successor, Robert Milot, did so only episodically, for he entered into conflict with the community that successfully replaced him.[13]

The seigneurs intervened in local disputes. Alerted by public discontent ("la rumeur publique"), the chapter's magistrate, the *procureur d'office,* instituted at least two dozen criminal proceedings against various villagers between 1709 and 1765, while the bailli heard a variety of minor suits at the seigneurial court in Cambrai.[14] Most of the village's civil litigation was handled by the officialité.[15]

The seigneurs named a local gamekeeper, who received a yearly stipend, a gun, a bayonet, and a uniform.[16] The Chapter's last warden would pay dearly for this garment. At seventy-six, he became Montigny's only victim of the Terror after accusations that he remained too attached to his silver buttons (which may have featured the Chapter's insignia). The warden's duties included the care of the seigneurial wood, the prosecution of all types of poachers, and when conflicts broke out over the planting of trees in the second half of the century he policed the paths as well, although, in fact, the community was responsible for forestalling the damages.[17]

Although the seigneurs wielded theoretically absolute power, the villages were run by local councils that effectively defended local interests, often against their lords. Montigny's village council consisted of a mayor, deputy mayor, first officer, two or more villagers, and a scribe who acted as schoolmaster as well as assisting the priest.

Local institutions were generally weaker in the north than in the south of France. This was especially true of Hainaut and Cambrésis, where the seigneurs named the mayors and councilmen.[18] Royal absolutism aimed to transfer this authority to the central government by increasing the intendant's prerogatives over communities. After 1700, only he could authorize a meeting of the inhabitants.[19] The Montignaciens then had to petition for permission to assemble in order to settle their numerous disputes with the village of Caudry or with their seigneur, even to sell logs from the communal wood.[20]

Nonetheless, it would be wrong to view the councils as completely powerless. There are no records of the actual running of the village, but we do know that, as elsewhere, the council oversaw property transfers, acted in loco parentis along with the seigneurs, and allocated tax burdens.[21] The council also regularly appealed for tax reductions as in 1660 when troops quartered in the village pillaged and ruined the crops, or in 1673 and 1674 when the council felt that the beer tax had been too steep.[22] The village authorities answered official queries and checked local stores. They attested to the lack of grain after the disastrous harvests of 1709 and of 1788.[23] In 1757 they entered a protest against farmers who kept pigeons.[24] They also regularly furnished villagers with affidavits, generally concerning their financial state—terribly poor or reasonably well-off—depending on the appeal at hand.[25] Their duties further included naming and paying the village's cattle and pig herders, choosing militiamen, and overseeing public charity, more specifically the lease of those *biens des pauvres,* the paupers' plots, donated by the Chapter.[26]

The parish had a churchwarden seconded by a vestry, and although we know little about their activities, the councilmen probably acted in a double capacity. It was the vestry that raised three thousand livres, selling *rentes* and eventually wood from the communal reserve, to pay for the rebuilding of the church in the 1740s.[27] Court costs incurred during a major lawsuit over gleaning rights meant further debts and further loans. In 1775 the community alienated its pastures for seven years to raise the necessary funds.

These village councils were often self-serving, but the task was not always pleasant. Mayors became personally responsible for the debts of the community, and it is not surprising that they tried to line their pockets with a little extra here and there. The priest accused them of collecting unwarranted fees for overseeing church accounts and leasing church land. Such "corruption" was not particular to Montigny. In Ligny a woman was prosecuted for daring to say that the mayor and council had dipped into the alms that rightfully belonged to the poor.[28] In Caudry in the late eighteenth century the inhabitants accused the seigneur and his council of falsifying the village's tax rolls.[29] The councilmen were replaced by order of the intendant.[30] Despite seigneurial and state interference, the inhabitants not only governed day-to-day affairs but scrutinized local officials. Northern communal institutions are usually regarded as weaker than southern ones, and the population as more passive.[31] The evidence of the law courts and appeals to the intendant, however, attest to a vigorous political life. As elsewhere in France, the community, sometimes rent by internal divisions, also united to do battle with their seigneurs, and this often happened with the support of outside authorities.

The political weight of lordship was thus light, and this also was true of its economic weight: the dues and monopolies that the seigneurs

Table 6. Value of Capons Paid as Part of Montigny's Seigneurial
Dues, 1588–1788

Year	Capons	Value of 1 capon in sous	Total value*	Entries	Average per entry
1588	112.3	10	56.03.0	52	0.5
1590	112.3	[8 deniers]	12.02.8	52	0.1
1597	112.3	6	33.17.0	[52]	0.3
1614	111	20	100.16.8	47	1.0
1641	103	20	—	45	[1.0]
1675	110.8	20	110.16.8	47	1.2
1698	120.3	28	144.08.0	46	1.6
1712	120.3	20	120.06.8	46	1.3
1717	110.8	24	133.00.0	46	1.4
1763	110.8	28	155.03.4	48	1.6
1787	111.1	30	167.06.0	49	1.7

Source: 4G2447, 6557, 6558, 6575, 6604, 6633, 6656, 6670, 6675, 6720, 6744.
*Florins: half the value in livres.

collected within the village. Unlike most lay seigneurs, the Chapter had little interest in enforcing its hunting monopoly within the village, and its onetime monopoly on baking had disappeared by the eighteenth century. Only the Chapter's milling monopoly and a jumble of seigneurial rents survived in the prerevolutionary period. In all, the latter produced only 80 livres in cash and about 150 livres in kind—in other words, about 4 livres a year for the forty or so contributing households. During the seventeenth century, dues had increased substantially, and the rise can be traced in the changing value of capons that formed the bulk of those dues. After 1700, dues remained practically unchanged (tables 6 and 7).[32]

On the whole, the weight of Montigny's seigneurial dues seem light. The *terrage* had vanished, a victim of seventeenth-century refusals to pay, and most plots carried neither *cens* nor *rente*. The *lods et ventes* payable on property sales were always low in ecclesiastical villages.[33] Inflation also had reduced the significance of these dues. In the eighteenth century the Chapter concentrated its efforts on its subsidiary privileges and placed less emphasis on monetary ones. A telling sign is that the payments elicited only passive resistance (nonpayment), while the tithe and royal taxation excited more vigorous protests. On the other hand, seigneurial interest in local resources awakened opposition. Troubles erupted in

Table 7.   Seigneurial Dues Collected by the
Cambrai Chapter in Montigny, 1698–1787

Year	Total in florins	Entries	Average per entry
1698–99	81.6	46	1.8
1717–18	89.2	46	1.9
1739–40	77.0	48	1.6
1754–55	88.05	48	1.8
1763–64	92.05	48	1.9
1768–69	95.05	49	1.9
1787–88	105.10	49	2.1

Source: 4G6656, 6675, 6696, 6711, 6720, 6725, 6744.

midcentury when the Chapter asserted its exclusive right to roadside tree-planting and took the inhabitants to court. The villagers proved willing to do battle when they felt themselves ill-used.[34] On the other hand, there is no evidence of the peasants interfering with the collection of the rente, and the Chapter's own light-handed approach emerges from the list of arrears that accompany each account. Late payments eventually gave way to "reductions" that canceled debts and cleared the records. One plot, marked down for twelve florins since 1738, had originally owed ten capons, six deniers, and one mencaud of wheat. This amount had already been adjusted downward in 1616, and by 1763 it dropped to a mere two florins.[35] If there was seigneurial reaction, it did not focus on petty dues.[36]

Seigneurial dues had lost their value for several reasons: inflation, the peasants' refusal to pay, and lax administration. Given its manpower and extensive apparatus, it was easy for the Chapter to keep accounts, but these were entered late and only occasionally updated. (Tenants, for example, were still listed years after they died.) The Chapter's accounts convey a sense of carelessness about financial details mingled with sudden bursts of efficiency that seem more typical of a lumbering machine than of conscious attempts to cash in on dues before the thirty-year legal prescription. In 1769, for example, new registers were compiled for fiefs held in Montigny, Caudry, Caullery, Cattenières, and Niergnies which showed that many heirs had not claimed them officially and therefore had not paid the Chapter the appropriate dues. The baillis were instructed to invite "all fief-owners to perform their duties as vassals" or face the seizure of their property.[37] Periods of rather benign neglect therefore oscillated with vigorous prosecutions, yet, in all, it was less onerous for a village such as Montigny to be under the lordship of a powerful and less exacting ecclesiastical institution than that of a more demanding resident seigneur whose revenues were directly dependent on squeezing his few peasants.

If seigneurial dues were economically trivial for lord and villagers alike, this was not the case with the tithe owed by all residents in the village. The tithe owed to the church was clearly resented, and this was especially true of the manner in which it was taken. The tithe varied between 6 and 8 percent (one-thirteenth rather than one-tenth) and it was collected in the fields; crops could not be removed until the passage of the official assessor, the *tourneur*. This led to inevitable conflicts between producers and tax collectors.[38] "Our grievance and request for payment rest on the fact that the defendant carted part of his wheat without warning the assessor. . . . The tither should not have to come after the peasant has removed his crop nor be expected to trust in the good faith of peasants who look upon the tithe as an odious exaction and who therefore try to evade it as much as they can."[39] Everything was subject to the levy, from major crops to garden produce. In Montigny the "lesser tithes to be collected throughout the parish and on all the enclosed arable . . . at eight percent" included "dry clover, hay, hops, camomille, *oliette,* colza, apples, pears, nuts, cherries, plums, wool, sheep, lambs, pigs, chickens. . . ."[40]

The villagers' opprobrium was generally directed toward the wealthy religious bodies that pocketed the tribute or the farmers who collected it. In both cases the revenue either left the village or enriched an already opulent personage. Consequently, there was less resentment when the community obtained the contract and funneled the surplus locally.[41] Dissatisfaction ran as high, however, when the priest held the farm— which he did most years up to the 1740s. Only communal control seemed to mitigate the sense of unwarranted exaction.

In the first half of the eighteenth century the abbey of Honnecourt allotted the priest the revenues of the tithe as long as he paid the assessors, provided for the upkeep of the church and presbytery, and gave the abbey one hundred livres annually.[42] He also received the income of thirty-two mencaudées attached to the benefice. In the 1740s he ceded the tithe to the abbey in return for an annual stipend.[43] The Chapter's farmer took over the lease. Conflicts over tithes may have persisted—without generating lawsuits—but the transfer reduced some of the local antagonism against the priest. Other grievances survived. As in other French villages, the council expressed the inhabitants' resentment of the service fees (ranging from five to twenty sous) that the priest charged for performing various duties, such as masses for the dead.[44] His attempts to swell his revenues (or from his point of view to salvage them) led to open conflicts with his flock. Disputes centered on the lease of the thirty-two mencaudées attached to the benefice, which local officials were supposed to oversee gratis. By violating this rule, they cut into the curé's income, and he successfully sought redress. Such conflicts, whether motivated by greed or by need, ceased after 1750. Despite his complaints, by the local yardstick the curé's parcels ranked him among Montigny's major landowners. This property afforded him an income of 460 livres, three times the wages of weavers in this period.[45] This was enough to divide him from his parishioners. Once their situation improved in the second half of the eighteenth century, there were fewer conflicts. This peace within the village also may have reflected a better quality of incumbents: that is, men who were not as rough, promiscuous, or tightfisted.[46] Nonetheless, neither the priest's character, fiscal exactions, nor his economic status appeared to have affected the villagers' religiosity, or at least not directly. Church attendance remained high, and the church itself was expanded in the 1740s. The population continued to distinguish between the office and its worldly representative.

In the middle of the eighteenth century, church and seigneurs claimed about one-tenth of an average household's income. A weaver and his wife earned approximately one hundred florins a year, and of that the seigneur took two florins, the tithe collector, ten. In that same period the public purse claimed another fifteen and a half florins. The peasants of Cambrésis paid a number of direct taxes, or tailles, but their burden was lighter than in nearby regions. While taxes in the North rose 38 percent between 1777 and 1789, Cambrésis's per capita contribution of four to five livres (like that of Flanders) fell below that of Maritime Flanders (which came to five or six livres) or neighboring Hainaut (where it reached six to seven livres).[47]

Direct contributions consisted of a personal or head tax, a corn tax (*moulinage*), property tax, stamp tax (*contrôle des actes*), and a militia tax. The *aides* then combined indirect taxes on consumption, most notably on spirits. An occasional *dixième* or *vingtième* (one-tenth and one-twentieth), proportional to revenue, swelled these contributions in the first half of the eighteenth century. From "extraordinary," they became regular levies after 1749.

In 1786 Montigny's total assessment came to 1,300 florins. This was the sum demanded by the Cambrésis Estates, following its negotiations with the central government, and it included all of the above-mentioned taxes with several supplements.[48] Each household in the village was responsible for a fraction, calculated at various rates. Some of the taxes involved four patars per mencaudée, or twelve patars per head, but the biggest contribution, the aide extraordinaire, required thirty-five patars per head and thirty-five patars for specific numbers of animals, land, and, above all, looms. If not fully progressive, this system at least insured that the rich farmers paid their proportional share. The latter were not particularly eager to bear such a heavy burden, and in the 1770s Montigny's farmer-mayor single-handedly raised the basis for property assessments from ten mencaudées (or less) to units of twenty (or less). This reduced the large landowners' taxable units, and, since the sum allocated the village remained the same, consequently raised the taxes of the majority of the peasants, whose tiny parcels still figured as one unit. The inhabitants successfully protested against this measure. The large farmers proved unable to control the village, and to the end of the Old Regime direct taxation continued to weigh lightly on the poor.

Altogether, few tax records survive for Montigny.[49] Nonetheless, they demonstrate that taxation weighed less heavily on villagers as the eighteenth century advanced. In 1744 a complete evaluation demonstrates that the inhabitants contributed 700 florins, or 15.5 florins per household, at a time when families earned about 100 florins a year.[50] Some forty years later, the local assessment came to 1,300 florins (the remainder paid by nonresidents). This marked a hefty rise, yet amounted to only 8.8 florins per family, for the number of households had tripled from 45 to 148.[51] What is more, the average weaving households now earned 150 to 170 florins. For weaving families, the tax rate had fallen by two-thirds, from 15 percent to 5 percent of yearly income. The major farmers were the least affected by this improvement in the tax situation, since their holdings continued to be the largest and most heavily taxed.

It is true that in wartime, at the beginning or in the middle of the century, extraordinary taxes rose suddenly as the rate applied doubled or tripled. In Montigny this represented a jump from 119 florins to 332 during the War of Austrian Succession.[52] Such demands lessened, however, as the government relied more heavily on loans. Besides, the really onerous charge in wartime had been the billeting and exactions of the troops.[53] These demands ceased in the eighteenth century. They had, however, weighed heavily on the population in earlier periods. In 1646, at the end of the Thirty Years War, Montigny asked their Spanish over-lords for help: "And one must consider the billets that the community provided both the foot and mounted soldiers who passed back and forth both from the garrisons in Cambrai or on their way to face their enemies to reconnoitre or to carry out orders, for which we cannot in good faith estimate the cost . . . the said community has suffered repeatedly and we leave it up to you to gauge how much. . . ."[54] A bill followed listing the various tributes from the villagers, including 494 florins "for an entire year's contribution to the enemy," while "the hay, oats, and cash paid out to subsidize the soldiers' three rations and their winter quarters at 45 florins a month amount to [270 florins] for six months." To this they added 90 florins for four summer months (at 22.5 florins). Altogether, the village spent 1,236 florins 18.5 patars on war-related expenses and 100 florins 15 patars for ordinary taxes. By comparison, eighteenth-century villages enjoyed excellent conditions.

Even in the eighteenth century the state continued to demand personal service. Lists of men able to serve regularly appear in the village's records, at least in the first half of the century.[55] An occasional mention in the parish records reveals the career of arms, but presumably, given the harshness of military life, there were few volunteers.[56] Though the province was theoretically free from forced labor on the roads, the intendant regularly requisitioned carts and men for various duties.[57]

In fact, local authorities used such exactions to control troublesome figures in the village. In 1744 the mayor and council certified that Philippe Joseph Bens, aged thirty-eight, and Pierre Philippe Paul, aged thirty-seven, "have agreed of their free will . . . to serve as *pionniers* as long as their services might be required."[58] The very same council would later describe one of them as a "ne'er-do-well suspected of a number of thefts." In 1748 the council complained that a year earlier Pierre Philippe Paul had appeared in the village with some low-life female companion: "We went over to his house to chase them out of the village but he had the nerve to threaten us and to tell us to go away or else he would throw one of us down, and on the night of the ninth to the tenth of November of the year 1747, they were still in the village. He then became violent once again, in defiance of the King, and interfered in the execution of a sentence against his sister who was in arrears in her tax payments and forcibly removed the pledge locked up in the local sergeant's house."[59] The rescue of his sister's pig, seized by order of the Estates at the request of Montigny's tax collector, cost Pierre Philippe Paul two months in jail on bread and water.[60]

The survival of the Estates of Cambrésis offered Montigny further protection against royal fiscality. The village council petitioned for lower rates whenever it felt that the village had been overcharged. Assessed forty-two florins for the mencaudée tax in 1660, the "manans and habitans de Montigny" informed the Estates outright that since the troops lodged in the village had ruined the crops and grabbed the better part of the harvest, "they had no intention of paying."[61] Twenty-five years later, they deemed the moulinage similarly outrageous.[62]

One of the principal functions of the provincial Estates was in fact to negotiate with the royal government for lower rates for its inhabitants. In 1754 we find this addendum to a circular tabulating the number of horses in each village. Montigny's council was informed that if it felt overassessed for the 1750 vingtième and desired a refund, it had to make an immediate request.[63] A reduction, certainly neither the first nor the last, was granted in 1775. "The gentlemen of the Estates have agreed that the sick of the village of Montigny pay only half of their taxes for the year 1774."[64] The process, negotiated by the Estates, was more systematic than in some areas of France where villages individually petitioned a beleaguered intendant for rebates.[65]

More vexing than direct taxes were indirect taxes, and these did become more onerous. Royal income from indirect taxation rose from one-third to one-half over the eighteenth century. The two major indirect taxes collected in Cambrésis consisted of the *pied fourché,* raised on the sale and slaughter of animals, and the *aides,* levied on the consumption of spirits, cider, wine, and beer. The last aroused the most bitterness since it was twice as dear on beer consumed at a publican's as on the private supplies by the barrel favored by the rich.[66] There was no salt tax in Cambrésis, which lay outside the barrier of the General Farms, but salt and tobacco were rationed within three leagues of Picardy, a zone that included Montigny.[67]

In each village within these limits, the provincial Estates accredited a single salt and tobacco seller, a person of means whose property yielded at least fifteen livres a year. The local supplier had to purchase the village's provisions in Cambrai, keep registers, and provide a bond for the goods. Montigny's suppliers were usually involved in other forms of trade.

Charles Huguet, who held the post in 1737, sold the grease used by weavers; Jean Adrien Cauchy (1730), Louis and Philippe Pigou (1749–53), and Jean Pierre Lantier (1754–69) marketed cloth.[68]

Cloth, in fact, was subject to an urban toll tax. Weavers from the countryside paid five sous for every piece of cloth they brought to Cambrai and the same amount in duty when they crossed the border of the Five Great Farms in order to sell their pieces in Saint-Quentin, the major market for the area.[69]

If these indirect taxes did not lead to outright rebellion, there were many instances either of tax evasion or of more insolent provocation.

> It is a fact that Isidore Delacourt, resident of Montigny and who has three salt consumers in his family has been marked down [in the register] for 45 pounds of salt a year. But he bought none from the salt vendor between the first of January to the 22 of April. . . . All the circumstances prove that the said Delacourt is indeed guilty and that he purchased salt for his ordinary and extraordinary needs from someone other than his parish's vendor, which goes against article 10 of the Royal Decree . . . so that he must be considered a smuggler and be condemned to the 200 livre fine as set down . . . in the salt tax ordinance ["l'ordonnance des gabelles"].[70]

The General Farms' interference with local liquor consumption gave rise to the most incidents. In 1755 clerks of the Farm accused one of Montigny's publicans: "Louis Lenglet was coming out of his house carrying a glass bottle . . . which he did under his apron; the said bottle was full of illegal *eau de vie* which he tried to hide in his barn . . . he broke the bottle against the barn door before our very eyes in an attempt to cover up his fraud."[71] The officials summoned a councilman to witness the results, showing him the liquid running down the barn wall and the segments of glass that still smelled and tasted of liquor. They poured some on his palm, and he recognized the flavor, but when the time came, both the municipal officer and the accused refused to appear in court, denying the clerk's allegations. There was no love lost between the villagers and officers of the Farm. Pouring away the evidence was the most obvious course. In 1782 the wife of Léonard Delacourt, "publican and retailer of *eau de vie* in Montigny, well-known to the agents of the Farm for his illicit sales for they have caught him at it more than once," wrenched the bottle from the officials' hands and smashed it. A year later, the wife of another Montigny wine seller did the same, heedless of the 100-florin fine.[72] "When the wife of the said Godart caught sight of the agents she yelled out in a clear and intelligible voice: drink up, here come the clerks. Some emptied their glass, others spilled out the contents and the wife of the said Godart took a white glass bottle containing some six cupfuls and emptied it into a bucket of water."

What was at stake here was the resentment of consumer taxes and the salt and liquor monopolies that restricted purchasing and forbade home-made brews. The Montignaciens repeatedly complained that their annual beer tax was too steep, but even in this regard their situation improved visibly over the eighteenth century. In 1674 they were charged about two hundred florins despite their claims that they drank no more than a hundred florins' worth. In 1747 the same tax again cost them two hundred florins, but by then the population had doubled.[73] It was the vigilance of the Farms, however, that riled them: their invasion of private domain, their right to search wherever they pleased.

But geography favored the residents. Such a border region could not but nurture fraud, smuggling, and contraband be it in foodstuffs, drink, or cloth. In a village where seigneurial dues were not heavy, and in a province where the Estates tried to protect the inhabitants from the worst excesses of royal taxation, it was the tithe and the *aides* that were most vigorously defied.

Outside authority weighed relatively lightly on Montigny. The seigneurial system was in retreat; despite its wealth, the Cathedral Chapter levied only trivial dues on the village. Far more important were levies of other kinds—the church's tithes and the state's taxes. Yet the village's growing population and prosperity during the eighteenth century made even these burdens bearable and far less onerous than they had been in the seventeenth century.

In these respects, Montigny was clearly favored over most regions of France. Cambrésis's recent addition to the kingdom and the continuing vitality of its Estates protected it from some royal demands. Regional differences, however, should not be overstated. Despite a few notable exceptions, feudal dues altogether weighed more lightly on French peasants in the eighteenth century, and the state became less burdensome.[74] Like Montigny's residents, most French peasants suffered less from the institutions set over them in the eighteenth century than had been true in earlier times.

II

THE

LAND

3

Landholding

Historians dealing with rural society have placed landownership at the center of their understanding of the peasantry. One of the arguments of this book, however, is that the peasantry's relationship to the land was shifting and complex. It depended to a large extent on broader economic forces and involved a continually renewed series of decisions. The peasants speculated with land when they needed to and manifested a supple approach to its ownership. Such uses of the land do not easily fit conventional models, for these usually presume the prototypical peasant to have been self-sufficient, even if only a minority actually managed to be autonomous and make their living primarily off the land. For the majority of peasants, recourse to supplementary sources of income was a necessity. The pivotal question for many scholars remains how this affected their outlook. Some believe that the peasantry remained bound to the soil and yearned for a parcel of land. Others concede that the peasants adapted to new circumstances, but that this lent them a different identity. They became rural artisans, detached from the agrarian community, and, in their most successful guise, mediators between city and country, further removed from the rest of the peasantry.[1]

Yet the success of peasant diversification has not received sufficient attention. The pauperization of the countryside, tied in part to extreme parcelization, is one of the fundamental arguments of the theory of proto-industrialization.[2] Peasants with little or no land, searching for supplementary incomes, turned to industry as a way of relieving their poverty. In the long run, so these theorists argue, this new source of revenue encouraged them to marry younger and to reproduce faster, thereby exacerbating an already difficult situation. They strained resources beyond their limits and eventually moved from relative deprivation to actual proletarianization.[3]

I do not contest the fact that peasant proprietorship declined over the eighteenth century and that the process became especially evident in the last decades of the Ancien Régime. The decision to stay in the village was crucial since it meant that patrimonies were shared among more resident heirs than previously had been the case. What is more, peasant access to land remained limited. In villages such as Montigny, peasants were left with those portions of the arable that had been disdained by nobles and

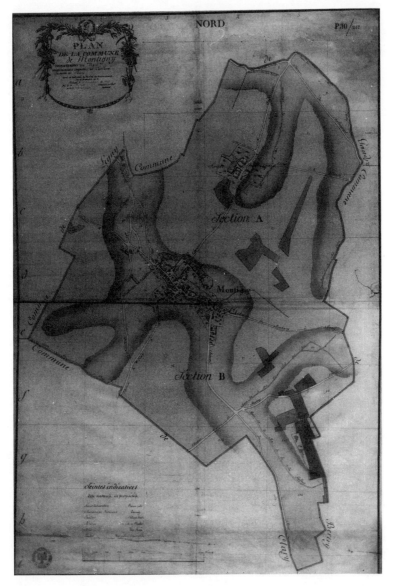

Figure 7. Map of Montigny, 1806 *Photo Populu, Archives départementales du Nord, Plans Cambrai.*

ecclesiastics alike (fig. 7). In other regions of France, bourgeois investors further reduced the peasants' share. Montigny and southeastern Cambrésis had attracted few such buyers, principally because the land was not very fertile and the best that was available was already in the hands of lay or clerical seigneurs. Since the amount available to the peasantry remained essentially the same, portions grew smaller as population rose, and by the end of the century many families survived on tiny plots. Yet the results were not disastrous. Wages from industry and the profits from trade allowed many peasants to live independently. Some invested in land; others disengaged themselves from it. In doing so, they expressed their trust in the reliability of industrial incomes. This belief would be hard to shake. Nineteenth-century weavers proved more reluctant to abandon their handlooms than they had been to abandon the land.

Reliance on industry and withdrawal from agriculture in villages such as Montigny began as a response to the late seventeenth- and early eighteenth-century crises. Although the peasants might appear to have been more secure than in the eighteenth century since there were larger numbers of self-sufficient farmers, this is not the case. Wars and epidemics had lowered population and consequently extended the size of individual holdings, but conditions were hard. High taxation and constricted markets hampered the development of the agricultural sector. A number of families emigrated, and the turnover of names in the Chapter's registers from the sixteenth to the early eighteenth century is suggestive. Of the thirty-six family names in late sixteenth-century Montigny, only three survived into the eighteenth century.[4]

Such population losses meant that in the mid-1680s a quarter of the village's forty or so households had sufficient land to be considered independent; only four had no arable, and three of these were women. By 1692 the number of households had fallen to thirty-seven, and eight young men were said to be off at the wars.[5] In 1701, conditions were so appalling that the village contained only twenty-four taxable households and eighteen beggars. By 1708, thirteen of the twenty-seven households included on the tax roll could pretend to independence, while seven others had no land at all. This is our last vision of a predominantly farming community, with a large number of middling, independent farmers, along with a handful of large farmers and a sizable proportion of landless. The eighteenth century would see the erosion of such classifications. Middling and small farmers disappeared, attracted by rural industry. The importance of land declined as new opportunities arose and old ones seemed less and less viable. Such, for example, was the lesson of the agrarian crisis of the 1740s, which marked the final decline of Montigny's subsistence farmers. It is no coincidence that peasant-weavers abandoned the land most readily in the 1780s, in a period of prosperity, when they felt it was economically feasible for them to do so. Even then, the process was not as one-sided as the averages would suggest. Not all weavers gave up the land, and, quite the contrary, successful ones built up patrimonies both for financial security and as profitable investments.

The Pattern of Landownership

Cambrésis contained vast ecclesiastical properties. The church owned 40 percent of the soil, the nobility 14 percent, the bourgeoisie 10 percent, leaving about one-third to the peasants.[6] In nearly half of the province, the church owned even more property, and there were only nine villages where it possessed less than 12 percent of the land. The southeastern regions of Cambrésis, where Montigny was located, had the poorest soil. As such, these regions had been less attractive to the religious foundations that had appropriated the more fertile lands. Nobiliar property, consequently, was more prominent in this area. In Troisvilles, for example, the seigneur, Cordier, owned 41 percent of the village, and in Ligny and Audencourt titled families likewise controlled most of the land.[7] Yet clerical property, even if not choice, remained important. It prevailed in Bertry, Caullery, and Clary, villages situated next to Montigny. In Montigny itself, because of donations in the early Middle Ages, 46 percent of the land was in the hands of the church. One nobleman, seigneur of nearby La Bruyère, held another 9 percent, and the peasants 41 percent.[8] Historical accident thus ensured that ecclesiastical ownership would remain substantial even in poor southeastern villages like Montigny. Peasant landownership in these parts surpassed the provincial average as well, for bourgeois property remained insignificant.[9]

In eighteenth-century Montigny, peasant parcels were scattered over a territory of about nine hundred mencaudées, or three hundred hectares.[10] Estimates vary with the source consulted. Fiscal rolls tend to exaggerate, while local pleas for tax reductions attempt to minimize the total acreage that shaped most assessments. Some documents include only the arable, others only land owned by local residents. They nonetheless indicate that Montigny covered between nine hundred and one thousand mencaudées during the early modern period. This land belonged in part to the local inhabitants and peasants of surrounding villages and to outside bodies.[11]

The biggest landowner was the village's seigneur, the Chapter of the Cambrai Cathedral, followed by the abbeys of Cantimpré and Prémy, and

Table 8. Land Distribution in Montigny in 1728, 1750, 1754 (in mencaudées)

Owner	1728		1740		1754	
	Amount	Percentages	Amount	Percentages	Amount	Percentages
Clerics						
Chapter	153.5	20.0	153	16.0	174	16.0
Cantimpré	144	19.0	141	14.5	125	12.5
Prémy	30	4.0	37	4.0	37	4.0
Chapel	11	1.5	18	2.0	18	2.0
Parish	50	6.5	43.75	4.5	43	4.0
Priest	42.5	5.5	32.5	3.0	32.5	3.0
Poor	16	2.0	15	1.5	15	1.5
Guillemains	—	—	—	—	30	3.0
Subtotal		58.5		45.5		46.0
Nobles						
de Baralle	96	12.5	92	9.5	92	9.0
de Rieux	—	—	28.5	3.0	28.5	3.0
Other						
Fievet	—	—	—	—	3	0.3
Peasants	224.5	29.0	412.5	42.0	414.75	41.0
Total	767.5	100.0	973.25	100.0	1,002.75	99.3

Source: C suppl. 524.

the Guillemains at Walincourt. The Chapel of All Saints, administered by the Chapter, also owned some parcels, as did the parish church and the abbey of Honnecourt (table 8).[12]

An examination of plot size, rather than landownership,[13] does not alter this overall picture. Large farms continue to stand out among a multiplicity of small plots that remained in peasant hands. Montigny proper contained two such sizable estates. The largest, a 155-mencaudée (approximately 50 hectares) leasehold known as La Trappe, belonged to the seigneurs, the Chapter of Cambrai. The second, measuring roughly 140 mencaudées, belonged to the abbey of Cantimpré. Yet another 90 mencaudées (30 hectares), the seigneurie of La Bruyère, were loosely attached to Montigny's parish. This was the village's only lay lordship and in the late eighteenth century belonged to Adrien Mairesse, esquire, a barrister.[14] These three properties occupied a total of 385 mencaudées, or more than one-third of the village's territory. Usually, though not always,

Table 9. Percentages of Montigny Inhabitants with Less Than Twenty-five Mencaudées, 1686–1787

Year	Percentages
1686	82.5
1708	66.7
1744	86.7
1750	87.3
1787	96.1

Source: C suppl. 524.

they were leased as single units so that a significant segment of the arable was farmed by a very few individuals.

In his study of the peasants of the Nord, Lefebvre maintained that a Cambrésis peasant needed at least eight hectares, or approximately twenty-five mencaudées, to be independent, that is, without recourse to a secondary occupation.[15] The few surviving tax rolls for Montigny show that between 1686 and 1787, only a minority were in such a position (table 9). Many, in fact, survived on far less.

In the late seventeenth and early eighteenth centuries one-fifth to one-third of the peasants of Montigny enjoyed the economic independence defined by Lefebvre. Less than 4 percent of the population could claim the same in the late 1780s (table 10). The proportion of middling and

Table 10. Percentages of the Population (P) and Percentages of the Land (L) Occupied by Montigny Residents, 1686–1787

	0–4m		5–24m		25–99m		More than 100m		Total	
Year	P	L	P	L	P	L	P	L	P	L
1686	23	2	61	29	10	25	8	45	102	101
1708	38	1	27	14	23	32	11	54	99	101
1744	40	5	45	27	11	46	2	23	98	101
1750	29	4	58	35	9	30	4	30	100	99
1787	72	12	24	32	2	16	2	40	100	100

m = mencaudées
Source: C suppl. 524, C états 288.

Table 11. Percentages of Landless and Owners of Gardens According to Montigny Marriage Contracts, 1700–1790

Period	Number of contracts	Landless		Garden		Total	
		Number	Percentage	Number	Percentage	Number	Percentage
1700–1719	23	1	4.3	4	17.4	5	21.7
1720–39	29	1	3.4	1	3.4	2	6.9
1740–59	37	—	0	4	10.8	4	10.8
1760–79	28	1	3.6	8	28.6	9	32.1
1780–90	30	6	20.0	12	40.0	18	60.0

Source: Cambrésis notaries.

subsistence farmers, with holdings of five to twenty-four mencaudées, who typically supplemented their income by tilling other people's land and dabbling in various crafts, diminished as well. From 60 percent of the local population in 1686, they fell to 25 percent in 1787. At the bottom of the scale, the proportion of peasants who owned less than five mencaudées rose from one-fifth to three-quarters over the same period. There, too, the major shift occurred in the latter part of the eighteenth century.

Marriage contracts show a similar trend toward smaller and smaller holdings. The 172 available Montigny marriage contracts, and an additional 140 from nearby localities, establish that by the 1780s three-quarters of newlyweds had marriage portions of less than one mencaudée.[16] The subdivision of plots applied equally to gardens.

As the eighteenth century progressed, ordinary residents of Montigny owned steadily less land, and an increasing number owned either none at all or only a small garden, usually one-quarter of a mencaudée. One-fifth of Montigny's newlyweds had been in this position in the early eighteenth century. Again, by the 1780s this was the case of nearly two-thirds. By the end of the last decade of the Old Regime, then, a majority married either with no land at all or with nothing but a house and vegetable patch (table 11).

The Pattern of Land Sales

With fragmentation came an active land market. Prices remained stable until the 1720s and then increased substantially. Altogether, the value of

Table 12. Average Price of a Mencaudée of Land in Montigny,
1679–1789 (in florins)

Period	Sales	Gardens	Average price	Arable	Average price
1679	2	—	—	2	52.81
1680–89	2	1	412.00	1	105.60
1690–99	10	1	864.00	9	111.80
1700–1709	10	2	433.34	8	106.74
1710–19	3	—	—	3	93.16
1720–29	40	6	752.18	34	187.84
1730–39	52	3	370.56	49	205.85
1740–49	30	3	575.11	27	244.36
1750–59	64	9	1,411.57	55	258.20
1760–69	121	24	754.24	97	238.68
1770–79	50	11	1,148.73	39	327.41
1780–89	15	5	1,526.17	10	478.38

Source: 3G887–90 Chapter of Cambrai *embrefs.*

real estate rose significantly in the century between 1680 and the Revolution (table 12).[17] This was as true of Ligny and Cattenières, a Cambrésis village close by, as of Montigny (table 13). Prices quadrupled in nominal value. If we allow for inflation and currency fluctuations, the real value increased perhaps two and a half times.

Sales were, of course, motivated by the economic climate. They increased dramatically in Ligny, for example, during that harshest of years, 1709. On the other hand, the next major agrarian crisis, that of 1740, however difficult, did not bring on similar sales. If anything, the combination of agrarian and industrial crises in the 1740s and 1750s made peasants cling desperately to what little they had. There appears to be no consistent correlation between crisis, indebtedness, and land sales. Rather, crises interfered with expectations and turned what was usually intended as short-term borrowing into more serious indebtedness.

Loan sharks are believed to have been key actors in the expropriation of the peasantry, lending them money and, once they defaulted, taking away their land. In both the seventeenth and eighteenth centuries, Montigny's inhabitants mortgaged land to raise money. In the earlier period they borrowed most frequently from institutional or urban lenders. The Dames de Saint-Lazare at Cambrai, for example, appeared more than once, as did other religious foundations and priests. Local notables also came forward with loans.[18] By the middle of the eighteenth century there

Table 13. Price of One Mencaudée of Arable in
Montigny, Ligny, and Cattenières, 1658–1789

Period	Montigny	Ligny	Cattenières
1658–69	—	81	—
1670–79	49	56	—
1680–89	99	97	—
1690–99	105	71	105
1700–1709	100	100	100
1710–19	87	123	109
1720–29	176	—	141
1730–39	192	—	176
1740–49	229	194	231
1750–59	242	—	—
1760–69	224	242	—
1770–79	307	—	357
1780–89	448	481	483

Base: 1700–1709 = 100
Source: 3G887–90, 3G864–75, 3G794–98, Chapter of Cambrai
embrefs.

was a noticeable shift to rural moneylenders and, most specifically in the
case of Montigny, to one Jean François Clais from the village of Esnes. He
provided loan after loan, at the regular rate of 4 percent current for rentes
(annuities) on property. He did so, undoubtedly, at some risk to himself,
but not in order to expand his property. He seemed to anticipate regular
returns rather than defaults, and, when he bought land in the village, he
chose those parcels that he judged attractive, not those that were mortgaged to him. He did not repossess land directly. When arrears accumulated unreasonably, the plots were either put up for auction or sold with
the rente still attached.

   If economic crises did not lead to land sales, what did? The peasants
themselves viewed the process in very personal terms. We see this in the
pleas that widows and widowers addressed to the local authorities. They
needed to describe their motives because the law required that they name
tutors for their underage children whenever they sold patrimonial holdings. They had to demonstrate that their offspring's inheritance was not
disposed of frivolously. The sellers told stories of personal woe. They
related their present distress to the lengthy illnesses of their spouses or (in
some cases) of their children, which had occasioned great expense and
led to unfortunate borrowing. It was only then that economic conditions
such as the dearness of grain or excessive taxation were invoked to

account for the arrears that had put the household in jeopardy. The only way to repay these debts and ensure the future welfare of the family—in some cases the money was intended for the children's apprenticeship— was to sell some property.

Even though illness proved an acceptable explanation, other troubles were mentioned as well. Farmers blamed crop failures, and merchants pointed to industrial crises. Misery was not sufficient cause. The integrity of the household had to be preserved, and the supplicants stressed that sales would secure the household's continued viability. Land was sold to repay debts and to allow the individuals to pursue their work. One widow explained that she had to replace eight horses that had died; otherwise, she would be forced to give up her lease. Another widow, that of a Cambrai weaver, had to sell land in Montigny to keep buying thread. Business had been slow, and she was presently overstocked, but if she suspended her purchasing, she might as well close up shop. The trick was to appear to act sensibly. Despite the apparent contradiction, one could get rid of family holdings in order to ensure the family's survival. The village authorities did not care to have more paupers on their hands. On the other hand, they never turned down such appeals.

Yet another set of factors affected land sales: family and inheritance. Familial considerations weakened over the century, and we can see this through a closer examination of two sample decades, the 1730s and 1760s. In Montigny, much of the land "sold" in the first half of the eighteenth century still entailed family settlements. In the seventeenth and early eighteenth centuries, not all siblings stayed in the village. A number moved away, usually to nearby villages, and this led to property exchanges and transactions among the heirs. Those who remained in the village took over the family holdings and paid off their brothers and sisters (this was an area of partible inheritance) through a formal deed of purchase. Often the sale of Montigny was balanced with a purchase in the new village. We know this because buyers and sellers with children, who disposed of inheritances or dowries, had to find suitable replacements. At times, these emigrants sold land to strangers. Sentimental attachments to the old homestead never stood in the way of active transfers of property. Land was important, indeed, but not necessarily the land of one's ances- tors. We are far removed from imaginative reconstructions that view the peasant as viscerally attached to his property: "[What] came through . . . was his immense grief, hidden resentment and appalling heartache at giving up his land which he had so greedily cultivated, with a passion

Table 14. Land Sold to Residents and Nonresidents in Montigny in the 1730s and 1760s

	1730s		1760s	
	Number	Percentage	Number	Percentage
Residents to nonresidents	—	—	6	5
Residents to residents	23	41	52	47
Nonresidents to residents	29	52	49	44
Nonresidents to nonresidents	4	7	4	5
Total	56	100	111	100

which can only be described as lust, and had then added to, with an odd patch of land here and there at the cost of the most squalid avarice."[19]

By the second half of the eighteenth century, as more and more people turned to cottage industry and fewer migrated, there were fewer such family arrangements. Inheritances were now parceled out within the village. As the number of owners grew, so did the incidence of sales. A real land market appeared, on the one hand, while on the other, with reduced emigration, people established firmer bonds with their terroir. The reasons for selling remained the same: some people still emigrated; others contended with poverty and indebtedness brought on by personal tragedy, economic crises, or recklessness (buying too much land was one such excuse). Absentee landlords could not necessarily count on profitable returns from rentals because of the difficulties associated with leasehold (known locally as the "ill will" of renters).[20] This and rising land values made selling land more attractive than owning it, and discouraged urban takeovers of peasant property. These factors meant that land continued to come up for sale, and, as a result, rich weavers or newcomers with money had no difficulty establishing themselves in the village.

In the 1730s, 44 mencaudées of arable changed hands, a mere 5 percent of the village; in the 1760s this figure was 130.5 mencaudées (table 14).[21] This last total represented one-third of the arable belonging to the peasants. The buyers were primarily local residents. Outsiders bought infrequently and, when they did, seemed only too keen to resell.

The price varied depending on the buyer. Land sold among local inhabitants cost more than land sold by nonresidents to residents (table 15). In 1730 familial transactions had an important place in the land

Table 15. Price Variations for One Mencaudée of Land Sold in the 1730s and 1760s

	1730s			1760s		
Type of sale	Total land sold (m)	Total amount paid (fl)	Average price (fl)	Total land sold (m)	Total amount paid (fl)	Average price (fl)
Resident to nonresident	—	—	—	35.5	7059	199
Resident to resident	14.5	2862	202	31.5	7418	236
Nonresident to resident	22.5	4135	184	62.3	10565	170
Nonresident to nonresident	7.3	747	103	1.3	433	347
Total	44.3	7744	175	130.6	25475	195

m = mencaudées
fl = florins

market. A slight majority of sales went to family members, and they obtained a better price. Homesteads in particular were reserved for siblings. In the 1730s, 60 percent of sales from nonresidents involved houses and yards (nine out of fifteen sales; while only one yard was sold outside the family). Besides such family arrangements, when land changed hands within the village (resident to resident), it rarely went to relatives. Such family dealings accounted for only 9 percent of local transfers, and 91 percent of in-village sales were made outside the kin group. In the 1760s, as more people stayed in the village, the number as well as proportion of in-village sales rose considerably. Seventeen of those sales (33 percent were to family members—seven of these still consisting of houses and yards, the favored family property. The majority of sales, 67 percent, however, did not involve relatives (in this case thirty-five sales, seven of them gardens). Even emigrants no longer seemed to favor their relatives. Of the forty-nine nonresident to resident sales, only 20 percent involved family members.

Yards sold for such erratic sums and came in such uneven sizes that a pattern is hard to discern. The average price of a mencaudée of arable fluctuated as well. This sometimes reflected private arrangements or inheritance or debt settlements (land was cheaper when it came burdened with rente) as well as variations in quality. This assessment of the productivity of different plots stands out quite clearly when a number of parcels were simultaneously put up for sale. Each segment fetched a different price. Yet perhaps the most surprising feature of the sales is the fact that family members ceased to pay less for land. In the 1730s family members paid about 20 percent less (an average of 165 florins) when they bought from nonresidents and 405 florins when they bought from relatives in Montigny itself (but this involved a tiny sample of two sales). The average sale price for people who were not related was 215 florins in the first instance and 205 florins in the second. In the 1760s the difference vanished. As the proportion of sales outside the family increased, the status of family members altered. These were no longer considered privileged buyers, especially where the arable was concerned.

If land sales were provoked as much by duress as by choice, the process was not irreversible. People sold land at some points in their lives and bought it at others. Land was not a sacred entity, and there was no special attachment to ancestral plots. These were sold, exchanged, and mortgaged not merely in times of crisis, but as investment strategies: to obtain funds to run a business or a farm, or to provide for children.[22] There was some eagerness to have something to pass on to one's descendants, but this did not stand in the way of other calculations and needs.

People who did well bought land. Some of their reasons may have been sentimental, or traditional, as they looked to the sort of independence that landownership promised. At the same time, as they well knew, land was the basis of credit, the security that helped to raise loans. By the middle of the eighteenth century, then, the peasantry was readier to view land as a commodity.

Peasant landownership declined in eighteenth-century Montigny, repeating patterns that historians have seen in other regions of France. These scholars have tended to view peasants' disengagement from farming as evidence of increasing pauperization. This book argues against that view. Although important elements of this argument can come only later, we should note at this point that land was bought and sold over the course of a family's lifetime, as circumstances dictated. Moreover, the land bought in Montigny went primarily to local residents or to neighboring villagers. Sales were not the result of expropriation either by urban dwellers or rural loan sharks. The Montignaciens themselves were able to come up with the funds necessary to purchase progressively more expensive plots. This process was not unique to either Montigny or Cambrésis, but what is clear is that in this particular case the rise in prices did not derive exclusively from the pressures of a growing population. People wanted land because it provided security, status, and borrowing potential. Land, for them, involved a whole set of decisions, which related as much to their diverse concerns and varied sources of income as to traditional expectations.

Appendix A

Table A-1. Landownership in Montigny Based on Marriage Contracts, 1641–1790

	Percentages					Number of
Period	Under 1m	1–4m	5–19m	20–99m	Total	contracts
1614–99	21	41	24	13	99	29
1700–1719	30	39	21	9	99	23
1720–39	18	43	29	11	101	28
1740–59	33	39	20	8	100	36
1760–79	66	19	15	—	100	21
1780–90	75	14	8	4	101	28

m = mencaudée
Source: Cambrésis notaries.

Table A-2. Landownership in Nearby Villages Based on Marriage Contracts, 1720–90*

	Percentages					Number of
Period	Under 1m	1–4m	5–19m	20–99m	Total	contracts
1720–39	25	—	50	25	100	4
1740–59	33	66	—	—	99	6
1760–79	58	35	4	2	99	48
1780–90	73	23	3	—	99	81

*The sample included no contracts prior to 1720.
m = mencaudée
Source: Cambrésis notaries.

The size of holdings sold from 1679 to 1789 confirms the pattern toward greater fragmentation.[23] A clear shift to smaller parcels is noticeable from the 1730s on, when the bulk of sales came to involve plots of less than one mencaudée.

Table A-3. Percentages of Sales of Arable and Garden Plots, 0 to More Than 10 Mencaudées, 1679–1789

Period	N	0–1 garden	0–1 arable	1–1.9 arable	2–4.9 arable	5–9.9 arable	More than 10 arable
1679–99	14	14	29	14	29	7	7
1700–1709	11	9	18	36	27	9	—
1710–19	7	29	—	29	43	—	—
1720–29	43	21	44	16	14	2	2
1730–39	62	14	82	6	8	—	—
1740–49	32	15	69	6	9	—	—
1750–59	81	21	69	7	1	1	—
1760–69	128	19	64	10	5	1	2
1770–79	59	21	53	19	3	3	2
1780–89	17	30	58	6	6	—	3

Source: 3G887–90 (Chapter of Cambrai—Montigny *embrefs*).

Land distribution can also be related to occupation despite the concern that distinctions in this matter may be tautological. Ploughmen (laboureurs) quite naturally tilled more land than day laborers, and people with little or no land looked for other ways to make a living. Cottage industry and agriculture were the major spheres of activity in eighteenth-century Montigny, and the village included the usual smattering of artisans. In analyzing the relationship between occupation and landownership, these pursuits have been broken down into five categories. Farmers divide into two separate groups: independent farmers (laboureurs, *fermiers,* and censiers) in category one, and subsistence farmers (*ménagers*) in category two. They are followed by a variety of agricultural laborers in category three (*manouvriers, journaliers, valets de charrue,* or *batteurs en grange*). Fine linen weavers and the very few cotton weavers combine in category four. Village artisans appear in a fifth category. A sixth merely gathers those whose profession could not be determined. Occupations do not figure on tax records and those used here came from parish registers, marriage contracts, and, in some cases, from the declarations of trial witnesses. Since the earliest parish registers have been lost, and the remaining information is at best scanty, it proved impossible to determine the type of work done by one-fifth of those listed in 1686. Nonetheless, the trend is clear: by 1787 plots in each category had grown smaller. Large farms are one exception since they were rarely subdivided.

Table A-4. Land Ownership in Montigny According to Occupation, 1686–1790

	Tax Records				Marriage contracts	
Year	Population (%)	Land (%)	Average plot (mencaudées)	Period	Number of contracts	Average plot (mencaudées)
			Independent farmers			
1686	27.5	72.6	58.20	1700–1719	1	—
1708	35	82	73.00	1720–39	3	—
1744	18	73	72.60	1740–59	1	41.5
1750	16	60	62.77	1760–79	0	—
1787	6.6	59	69.10	1780–90	1	—
			Subsistence farmers			
1686	12.5	6.7	11.80	1700–1719	no surviving contracts	
1708	11.5	4	11.25	1720–39		
1744	4	2	7.00	1740–59		
1750	2	.3	2.75	1760–79		
1787	1.3	.9	5.50	1780–90		
			Farm laborers			
1686	12.5	0.5	4.50	1700–1719	3	3.67
1708	—	—	—	1720–39	—	—
1744	—	—	—	1740–59	2	.875
1750	—	—	—	1760–79	2	.25
1787	6.6	2	1.90	1780–90	3	.25
			Weavers			
1686	17.5	8.7	10.90	1700–1719	16	3.2
1708	31	2	1.75	1720–39	22	4.8
1744	56	19	6.12	1740–59	24	3.9
1750	62	27	7.35	1760–79	12	1.7
1787	62	28	3.55	1780–90	21	1.1
			Village artisans			
1686	20	7.7	8.50	1700–1719	3	23.21
1708	11.5	6	15.00	1720–39	3	3.00
1744	18	5	5.25	1740–59	5	5.00
1750	20	13	10.86	1760–79	7	3.40
1787	19	9	3.66	1780–90	3	2.85
			Unknown			
1686	20	3.7	4.20	1700–1719	—	—
1708	11.5	1	3.00	1720–39	—	—
1744	4	3	1.00	1740–59	1	.25
1750	—	—	—	1760–79	—	—
1787	4.6	1.4	2.40	1780–90	—	—

4

Tenancy

Nobles and ecclesiastics owned one-half of Montigny's territory. They had done so for centuries, with remarkable stability. Gentlefolk periodically sold land, usually to other gentlefolk; the church held fast to its properties. As we have seen, these practices constricted peasant holdings and meant that peasants could acquire land only at the expense of other peasants. On the other hand, the arable was tilled in its entirety by the local population. Absentee owners rented out their domains to a small group of resident tenant-farmers. The latter did not sublet, as was often the case in other provinces. The so-called *fermiers-généraux,* when they did appear in this area, did not speculate on leases, although they collected the tithes and the seigneurial dues. They worked the land themselves and tried to accumulate a maximum number of rentals. The existence of large farms thus did little to assuage the average peasant's need of land; it created, instead, an oligarchy of powerful, rich farmers. What is more, a significant proportion of smaller properties were let to the same group of tenant-farmers and laboureurs. In this way, they managed to control most of the village's grain production. Nonetheless, a share of smaller plots regularly went to ordinary villagers. This permitted some, at least, to retain or expand their involvement in agriculture.

The four large farms in and about Montigny remained in the hands of the same few families, generation after generation. In the few cases where tenants were dismissed, they were replaced by local farmers who, especially in the latter part of the century, made a big push to extend their individual hold over large properties. No totally new families arrived on the scene. When heretofore unknown names appear on leases, they prove to be those of the new spouse of the previous tenant's widow, or of a daughter who inherited the tenancy. In any case, it soon turns out, these men came from similar farming families in the region, weaving a complete web of kinship.

It is possible to trace this dynastic control in all of the Montigny farms. In 1675 Calixte Gabet farmed the Cambrai Chapter's domain of La Trappe, and he passed it on to his daughter Anne when she married in 1678.[1] She and her husband, Michel Malesieux, occupied it until 1701 when they ceded it, in turn, to their son, Antoine.[2] In 1711 Antoine's widow appeared as the farmer, and, when she remarried, the land went to her husband, Moyse Crinon, and remained in the Crinon family until Charles lost it in 1763. Whether by mismanagement or ill luck, Charles, who had taken on a prosperous domain in 1750,[3] accumulated debt upon debt and in 1763 had to surrender the farm to Robert Milot (who already occupied one-quarter of Le Troncquoy) and a Caullery farmer, Henri Mairesse. When Milot died in 1781, his son, Jacques François, took over the lease, which he still held in the 1790s.

The Malesieux family, which briefly occupied La Trappe, held other leases as well. From the turn of the century to his death in 1755, François Malesieux leased 37.5 mencaudées from the abbey of Prémy and another 12 from the Chapel of All Saints. He left both to his daughter, Marie Reine.[4] She passed on the rental to her second husband, Claude Cardon. On the eve of the Revolution the properties formed the dowry of their daughter, who married the laboureur Pierre Bisiaux. Both of these men were newcomers to the village.

Other Malesieux appear as tenants of La Bruyère. In 1681 Pierre Henninot inherited the lease from his parents. On his marriage to Catherine Dubois, his brother and brother-in-law recognized his right of occupancy.[5] Widowed before 1705, Catherine appeared as defendant in a dispute over tithes, and she still held the domain in 1713.[6] In 1720, however, the Taine of Ligny negotiated its transfer with the proviso that an unnamed compensation be paid to Pierre François Henninot, son of Pierre and Catherine.[7] The document does not mention if and how he forfeited the tenancy, and parish registers have him working as a weaver in Montigny.[8] His sister Marie Marguerite and her husband, Jean Philippe Malesieux, somehow recovered at least a portion of the farm. In 1749 their sons shared the land, although the eldest eventually farmed it alone.[9] At his death in 1789, Pierre Philippe Malesieux figured in the parish register as "former farmer of La Bruyère," although the Tamboises had long since replaced him, followed by yet another Troncquoy farmer, Louis Petit.[10] The last still occupied this land during the Revolution, although its master had fled.[11]

Another Montigny family, the Labbés, farmed the 102 mencaudées that the abbey of Cantimpré owned in the village. Michel Labbé and his wife occupied the properties and bequeathed them to their son, François, when he married in 1677.[12] He subsequently gave them to his heir, Antoine, in 1733, who handed them eventually to his own son, Jean Baptiste, in 1771.[13] This provides one instance where tenure descended in a direct line, rather than through the remarriage of widows, as was the case for the other farms. In fact, the family made very clear provisions for this. When Jean Baptiste married Marie Rose Malesieux in 1787, the marriage contract stipulated that should he die, she would continue to run the farm until one of their children was old enough to take it over. Should she remarry, she would be entitled only to her personal belongings.[14]

François Labbé's other son, Antoine's brother, received a piece of twenty-four mencaudées, detached from the Cantimpré holdings, when he wed Marie Agnès Guille in 1718.[15] His wife's lease of the twenty-six mencaudées belonging to the Guillemains, which her father had held since at least 1683, compensated him for his lesser share of the Cantimpré farm, as did the fifteen mencaudées leased from the parish and poor.[16] A widow in the 1750s, Marie Agnès continued to lease the Guillemain and Cantimpré properties, and in 1772 her two sons took them over.[17]

The Troncquoy farms, totaling 550 mencaudées (175 hectares or so), located northwest of Montigny, formed part of the parish of Caudry until the middle of the eighteenth century when they joined Montigny's parish. The information on its tenants is therefore more tenuous for the early period. In the second half of the century its close ties to Montigny provide a clearer picture. Despite the variety of surnames, on this estate women again hold the key to familial retention of leaseholds.

In 1680 Pierre Ledieu and Antoine Crinon, occupiers of one of the three farms, went bankrupt. Pierre then stated that he had inherited the farm from his father.[18] Their goods and chattel were put up for auction, but relatives, who were farmers in nearby villages, bought them and evidently helped to set the two men on their feet again, for in 1701 they held the contract to Caudry's tithes.[19] It was common for families to support defaulting members. In July 1702, when the crops harvested by Jean Defontaine, a Caudry farmer, were going to be seized, his sons-in-law paid the arrears.[20] Later in the century the brother-in-law of another Troncquoy farmer, Louis Petit, similarly covered his debts.[21]

In 1706 three farmers, Antoine Crinon, Marie Sellier (widow of Pierre Ledieu), and Philippe Leclercq, occupied the farms. Marie Sellier had leased one-quarter since 1705. In 1722 she finally signed a new contract after years of unofficial tenure. Her son, Pierre Joseph Ledieu, and his wife, Marie Godecaut, replaced her in 1731. We know little else until 1750 when Robert Milot took over the collection of Caudry's tithes. He had married Marie Godecaut and settled on the farms. Robert Milot, and later his son, Jacques François, rented one-quarter of Le Troncquoy and two-thirds of the Montigny estate of La Trappe until the end of the century. The Crinons continued to farm the second quarter of Le Tronc-quoy. Philippe took over from Antoine, followed by Louis Petit who married Philippe's daughter, Marie Jeanne Crinon.[22]

Philippe Leclercq occupied the remaining half of the estate, which he inherited from his mother in 1718. His widow then leased it in 1726, 1745, and 1754, joined eventually by her second husband, Pierre Joseph Tamboise. Their son, Pierre Aubert Tamboise, and his wife and later widow, Anne Joseph Fontaine ("la veuve Tamboise"), leased this portion from the 1760s to the 1820s.[23]

These cases show how the biggest tenant-farmers were able to maintain their hold over rental properties for most of the period and hand them to their chosen successors, be they spouses or offspring. Wills and dowries indicated that the owners' consent would be needed, and, in fact, these rarely interfered. Even in cases of near-bankruptcy, farmers could count on the support of their kin. Though farmers might spread their tentacles and accumulate small plots and even occupy land in other villages—as was the case of the Tamboises or Milots—no single family was ever able to monopolize either the whole of Le Troncquoy or to collect an overwhelming number of leases. They tried. At the end of the Old Regime, the Troncquoy farmers took over the seigneurie of La Bruyère.[24] Nonetheless, some sort of equilibrium was repeatedly struck.

One may wonder why this was so and how owners intervened in this process. For, if renting to a wealthy, well-established farmer was attractive, it was also in the owners' interest to bring in competitors. This would explain the surprising favor accorded to widows' second husbands who often took over the previous lease instead of the deceased's rightful heir. Widows held on tenaciously to their tenancies, sacrificing sons for whom they found monetary compensation or advantageous marriages. The family, rather than the lineage, remained in place, with its extensive kin networks. In a region where (as we shall see in detail) tenants could only be dismissed with great difficulty, owners would have welcomed such opportunities to introduce new blood. Newcomers would have to be legitimized by signing new contracts, thus allowing for a raise in rent that might otherwise have been more difficult to obtain. The system, again, allowed for considerable manipulation. From the community's point of view, these new arrivals also ensured that even if a regional oligarchy remained in place by means of intermarriage, one dynasty did not become all-powerful within a single village.

Smaller Leases

Various religious bodies also owned small properties in the village of Montigny. Fifty or so yards belonged to the seigneurs, the Cathedral Chapter, and had long been transferred to the peasants in the form of perpetual or long-term leases. It was on this land that they built their houses and kept kitchen gardens, and it was on this land that they paid seigneurial dues. The paperwork generated by the sale of *biens nationaux* during the Revolution shows that the abbey of Cantimpré possessed a number of similar plots in the village. Besides this seigneurial tenure, however, there were small properties available for rent. These encompassed, for one, the aforementioned land of the Guillemains or the smaller Cantimpré farm. They were tilled by small tenant-farmers and local laboureurs. Parish property was open to public bid every nine years, as were the curé's ten hectares. Peasants also rented land to other peasants either because they had left the village, because they were too old to till it themselves, or because they did not own the proper implements.

The 1787 tax roll, surviving leases, and parish records give us a picture of the small property renters on the eve of the Revolution (table 16). Those documents show that they could be found in all but the lowest tax categories.[25] A similar combination of farmers and artisans appears in the disposal of Montigny's clerical and parish property (table 17).

These small holdings could potentially increase the average peasant's or artisan's access to land, and in some measure that proved to be the case, despite one major limitation. The village's farmers usually held between one-third and one-half of the available rentals, an arresting fact that demonstrates their continual eagerness to secure land and expand production. Not even the richest disdained such parcels. Nonetheless, the periodic auction of parish leases and other lots afforded the more prosperous merchants, weavers, and artisans a continued place within the farming community. They could, moreover, speculate with their own patrimony (mortgage or sell it, that is) with some assurance that they would find some land to rent. Their optimism rested on two factors. The first was pure observation: the plots remained open to bidding so that every two or three years, as different parcels came up for renewal, they could compete for new leases. The second involved a creative use of tradition. The assumption that families retained rights to leaseholds, a phenomenon I will discuss in detail in the section that follows, meant

Table 16. Distribution of Small Property Leaseholders

Amount of taxes paid (in florins)	Taxpayers	Leasors	Occupation of leasors
more than 49	5	5	farmers
26–49	0	0	—
20–25	5	5	1 farmer, 3 weavers, 1 merchant
19	1	0	—
18	0	0	—
17	3	2	1 farmer, 1 merchant-weaver
16	3	2	2 weavers
15	4	3	2 weavers, 1 shepherd
14	1	1	1 cartwright
13	3	2	1 weaver, 1 farm laborer (?)
12	5	5	1 farmer, 3 weavers, 1 unknown
11	4	2	1 weaver, 1 clockmaker's widow
10	6	4	3 weavers, 1 carpenter
9	2	0	—
8	14	7	1 farmer's widow, 3 weavers, 1 carpenter, 1 mason, 1 tailor's widow
7	10	6	3 weavers, 1 clerk, 1 merchant, 1 blacksmith
6	12	4	4 weavers
5	13	3	3 weavers
4	20	6	1 ex-farmer, 4 weavers, 1 cabinetmaker
3	14	8	5 weavers, 3 farm laborers
2	9	0	—
1	15	0	—
less than 1	4	0	—
Total	153	65	

that natives, spouses, or heirs could presume on some ancestral claim to rentals, a claim they would be sure to keep alive. The continuity of familial tenure attests to this. Sons, sons-in-laws, second husbands took over parcels. Yet, although one can trace these relationships, they cannot be predicted. Who would take over what, or which family would choose to avail itself of such opportunities, depended on individual strategies: how many heirs survived, how many stayed in the village, how the patrimony was shared, who remained eager to till the land.

The mixture of claims that went into rentals placed constraints on both owners and tenants, but it need not be automatically ranged within

Table 17. Occupations of Leaseholders of Priest's Land (1726, 1730) and of Parish Property (1778–88)

Year	Occupation	Amount in mencaudées	Leased land (%)
1726	3 farmers	8	40
	7 weavers	7	35
	1 blacksmith	2	10
	1 publican	2	10
	1 shepherd	1	5
1730	2 farmers	5.5	18
	9 weavers	9.75	32
	2 Bertry residents	9	30
	2 carpenters	3	10
	1 blacksmith	1	3
	1 clerk	1	3
	1 forester	1	3
1778	3 farmers	3.4	40
	2 weavers	2.1	24.5
	1 blacksmith	2	23
	1 cotton merchant	1.1	12
1780	4 farmers	8.5	47
	6 weavers	6.5	37
	1 merchant-weaver	2	11
	1 cabinetmaker	1.25	7
1785	3 farmers	5	37
	6 weavers	7	52
	1 mason	1.5	11
1787	3 farmers	2.5	30
	3 weavers and 1 laborer	2.7	32
	2 merchants	2.1	25
	1 blacksmith	1	12
1788	5 farmers	10	48
	7 weavers	7.25	35
	1 merchant-weaver	2.5	12
	1 cabinetmaker	1.25	6

Source: 7H154 (1726, 1730), L5062 (1778–88).

the rigid workings of a moral economy. Rentals belonged, instead, within a broader system that integrated old and new approaches to property. If one could count on the security of rental property, it became easier to put one's own personal property to speculative uses.[26]

Mauvais gré

Although rentals potentially increased the supply of land, the tendency to presume on a family's perpetual right to leaseholds complicated matters. Landownership and tenancy were often confused both in the public mind and in official documents such as tax records or dowries. Leased and rightfully owned strips were passed on to heirs regardless of their origin, and tenants regularly refused to surrender properties at the termination of their leases. This state of affairs was known to the authorities as *mauvais gré* (ill will) and characterized these border provinces. It survived in Cambrésis despite attempts by both government and owners to moderate its effects.

In fact, leases were handed down from father to son, especially in the case of large domains, and the occupiers came to regard the land as their own.[27] The farmers believed that they had a *droit de marché,* a right of occupancy, and refused to vacate the premises at the end of their terms. They avenged themselves on anyone who either bid against them or who managed to take over their leases. Penalties for refusing to abandon a holding at the end of the contract ranged from loss of seed, labor, and the payment of one year's rent, to the death sentence.[28] This testified to the tenacity of the tradition.

> Warning that anyone bold enough to do any harm to the Owners or to their new Farmers, or to their Belongings, be it directly or indirectly, will be considered as and punished for disturbing the public peace and become liable to the most severe penalties, even death, in the case of homicide, fire, or other ill-treatments, in conformity with the Ordinance issued by the Parlement of Tournay, on 20 July 1682, and to set an example and inspire terror in others, none will be pardoned for this.

The custom discouraged rentals and deflated rents, a fact that worried the central authorities who expressed their concern in a series of edicts. A 1724 proclamation stated:

> All this while farmers have stayed on these properties, generation upon generation, paying only minimal rents to the owners, growing accustomed to treating this land as their own, and refusing to renew their leases or to adjust the rent to prevailing circumstances, or to allow themselves to be replaced, threatening to burn out or to kill anyone who held a lease that would dispossess them . . . so that considering these holdings as their true patrimony, they sell them to whomever they please, often at their true value, endow their children with part or all of these properties when they

marry, or divide them in as many lots as they have heirs, and, should the division be contested, have it adjudged publicly to the highest bidder, and given their common interest, they always support one another.[29]

We have one example of how such intimidation worked at the local level: "Last Thursday, 29 of July, the day that the crops on thirty-six men-caudées were to be sold at public auction on the request of the abbé Josset . . . the sons of Michel Millot were heard to say very angrily that the first devil who dared to place a higher bid on their father's farm would be torn to bits . . . and that that day and on the following days the abbé Josset was kidded in the village that he had been taken (bien gouré) and that the crops had gone for half their value."[30] In 1679, 1707, 1714, 1732, and 1747, edicts attempted to curb such defiance.[31] The persistence of the authorities proves the frequency of the offense, at least until the middle of the century when owners appeared to regain some control. The change is manifest in Montigny. The continuity of families renting the farms of Le Troncquoy, in its immediate vicinity, demonstrates the monopoly mentioned in the edict, yet in the 1760s the Chapter succeeded in dismissing the tenant of La Trappe, the biggest rental within the village itself: "Charles Crinon . . . is ordered to relinquish his farm immediately and to allow the person to whom the Chapter will lease the estate to till the plots lying fallow."[32] The seigneur of La Bruyère similarly forced the widow Tamboise to quit his lands in 1786.[33]

Confrontation lurked behind all forms of rental. In 1771 and 1774 Pierre Aubert Tamboise and Robert Milot, two of Le Troncquoy's farmers, and Jean Charles Fontaine, their homologue at Le Coquelet, peacefully yielded their contract for the local tithe collection to Philippe Taine of Caudry.[34] The transfer of similar revenues to Jean Bracq of the same Caudry in 1723 had gone quite otherwise.[35] He confronted an angry community, as did the Chapter's man who had been delegated to oversee the bidding. Joseph Ledieu of Le Troncquoy was heard to whisper: "You are well aware, Sir, of what happened thirty-six years ago in our village . . . over a similar dispute involving the tithes . . . the farms of Le Troncquoy were set on fire and several people were sent to the galleys . . . and Ledieu went on to tell the witness: well, then, worse could happen or something worse might well happen." When that night a few gunshots were loosed by Bracq's window, and his two tithe collectors resigned, the farmer appealed to the Chapter for help. Something must have been done, for he gathered the tithe and in 1727 renewed his bid, undaunted by repeated threats.[36]

Witnesses admitted that there was nothing unusual in such goings-on. A farmer and weaver from Caudry described how nine years earlier his father "had been badly wounded by the children of the old tithe-holder because the village council, of which the witness's father was a member, had taken over the tithe." Caudry's clerk, contradicting his own evidence, maintained that violence flared whenever members of the village council lost the lease. This had been demonstrated years before when Jean Denimal, then the tithe farmer, had made his relatives burn down Le Troncquoy because one of its occupants, Pierre Ledieu, sat on the council that successfully bid for the contract.

The disputes over Caudry's tithes illustrate the conflicts between the community (or the oligarchy that spoke in its name) and the farmer bent on individual profit. The methods were those invoked in cases of mauvais gré. As André Cottiau, farmer at Le Coquelet, put it: "the same thing happens when someone takes over another person's land and they end up cutting each other's throats."[37] Yet the uproar in Caudry failed to intimi-date the bidder. It did, sixty years later, in Clary, but the farmer's son was eventually indicted for the violence and mauvais gré displayed when his family lost its lease.[38] While Montigny avoided such outbursts, several lawsuits involving local inhabitants show how landowners could raise the issue of ill will to win their case.

On 12 July 1736 Charles Delacourt, a laboureur, answered the charge that he refused to leave the eighteen mencaudées that he leased from Guillaume Lecocq in Clary: "The defendant really stopped farming the land owned by the plaintiff and even agreed in writing that [the latter] be allowed to hire whatever new farmers he wanted. The plaintiff then publicized that his land was for rent and the notices mentioned that the defendant had given it up. But in the course of the negotiations, [the owner] let it be understood that until he found a new farmer, [the present occupier] should continue to till his fields."[39] A year later, with the harvest at hand, the farmer wished to bring in his crop and demanded to be paid for his seeds and his labor. The owner's version differed some-what. According to him, the two had bound themselves by an unwritten agreement, following the official expiration of the lease, but Delacourt refused to pay the new rent "and tried to push his master around" (*a pretendu donner la loy a son maître*). On 29 July 1737 the court sided with Lecocq and ordered Delacourt to vacate the eighteen mencaudées and pay double rent for 1737.[40]

The spirit of these disputes reveals itself clearly in another case. In

1768 Jean Pierre Lantier, a Montigny merchant-weaver, was taken to court by his brother-in-law for occupying six mencaudées "without a lease and against the wishes of the plaintiff who wants to dispose of them as he likes."[41] On 9 April, Lantier had to abandon the parcels, but the parties nonetheless reached a settlement. At that point the plaintiff admitted that "if he had requested that [the defendant] give up the land, it was only to gain peace of mind, and to settle those difficulties that had always arisen over the rent which was only paid after a great deal of fuss." Since Charles Delacourt continued to occupy the Clary plots and Jean Pierre Lantier to farm the six mencaudées, the threat of prosecution for mauvais gré became less a means of ridding oneself of tenants than a way of enforcing rent increases, with the judiciary guaranteeing their collection. Despite its apparent inflexibility and its seeming subordination of economic uses of the land to the needs of the family and to static expectations, the system of mauvais gré allowed room for negotiation.[42]

Rents

Rents on these properties, as on other small plots, were varied. They might be set in cash or in kind. The length of occupancy (as one might predict from the custom of mauvais gré) probably played a greater role in setting the amounts than the status of the taker. The powerful were not necessarily favored, except by dint of seniority. The Cantimpré farmer Jean François Labbé was able to secure his tenure of church parcels in 1778, 1780, 1785, and 1787 at the lowest rate at each public bid. Jacques François Milot, the wealthiest man in the parish, also owed just under the average of 1.4 mencauds of wheat (per mencaudée) as his rent in 1780, but slightly over the average in 1785. Another middling farmer, Claude Cardon, paid slightly more than the average in 1780 and more and less, respectively, in 1778 and 1787. The former censier of La Bruyère, Pierre Philippe Malesieux, had the dubious honor of paying the highest rate in 1778, though he had fallen on hard times and paid only four florins in taxes. In 1780 this lot fell to the widow of a weaver (who paid twelve florins in taxes); in 1785, to a mason (eight florins); and in 1787 to the farmhand Pierre Martin, (three florins) along with the weaver André Godart (seven florins) when both owed a record of 3.1 mencauds for each mencaudée. Joseph Petit, recently ensconced at one of the farms of Le Tronquoy, however, paid nearly as much (three mencauds) when he first

Table 18. Average Number of Mencauds Due
Annually for Small Leaseholds (per mencaudée)

Leasor	Year	Amount
Priest	1726	1.40
Priest	1730	1.56
Priest	1744	0.94
All Saints	1751	1.00
All Saints	1770	1.16
Priest	1776	1.14
Church	1778	1.60
Church	1780	1.40
Church	1785	1.67
Church	1787	2.05

Source: L5062, 5G545, 7H154, 4G3297.

rented parish property in 1788. More important than such specific variations, however, was the steady upward pressure of rents throughout the century (table 18).

In the seventeenth century, leases of small property in particular took the relationship of mencaud (the measure of volume) to mencaudée (the measure of surface) as their starting point. This meant that someone who rented a three-mencaudée plot paid three mencauds of wheat (whenever it grew wheat, that is, meaning every three years).[43] Such calculations persisted well into the next century. In 1768 the seigneur of Bertry leased the farmer Pierre Aubert Tamboise twenty-three mencaudées, on which he owed twenty-three mencauds of wheat.[44] Furthermore, fiscal records continued to presume such a relationship. Leases in both Bertry's and Troisvilles's 1755 tax rolls, for example, were valued at one mencaud per mencaudée.[45]

Starting in the eighteenth century, however, we find leases conceived on a different basis that gauged productivity more accurately. In 1738 a lease of 2.25 mencaudées set the rent at 5.25 mencauds per mencaudée. When, a year later, Montigny's priest rented out some land, he charged 9.5 mencauds of wheat on 1.25 mencaudées, 6.5 mencauds on another mencaudée and 2.5 mencauds on half a mencaudée (still every three years). This last rate of 5 mencauds per mencaudée approached that of another lease. In 1749 a retired weaver leased a laboureur a 2 mencaudée plot for 11 mencauds of wheat. The same man again rented 7.25 mencaudées in Caudry in 1753 at 5 mencauds per mencaudée (whenever they grew wheat). In 1762 those very plots were divided into 3 men-caudées that brought in 4 mencauds per mencaudée and the remainder that owed 5 mencauds. On the whole, prices in Montigny continued to hover between 5 and 6 mencauds (or 1.3 to 2 mencauds a year). Similarly, in 1788 a Clary widow leased several plots located in Montigny and Ligny to two weavers. The rent on 1.3 mencaudées came to 5.5 mencauds of wheat, on 1.5 mencaudées to 4 mencauds, and on the last mencaudée to 6 mencauds. Finally, the 6.5 mencaudées (divided into three uneven rotations) leased by one Montigny weaver to another in December 1789 cost him 13.5 mencauds annually.[46]

How can one account for these changes? Did a moral economy prevail that set natural limits on rentals in the seventeenth century that were broken in the eighteenth, or did this relate directly to increases in output? The seventeenth century functioned with a rough estimate of proper rents that married traditional ways of thinking with empirical observation. The mencaud/mencaudée relationship defined peasants' presumed ability to pay; it did not attempt to establish actual productivity. We can say this all the more assuredly since the yardstick was applied to all rentals more or less uniformly. Yet it was not completely divorced from reality, bound by some timeless imperative. It did, in fact, reflect the depressed conditions of the seventeenth century and the impoverished nature of village agronomy in this period. In the eighteenth century these relations altered. Rents, whenever possible, became more attuned to productivity and fluctuated, falling around or below one mencaud but also climbing as high as seven mencauds per mencaudée (or more than two mencauds a year—that is, double the previous standard). This expressed, as we shall see, an improvement in overall conditions as well as a rise in yields.

For most of the century, rents on large estates rose sporadically, and the signing of contracts appeared somewhat haphazard. Sons and spouses took over leases at the death of the previous occupier or the marriage of his successor in the cavalier manner encouraged by mauvais gré. They had to seek the consent of the owner to legalize the transfer, but they often let time slip by, and, indeed, whenever proprietors lacked either the energy or the nerve, nine-year leases could well stretch out to a dozen years or more; prices might remain the same for several decades.

Rents rose, nonetheless: some indeed, as we have seen, through the coercion of the law courts. Relations between the judiciary and the landowners were not tight enough, however, to secure the rack rents or high entry fines that had, at times, prevailed across the Channel.[47] The

Table 19. Cash Owed on Properties Owned by the Abbey of
Anchin, 1692–1778

Farm	Year	Amount due (florins)	Increase (%)	Overall increase (%)
Coquelet	1692	389		
	1705	389		
	1751	600	+54	
	1778	1050	+75	170
Le Troncquoy	1705	240		
(1/2)	1718	240		
	1727	240		
	1745	350	+46	
	1754	628	+80	162
Le Troncquoy	1715	122		
(1/4)	1722	122		
	1731	176	+44	
	1758	314	+78	
	1767	314		
	1776	400	+27	227

Source: 1H669.

parallel systems of justice that evolved in France account for this difference, since individuals and communities could appeal to the state and
play off opposing interests in ways they could not in England.[48] Provincial courts might overturn seigneurial rulings, while the king protected
his revenues by siding with the peasants.

Increases were regularly registered, nonetheless, and all the more
clearly if one totes up the subsidiary payments demanded of the tenant.
The abbey of Anchin's leases for Le Troncquoy and adjoining Coquelet
show that although the amount owed in wheat remained constant (208
mencauds for half of Le Troncquoy and 104 for the remaining quarters),
the peripheral cash dues and sundry items rose by the middle of the
eighteenth century (table 19).[49] These included the number and quality
of sheep, the "accountancy fees" that were tacked onto the contract, and
various *corvées* that came with the property, such as the carting of goods.
There was a substantial gratuity or entry fine, paid at the signing of each
new lease. I have combined all these expenses and divided them by the
nine years of the contract in order to trace the rise in rent, which might be
overlooked if one focuses on the apparent stability of payments in cereal.

Table 20. Rent Due on the Cantimpré Farm, 1705–92

Year	Surface in mencaudées	Mencauds	Increase (%)
1705	144	64	
1754	102*	56.5	+25
1772	102	80	+42
1792	102	80	

*The farm had been divided into two lots.
Source: 4G2438, C suppl. 524, 37H229, 1Q125.

The abbey of Cantimpré most likely also increased its subsidiary fees over the century. It did not record the changes, however, and surviving leases only state the amount charged in wheat (table 20).

The Chapter leased its property of La Trappe for a fixed cash rent until 1783 when it imposed what would become a far more profitable remittance of 240 mencauds of wheat. The entry fines added another 51 florins 13 patars annually, although the farmers paid the full sum, that is, 465 florins and 15 patars, the first year of their new contract.[50] A sample from the Chapter's account books illustrates the movement in rent and, more specifically, the rise in the very last years before the Revolution. The increase can be calculated precisely since the clerk entered the date and amount for the sale of each portion of grain collected from the villages.

Table 21 shows that there was a steady upward movement throughout the century, so that the Chapter collected 189 percent more in 1779 than it had a century earlier. This does not take into account the extraordinary jump of the late 1780s when rents rose another 211 percent. Other farms followed the same course. Raises for Le Troncquoy and Coquelet ranged between 162 percent and 227 percent, as did those for three other domains in the region. Payment on the first of those properties increased 186 percent between 1675 and 1774, while the two others appreciated 111 percent (one between 1709 and 1784 and the other between 1708 and 1779).[51] The Cantimpré farm in Montigny, where payments remained in kind throughout the century, saw a rent increase of 77 percent between 1705 and 1792. These amounts surpass the estimated doubling or even trebling of rents that Ernest Labrousse suggested for the whole of France between 1726 (when the currency stabilized) and the end of the Ancien Régime.[52] They approximate rather the 208 percent that Wilhelm Abel used for France for that same period.[53]

Table 21. Rents Due on La Trappe, 1675–1787

Year	Amount due in florins, patars, and doubles	Price of 1 mencaud of wheat (florins)	Cash dues expressed in mencauds of wheat	Increase or decrease (%) Cash	Increase or decrease (%) Wheat
1675	150.00.0				
1698	162.10.0	4.00.0	40.3	+8	
1703	162.10.0	1.10.0	108.3		+169
1717	162.10.0	1.08.0	116.0		+7
1735	200.00.0	2.16.0	71.5	+23	−38
1745	288.00.0	2.04.0	131.0	+44	+83
1757	350.00.0	6.00.0	58.3	+22	−55
1763	350.00.0	3.04.0	109.3		+87
1765	433.09.0	3.16.0	114.0	+24	+4
1779	433.09.0	3.16.0	114.0		
Total				+189	
1783	880.17.0	3.09.12	240.0	+103	+110
1784	1,491.15.0	6.00.0*	240.0	+70	
1785	1,323.15.0	5.06.0	240.0	−11	
1786	1,020.00.0	4.05.0	240.0	−23	
1787	1,347.15.0	5.08.0	240.0	+32	
Total				+211	

*In their records for 1785, 1786 and 1787 the Prévôtés du Cambrésis name a different price for the sale of the farm's and the village's wheat.
Source: 4G6656–6744, Accounts of the Prévôtés du Cambrésis.

These figures show how mauvais gré could defer but not stop rent increases. On the other hand, the custom gave takers a security of tenure that would encourage them to invest in the property. They therefore experienced something akin to the favorable conditions associated with eighteenth-century England.[54] Lessees enjoyed long-term occupancy; they reaped the profits from rising grain prices.

Another look at the leases for La Trappe, the Chapter's farm, shows how the conversion of cash payments into their equivalent in wheat often favored the tenant. Even if the set amounts stagnated or increased only gradually, the corresponding values wildly fluctuated. The Prévôtés du Cambrésis (receivers of two-fifths of one-third of the rent for La Trappe) recorded the sale of wheat collected in the villages each fall as partial payment of seigneurial dues. They evidenced the movement presented in table 22.[55]

Over the ninety-six-year period (there are no data for 1729), wheat

Table 22.　Value of One Mencaud of Wheat Grown in
Montigny, 1691–1787 (in florins, patars, and doubles)

Year	Amount	Year	Amount	Year	Amount
1691	1.12	1724	3	1757	6
1692	3	1725	4	1758	3.12
1693	4	1726	4	1759	3.04
1694	4	1727	3	1760	4
1695	3	1728	1.18	1761	3.04
1696	2	1729	—	1762	3.12
1697	3	1730	2.10	1763	3.04
1698	4	1731	4.10	1764	2.16
1699	5	1732	2.04	1765	3.16
1700	3	1733	1.16	1766	3.09.12
1701	2.08	1734	2	1767	2.16
1702	1.12	1735	2.16	1768	6.10
1703	1.10	1736	2.08	1769	5.09.12
1704	2	1737	2.12	1770	6
1705	2	1738	3.12	1771	5.04
1706	2	1739	3.16	1772	4.12.06
1707	1.10	1740	7	1773	5.16
1708	1.13.12	1741	4	1774	5.08
1709	4	1742	3.10	1775	6.00.03
1710	3	1743	2	1776	4.09.12
1711	1.08	1744	2	1777	4.05.12
1712	4	1745	2.04	1778	4.03
1713	4	1746	2.16	1779	3.13
1714	5.15	1747	3	1780	3.13
1715	5.06.12	1748	3.12	1781	4
1716	1.06	1749	4	1782	3.05
1717	1.08	1750	4.10	1783	3.09.12
1718	1.11	1751	4	1784	6.13.12
1719	2.08	1752	4.12	1785	5
1720	2.14	1753	4.04	1786	4.05
1721	1.10	1754	3.04	1787	5
1722	2.12	1755	2.12	1788	—
1723	3.12	1756	2.08	1789	—

Source: 4G6656–6744.

averaged a price of 3 florins 10 patars. Almost half of the time (forty-five years) the value fell below that, although this occurred primarily in the first half of the century (thirty-seven of the forty-five years). Wheat fetched an average of three florins between 1691 and 1750, and in 1691, 1702–3, 1707–8, 1716–18, 1721, 1728, and 1733 the price dropped beneath two florins. Consequently, the Chapter's tenant had to sell more grain to pay his rent. The average between 1750 and 1787 jumped to 4 florins 5 patars, a rise of nearly 50 percent, although the value fell below that level twenty-one times.

The value of a mencaud spiraled in times of crises, reaching 4 florins in 1693–94, 5 florins in 1699, 4 in 1709, and 5 florins 15 patars in 1714–15. The highest recorded value, excepting the very late 1780s for which we have no precise figures, came in 1740 when prices rose to an extraordinary 7 florins per mencaud. After a lull, wheat increased to 6 florins in 1757, and again in 1768, 1770, 1775, and once more in the mid-1780s. This meant that the Chapter's farmer, Moyse Crinon, disbursed the least in 1740 when his rent came to a mere 28.5 mencauds of wheat. Yet farmers did not necessarily rejoice in periods of dearth, for they had to keep seeds, feed their families and workers, and pay taxes and rent out of a reduced crop. On the other hand, whatever surplus they took to market brought in handsome returns.

Through the 1770s, then, conditions favored the farmers. In the mid-1780s, however, the Cambrai Chapter reacted to rising grain prices and succeeded in converting its leases from cash to kind in order to reap some of those profits. One should note that Montigny's new contract was drawn up at the expiration of an eighteen-year lease where wheat had averaged 4 florins 12 patars but had dropped by one florin in the last four years. The newly established payment of 240 mencauds instantly doubled both the amount in wheat and what had been its cash equivalent.[56] A year later, the rent had risen by yet another three-quarters—an amount that more than trebled the previous lease.[57] Looking back at the lease of La Trappe (after 1783) and recalling that only one-third of the 157 mencaudées (50 hectares) grew wheat each year and adopting the conservative yield of 5 to 1, we find that the entire crop would have been turned over to the owners.[58] Even with a yield of 6 to 1, more than 80 percent would have been lost to the tenant, and this not including expenditures on seeds, tithes, taxes, wages, upkeep, and personal provisions for the farmer.

Hugues Neveux argues that rent in Cambrésis took 40 percent of the crop.[59] This brings it close to sharecropping, all the more so if owners sometimes provided the seed, as the squabble between Charles Delacourt and his landlord implies. In other parts of France, such as northern Burgundy, the owner collected one-third of the produce.[60] In the Paris region in the early seventeenth century, landowners could expect about 20 percent.[61]

The average yield of 5 to 1 on which Neveux based his calculations would, as he himself agrees, be surpassed on better land, especially on the better-cultivated domains. It is therefore more than likely that Montigny's yield was twice as high on the Chapter's farm. The rent, then, would drop to a more appropriate percentage. By the same token, earlier payments would diminish accordingly.

Conditions improved for the farmers in the middle of the eighteenth century, even for those who had suffered more than they had benefited from the 1740 crisis. They grew richer. This in turn encouraged and financed further expansion. It was in this period that the Troncquoy farmers began to accumulate leases and tried to monopolize village pastures.[62] Yet some failed. The unfortunate Charles Crinon forfeited his lease of La Trappe at this very juncture. When he took it over from his father in the 1750s, the farm was reported to be prosperous. Yet year after year he had trouble meeting his commitments, and the Chapter eventually evicted him. His father replaced him for a brief period, and then two nearby farmers took over the lease. The fact that relatives did not prop up this foundering member meant that he was considered hopelessly incompetent rather than temporarily distressed. Success was not a foregone conclusion, therefore, but the years of moderate rents and rising grain prices proved a springboard to those able to take advantage of them. The rent increases of the 1780s, whether they were fair adjustments or not, represented huge outlays for tenant-farmers, a redirection of their profits into the pockets of the landowners. This would aggrieve them and involve them in the rural discontent that accompanied the early phases of the Revolution.

None of the leases mentioned here made any reference to payments in the spring crop (usually oats or barley). In the case of the Chapter's last lease, therefore, the entire amount would have accrued to the farmer. In the long period of cash payments he would, of course, have used some of this income to pay his rent. Crop rotation and the stores of grain described in inventories suggest that one-third of the arable was devoted to fodder crops.

The average price for Montigny oats on the Cambrai market between 1691 and 1787 was 2 florins.[63] Between 1691 and 1751 it came to 1 florin 16 patars, and between 1751 and 1787 to 2 florins 10 patars, an increase of 37 percent over the earlier period. The pattern in Montigny reflected that of the rest of France calculated by Labrousse (table 23). Labrousse's estimates show that in France as a whole prices for oats rose more than wheat prices. This was true in Montigny as well. When the farmers of La

Table 23. Increases in the Price of Wheat and Oats

	1726–41	Labrousse 1771–89	Montigny 1771–87
Wheat	100	156	145
Oats	100	174	163

Base: 1726–41 = 100
Source: 4G6656–6744; Labrousse, Histoire économique et sociale de la France, II, 399.

Trappe signed their lease in November 1783, the price of one *rasière* of oats nearly equaled the value of a mencaud of wheat. This might well have eased the farmers' way into signing over the bulk of their wheat crop.

Tradition and innovation were not necessarily at loggerheads in leasing arrangements. Mauvais gré provided farmers with a personal security of tenure that gave them a stake in its prosperity. It did not, despite the wails of owners and the worries of authorities, prevent rent increases. As we have seen, rents rose throughout the century, dramatically so in the 1780s. Owners, in fact, understood this fact and used the courts not to replace tenants (although sometimes that might prove necessary) but to ensure that they paid higher rents. And tenants accepted the courts' verdict and complied. Mauvais gré, with its arsenal of threats and vengeance, was not directed against landlords but against fellow farmers. What the tenant wanted was his farm. As for the rest, he would apply pressure to keep the rent down but eventually come to some understanding with the owner.

For most of the century, the farmers in and around Montigny owed similar rents. Except in unusual circumstances, the Chapter's cash payments translated into 100 to 130 mencauds of wheat, which compares more or less to the 104 mencauds that the Troncquoy farmers paid for an equivalent amount of land, or to the sum, prorated, paid out by the tenant of Cantimpré.[64] Rising demand from a growing population stimulated production, all the more so once grain exports received official sanction. The tentative improvements in agriculture described in chapter 5 raised yields and ensured the village's continued self-sufficiency. They also provided a marketable reserve. Such developments benefited the major farmers but they also attracted local merchant-weavers who invested in agriculture.

In the second half of the eighteenth century, weavers who leased small properties also reaped some of these benefits since they managed to stay afloat. If conditions had worsened for the peasant, as the immiseration thesis contends, such land would have fallen to rich farmers or led to indebtedness and bankruptcy. In fact, this did not happen. Since a great deal of work was expended on the wheat fields, this suggests that something made all this effort worthwhile. Surely, peasants did not work themselves to the bone only to deposit their entire crop in their landlord's barn in the hopes that the following year's oats crop would bring in a few florins. Did a rising population and growing competition for land compel them to put up with appalling conditions? One explanation may be that such rentals simply allowed peasants to speculate with their own land. That is, they could mortgage their property, or sell it, with some assurance of finding alternate plots. Rentals then permitted speculation with other landed assets; income from trade or from weaving contributed to monstrous rents. The tenant did not starve the year that he paid his wheat dues; he could support himself in other ways. And, as we have seen, the spring crop remained at his disposal. Some of the produce would go to feed his own animals; the remainder would be sold.

Yet there was a dark side to all of this. The authorities regularly requisitioned fodder, and the peasant was never free from the worry that he would have to contribute his produce, especially in these border regions. In September 1744, Montigny provided 170 rasières of oats and less than six months later had to come up with an additional 400 bundles of straw. This pattern was repeated for the remainder of the war, although the amounts varied.[65] As oat prices rose, the gamble became more attractive, despite the fear of government incursions. If we compare the inventories of farmers in the 1680s with those of the 1780s and 1790s, the contrast is striking. Oats and other fodder crops matched the supplies of wheat, whereas they had filled no more than one-tenth of stores in the late seventeenth century.

Oats rose significantly only in the latter part of the eighteenth century and so cannot fully account for the peasants' ability or willingness to pay high rents. Despite the speculative aspect and the combination of incomes, the most likely explanation remains that yields were in fact rising and that, unlike in the previous century, peasants and farmers were indeed in a position to adjust rent to output, however much they resented the process. Higher rents were first applied to small tenancies, which proved more vulnerable to such manipulation, and only subsequently to larger estates.

Appendix B

The account books of the Prévôtés du Cambrésis include the sale of several bundles of oats they collected annually in the village as part of their seigneurial dues, and they show the following movement in prices.

Table B-1. Value of One Montigny Rasière of Oats, 1691–1787 (in florins, patars, and doubles)

Year	Amount	Year	Amount	Year	Amount
1691	1.04	1724	2.08	1757	2.10
1692	2.08	1725	1.16	1758	2.08
1693	2.10	1726	1.06	1759	2
1694	2.10	1727	2	1760	2.04
1695	2	1728	1.10	1761	1.12
1696	1.10	1729	—	1762	1.18
1697	1.04	1730	2	1763	2.08
1698	2	1731	2.04	1764	1.12
1699	1.18.08	1732	1.16	1765	2
1700	1.08.15	1733	1.06	1766	2
1701	1.04	1734	1.04	1767	2.08
1702	1.04	1735	1.08	1768	2.16
1703	1.04	1736	1.10	1769	1.18
1704	0.18.12	1737	1.06	1770	2.10
1705	0.18.12	1738	1.10	1771	2.12
1706	1.07.12	1739	2	1772	3
1707	1.06	1740	3	1773	3.08
1708	1.03	1741	2.12	1774	2.10
1709	1.18.08	1742	2.10	1775	2.16
1710	1.08.15	1743	1.12	1776	2.12
1711	2.08	1744	2.04	1777	2.16
1712	2.06.02	1745	2.04	1778	2.17
1713	2.08	1746	2	1779	2.11
1714	4.13.12	1747	2	1780	2.07
1715	1.07	1748	2.05	1781	2.16
1716	0.17.04	1749	2.04	1782	2.12.12
1717	0.16	1750	1.16	1783	3.06
1718	1.02	1751	2	1784	2.18
1719	1.10	1752	2.08	1785	3.17
1720	2.14	1753	2.08	1786	3.02
1721	1.04	1754	2.00.12	1787	3
1722	1.12	1755	1.16	1788	—
1723	2.08	1756	1.12	1789	—

Source: 4G6656–6744.

5

Agriculture

Did France experience an agricultural revolution in the eighteenth century? There was a time when the debate on this question grew quite heated. Takeoff models were proposed and then refuted. For some, the French countryside flourished in the eighteenth century, galvanized by large-scale farming and by the progressive outlook of its farmers.[1] There, England offered the dynamic prototype. Others posited long-term brakes and disabilities that continued to afflict the French rural economy.[2] Once the English themselves began to debunk the notion of a spectacular takeoff and to suggest more gradual changes, this in turn altered the perception of the French situation.[3] Some even argued that French growth paralleled that of Britain. Yet, for all that, the notion of French retardation has not been laid to rest. The arguments have shifted somewhat so that there is less exasperation at the clinging to routine and greater attention paid to rational choices. The French lacked proper economic incentives to innovate (for innovation remains the mainstay of such arguments) or the proper terrain. Whatever the framework, the answer remains the same: there was no agricultural revolution in France in the eighteenth century.

The North of France has figured prominently in these discussions. Flanders had been the cradle of progress with its very early transition to multiple crop rotation and its intensive agriculture. Yet it had failed to inspire the rest of the country. Elsewhere, and especially in areas of open farming, biennial and then triennial rotation remained the norm, with the heaviest emphasis placed on wheat production demanded by landlord, tither, and tax collector. The North, then, seemed to bring into focus most acutely the deficiencies of the French rural economy.

Cambrésis in particular, because of its well-preserved ecclesiastical records, attracted the attention of scholars. Hugues Neveux mapped its decline, as he calls it, over the fifteenth and sixteenth centuries, though he agreed with Le Roy Ladurie that the eighteenth century saw the dawn of a new era.[4] Michel Morineau made the diocese the prototype of long-term immobilism, even if his version was rosier than Neveux's.[5] Yields rose and fell, stagnated, jumped, or declined. This had little to do with innovation or peasant outlook. The outcome was geographically determined. The soils of Hainaut and Cambrésis could produce high yields, and they had done so from time immemorial. The eighteenth century brought no changes, spectacular or otherwise. When the peasant set his mind to it (weather helping) and used the tools at his disposal, he could reap returns that were as plentiful in the eighteenth century as they had been in the fourteenth. The process was one of *restoration* rather than revolution.

How is one, then, to gauge the performance of French agriculture in the eighteenth century, and that of Cambrésis in particular? Improvements were indeed more gradual than revolutionary, and innovations slow to penetrate. Yet methods of cultivation did improve, especially once the capital available to the big farmers increased. As a result, large farms grew more productive, raising both yields and revenues. Since the changes of the eighteenth century occurred within a social setting similar to that of seventeenth-century stagnation, a reexamination of the brakes on French productivity and of the limitations of open-field farming would seem to be in order.

Hugues Neveux attributed Cambrésis's decline to the noncapitalist mentality of its big farmers. In his view, they concerned themselves less with profit than with status and, once they established themselves at the top of the rural hierarchy, focused their energies on maintaining their social and political hegemony and paid less attention to economic success. Mauvais gré to the rescue, they became entrenched. Neveux shares the common assumption that a change in outlook, rather than a change in opportunity, eventually roused the farmers from their complacency. If we focus, instead, on the economic potential of any given period, then the farmers' responses retain cogency as well as continuity. The eighteenth century provided incentives for improved husbandry that had been lacking in the seventeenth century. A whole series of factors involving rents, yields, implements, population size, and marketing intervened. None of these can individually account for the transformations. It was their combination that created a new momentum.

Cambrésis because of its traditional agriculture offers a good vantage point for examining eighteenth-century transformations. The village of Montigny is especially significant because it lay in an ill-favored part of the province. The land was not sterile, but hard to work. In the eighteenth century an increasing number of peasants would find it more profitable, therefore, to abandon the land in favor of industry. Those who continued to till it, on the other hand, did so with progressively better results. The continued interaction between agriculture and industry forms one of the major arguments of this book. Thus, because of weaving, the village's population grew, and this brought on agricultural improvements, especially on the large farms. Profits from agriculture were diverted into trade, just as those from textiles wound their way back to the land. Weavers continued to till the soil, richer ones as independent farmers, poorer ones as agricultural laborers. Industry did not displace agriculture; rather, it stimulated it.

The Quality of the Soil

In 1750 the Cambrésis Estates drew up a list of the ninety-one villages in the province, jotting beside each name the quality of its soil. The memorandum served for their assessments of the vingtième tax.[6] They found that five localities had very fertile soil, that nineteen had good land, twenty-seven mediocre, thirteen bad, fifteen very bad, one average, while eleven contained a mixture of these types. The villages surrounding Montigny, Bertry, Caullery, Clary, and Ligny ranked along with Montigny in the very poor category.[7] Troisvilles, located northeast, proved merely mediocre, as did the large farms in the vicinity: Le Troncquoy and Coquelet, as well as a hamlet of Caudry by the name of Borneville, which lay in Cambrésis. Caudry itself, just north of Montigny, had for historical reasons remained an enclave of the province of Hainaut and was not evaluated.

The Montignaciens themselves concurred with this description they had affixed to the 1750 tax roll: "Our territory covers 973 mencaudées at most, and, among them . . . there are 111 mencaudées of wastes, roads, barren areas, and ravines that produce nothing and are only used to pasture animals or as fast-flowing waterbeds. . . . Among the 862 mencaudées, 515 produce little because their soil is hard, wet, and chalky and yields at most 266 livres a year. The remaining 374 mencaudées of somewhat better soil (qui est le plus passable) yield about 336 livres a year."[8] Sixty percent of the soil, then, produced but little. In 1795, 579 mencaudées of arable were similarly divided into good, mediocre, and poor soil. Once again, the poorer terrain took up 55 percent of the total (319 mencaudées), the passable 33 percent (190 mencaudées), with only 12 percent (70 mencaudées) considered any good.[9]

As late as 1829, the departmental yearbook placed the district of Cambrai, to which Montigny belonged, as sixth out of seven in terms of fertility, outdistanced by the districts of Lille, Douai, Valenciennes, Hazebrouck, and Dunkerque (in that order) and followed by only the easternmost district of Avesnes, devoted primarily to pasture.[10] As in 1750, the Montigny region (the canton of Clary) was described as one of the most backward, not merely of the district but of the whole department: "This canton is one of the poorest in the department. There is much industry and little agriculture, most of the workforce depends on manufacturing for its survival."[11] Whereas the eighteenth century stressed the nature of cultivation, the nineteenth century focused on geological features. "Clay and silt predominate in the direction of Bertry, Clary, and Caudry."[12] In 1869 a geologist speculated that, besides lying on a small ravine, Montigny had "wells . . . 30 to 35 metres deep. Along the northern and southern elevations, one would quite likely come across Clary clay or even sand, but find the whole covered with alluvial deposits."[13] This layer gave Cambrésis its potential fertility—but in Montigny it appeared only in patches.[14]

The best soil in the village was found on the western side, on the left bank of the Riot Miquel, a stream that curved north toward Caudry. This more fertile belt covered, at most, one-third of the surface.[15] The chalky right bank was partially wooded. In the northeast, things did not look so bright. The place names were suggestive. One segment was known as the "potter's land," other spots as "the big gulley," "the hard lands," "the sandpit," "the gravel pit."[16] They spoke of that poor, impermeable soil that eighteenth-century occupiers dismissed as hard, wet, and chalky (fig. 8).

Owners of large properties dominated what good land there was. Even then, half of this soil could be considered no better than poor. The Chapter estimated that 49 percent of the 143 mencaudées that made up its estate were of low quality, 42 percent were average, while 9 percent remained uncultivated.[17] The abbey of Cantimpré and La Bruyère exhibited similar characteristics. We lack comparable data on the farms of Le Troncquoy, although it was considered better land.

The smaller holdings of the abbeys of Prémy and the Guillemains, on the other hand, lay at the eastern and less favored reaches of the village, toward Bertry. That village, like Montigny, would continue to leave much of its land fallow in the nineteenth century.[18] There, poorer plots prevailed. They made up 59 percent, with another 27 percent of average quality, and 13.5 percent that never came under the plough. The villagers' parcels belonged in the same category, not surprisingly, since the seigneurs had kept the better soils, leaving the poorer ground to the peasants and later buyers.

Figure 8.   Location of Montigny's Arable   *Source:* Duthoit, *Montigny-en-Cambrésis.*

Extent of the Arable and Crop Rotation

Cambrésis remained a region of triennial rotation and open-field farming. One-third of the arable, the first section, or *saison,* was sown in wheat, or *bleds.* This usually meant wheat, rye, and a mixture of the two, known as *méteil,* or maslin, probably in a 60:40 ratio, as well as a bit of barley.[19] The second section, sown in the spring, was known as *mars,* and its produce was often referred to as *marsailles.* On it grew a mixture of oats, barley, vetch, with a sprinkling of clover, sainfoin, and poppy distributed among the main crops.[20] One-third of the land lay fallow.

In the early eighteenth century, the region continued to produce traditional crops: wheat, rye, maslin, barley, oats, buckwheat, peas, beans, and lentils.[21] In November 1794 Montigny still retained some measures of wheat and maslin, barley, and a tiny portion of plain rye. There was much straw, a bit of oats, and a lot of clover.[22] Only three people had oats, and that crop represented only 8 percent of the recorded storage. Two of these people were farmers, but of course armies regularly requisitioned fodder in this war-torn zone.

In June 1795 Montigny listed the following amounts under cultivation (in percentages):[23]

wheat	2	
rye	4	
maslin	23.5	total: 29.5
barley	5.0	
oats	9.0	
vetch	45.0	
clover	2.5	
hay	0.9	
oil poppy	0.5	total: 62.9
beans	5.0	
potatoes	1.0	
peas	0.1	total: 6.1

The very low wheat figure reflected a poor harvest that the village had attempted to counter by planting oats and buckwheat in the spring.[24] The next complete breakdown, in 1836, shows that 61 percent of the territory was cultivated, as had been the case in the Old Regime, for 26 percent still lay fallow, while 3.5 percent consisted of woods, another 7 percent of pastures, and the remaining 3.5 percent of kitchen gardens.[25] The 353 hectares of arable were distributed as follows (in percentages):

wheat	38.2	
maslin	8.5	
rye	8.5	total: 55.2
barley	11.3	
oats	17.0	
oil poppy	14.1	total: 42.4
potatoes	2.3	total: 2.3

Wheat had become the main crop, although the village still grew rye, barley, colza, poppy, and potatoes.[26] Whereas in 1794 maslin had outdistanced wheat by 3:2, in 1836 the ratio had shifted to 4.5:1 in favor of wheat. Since the more resistant rye plant had been sown so that it could support the more fragile wheat stalk, the switch meant that the region now grew a sturdier and healthier strain of corn.[27] There were altogether fewer varieties of crops, and these were produced in larger quantities that reflected a growing specialization and commercialization. Montigny's increased production of colza or poppy oil directly manifests this trend. Demand for this cheap alternative to olive oil grew from the 1790s until the 1840s when it crumbled in the face of foreign imports.[28] At the same time, the rise in wheat production catered specifically to the ever-growing popularity of white bread. The creation of enclosed pastures, on the other hand, accounts for the relative decline of fodder crops.

The cultivated space expanded and contracted. In 1672 the Montigny authorities stated that its territory consisted of "three rotations of about 300 mencaudées," with "80 mencaudées that were never ploughed because they were sterile, heath, or abandoned" and 34 mencaudées of gardens.[29] In 1684 the cultivated area had grown to 924.5 mencaudées, leaving only 34 (3.5 percent) that "were never tilled and remained idle the year round." In 1686 the arable spread over 952 mencaudées 10 pintes "in three sections including various barren parts that have been ploughed and planted with a spring crop." The area under cultivation had reached its utmost extension. These forays into the "badlands" exemplified the periodic recourse to extensive agriculture, one that the Physiocrats would pointlessly encourage in the middle of the eighteenth century, since such land produced little, or produced only for a short period.

In 1709 the first section shrank from its average of three hundred mencaudées to a mere two hundred or so. After the terribly cold winter, the village had no grain left and begged for seeds: "There is no wheat left from 1708 and none from 1709 and our examination of the portion that will be sown this fall shows that we will need 220 mencauds of wheat to sow the said fields."[30] That harsh winter, following upon decades of warfare, reduced the arable by one-third. As far as can be observed, the village never fully recovered. The shrinkage of the arable was the logical abandonment of a fundamentally infertile soil. As the eighteenth century progressed and industry offered other means of survival, it seemed pointless to persevere where the rewards were few.[31]

The poverty of the soil explains why in 1836, 149 hectares out of 572 (26 percent) still lay fallow, while the proportion had fallen to 12.5 percent in Troisvilles, 4.5 percent in Ligny, 3 percent in Caudry, 1.5 percent in Clary, with only Bertry, among these other neighbors, coming close at 20.5 percent.[32]

Strictures against ploughing the fallow occur in all eighteenth-century leases. "[Do not] leave [the said land] unploughed nor let it bear any of those grains which are not common in the region and county of Cambrésis as well as have them bear only three spring and three fall crops without permission to change the cycle or rotation."[33]

In the seventeenth century, village-wide rotations persisted, and the arable was always described in those terms. In 1672, therefore, the local authorities declared that the arable consisted of three hundred mencaudées "à la sole," or of three sections of three hundred mencaudées.[34] Similarly, the tenures of large farmers were commonly expressed in multiples of three, as in the entry for Antoine Malesieux on the 1708 tax roll, which read "45 mencaudées à la sole," or a tenure extending three times forty-five mencaudées. In the 1680s, tax documents split the arable into three sections, which, once individual entries have been computed, display the following proportions (in percentages):

	First	Second	Third
1684	37	31	32
1685	36	32	32
1686	32	34	34

The first section, bearing the major crop, appeared slightly overextended when peasants with only tiny parcels declared none left idle. Three of them had no fallow in 1684, but in 1686 (when the figure reverses) one reported some untilled land. What is more, that same year another claimed no crops at all, arguing that all his land had lain "en riez," that is, had been left uncultivated.[35] On the whole, however, the villagers reported parcels in each of the three parts, even if the dimensions did not always scrupulously coincide.

In the early eighteenth century the *Bans politiques* that regulated the countryside assumed that the arable was divided into three distinct parts. Article XVII ordered sheep to be taken to pasture "by the main roads that lead to the section [singular] lying fallow": "enjoignant de les conduire par les grands Chemins qui mènet du côté de Sol à Gachères."[36] As far as the authorities were concerned, the fallow covered a single compact area.

This system of rotation accorded well with other aspects of Montigny's rural economy in the early eighteenth century: the absence of a land market and the conventional relationships surrounding land and rentals. Like these other aspects of the traditional economy, rotation schemes broke down after 1740.[37] The language of official records changed, and tenures were no longer expressed in multiples of three but in whole figures, even if the land remained divided in three sections. Thus, in 1798 Jacques François Milot, the farmer of La Trappe, grew "wheat and rye" on one section, "oats and fodder" on the second, while a third lay fallow.[38] New taxes based on income, such as the dixième or vingtième, placed more emphasis on the differing value and productivity of plots and replaced the previous schema where one rate had applied to wheat fields and half as much to oat fields. In fact, we only know about Montigny's division of the arable in the 1680s because the Estates contended that there were discrepancies in the village's declarations of its first and most highly taxed section.

Notarial records afford some insight into actual practices. To begin with, rotation in the eighteenth century rarely involved sections of equal size. Instead of the multiples of three, referring to so many mencaudées "à la sole" of the tax records, the land was often described as divided into three rotations of unequal size, "en trois roies inégales." Moreover, the land was not necessarily incorporated within village-wide rotations. Leases show that although triennial rotation persisted, it sometimes functioned within discrete units. The seigneur of Bertry rented the Troncquoy farmer Pierre Aubert Tamboise twenty-three mencaudées. They came in two separate plots. The larger field, measuring eighteen mencaudées, was itself divided into two sections: one planted with the spring crop and another that lay fallow. Wheat grew on the other five-mencaudée plot.[39] When the Montigny merchant-weaver Charles Antoine Dubois sold a fourteen-mencaudée fief in 1781, it included within it the three standard rotations. A previous lease of the same parcel described it as divided into three unequal rows.[40]

Rotation was clearly associated with good husbandry, more specifically with the preservation of soil fertility. Farmers followed a three-year cycle, planting some fields with the spring crop and others with the main crop, while letting other portions rest, according to an age-old ordering that they repeated year in, year out. Yet the "trois roies inégales," the periodic extensions and contractions of the cultivated surface, attest to a greater degree of flexibility than might otherwise be supposed. We cannot know with absolute certainty how peasants used their land in the eighteenth century. It does appear, however, that they exercised some personal control and that there was room for variation.

We know, for example, that some reduced the fallow in the latter part of the eighteenth century and introduced new crops, sometimes with the express encouragement of agronomically minded owners. In March 1777, when Adrien Mairesse, seigneur of La Bruyère, leased his lands to Pierre Aubert Tamboise, he threw in the twelve mencaudées of his personal domain (*réserve*) with the express condition that these would be cultivated at all times, that is, "refroissées" in local parlance.[41] Traditional crop rotation had been at least partially abandoned.

In some areas it had been abandoned altogether. The village of Etrun declared in November 1790 that it opposed sheep grazing because its territory was not rotated (*notre terroir n'est point assolé*) and the animals would be likely to damage the crops.[42] In most areas the fallow was open to common pasture after the harvest under the strict guidance of herders who moved the beasts from place to place and made sure that they did not trample the cultivated ground.[43] The fact that villagers continued to worry about such depredations suggests that the arable was not divided into exclusive, distinct areas.[44] Sheep would be most tempted to wander off if they found something attractive to chew on. They could do so only if cultivated fields mingled with fallow ones.

The responses to the 1790 government survey that inquired about the advantages and disadvantages of allowing the landless to pasture animals in the village thus offer a possible gauge (in the absence of other evidence) of how far rotation had been abandoned. Thirty-two answers survive for Cambrésis. In one village the inhabitants were divided on the question, but nine others expressed their approval, four on the grounds that more sheep would provide more wool and more meat, and the others with the argument that it would offer added resources for the needy.[45] Two-thirds of the responses, that is, twenty-one localities, denounced such grazing because it harmed the crops. The argument was that since there were no common pastures, the sheep belonging to the landless would naturally feed on other people's produce. No one mentioned the fallow section. There is reason to believe, therefore, that two-thirds of Cambrésis villages had followed Etrun's example and abandoned village-wide rotations. Individual usages and choice prevailed over long-standing habits.

Scattering

These very rotations had at one time dictated that peasants own fields in the various sections, and that their holdings, therefore, be scattered.[46] This scattering persisted in the eighteenth century. The land was neither formally redistributed nor reorganized into more compact units.[47] Part of the reason is that although individual peasants owned a number of tiny strips dispersed throughout the countryside, these were in fact already incorporated within larger blocks that were farmed jointly by the co-owners.

No land survey of the village of Montigny survives prior to 1806, but in the 1760s the Chapter commissioned a map of the village's roads, which designated some of the plots that lay alongside.[48] The thirty-two parcels singled out on the map depict an irregular patchwork of rectangular fields, with an occasional corner jutting out to encroach on the neighboring field. These oddly shaped rectangles, squares, and diamonds covered between two and twelve mencaudées each. Some belonged to the Chapter and were occupied by its farmer, Moyse Crinon. Others were shared by groups of villagers whose names figure on the document itself. The type of crop being raised on the fields and the direction of the furrows may have demarcated one set of parcels from the next, but otherwise, except for the odd rock here and there, only the trained eye could perceive where one property ended and the next one began. This remained an area of open farming.

Fragmentation and scattering, therefore, continued as the norm. The Chapter's 160 mencaudées divided into thirty-four separate lots in 1670 as well as in 1765. Some, as the map showed, lay one beside the other; others, if we go by the stated limits (that is, on whose land they abutted), were at opposite sides of the village. Other large estates, such as those of La Bruyère, Cantimpré, and Le Tronquoy were more compact. None came in a single piece, but the lots tended to be fewer and larger. The Cantimpré farm, for example, had been split in the early eighteenth century so that 18 mencaudées had been carefully carved out of its three main lots of 84.5, 17.5, and 17 mencaudées. La Bruyère likewise divided into five sizable units, the smallest containing about 25 mencaudées.[49]

Families attempted to share good and poor soil equitably. Wills, for one, aimed to distribute plots of comparable quality among heirs. Nonetheless, whenever possible, siblings kept this property in common, undivided ("à l'indivise"), though each held a recognized and fully delineated strip. This practice had been more widespread in the seventeenth and early eighteenth centuries, when larger parcels prevailed and people reasonably assumed that units would be reconstituted through early deaths, departures, or intermarriage. Shared plots became more rare as the eighteenth century progressed. Then, the patrimony fragmented as more people remained in the village. Subdivision, in long furrows, no longer made much sense, and the plots were distributed, one to each heir, rather than shared. At least, that is what emerges from the grid of inheritance. In practice, units such as the ones featured on the Chapter's map continued to be tilled in common by a number of co-owners who had, probably, originally been co-heirs.

The division of large rented estates such as the Cantimpré farm performed the similar purpose of partitioning diverse soils bearing different crops. There, the older brother had kept most of the tenancy, and eighteen mencaudées were carved out for the younger. He received three strips of equal size in different parts of the property, representing the three rotations. The Chapter's farm, on the other hand, embodied accidental dispersal since the tenancy known as La Trappe, in fact, assembled the remainder of the Chapter's medieval domain. Some of this land had fallen into private hands, but the Chapter had retained parcels that it rented out, mostly to a single farmer. Even if such scattering did not necessarily impede proper husbandry,[50] it hindered large-scale improvements. It explains why peasants should want to till their strips within larger, "undivided" units. The nature of the soil, heavy and demanding, provided a real incentive to pool manpower and resources.

Ploughing and Harvesting

Even if Montigny was no farmer's dream, its soil did not totally lack potential. Some areas were impossibly arid and remained uncultivated even in the mid-nineteenth century. Yet most areas were not beyond redemption. They demanded, rather, a lot of work and proper implements. "All the necessary conditions seem to converge to give this region an almost entirely fertile soil destined for plentiful harvests. It shares such advantages with many other regions. But what truly distinguishes it is the human labor that slowly freed the land of its savage features, and the effort of generations of farmers that finally managed to domesticate it."[51] What the geographer Albert Demangeon attributed to the region as a whole applied all the more to a less favored village such as Montigny. Farming, therefore, had both natural and social limitations. The farmer's success depended on the quality of the soil, on the one hand, but on the other it rested on the means at his disposal, that is, his ability to renew his material and invest in improvements.

The hard Cambrésis soils received three ploughings. The local peasantry used a light plough called a *binot* as well as a heavier plough known as the *harna,* which required four horses to pull it. The ground was also broken at three different intervals by means of a harrow made of iron prongs. The area destined for the winter crop received the most attention.[52] The wheat plant was delicate and required greater care than secondary grains like oats or barley that were planted on the second section. The demand for wheat never slackened, and it was used to pay the bills. It therefore warranted all the efforts expended on it.

Right after the harvest, the peasants would turn over the areas lying fallow. They dug furrows that opened up the ground. Frost, or the alternation of freezing and thawing, pushed excess water to the surface, thus draining the soil and readying it for cultivation.[53] After the winter, vigorous harrowings broke down the ridges. A layer of fertilizer then covered the ground. The second ploughing came in May, followed by another in September. One month later, the land got a final harrowing just before being sown by hand. A roller pressed down the seeds and later the roots inside the earth.[54] The parts bearing the spring crop suffered from relative neglect since the grains they carried grew far more easily. The soil was only ploughed and harrowed once after the winter.

The humid climate of the region and the uneven quality of its soil could cause drainage problems, but what the peasant feared most were extreme variations in the weather, sudden frost, excessive rainfall, seasons either too cold or too hot. The crops grew best in moderate temperatures that warmed gradually in the spring and then slowly cooled in the fall.[55] Since such optimum conditions were not always met, the fields demanded a lot of attention. Humidity, for instance, bred weeds that had to be pulled each spring by men, women, and youngsters.[56] Time and again we are reminded of how much the region's fertility depended on this ceaseless labor.

Every lease stipulated that the tenant spread fertilizer.[57] Although full manuring probably took place only once every nine years, that is, once during the life of a contract, the prefect Dieudonné was more generous in his estimate, although he reproached this district for its laxity in dressing the soil: "The clay surfaces are only manured once every nine years, and the cold, humid, rocky and silty soils every three to six years. One should note, however, that in the meantime, ashes or lime have been spread on the crops."[58] The chalky ground provided an alternative source of fertilizer for the clay soils. In 1716 Antoine Crinon, tenant at Le Troncquoy, purchased a load of ash in Le Cateau, which he presumably scattered on his fields.[59] The folding of sheep on the fallow was another way to invigorate the soil. The lease of La Bruyère stipulated that the takers would "during the said period keep at their own expense at the said place of la Bruyère the number of sheep needed for the enrichment and improvement of the land."[60] Every major tenant-farmer in the region kept large flocks of sheep, and the right to pasture on Montigny's commons would give rise to bitter conflicts in the eighteenth century.

The custom in Cambrésis was to spread one mencaud of seed over each mencaudée,[61] and that is what the curé requested for his own land that same year:

> Above that I need 29 mencauds to sow on my land. I need 12 for the plots that I cultivate myself and 17 to advance to my Caullery farmer because he rents 17 mencaudées in three sections (*à la sole*) and I plough 12 in Montigny's parish, [I also need] 10 mencauds of barley because I'm slowly selling [my supply] to my parishioners so that they can make bread and my two horses use 6 rasières of oats which is why I don't have enough to meet my household needs until All Saints Day."[62]

The main crops were harvested between the end of June and late September, but some unripened oats, vetch, or rye reserved for animals could be gathered as early as April or May.[63] The preferred instrument was the scythe, which, unlike the sickle, only adult males could wield. While the men cut the stalks, women and children trooped behind them, bundling the corn into sheaves that they piled in groups of ten. The reapers then awaited the passage of the tithe collector. Once he had carried off his portion, the remainder could be stored in barns and left to dry. It was threshed throughout the year as the need arose.[64] The portion of the stalks still standing and the grain that had fallen to the ground were gathered by gleaners in the forty-eight hours after the removal of the crops (though no earlier than 20 September). Once the period allotted for gleaning had passed, the land was turned over to the pasture of animals.[65]

Implements and Methods

In the early nineteenth century the prefect Dieudonné estimated that only 1 percent of all the land in Cambrésis (including gardens) was worked by hand.[66] The rest required ploughs and animal traction. Because most peasants could not afford these, they either reaped a meager crop since this harsh terrain demanded careful cultivation, or they paid the tenant-farmers to plough their fields. The shepherd Philippe Lenglet, for example, noted in his marriage contract that his uncle would subsidize the tilling of his parcels. In 1761 Jean Philippe Taine and his wife, Rose Bugnicourt, farmer-weavers from Clary, reported that various inhabitants owed them 107 florins for the thirteen fields they had ploughed. These ranged from one-quarter to two mencaudées each, for which the farmer charged them about ten florins per mencaudée.[67]

But the farmers were not always reliable. Taine went bankrupt, leaving his clients in the lurch. In 1727 Marie Michelle Malesieux accused Moyse Crinon, the Montigny farmer whom she hired to till her fields, of careless-ness in tending to her six-mencaudée plot.[68] Jean Douchez, who had been Crinon's ploughman (*valet de charrue*) for six years, recalled that something was always neglected when it came to those six mencaudées: "One year, he limited himself to turning them over after the harvest and then sowed them in that state without bothering to build and break the ridges as he ought to have and as one always does, for the land must always be turned over before St. John's Day and then after the harvest it is built up and broken before it is sown." The plots, therefore, had only been ploughed lightly once with a binot, and this was clearly deemed insufficient and contrary to good husbandry.

The attraction of seasonal employment on the large domains also led peasants to neglect their own plots. The farmers would hire peasants to weed in the spring, but mainly to harvest in summer and then help thresh come fall and winter. This ready supply of workers proved a boon for the big farmers. They were assured of a cheap (or cheaper than imported itinerant work gangs), reliable, and dependent work force that encour-aged an intensive use of labor. The peasants, meanwhile, benefited from the security of such supplemental income. By the middle of the century some villagers married with nothing more than a room on the family homestead, a loom, and the scythe they carried to the farmer's fields.[69]

The big tenants had always relied on local inhabitants. In 1705 Etienne Lenglet, a thirty-seven-year-old Montigny weaver, called on to testify in a dispute, described himself as an *aoûteur*, an August worker, on the farms of La Bruyère, occupied by Catherine Dubois.[70] Pierre Bracque, a Caudry weaver, had been employed at Le Troncquoy as Antoine Crinon's "aousteur" for twenty-four years "or thereabouts and even from an early age when his father worked there doing the harvest" (again as "aousteur"). So had Pierre Defontaine, while Antoine Bricout, sergeant of Caudry, aged sixty-four, stated that "he had done his August for Antoine Crinon going on forty years or so."[71] Most villagers presum-ably participated in the harvest, but there is no record of their number or wages.

Though symbiotic, the relationship between employer and worker did not entail sentimental attachments. In the eighteenth century the increase in population and expansion of the labor force allowed the union of Le Troncquoy and Montigny. The farmers detached their farms from Caudry, joined the parish of Montigny, and began to employ Montigny harvesters rather than laborers from Caudry. The switch created no lasting bonds. The dependence on a local work force ceased with the Revolution, despite violent protests from the villagers. The Troncquoy farmers hired Flemish crews that handled a more efficient harvesting tool, the *piquet*.

The ownership of expensive implements distinguished the large tenant-farmers and labourers from the mass of the peasantry. None was so aware of the discrepancy as Montigny's priest, François Lagrue, who voiced populist sentiments against the pretensions of the farmer of La Trappe. He refused to provide Charles Crinon with a "certificate of poverty" that would allow the farmer to seek a papal dispensation to marry his niece without paying the appropriate fee.

> If the son of the leading farmer of the village, who has been promised a mere 3000 florins when he weds, is considered poor and merits such a certificate, how would you describe those who have no land of their own, who cannot afford horses and ploughs, who, in order to earn their daily bread hire themselves out as laborers, and who always bring to the altar no more than their bodies and a bundle of rags?
>
> The plaintiff's father has a beautiful, large farm, one of the best built, besides which he owns both patrimonial and inherited plots. He rents a large domain that always requires two ploughs and sometimes even three and on top of that he collects the tithe which he may call insignificant but which is in fact considerable.[27]

The farmer who mustered horse and plough belonged to a different world from that of the ordinary peasant. The loss of these attributes of course signified his downfall. When the Chapter of Cambrai dismissed the same Charles Crinon as farmer of La Trappe, their overseer stressed his lack of horses: "Given his well-known insolvency and the fact that he has lost his horses and even his house, . . . he is presently really and truly ruined."[73] As farmers renewed and augmented their stock of implements over the eighteenth century, the gap between rich and poor peasant became even more marked.

In 1680 Pierre Ledieu and Antoine Crinon of Le Troncquoy, victims of hard times, the miseries of war, and the "evil eye," proved incapable of paying their arrears and of stopping the sale of their newly acquired horses and cattle.[74] The inventory at the time of the auction listed their possessions:

Ledieu		Crinon	
5	horses	4	horses
2	heifers	1	colt
2	cows	2	cows
30	sheep	16	sheep
2	sows and 9 pigs	2	sows
1	cart	1	cart
1	plough	1	plough
		1	harrow
20	rasières of oats	30	rasières of oats
200	sheaves of wheat	221	sheaves of wheat

This was not unlike the assortment one would find on smaller farms. In 1678 the farmer of La Trappe owned three horses, a plough, carts, and harrows, while the widow of a Montigny laboureur possessed three horses as well but only one cart, plough, and harrow. He farmed a 150-mencaudée property, she leased thirty-six.[75] In the first half of the eighteenth century this configuration changed little, and tax records both in Montigny and in the neighboring villages disclose that farmers continued to own no more than three to four horses, meaning that they had no more than a single plough team.[76]

When the Montigny laboureur Antoine Labbé married in 1733, he inherited a similar (nondetailed) assortment: "horses, one cart, one plough, two harrows, ploughing instruments, oats, fodder, sheaves, threshed and unthreshed wheat."[77] The 1744 tax roll ascribed three horses to him as it did to his brother Michel, another local farmer. Charles Delacourt, the Montigny laboureur who got into trouble over mauvais gré, owned three horses when he wed in 1728 and the same in 1744.[78] In 1736 a laboureur from Fontaine au Pire who married the daughter of the Montigny farmer Moyse Crinon received horses, carts, harrows, heavy and light ploughs, and all the implements commonly used with two ploughs. His movables also included a flock of sheep, cows and a bull, pigs, and chickens.[79] The stock of the bigger farmers still recalled those of their humbler counterparts.

By the middle of the century a change nonetheless began to take place, first with an increase in the number of horses owned by the biggest farmers. Already in 1744 the farmer of La Trappe, Moyse Crinon, had owned six horses, that is, twice as many as the other farmers in the village—a number that matched the size of his tenancy. In the period that follows it became more and more usual for farmers to declare ten, twelve,

fifteen, twenty-four, and even forty-five horses, as was the case for one
fellow in Neuvilly in 1777.[80] In Ligny in 1745 the leading farmer owned
eight horses.[81] Four decades later, a local farmer left behind the following
assortment:

		Value	
		(florins)	(patars)
a	first team of 6 horses	436	8
a	second team of 6 horses	296	16
7	heads of cattle (8 other cows had just been sold)	200	
7	pigs and 1 sow	68	4
50	fowls	—	
900	sheaves of oats	116	
800	bales of fodder, wheat, oats	144	
1,500	sheaves of wheat	262	10
agricultural implements made of wood and iron			
3	or 4 carts or wagons	208	15
5	harrows	19	14
2	ploughs	36	
3	binots	30	
2	rollers (*ploutoirs*)		
	and a medley of unspecified smaller tools	2	8[82]

There were butter churns in the dairy and beer barrels in the cellar, but
despite the farmer's prosperity, a sense of shabbiness pervades the inventory. The notary who estimated the belongings noted that some of the
horses were blind, while others suffered various ailments, that the furnishings were damaged, the crockery chipped, and most of the linen old
and used.

The number of animals, especially horses, increased but their quality continued to vary. From the end of the seventeenth century to the
middle of the eighteenth, communities insisted that farmers owned
both good and wretched creatures. "Jean Philippe Malesieux has two
horses capable of work (en estats de faire les service) and two that ought
to be counted as one."[83] This applied to all of the local farmers who
had more than two horses. The twelve horses mentioned in the Ligny inventory ranged between five and eighteen years of age and were valued
at nineteen and 120 florins. The fourteen horses of another Cambrésis *fermière* were worth a total of 650 florins, but again with a wide
variation.[84]

	(florins)	(patars)
8 horses	400	
3 colts	160	
2 other colts	86	8
1 other colt	4	16
2 bulls	60	
1 ox	72	
1 calf	48	
6 cows	288	
1 donkey	10	
6 large pigs	72	
14 piglets	56	
chickens, pigeons, ducks	30	
147 sheep at 6 florins each	882	
3 carts	180	
2 ploughs, 3 binots, 4 harrows		
3 rollers (*ploutoirs* and *rouleau*)	42	

This inventory immediately highlights once again the heavy investment in horses and the high cost of animals when compared to farming implements. There, the real expense was iron. The wood in all of the Ligny farmer's agricultural implements came to 87 florins, but the iron components were valued at 197 florins.

Farmers in Montigny also expanded their stock. In 1798 Jacques François Milot, tenant both at Le Troncquoy and La Trappe, suspected of having emigrated during the radical phases of the Revolution, temporarily forfeited his farm. The authorities made an inventory of his goods.[85]

furniture and household goods	94	francs
6 horses	648	
3 cows, 4 heifers, 2 calves	200	
5 piglets and 1 sow	64	
30 fowls	26	
1 cart, 2 harrows, 1 plough, 2 binots,	170	
1 *brabant*		
500 bales of fodder and 600 sheaves	135	
farmhouse and outbuildings	8,000	
necessary repairs requiring	8,000	

He not only owned a greater number of ploughs than his predecessors but a greater range that included the brabant, a very light plough used in the Lille region that was pulled by only two horses. The lack of sheep was only temporary, for in 1836 Montigny had a total of 360.[86] Jacques François Milot was Montigny's wealthiest farmer. He had an estimated capital of 100,000 livres (in preinflationary 1790 value), yet his farm implements seem modest in comparison to those left behind by his Ligny counterpart. Since the local authorities drew up the inventory of Milot's belongings in the midst of war, following upon enemy pillage, and since the inhabitants were not above a bit of patriotic looting, it is more than likely that his equipment resembled that of the Ligny farmer rather than that of his predecessors a century earlier.

By the middle of the century the growing prosperity of the farms brought on a renewal and extension of agricultural implements. Husbandry too showed signs of improving. In 1786 a dispute over contracts and seed provision pitted Joseph Petit of Le Troncquoy against Amand Moity, a Bertry farmer.[87] In the process, Petit proved that he "ploughed, sowed, and fertilized" the land as well as "finished the ploughing on three and a half mencaudées and harrowed five times." The basic number of harrowings, at least, had increased beyond the customary three. Altogether, the land received better care at the end of the period as we learn from one of the region's small farmers.[88]

> Memorandum of the work that I performed on a piece measuring four mencaudées that I rented from Madame Patoux who forced me leave it [mavoir fois donner un degistement] after I ploughed the fallow [apres les avoit poussé en gacher] as I did for myself and so gentlemen I will tell you what my wages should be:
>
> 1. for a row ploughed with the *binot* at 30 patars and for two harrowings at 10 patars the harrowing makes 3 florins 10 patars.
> 2. having ploughed (*gacré*) with two irons makes 5 florins.
> 3. having ploughed (*terché*) with a *binot* and pressed it down (*rebatu*) twice makes 3 florins 10 patars.
> 4. then having broken the ridges with two irons and harrowed four times makes 7 florins.
> 5. after having broken the ridges, I ploughed (*terché*) again with the *binot* and went twice with the harrow which makes 3 florins 10 patars.

The gacre and terche refer to those ploughings on the main section known as *gachérée,* or *jachérée,* and "tierçage," for they were performed on the fields lying fallow (the French term being *jachère*). The plots were therefore given five ploughings, twice with the heavy plough with "two irons" and three times with the binot as well as eight harrowings.

We cannot really tell whether these were novel procedures or not. It is clear, however, that by the end of the eighteenth century they were widespread, so that a laboureur was expected to perform such tasks even on a property of the scale of Madame Patoux's, measuring four mencaudées. Such improvements raised productivity and allowed the region to feed a growing population.

Crops

Agricultural techniques improved, and the capital at the farmers' disposal increased. As a result, in the second half of the eighteenth century yields rose so that even Montigny with its harsh soil continued to feed a growing population. One could surmise that the grain supply that once wound its way to Cambrai and Le Cateau now remained in the village. Yet historians have shown that grain marketing networks expanded in this period and that rioting often accompanied exports of local corn.[89] In fact, southeastern Cambrésis as a whole remained self-sufficient in grain, and, as the authorities made clear, only exported surpluses. "The produce from [this canton's] land suffices in ordinary years to feed its inhabitants."[90] The excess was then sold in Cambrai and Le Cateau.

In June 1792 the commune of Montigny answered yet another of the innumerable and invaluable surveys sent out by the new Revolutionary regime. This one dealt with the state of its grain production. The village authorities declared that 2,900 mencauds of corn (bleds) went to feed the population, 700 mencauds of wheat were sown annually (this figure included Le Troncquoy), and to the query about "the average ratio between seed and crop: that one mencaud could bring in five making a total of 3,500 mencauds in the measure of Cambrai."[91] Not all of the villages in the canton volunteered such information. Clary, however, also declared that it took 875 mencauds of seed to reap its yearly crop of 6,000 mencauds, that is, a yield of 5.85:1.

These yields correspond to the averages encountered by other historians. In the poor soils of northern Burgundy yields oscillated between 3 and 5:1 in the eighteenth century.[92] For seventeenth-century Picardy the estimate is 5:1 or 6:1, with the figure rising to between 6:1 and 8:1 in the next century.[93] The average estimated yield for the whole of France in the eighteenth century still hovers between 5:1 and 6.62:1.[94] For Cambrésis, Hugues Neveux uses the same average return or harvest of 8 hectoliters per hectare.[95] Lefebvre believes that to feed the population, the average would have to have been at least twice as high, bringing it to

15 or 16 hectoliters per hectare, that is, 10 mencauds per mencaudée.[96] This doubling by an historian of the late eighteenth century of the estimate proposed by a Renaissance specialist would argue strongly for improved productivity over the eighteenth century.

The survey that was cited earlier confirms the rise in yields. The average return reported by Clary was to be outdone that very year. The villagers computed that they expected 8,000 mencauds from the 840 they had sown that year, bringing in a yield close to 10:1. Similarly, that same summer Selvigny, a village located southwest of Montigny, next to Clary, declared a yield of 11:1 even though it had been described earlier in the century as possessing (like all its neighbors) very poor soil.[97] Montigny, like Clary and Ligny, would show that yield in 1836 when the authorities next inquired.[98]

Since the large farms occupied the bulk of the good land, and the villagers had to make do with the poorer soil, the low productivity in the eastern part of the village combined with the greater fertility in the northwest might indeed have produced the paltry average yield of 5:1 at the end of the eighteenth century. Yet this averaging hides the fact that the village continued to feed itself. In 1685 the Montignaciens consumed 1,065 mencauds a year.[99] Since this information formed part of a plea to reduce the moulinage tax, it must be taken as a minimum. At that time the population ranged between 250 and 300 people, and thus the per capita consumption was of the order of 3.55 to 4.26 mencauds. In 1792, 600 inhabitants divided 2,900 mencauds, or an average of 4.8 mencauds per person.[100] The individual grain ration had increased by the end of the eighteenth century.

The population of Montigny tripled during the eighteenth century. The village nonetheless continued to feed itself, and the wealth of the farmers shows that they were not merely redirecting supplies that would have previously gone on the market. Successes of this sort were not only meaningful in the short term but brought about long-term changes. It cannot be denied that real agricultural breakthroughs came in the nineteenth century with chemical fertilizers and labor-saving machinery. Although there were fewer "innovations" than we have been accustomed to expect—involving, that is, more complex rotations, particular leguminous plants and particular types of fertilizers, drainage systems, and enclosures English-style—farmers nonetheless managed to overhaul production within the old structure.[101] The agricultural improvements that were tested on the large farms eventually trickled down to the plots tilled by the peasants. There, size proved less of an obstacle than capital.

For although the territory was fragmented, plots were tilled in common and in fairly large units that recalled the undivided patrimonies of old. The drawback for the small peasant remained the high cost of animal traction. If profits were to be measured, unless one were farming a large estate at a nearly stable or slowly rising rent, it made more sense from the middle decades of the eighteenth century onward to direct one's energies to industry and trade. This led in turn to a restructuring of the village's agrarian economy.

6

Rural Transformations and the Turn to Weaving

Previous chapters have described the complex changes that Montigny underwent in the eighteenth century. Population trebled as more young men and women found means to remain in the village; the weight of taxation and seigneurial dues fell. Though agriculture was not revolutionized, farming methods improved enough that the village could feed itself despite its growing numbers. Views of the land itself altered, as families increasingly treated their properties as a purely economic resource, selling readily to nonfamily members.

During these same years Montigny was transformed from a mainly agricultural village to an industrial one, oriented to the market. In the late eighteenth century the village's agricultural production rested almost entirely with its five large farmers. We have seen that this entailed no decline in the village's prosperity; on the contrary, the inhabitants were better fed and more secure as the eighteenth century advanced. But the experience of change requires closer study. Which social groups turned to weaving and why? How did new economic activities coexist with the old? How did villagers negotiate these changes, and what new attitudes, if any, did this adaptation require? Many studies of proto-industry have argued that it was the poorest who turned to weaving as other opportunities dwindled. In Montigny, both middling and small peasants chose to diversify. They did so as a response to the experiences of the first half of the eighteenth century, experiences that led to a restructuring of the local economy.

The Montigny of Colbert's time was still predominantly agricultural. Marriage contracts and tax records from the middle of Louis XIV's reign show the survival of small-scale farming, with middling and subsistence farmers tilling between ten and forty mencaudées.

A small population, kept low by emigration, tilled relatively large parcels, and a quarter of households made an independent living from farming. Typical of these small farmers was the widow Michelle Leduc, whose marriage portion of 1678 included thirty-six mencaudées "that she rented from several masters in return for grain" as well as three horses, a cow, cart, plough and harrow, and other farming implements.[1] The reconstruction of occupations for the 1686 tax roll (supplemented by notarial records) shows that fifteen of Montigny's forty families were directly involved in agriculture as subsistence, middling, or big farmers (ménagers, laboureurs, and censiers), that seven produced cloth, and six kept flocks. One resident may have been a carpenter, for his son would be; yet another was a laboureur, although he went by the title of "ex-mayor"; and there was one farm laborer. Nine occupations could not be determined, but they doubtlessly involved some form of craft or agricultural work. In other words, at the close of the seventeenth century the village was dominated by middling peasants. They were to disappear in the eighteenth century.

Sheepherding was the first of Montigny's agricultural occupations to experience severe difficulties. Nine families at the turn of the century counted shepherds in their midst: the Berleques, Delbarts, Denoyelles, Farés, Godarts, Hutins, Leclercqs, Lenglets, and Milots. These activities were curtailed in this period, and some men, like Jean Berleque and Jean Delbart, became subsistence farmers, while others turned to weaving. Only two descendants still tended sheep later in the eighteenth century: Paul Milot in Montigny and Alexandre Leclercq in Elincourt. In fact, the village, or rather its major farmers, imported shepherds from Caudry and from Bertry.[2]

The decline in sheepherding was directly related to the struggles over grazing grounds that flared in the seventeenth and eighteenth centuries. Large farmers sought to monopolize pastures. They tried to stop communal grazing on their own farms while at the same time attempting to extend their hold over communal pastures. The widespread concern over the depredations caused by animals and especially sheep wandering between the crops ensured popular support for the legislation that limited the number of animals allowed to graze on the arable to the amount of land tilled by the household (in one village the norm became one beast per mencaudée).[3] This meant, however, that peasants with little land ceased to keep flocks and that only the rich owned sheep. There remained one exception. Shepherds, hired by the big farmers, were given some sheep as part of their payment, and they tended these alongside their masters' flocks.[4]

Other peasants were hit by the agricultural crises of the early eighteenth century. War and heavy taxation increased the burdens on the peasantry, with deplorable results. The 1701 tax roll, with its litany of woes, reflected this dramatically. Montigny was reduced to twenty-four taxable households and eighteen beggars. Among the payers, one was "a poor, ruined tenant-farmer," another "a poor *ménager,* very aged, with no profession, unable to pay"; the blacksmith, too, was no more than wretched, as were the "poor servant of a shepherd" or the "poor orphan" apprenticed to a weaver.[5] The story was the same in all nearby villages. Ligny supported fifteen beggars. In Clary forty households depended on public charity, and twenty-three did in Troisvilles.[6]

Such poverty continued to plague the countryside, and in 1720 Troisvilles' tax roll still included five paupers "who had been reduced to begging."[7] Conditions at the end of the seventeenth century and the beginning of the eighteenth century were ripe for alternate sources of income; weaving would provide the foremost of these outlets. Other crafts also would proliferate in the eighteenth century as villages attracted or trained carpenters, cartwrights, masons, shoemakers, barrelmakers, spindlemakers, and seamstresses. Industry was gradually incorporated into household activities, though with varying intensity. Farmers and above all their younger sons took up weaving as a secondary activity, while other peasants turned it into their major occupation.

The mingling of artisanal and agrarian activities created hybrid groups, among whom agrarian pursuits dominated in the first half of the century, while artisanal ones took over in the second. Take the case of Nicaise Lamouret. When he represented his mother at an inquest in 1689, he described himself as a weaver. His mother then occupied twenty mencaudées. By 1694 he acted as Montigny's tax collector, and in 1708 he tilled 34½ mencaudées and also owned two horses. When his daughter married in 1732 he was no longer alive, but the marriage contract described him as a laboureur whose widow still worked several plots. His son, who farmed twenty or so mencaudées, also considered himself a laboureur. Although weaving may have remained a part-time occupation, it had clearly retreated to the background.[8] The youthful weaver had given way to the adult farmer.

For some laboureur families the growing reliance on industry expressed declining fortunes. For example, the circumstances of the Delacourt family, once among Montigny's self-sufficient farmers, deteriorated around the middle of the eighteenth century. Charles Delacourt had occupied 16¼ mencaudées in 1684 and twenty-five mencaudées two years later. In 1708 his son Jean Delacourt, then mayor, rented 141 mencaudées. His eldest grandson and namesake, Charles, inherited the leases of twenty-eight mencaudées in Caudry and seven in Montigny when he married in 1728. In 1743 Charles Delacourt occupied twenty-four mencaudées in Clary, and in 1744 held forty in Montigny. Meanwhile, two of his brothers became weavers and a third moved to the nearby town of Le Cateau. To preserve the economic integrity of the senior household, one heir pooled all of the leases. In this particular instance the two youngest siblings received no more than a part of the family home and several small parcels. Delacourt's sons (there were three), on the other hand, parceled out the patrimony, rented no land, possessed little property, and worked as weavers. Unlike their father, they rented land neither in Clary nor Caudry. The Delacourts had ceased being farmers.

In other cases the turn to weaving resulted not from the family's decline but from the specific difficulties of farmers' younger sons. Even the heir apparent had to endure a trying period when he felt the weight of paternal authority, had no independent status, and was treated no better than a farmhand. "The said Charles Crinon spends his days either loading dung or forking his father's hay, and can be found both in August and at other times working in the barn, or leading the plough, or else overseeing his father's workers. He follows the wagons when it is time to cart produce outside the village. In short not a day passes when he does not exert himself by the sweat of his brow on behalf of his father."[9] One Ligny groom fared even worse, for his marriage contract stated that he would continue to work for his mother, a local farmer: "The future husband agrees to lead his mother's horses as a good servant should and she will feed him and treat him as she would any ploughman."[10] This arrangement might actually have improved his status by providing him some remuneration.

An only son, Charles Crinon would come into his inheritance the day of his marriage. In fact, most leading farmers managed to provide for several children. In the early eighteenth century Antoine Crinon of Le Troncquoy passed his share of the estate to his eldest son, Philippe. Another settled in Cambrai. The second, Moyse, Charles's father, married the widow of the farmer of La Trappe and took over the Chapter's lease, a circumstance that propelled the "rightful" Malesieux heirs to make their living from weaving.

Since the eldest son usually took over the family's leases, the others had no choice except to leave the paternal roof in search of an equivalent position (by marrying the widow or only daughter of a farmer, for example) or else to stay and work for their sibling. Laboureurs who held several leases could have shared these equally among their offspring since this was, after all, an area of partible inheritance. Yet until the middle of the eighteenth century they favored one child. Charles Guille distinguished his daughter Marie Agnès (by his second wife) who, with the consent of the sons of a first union, received the lease of twenty-six mencaudées belonging to the Guillemains, fifteen mencaudées rented from the parish, and a house and garden held from the Chapter. What were the sons to do but seek other sources of income? Quite naturally, Guille's relations with his eldest son, Jacob, were strained. Jacob's name was struck off the contract the father drew with his new bride, although we can only guess at whose request. When Jacob's turn came to marry, his father merely agreed to till the five mencaudées brought by the wife for two years and to provide him once with the wheat growing on two mencaudées. And "the said Jacob promises to work for his father until St. Rémy's Day." At the time of his second marriage in 1727, Jacob Guille, although termed a laboureur, still owned no more than 3¼ mencaudées, although he probably leased more. Reinforcing the laboureur connection, his widow married the farmer Charles Delacourt whom we have encountered more than once.[11] The situation of such younger sons may not have improved dramatically in the following decades, but weaving became the great equalizer. Families that gave up farming for industry divided the patrimony. The major heir disappeared. He or she no longer obtained the family's leaseholds that had set him or her apart from other siblings.

These two contrasting strategies were especially clear in the case of the Cantimpré farmers. In the early eighteenth century the estate was split into a large and small concern that allowed both brothers to stay on the land. In the late eighteenth century, on the other hand, the same family confided the entire lease to the eldest son. Both of his younger brothers took to weaving. And indeed, when Jean Baptiste married, the status of his one surviving brother, the weaver Charles Antoine, was defined as follows: "He will be lodged, fed, and heated at the newlyweds' expense, in their own house, and receive the clothing and linen appropriate to his status, and be given each month three livres spending money and in return he will work as best he can for the benefit of the couple."[12] There were a number of possible scenarios, then. Younger sons who stayed on the farm and worked at the loom replaced one form of subservience with another. Yet sometimes their separate vocation might be parlayed into a measure of independence. Thus, Marie Agnès Guille's above-mentioned settlement stipulated that her other half-brother, Pierre, would be kept and fed on the farm and be granted the use of part of the weaver's cellar. Yet when he married, after his father's death, Pierre Guille was living on his own, in the house and garden salvaged as direct inheritance from his mother, with one mencaudée tilled for life by his brother-in-law, yarn, and the two looms left him by his father.[13]

Table 24. Number of Cattle Owners

Village	Year	Households with cows	Percentages
Clary	1743	65 of 149	43.6
Neuvilly	1777	65 of 239	27.2
Clary	1788	104 of 397	26.2

Source: C20969, C suppl. 524, C suppl. 474, C états 270.

By the middle of the eighteenth century it was no longer chiefly younger sons who chose the independence that textiles could offer. Weaving now provided a new alternative for all strata of the peasantry, especially middling farmers. The expansion of industry encouraged such a move, and the difficult circumstances of the middle of the century made it all the more attractive. The agricultural crisis of 1740 and the cattle murrain of 1744 weakened the middling farmers considerably and spelled the demise of the small subsistence farmer.

This is manifested in the decline in the ownership of animals that is one of the striking features of the eighteenth century (table 24). In 1744, thirty-four of the forty-five villagers listed on Montigny's tax roll owned cattle, and twenty-four families owned at least two. In 1746, after the disease had struck, all that remained were eight cows, eight heifers, and four calves.[14] In this instance, natural disaster only completed a longer process. Two-thirds of Montigny's dowries included cows or sheep in the seventeenth century, and one-third between 1701 and 1750; but only three contracts did so after 1750. The same pattern prevailed in nearby villages. Peasants were abandoning farming, then, and ceasing to rely on the subsidiary income provided by a cow or two.[15]

This change was uneven, and the 1740s saw a brief interruption of it. The outbreak of the War of Austrian Succession, and the textile crisis that followed, reduced alternatives and forced the peasants back onto the land. This is especially noticeable in the case of subsistence farmers, who suddenly appeared in large numbers in this period.

In the middle decades of the century parish records described eighteen villagers as ménagers. These men held very little property. Their parcels ranged from one to four mencaudées, while the two most favored held eight and thirteen mencaudées, respectively.[16] Few weavers in 1750 possessed as little land as these men. Ten weavers owned up to five mencaudées, fourteen between six and ten, five others between eleven and fifteen, while Jean Pierre Lantier, the village's leading linen merchant, held thirty.[17]

In one way it is tempting to conclude that the term ménager was purely idiosyncratic, reflecting the bias of the curé who entered their profession in the records. But the reality appears more complex. Laboureurs continued to exist, though reduced in number and importance, up to the end of the Ancien Régime. They farmed smaller ecclesiastical properties and accumulated leases from other nonresident owners or even local peasants. Ménagers, on the other hand, were not fixed in the hierarchy. They reemerged in the mid- to late 1740s when a double crisis hit the countryside. Low wheat prices strained the farmers, who employed fewer laborers. The rents paid for La Trappe can serve as indicators. In 1735, to meet his payments, the tenant-farmer had to sell 71½ mencauds, whereas in 1745 his lease (which had risen by 45 percent) required him to market nearly twice that amount (131 mencauds). If this were not enough, the blight that killed three-quarters of local cattle in 1744 further threatened the ménagers' livelihood.[18] Nonetheless, the peasants were in no position to abandon the land, for at that very time textile production crumbled as the war closed foreign markets. The crisis endured. "We sold no cloth for twelve years, the old weavers tell us."[19] The temporary closure of the industrial sector revitalized, willy-nilly, agrarian activities. In such circumstances, villagers held on to their land. Despite the hard times, there were fewer land sales in Montigny between 1740 and 1749 than during any other period between 1720 and 1780. Once industrial production rose again (from 1747 until the onset of the Seven Years War), the briefly resurgent ménagers returned to their looms.

Seven of them subsequently became weavers, three during the 1740s and the other four in the 1750s. The adoption of weaving by these peasants did not necessarily signal the family's social decline. Some (the Cauchys) became cloth merchants, while others (the Gueurys and Halles) introduced cotton to Montigny. Other ménagers became farm laborers or else craftsmen. One finds a mason, a forest ranger, and an alehouse keeper. Three died in this period while still working the land. A less lucky confrère ended up a beggar, which is how he appeared in the parish record at his death in October 1765.[20] In most cases these ménagers returned to the occupations they had been forced to abandon during the crisis. Two of them had been farm laborers when they married, an occupation they resumed in the late 1750s. Five other notarized contracts dating from 1712 to 1733 show that some of these other subsistence farmers had originally been weavers.[21]

This crisis of the 1740s seems to have been the last gasp of the old economy. Thereafter, an agrarian society gave way to one dependent on the corn production of its large farms and on the textile production of the majority of its nearly landless inhabitants. The middling and especially the small farmers had been either displaced or replaced. They had moved from a period of near self-sufficiency, when most could eke out a living from the land and from related activities, such as gardening or stock raising, to one in which they relied increasingly on industry to supplement and then provide the bulk of their earnings. They seemed unable to hold on to leaseholds and let them fall into the hands of more dynamic weaving families. As hopes of self-sufficiency—that is, the ability to survive from farming activities—receded, the peasantry retreated from the land. A threshold had been crossed beyond which it no longer seemed worthwhile to struggle to hold on to a farm whose viability was questionable.

Hence, the mid-eighteenth century seems to have brought a far-reaching change in peasants' views of the land. One sign was that families ceased to favor their eldest sons and increasingly divided the inheritance and the leaseholds among offspring, when they did not relinquish the latter altogether. Such parcelization, it would appear, reduced attachment to the soil. Once hopes of independent income from the land vanished, property could continue to be subdivided, for its function was now less to supply a living than to provide symbolic membership in the community. The periodic fragmentation of the soil that characterized the Western agrarian economy from the later Middle Ages on was not merely a Malthusian response or a Malthusian trap. Since peasants could not make a proper living from the land, they ceased to trust it, to believe in its potential. They needed proof that it could still ensure their survival. In the meantime, they turned to other means of support.

Such a choice had a powerful logic, given the poverty of the soil. Working the land required so much effort, so much investment in time and money (for ploughs and horses), that the peasant was better off concentrating on his garden produce (where intensive labor would reap better rewards) than struggling to produce a meager wheat harvest when he could survive as well if not better by weaving and working summers on the large farms. He might also choose to divert to other types of investments the money that had previously gone to the laboureur who tilled his parcels. Fragmentation, then, tended to reduce the productivity of small plots, and it might be presumed that yields on such fields actually declined, thereby increasing even more the village's dependence on its large farms.

Yet land did not totally lose its appeal. In the second half of the eighteenth century, peasants continued to covet properties, and successful weavers made frequent purchases. As agricultural activities became less important, land became valuable particularly for its capital-raising properties. Rental property passed from the laboureurs into the hands of competing farmers but mainly to men who had hitherto worked primarily as weavers and who were attempting to build up landed assets.[22] This accumulation first became noticeable in the 1730s and would provide the springboard for mercantile activities. By this period, for example, as many weavers leased church and parish lands as did farmers. Most of the village's linen merchants obtained loans on the strength of their real estate. Yet when the merchant-weaver Charles Antoine Dubois borrowed 6,000 florins in 1785, he mortgaged ten mencaudées of arable as well as his house and half-mencaudée yard, along with its "various barns and other farm buildings, furnishings, agricultural tools, horses and other beasts, looms and other movables."[23] This particular weaver, then, was both a farmer and a craftsman. Thus, while economically declining laboureurs became involved in weaving, by the 1780s a number of weavers did more than just invest in land. They also tried their hand at farming.

The replacement of the independent farmer by the combination of farmer-weavers again increased the peasants' reliance on the big farmers for their food supply and for some supplementary income. Investments in the textile trade made such new-fangled laboureurs prey not only to agricultural crises but to industrial ones. When the credit structure toppled in 1760, one such farmer-weaver, Jean Philippe Taine of the village of Clary, went bankrupt and so failed to till the plots of the sixteen families that relied on his labor.[24] Similar defaults by Montigny merchants showed the dangers of counting on such services. Pressed for funds, they might abandon farming altogether. Such was the merchant Charles Antoine Dubois's eventual fate, although he struggled to the last to salvage his double investment. Some, of course, managed to be successful at both, especially in the 1780s. Nonetheless, there was a good chance that the peasants' plots would be neglected or tilled less regularly and less thoroughly than they had been when such work represented one of the laboureurs' major forms of income. By challenging the laboureurs' claims to leaseholds and by inserting themselves into the rental process, weavers destabilized the agrarian economy before being either sufficiently wealthy or committed to the land to take their agrarian investments seriously.

By the middle of the century, therefore, the village's leading farmers not only controlled the best land—as they always had—but also reaped the benefits of a general restructuring of the village's economy. The disarray in the ranks of the laboureurs forced the local peasantry, more and more occupied with weaving and happily fragmenting its property, to rely even more strongly on the income earned by seasonal work and on the food grown by the farmers. This process enforced specialization and encouraged a rationalization of agriculture.

In the prerevolutionary decade, merchant-weavers invigorated the debilitated stratum of laboureurs and challenged the farmers' hegemony. The rural hierarchy of the late eighteenth century might, on the surface, then have recalled that of a century earlier. The village, once again, had a number of middling as well as big farmers, even if the ménagers had completely disappeared. But the group's membership had changed. The middling farmer of yore had been replaced by a group of rising weavers. A significant change had taken place in an apparently static structure.[25]

The peasants' fluid conception of landownership and their mitigated attachment to property raises the vexed question of rural pauperization. I have argued here that peasants indeed had less land at the end than at the beginning of the eighteenth century. For some, this meant impoverishment and perhaps even misery. For most, however, the shift was not so traumatic. Significantly, begging practically disappeared in the region. Paupers rarely crop up in parish records (none appear after 1765), and they are no longer mentioned in tax records past the middle of the century. In 1762 the village of Clary actually declared that "there were no disreputable sorts (*gens sans aveu*) and no beggars or other refugees in the village, except for an itinerant shoemaker who sometimes spent eight to ten days in the village who had taken advantage of a local girl whom he had promised to marry at the earliest opportunity."[26]

The social tensions associated with unremitting poverty lessened. The case of Jean Baptiste Ramette, a twenty-six-year-old day laborer, encapsulates this process and illustrates the possibilities that villagers enjoyed in the eighteenth century. In 1757 he was accused of shooting one of the farmer Charles Crinon's dogs.[27] The hounds had mauled his pigs when the pigs wandered into one of Crinon's fields. Crinon mustered the support of his men as well as that of the Troncquoy farmer Robert Milot against the culprit. Crinon's shepherd thus testified:

> Jean Baptiste Ramette is a man who is feared and mistrusted in the village. No one dares speak against him and no one dares resist him for fear of being beaten; he has been known to steal from Charles Crinon, his master, a farmer in Montigny . . . and everyone knows that only Ramette or his children could have done it and they are suspected of even worse in the village. The said Ramette supports a wife and four children and his only occupation is poaching. He doesn't own or rent any land and can only live by hunting and plundering wherever he can. He is a mean and angry man who, at the slightest provocation, takes out his knife and threatens your life.

But Ramette's neighbors, a weaver and a widow, refused to concur with this judgment. Whether from fear or solidarity, the first declared "that she has no knowledge that the said Ramette is feared or mistrusted," while the second abstained from commenting. His petty crimes that victimized the local rich did not arouse widespread opprobrium.

Though the Chapter's prosecutor investigated the character charges, interrogated Ramette about various misdemeanors, and established his weak economic position, he finally nailed him for his attack on Crinon, at knifepoint, in a Montigny tavern. During the inquest, Ramette described how he scraped out a living: "He and his wife survived by doing odd jobs and with the small allowance of wheat they received from the parish . . . lately, he had worked one day at Le Troncquoy doing some gardening, he had spent two days and a half brewing at Lafrance's and had delivered beer for different alehousekeepers and farmers in and around Montigny . . . during the winter he spun rough flax and in the summer he had nothing to do because there was no work." This society set little aside for the poor. The Chapter's charitable institution, the Office de l'Aumône, spent fifteen florins on Montigny and Caullery's poor in 1701, which rose to a munificent twenty in the 1720s.[28] The population therefore put up with the inconveniences of poachers, scavengers, and encroachers on public roads. While the seigneurs prosecuted, and victim hauled culprit before the courts, the remainder of the population took such misdemeanors in stride.

Jean Baptiste Ramette appears to illustrate the problems of poverty and rootlessness in the eighteenth-century countryside. He lived by an "economy of makeshifts," and he apparently expressed the social tensions that this created.[29] Yet at the end of his life he had become a respectable member of the community. Nicknamed *l'homme de fer* (the iron man) he eventually made a living from textiles. In 1798 he and his son, now worthy "linen manufacturers residing in the village of Montigny," would be called on as character witnesses on behalf of one of their workers, Jean Joseph Ruol, accused of stealing another weaver's materials.[30] The intervening decades had eased some of the difficulties of life in Montigny and elevated the Ramettes to respectability. While the young and the elderly, who were less readily prosecuted, could still be found foraging, weaving reduced the number of unemployed.

Cottage industry, then, could prove the antidote to rural poverty. In the second half of the eighteenth century, Montigny's population did not, however, view weaving merely as a means of staying alive. The spread of rural industry and the expansion of credit brought a new dynamism to the countryside. It created new opportunities for wealth and social advancement that had not existed in the purely agrarian economy of the seventeenth and early eighteenth centuries. Given these opportunities, it was not only the village poor who turned to weaving. Farmers' younger brothers and middling farmers themselves were tempted by it, readily relinquishing the ideal of subsistence farming. Montigny's history after 1750 illustrated how weak that goal had been and how quickly peasants could abandon it once viable alternatives presented themselves.

III

THE

LOOM

7

Weaving

Industry came relatively late to rural Cambrésis. The Flemish countryside had vibrated to the sound of looms as early as the fourteenth century when peasants in the Cambrai hinterland were still devoting their energies to tilling the land. This textile production had been closely subjected to urban control and had suffered from the declining fortunes of the Flemish towns and of the woolen cloths they produced.[1] In the late seventeenth century, industry spread anew from town to country in an effort to reduce costs and to evade an overly regulated guild system. Whether the high-quality linens, known in English as cambrics, were invented in Cambrai or introduced into the city in the fourteenth century is irrelevant for our purposes. By the eighteenth century this activity, which had once made the fortunes of the town, had relocated to the countryside. This reduced costs by 10 to 20 percent, depending on the type of cloth, for rural workers were paid less than their urban counterparts.[2] The dispersal probably began in the early to mid-seventeenth century but only spread with any magnitude in the eighteenth.[3] The retreat to the countryside affected old textile centers like Cambrai and Valenciennes. In the eighteenth century, urban production declined dramatically in favor of rural production, although the towns retained some marketing functions, especially for long-distance trade.[4]

Location of Textile Industry

If there were reasons why industry left town, we have also seen why it found a haven in the countryside. The poverty of the soil and its demanding husbandry made textile production a welcome supplementary and even alternative occupation (fig. 9). One finds a regional correlation between levels of fertility and the readiness to turn to textile production.[5] The soil evaluations of the Cambrésis Estates and a map of the region clearly indicate that the most productive land lay north and west of Cambrai and the Escaut River.[6] Fourteen of the villages with good soil, and four with mediocre soil, were located there. Seven other villages with mixed terrains and four of mediocre quality could be found southwest of the city, while only one village in the entire area was deemed poor:

Figure 9. Soil Quality of a Number of Cambrésis Villages

Aubencheul-au-Bac, at the very northeastern tip of the province. Even late in the eighteenth century, few people earned their living from cottage industry in these villages, even in those with poor land. Aubencheul-au-Bac, for example, had no weavers, and in the other villages only a minority of the inhabitants (the highest was 8 percent in Fontaine Notre Dame) wove.[7] The Napoleonic prefect Dieudonné counted the number of looms in the region and found few in that sector.[8] The only notable exceptions overlooked by the prefect were the villages of Bantigny and Flesquières (both with mediocre soils) where the 1790 tax returns show that 29 percent and 40.5 percent of the inhabitants wove cotton or wool rather than linens, that is, that they called themselves *tisserands* rather than fine-linen workers, or *mulquiniers*.[9]

The heartland of linen production, which divided into the finer *batistes* and somewhat rougher *linons,* lay to the east and south of Cambrai. There, weaving was a major occupation, irrespective of soil quality. Only two of the six villages with good land had no looms. The others— Saint-Hilaire, Quiévy, Rieux, and Saint-Vaast—supported large populations with a ratio of one loom per household.[10] Another populous village, Viesly (1,751 inhabitants) located close by, had a mixed terrain and more weavers than any other village of that soil type. There were also thirteen villages with mediocre land, and only three of these had little or no cottage industry, while the others reported a high percentage of looms.

While the poor arable was concentrated south and southwest of Cambrai, one miserable village lay northwest of the capital. Though on the eastern bank of the Escaut, Thun-Saint-Martin (like its neighbors Naves, Thun-Levêque, and Ewars and that other "bad" village farther west, Aubencheul-au-Bac) produced no textiles—at least none that appeared in Dieudonné's statistics. Two other villages with poor soil, Bantouzelle and Crèvecoeur, had no weavers, although a 1790 government survey showed that at least one contained a large body of spinners of both sexes. Of the twelve villages with the poorest soil, only one, Lesdain, to the west of the others, included few weavers, although nearly one-third of the inhabitants worked as spinners.[11]

One area stands out. A handful of villages south of Cambrai remained practically untouched by weaving, despite their proximity to the less fertile soils. Some such as Séranvillers had good soil. In others, it was of mixed quality as in Masnières, mediocre as Forenville and Wambaix, bad in Crèvecoeur, or very bad in Lesdain.

This confirms the observation that although poorer soils proved receptive to industry, this applied to the region rather than to individual villages. Whenever a poor agricultural area turned to cottage industry, it drew its more prosperous members into the network, whereas an area that was basically fertile had little call for industry, and the inhabitants of its less favorable parts had to find other sources of employment. They generally did so by working as field hands.[12]

The extent of peasant landownership does not seem to have played a decisive role in determining whether or not the village adopted rural industry. According to the data provided in Lefebvre's appendixes, in five villages with good soil, peasant property ranged from 26 percent (Raillencourt) to 36 percent (in Quiévy, a weaving village).[13] In five villages with mixed terrain, peasant property dropped to as low as 18 percent in Proville but rose to 47 percent in Viesly, another weaving village. While this might imply that peasant proprietors predominated in industrial villages, the figures for localities with mediocre land invalidate this conclu-

Table 25. Average Size of Peasant Holdings in Nine Cambrésis Villages

Village	Date	Soil quality	Average peasant holding (mencaudées)	Industrial status
Inchy	1791	very bad	.58	weaving
Etrun	1789	mediocre	1.0	nonweaving
Abancourt	1773	good	2.0	nonweaving
Vielly	1783	mixed	2.4	weaving
Bertry	1784	very bad	2.8	weaving
Esnes	1783	bad	3.2	some weaving
Quiévy	1785	good	3.2	weaving
Lesdain	1785	very good	4.9	nonweaving
Raillencourt	1765	good	5.5	nonweaving

Source: Lefebvre, *Paysans du Nord*, pp. 896–99; Dieudonné, *Statistique*, II, 278–80; C15428.

sion. Peasant landholding went from 15 percent in Béthencourt (weaving) and 17 percent in Flesquières (with its cotton or wool production) and Paillencourt (which had no industry), to 26 percent and 29 percent, respectively, in Villers-Guillain and Troisvilles (both weaving) and finally to 39 percent in Doignies (very little industry) and 40 percent in Etrun with its lone tisserand. The same was true of villages with very poor soil. Peasant landownership in such villages ranged between 21 percent and 39 percent: the lowest, Esnes, as well as the highest, Fontaine-au-Pire, producing linens (although Esnes had a lower incidence of looms). Inchy with its 58 percent weavers had the fewest peasant proprietors in the least fertile soil category; only 9 percent of the territory belonged to the peasants, whereas in Lesdain, which had little industry, such landownership rose to 42 percent.

The average size of the plots possessed by the peasants demonstrates the same variability (see table 25). Individual villages therefore could not determine the recourse to industry. If a commercial network was not already in place, attracted by the region's need for supplementary incomes, then the village, however poor and infertile, would not turn to proto-industry.

Spread of the Industry

Once the economic networks that weaving required were in place, all villages were drawn into it, whatever the prosperity of their agricultural

Table 26. Percentage of Weavers in
Montigny, 1686–1787

Year	Percentage
1686	17.5
1708	33
1744	56
1750	62
1787	62

Source: C suppl. 524, C états 429.

sectors. These networks determined the form as well as the fact of industrial production. Finer-quality batistes were produced in the valleys of the Ecaillon, Selle, and Erclin, closer to Valenciennes.[14] The sectors to the south and east, dependent on Cambrai and Saint-Quentin, manufactured slightly rougher and cheaper linen cloths—linons and gazes. As the networks solidified, this distinction grew firmer, and in the second half of the eighteenth century, Montigny and its neighbors came to specialize in these coarser products.

By 1700, weavers permeated the tax records, and it is possible to trace their progression in a village such as Montigny. In sixty years their number rose from less than one-fifth to nearly two-thirds of the working population. In Troisvilles in 1701, weavers made up 12.5 percent of taxpayers, 22 percent in 1720, and in 1743 the proportion had risen to one-third. Caudry listed no weavers in either 1701 or 1704 when the inhabitants were farmers and laborers, but in 1754 weavers made up 42 percent of the population and 52 percent in 1776.[15] In Clary 16 percent of taxpayers wove in 1701, and 32 percent in Ligny, a figure that had reached 44 percent by 1743. The marriage contracts for those two villages show that as early as 1674 and 1677, couples were bringing one or two looms to the newly formed household.[16]

Clary demonstrates the proliferation of looms in the second half of the eighteenth century when cottage industry became the major occupation. In 1743, 40 percent of the taxpayers shared a total of 94 looms. Half a century later, the same proportion owned looms, that is 40 percent of the local inhabitants, but they now represented 159 households rather than the previous 60, and 331 looms rather than 94. The number of weaving households had increased by 165 percent; the number of looms by 252 percent. Only 45 percent of weaving families now owned one loom, 33 percent owned two looms, and 21 percent owned three or more. The concentration was less marked in nearby Neuvilly. In 1777, one-third of households (35 percent) wove and owned a total of 120 looms. Some 69 percent had one loom, 21 percent had two looms, and 9 percent had three looms or more.[17] Weaving had become a full-time occupation in these villages.

Production

But this did not mean that agricultural work ceased to affect cloth production. The number of pieces taken to the Valenciennes stamping stations peaked in March, February, July, and September (in descending order), and the fewest appeared in August.[18] This curve more or less reflected the agricultural calendar, especially the quiet of the winter months. The need to have the cloth bleached before the November deadline explains the sudden rush in July and September that surrounded the major lull in August. Bleaching took place out of doors, and merchants would refuse pieces after 15 October, since the bleaching process required three weeks. Agricultural needs interfered with full-time production, but there were other hindrances such as the varying availability of yarn.

A survey carried out in 1790 provides firsthand information about the amount of time devoted to weaving in some of the province's villages and thus allows assessments of weaving's importance.[19] Experts agreed that it took a weaver three weeks to manufacture a piece of fine linen.[20] This means that in villages where the average household produced seven to fifteen pieces, weavers spent between five and ten months at the loom, assuming an even size of cloth.[21]

The weavers worked on their own or on rented looms in their own homes.[22] Occasionally, they worked in a master's workshop. In Ligny, for example, in 1743 two prosperous weavers had three and four assistants living with them.[23] The incidence diminished as more looms were introduced in the villages and more houses were fitted to accommodate them. A weaver usually received his loom as his dowry.

When Pierre Henninot married Marie Magdelaine Taine of Ligny, the wife's parents promised to build them a cottage with a cellar housing two looms. In Clary two decades later, in the 1730s, the bride's family provided space for four looms, and, as cottage industry spread, similar plans became commonplace.[24] Once the weavers' cellars were specifically built to hold four looms, they came to be used by more than one family

Table 27. Industrial Production in Cambrésis Villages

Village	Looms/ weavers	Information	Average	Looms*
Bantigny	25 looms	work 4–6 months	—	—
Blécourt	—	work 4 months	—	—
Caullery	40 weavers	8 pieces each	8	100
Crèvecoeur	20 weavers	240 pieces	12	110
Esnes	70 weavers	850 pieces	12	132
Fontaine au Pire	128 weavers	1152 pieces	9	176
Haucourt	21 weavers	250 pieces	12	65
Lesdain	6 looms	52 pieces	8.3	60
Ligny	152 weavers	1138 pieces (15 ells)	7.5	254
Montigny	60 weavers	440 pieces	7.3	124
Saint-Aubert	250 looms	10 pieces per loom	10	310
Saint-Souplet	66 weavers	792 pieces	12	290
Selvigny	55 weavers	825 pieces	15	114

*Cited by Dieudonné, *Statistique*, for 1789.
Source: L6651-2.

member. Marriage contracts often envisaged parents and newlyweds sharing the cellar and conceded the usufruct of looms to other unmarried children as well.[25] The cellars were in fact half-basements so that the actual lodgings stood a few feet above ground. These damp workshops were meant to keep the yarn, which was covered in grease, from drying too quickly. The looms were lined up along the wall so that the light which penetrated from the large tilted windows fell on the worker's right-hand side. The manufacture of fine linens required the use of small looms whose gentle motion prevented the threads from breaking. These looms were made of wood and cost relatively little. In 1782 the loom and utensils of a Bertry weaver were valued at twelve florins, at most a month's worth of weaving. In 1770 the weaver Jean Philippe Taine of Clary owned two looms, each worth seven florins, while a third, in poor condition, was estimated at no more than two florins.[26] By 1753, Montigny had enough weavers to warrant a full-time spindlemaker (*rosier,* or *rotier*) who supplied parts for the loom.[27]

Weaving fine linens was a difficult skill whose techniques were transmitted through the village during the early days of cottage industry. In 1730 Louis Pigou recounted how he had spent two years in Jacques Lefort's house in Montigny, "working for his own profit and only borrowing the cellar."[28] He had been seconded by Jean Lefort, nephew of

Jacques, who was cleverer in the art "of preparing the threads for weaving." While Catherine, Jacques's wife, knew how to warp thread, neither she nor her husband could weave. It was Jean who took charge, "working the loom by himself," although his aunt claimed that he had worked as her employee, manufacturing one piece after another on her behalf. He, on the other hand, maintained that he had set the threads, bought the yarn and distributed it, acted as master to other weavers, and often taken the product to Saint-Quentin and elsewhere. Several witnesses confirmed his account, vouching that after three or four years' training, Lefort had gone to work "in the cellar of his uncle's house, where he was then living" and where he supervised the work of fellow weavers. In the early eighteenth century, only a few inhabitants possessed the appropriate facilities. They shared them with other weavers to whom they passed on their expertise. In Jean Lefort's case, he trained the laboureur Louis Pigou as well as other villagers. As this know-how spread and each household built weaving cellars and installed its own looms, production acquired a family base as one generation trained the next.[29]

If Lefort's aunt could not weave, she was capable of warping the thread and of assisting her nephew at the loom. Montigny's 1701 tax roll includes one female weaver, "Michelle Denoielle, fine-linen weaver . . . head of household, separated from her husband."[30] Several such mulquinières would crop up in the parish registers over the century, but on the whole weaving remained a male occupation. Dieudonné assigned wives a subsidiary role, seconding their husbands when there was no one else to set the woof.[31] Widows, of course, were most likely to be independently active. Thus, the widow Boursier, with her sons' assistance, became one of Montigny's small-scale merchants.

Children helped their parents at least part of the time. In 1743 the curé of Ligny described the working arrangements of a number of weaving families.[32] These were considered either affluent or fairly well-off. Six employed one to four live-in helpers, twelve worked on their own, and one worked with his wife ("ils travaillent eux-memes dans leur maison"). Eight worked with their children ("qui travaille luy et ses enfans"), of which they had two to six each.[33] One weaver with four children, however, employed only one son ("ille travaille luy meme et un de see garsons"). The sort of domestic arrangements by which children worked at the loom from their tender years, described by Mémé Santerre for the end of the nineteenth century, may have prevailed two centuries earlier.[34] Whenever the young appear in documents, however, it is for some prank, squabble, or petty theft, such as stealing fruit or gleaning out of season, that finds them out-of-doors. Indeed, children were needed in the fields as much as in the home. All the witnesses called to testify in a dispute that opposed two of Troisvilles' seigneurs were able to do so because they had been in the fields that October day.[35] They included weavers and a weaver's son, aged eighteen, a sixteen-year-old spinner who herded the village's cows, as well as farmers, farm laborers, an innkeeper, and a surgeon.

As in the towns, young men went through an apprenticeship and joined the ranks of full-fledged weavers in their late teens. There were no formal stages, no masterships or mastership examinations. Part of the attraction of the rural venue was that it circumvented such restrictive guild requirements. Although journeymen occasionally figure in the records, adolescents are usually called workers and are presumed to be working for their parents. In the process of family reconstitution, I traced all godparents, and the earliest mention of a profession is eight years old for girls (spinners) and fourteen years old for boys (weavers).[36] Curés, from the middle of the century onward, tended more appropriately to call these youngsters "workers" (ouvriers) or refer to them as the sons and daughters of weavers. Some children, depending on the family's inclination, were described as schoolchildren (écoliers).[37] Charles Antoine Dubois, who appeared as a worker at the age of thirteen, had become a weaver by the time of his wedding five years later.[38] Though the evidence remains scanty because the curé did not always include the godparents' professions, it is clear that training began early. According to Dieudonné, boys began their apprenticeships around the ages of eleven or twelve. They earned eight to ten francs a month by the time they were fourteen, and twelve to eighteen francs at eighteen.[39] Because of the brittleness and fineness of the thread and the difficulty in producing a smooth and even cloth, weaving fine linens required training and skill. By the time boys reached seventeen or eighteen, the community deemed that their skills had matured sufficiently for them to be considered full-fledged weavers.

A weaver received ten francs for a gaze, fifteen for a linon, and eighteen for a batiste.[40] Once we convert these amounts to florins, a Montigny gaze weaver could count on twelve to sixteen florins per piece.[41] The twenty sous he earned a day represented double the income of a spinner and slightly more than the wages of an agricultural laborer, who took home ten to fifteen sous when he was fully employed.[42] In times of difficulty, wages might be much lower. In Caudry in 1791, with its three hundred looms, a hundred farm laborers, and four hundred spinners, the fine-linen workers were said to earn ten to twelve sous a day, while spinners were left with only twelve to fifteen sous a week once they had paid for their flax, oil, and heat.[43]

In this region, spinning was an occupation usually but not exclusively relegated to women, who acquired these skills very young.[44] They began the process by combing the flax, separating the two-thirds of finer strands from the one-third of waste (étoupe) that would be spun as well, yielding a coarser thread (lin de gros) that would go to make common cloth (*toiles de ménage*). The work was done by handwheel, and the spinners took two to three strands, which they pulled into a very fine but even thread, wetting their fingers all the while from a bowl of water placed over the wheel or else using their saliva. Once they had produced an appointed amount of yarn, the spinners transposed it onto bobbins, which they brought to a weaver for warping. Sixteen threads formed a *portée,* and twelve to fifteen *portées,* depending on the cloth, then made up a *quart,* each *quart* consisting of two hundred threads.[45]

The finest and lightest thread fetched the highest price. A spinner of fine yarn could earn nine sous a day on the average and a maximum of eight sous for the coarser variety, although, as we have seen, it is unclear if this represented her net or gross earnings. Cloth was rated according to a numbering system that defined its quality and its price. The higher the number of threads (calculated on the basis of *quarts*), the finer the product. Thus, if the warp contained eighteen *quarts,* the cloth would be known as number eighteen, and this is how it would appear in records and registers. The maximum fineness varied depending on the type of cloth.

Batistes numbered from ten to twenty-eight, gazes from four to sixteen, and linons from five to twenty-two. Batistes usually measured twelve and a half ells with a two-thirds width; gazes, fourteen and a half ells and three-quarters width; and linons, fifteen ells and a variety of widths.[46] The common cloth (toiles de ménage), fashioned from leftover flax, could stretch as much as seventy-nine ells, or more than fifty meters.[47]

The basic distinction among finer linens rested on the thickness of the weave. Batistes were tighter yet finer than the lighter and looser linons (hence their other name of *clair*).[48] Cuffs, handkerchiefs, and the collars favored by ecclesiastics and other notables were made from batistes, while linons and gazes tapped a broader market by serving for such female apparel as kerchiefs and other headgear.[49] While Cambrai's clerical and monied elite absorbed some of this finer production, nine-tenths of the cloth was sold abroad. France bought one-quarter (Cambrésis lay beyond its customs barriers). Britain, Brabant, the Low Countries, Germany, the Baltic, Italy, Spain, Portugal, and the French islands purchased the rest.[50] The weavers themselves used the linen waste to fashion rougher skirts and other garments.

While, on the whole, production rose throughout the eighteenth century, cycles in popularity affected the relative demand for these cloths and especially of the finer batistes that sold less well at the end of the Ancien Régime when public preference shifted toward the lighter and cheaper linons. The shift in public taste had clear repercussions on Montigny and its neighbors. These villages had manufactured both batistes and linons in the first half of the eighteenth century. Marriage contracts permit us to trace this phenomenon because donors who offered the young couple yarn as part of their dowry sometimes specified for what type of cloth. Thus, in the earlier part of the century, batistes were mentioned five times (with a fineness of 18 and 20); claires, or linons, four times (13, 13, 15, 16); while eight pieces ranged from 13 to 17 and could equally have referred to batistes or linons.

Fabrics appeared in fourteen more contracts after 1766 (most frequently in the 1780s); ten mentioned gazes (with a fineness of 8 to 11); two others called 7 and 10 were also probably gazes, which left only two instances of linons with a fineness of 14 and 15. The shift to gazes mirrors the changes in demand for these materials as well as a change in Montigny's orientation away from Valenciennes and Cambrai, the respective centers of batistes and linons, to Saint-Quentin, the heart of the gaze industry. The village proved remarkably flexible in its adaptation to the new product (invented in 1765). The manufacture of gazes is mentioned in a marriage contract as early as 1766.

This switch, characterized by a reordering of marketing networks, was mediated by local merchants rather than imposed on the villages by urban putters-out. This process will be examined more closely in a later chapter, but here it should be emphasized that such adaptability on the part of the population demonstrated its flexibility rather than its declining skills. Gazes were coarser than either batistes or linons, but in all three cases the material was fine linen that demanded delicate manipulation. The huge increase in production of such cheaper cloths, which made the fortunes of Saint-Quentin, reflected the growing demand for such products rather than deteriorating standards of manufacture.

Spinning

Flanders was noted for the quality of its flax, and it was to Flanders that the villages in the region turned to obtain their raw materials. The best flax came from Fenain, Sommain, Erre, and Wallers, in that order, and their fame rested on the purity of the waters that washed the plant.[51] Montigny bought its flax in Fenain and Marchiennes, while other Cambrésis villages included Iwuy, Sommain, Wallers, Erre, Thun-Saint-Martin, and Cambrai among their sources.[52] Most villages spun both coarse and fine linen, and it has been estimated that the region supported five spinners for every weaver.[53] Yet this ratio was deemed insufficient, all the more so, urban clothiers complained, because the English were cornering local supplies illicitly, since yarn exports were forbidden. It was cheaper for these foreigners to get hold of the yarn and have the cloth manufactured in England or Scotland than to purchase batistes through the legal channels and face high customs duties. French manufacturers who needed a cheap and steady supply naturally resented these contraband activities and saw them as the cause of local shortages.

In fact, yarn production lagged behind demand and restricted cloth production to a part-time occupation. The 1790 survey provides useful information about spinning and the production of fine-linen threads in the province. Table 28 indicates that the higher the population, the greater the output, simply because of the greater number of hands. Yet the lower average production of twelve to fifteen *quarts* per spinner occurred in fairly populous manufacturing villages, and this suggests that the women assisted the men at the looms and had less time at the wheel. They therefore relegated such work to the young, the widowed, or the aged. This contradicts one of the suggested proto-industrial models that would have called for all phases of production, from the growing of the flax to its spinning and then weaving, to be concentrated in the household where the wife and children provided all of the yarn needed by the adult male weaver.[54]

Whatever the number of *quarts* required for one piece—be it ten or thirty—only two villages manufactured enough thread for their weavers. One should note that the number of *quarts* represented only the amount contained in the warp, and that the entire piece would of course have required extra thread for the woof (see table 29).

Crèvecoeur and Lesdain produced surpluses because they were only marginally involved in weaving. All of the other villages needed to purchase extra supplies of yarn, although Haucourt and Saint-Souplet

Table 28.   Spinning in Cambrésis Villages

Village	Land	Population	Spinners	%	Looms	Quarts	Average
Abancourt	good	485	210	43	—	600 (fin) 530 livres (gros)	3
Banteux	—	495	98	20	—	4,800	49
Bantigny	mediocre	348	100	29	—	4–10 livres	?
Béthencourt	mediocre	610	100	16	134	12,000–13,000	12/13
Caullery	very bad	427	120	28	100	3,000	25
Crèvecoeur	bad	1,399	400	29	110	13,312	33
Cuvillers	good	317	45	14	—	—	4 livres
Déhéries	good	62	19	31	12	380	20
Esnes	bad	1,073	223	26	132	4,014 (fin) 550 livres (gros)	18
Elincourt	very bad	1,169	300	26	84	6,000	20
Etrun	mediocre	565	80	14	—	2,000 livres	25 pounds
Ewars	very good	458	158	35	—	4,000	25
Fontaine au Pire	bad	834	219	26	176	3,168	15
Fressies	average	771	180	23	—	3,240	18
Haucourt	very bad	246	72	29	65	2,592	36
Hemlenglet	mediocre	540	140	26	—	—	—
Honnecourt	—	1,575	300	19	60	9,000	30
Lesdain	very bad	755	214	28	60	8,560	40
Ligny	very bad	1,124	183	28	254	3,000	25
Malincourt	—	744	60	8	108	780	13
Montigny	very bad	464	60	13	124	900	15
Morenchies	good	85	20	24	—	300	15
Neuville-Saint-Rémy	good	552	80	14	—	120 livres	
Paillencourt	mediocre	1,141	150	13	—	*	30
Raillencourt	good	493	72	15	—	3 months	—
Ramillies	good	391	60	15	—	800	13
Sailly	good	550	100	18	—	3,600	36
Saint-Aubert	mediocre	1,548	600	39	310	3,600	6
Saint-Hilaire	good	1,380	200	15	302	6,400	32
Saint-Souplet	very bad	1,351	200	15	290	—	52
Sancourt	good	298	73	25	—	—	—
Selvigny	very bad	523	150	29	114	6,000	40
Thun-Saint-Martin	bad	737	130	18	—	3,380	26
Tilloy	good	154	40	26	—	100 livres	—
Walincourt	bad	1,372	400	29	297	18,400	46
Wambaix	mediocre	399	88	22	30	1,132	13

*One quart per week for seven months.
Source: L6651-2, C15428; Dieudonné, *Statistique*, II, 278–80; III, tables.

Table 29.   Cloth Manufacture Based on Yarn Production in the Villages

Village	Declared quarts produced	Actual number of pieces made using			Actual number of pieces in 1790
		(10 *quarts*)	(20 *quarts*)	(30 *quarts*)	
Caullery	3,000	300	150	100	360
Crèvcoeur	13,312	1,331	666	444	240
Esnes	4,014	401	201	134	850
Fontaine au Pire	3,168	317	158	106	1,152
Haucourt	2,592	259	129	86	250
Lesdain	8,560	856	428	285	52
Ligny	3,000	300	150	100	1,138
Montigny	900	90	45	30	440
Saint-Aubert	3,600	360	180	120	2,500
Saint-Souplet	10,400	1,040	520	347	792
Selvigny	6,000	600	300	200	825

could have gotten by with local production if they just manufactured rough linens. The others had to obtain their quotas from urban or rural merchants who bought thread from nonmanufacturing areas. Thus, the spinners of Etrun declared that they sold their yearly output of two thousand livres of fine yarn to weavers and merchants from other localities.[55] Jean Pierre Lantier, Montigny's leading merchant-weaver, secured his own supply by employing a network of spinners. He owned at least a hundred spinning wheels.[56]

If a weaver produced an average of seven to twelve pieces a year, each one would need to provide from one hundred to three hundred *quarts* of yarn annually, depending on the type of cloth. Given an average individual output of fifty-two *quarts* a year, every weaver had to rely on the work of four if not eight spinners. The limited supply of yarn restricted cloth production altogether and could well have influenced the recourse to coarser and looser materials. In any case, it kept weaving a seasonal occupation. The expansion of the industry necessitated either the extension of spinning networks or mechanization of the process. Cambrésis in the late eighteenth century provides a perfect example of the bottleneck effect that led to the invention of labor-saving machinery. Such technological innovations were not applied to linens until the middle of the nineteenth century, however. Linen threads proved too delicate and brittle for the mechanical devices that worked so well for cotton.

It is of course true that when village authorities counted local spinners, they made a rough estimate of the number of matrons and girls for whom this was a steady occupation. In fact, in Montigny as elsewhere, most women spun, and, when asked their profession, all women declared they were spinners, that is, unless they were specifically occupied otherwise as midwives, farmers, or merchants.[57] Since they used a wheel rather than a spindle, they had to allocate specific times to spinning and did not spin as they walked, for example. In March 1802 a bloody assault took place one morning in Clary, and a number of people answered the shouts of the elderly victim. Four women had been spinning, their ages forty-four, twenty-one, seventeen, and twelve.[58] The number of spinners therefore would have exceeded the sixty reported by Montigny. But few worked full-time, and many assisted their husbands at the loom or in the fields. The Caudry authorities counted four hundred spinners, but "half were busy with domestic chores."[59]

Although women turned to spinning in their spare time, they regularly gathered to spin. In 1707 Montigny's curé testified in a paternity suit and described the way the young congregated in the house of a local matron. "The girls get together to spin and the boys then come by to kid and laugh with them."[60] An accusation of infanticide in Bouvignies was countered by a similar observation. "Young men showed up at the spinning gatherings in her house, as they always do."[61]

Standard of Living

In the lawsuit cited earlier between Jean Lefort and Catherine Lefort, the latter refused to pay her nephew for the cloth he had manufactured in her cellar, arguing that "every one knew that the loom can barely feed the weaver. If there are any profits to be made it is in the cloth trade and even then it needs to be carried out on a larger scale than that ever attempted by the plaintiff." She felt he should be content with the room and board she had provided for twenty years. Moreover, he must have earned plenty, for "no sooner had he learned to weave than he was off to the tavern where he squandered large sums."[62]

Catherine Lefort contradicted herself by insisting on both her nephew's extravagance and his miserable earnings. Altogether, however, she stressed the weavers' dreary existence: "we have seen how so many of these workers' children are forced to beg because their fathers barely make six sous a day." The inspector of manufactures responsible for the region stretching from Valenciennes to Saint-Quentin, Jean Baptiste Crommelin, held equally bleak views about rural production. A victim of a bankruptcy in 1759 that had ruined his Saint-Quentin firm, he denounced rural competition for destroying urban trade, and he vituperated against rural weavers who were foolhardy enough to believe that they could make a living by manufacturing and selling cloth.[63] He spent his career lobbying for stringent controls over rural production, and the occasional bursts of restrictive legislation that one finds for the region were attributable to his efforts. Year after year he sent the government reports on production, based on the number of pieces that had passed through the official quality controls. This failed to include the unregulated rural production that he wished to dismantle, except when he felt particularly outraged. Even if he proves a reliable witness of urban decline, his picture of overall production and of activities in the countryside is misleading. When he notes that prices are down, that the markets for linens have dwindled, especially in Cambrai, we are left to wonder whether this is a universal phenomenon, affecting town and country alike, or whether it touched only urban centers. It is true that his relish in describing the discomfiture of rural producers was such that he must have been right about some of the cyclical downturns. For the industry was subject to fluctuations.

Cloth production was prey to short-term recessions, affected by international markets and levels of demand. We can follow the slumps caused by the Seven Years War and the subsequent recoveries of Cambrai and Saint-Quentin. In Cambrai the number of stamped cloths fell from 13,504 in 1755 to 9,300 in 1760 and 6,770 in 1763 before rising to more than 11,000 by 1769, 15,000 in 1776, and 20,000 in 1783.[64] Saint-Quentin experienced similar fluctuations. From 108, 834 cloths in 1756, the number dropped sharply to 72,112 in 1760, only to pick up again rapidly to 99,628 the following year and reach 107,705 in 1763. As low as 75,798 in 1769, the number of pieces rose to 108,581 in 1774, then dropped once more for four years before a strong showing in the 1780s when 144,218 pieces were stamped in 1785. By 1788, in the wake of the Free Trade Treaty with England, the Saint-Quentin total had been reduced once more to 105,681 pieces.[65]

These periods of recession and retrenchment could prove devastating for the weavers, some of whom never recovered their losses. These effects will be traced in the following chapters. Nonetheless, the picture of gradual and inevitable impoverishment propounded by Crommelin or the widow Lefort is misleading.[66] Rural industry brought with it new risks but also a new source of income. The weavers' profits increased in the eighteenth century.

Table 30. Average Number of Children in Montigny Households

Period	Completed families		Incomplete families	
	Births	Survivors	Births	Survivors
1700–1750	6.8	4.7	6.2	5.1
1751–70	4.9	3.3	3.5	2.2
1771–90	6.9	4.8	4.6	3.2
1791–1810	5.9	4.3	5.4	3.5
1811–20	—	—	4.0	2.9

By the 1780s, weavers were making eighteen sous a day, that is, three times more than the amount Catherine Lefort estimated in the 1730s.[67] Even if she blackened the picture to strengthen her argument, and supposing that actual wages had averaged ten sous, then the weaver's income of eighty florins (for eight pieces of cloth) in the first half of the eighteenth century when wheat averaged three florins would have provided him with thirty-three mencauds of wheat if his wife's earnings of another twenty or so florins did not fluctuate. With an income of eighteen sous a day, and his wife's fifteen *quarts* of the best-quality yarn worth thirty sous, or an additional twenty-five florins, the weaver's household in the latter part of the century would earn 150 to 170 florins. At the average price of 4 florins 5 patars, this would have bought about forty mencauds. Real income had risen by 20 percent.

Nor was this prosperity compromised by increasing family size, as some theorists of proto-industrialization have suggested. For Franklin Mendels, for instance, the cottagers did not envisage profit-making but instead made human capital their main investment and had more children; in other words, whatever gains industrial work offered were lost to population growth. The average Cambrésis household at the end of the eighteenth century, however, contained 4.8 members in agricultural areas and slightly less, 4.7, in areas with rural industry.[68] In Montigny, family reconstitutions show a drop in the number of children in the 1750s and 1760s and again at the end of the century, caused in part by the revolutionary upheavals and imperial campaigns (table 30).

In the eighteenth century, Montigny's population went from about two hundred to about six hundred inhabitants. This phenomenon involved changes in strategies concerning the mobility and marriage of family members. More siblings stayed in the village, and a greater proportion of them married. They did not raise more children or even have them closer together. There is no apparent correlation between the cheapness of wheat and industrial output in the region. Production responded to demand, that is, to expected demand. Slumps came when markets were glutted, and this eventually translated into underemployment. Otherwise, the weavers worked and sold their pieces. They looked for profits, and trade offered them the opportunity to better their prospects.

By the late eighteenth century, two-thirds of Montigny's male population were weavers. Weaving had spread throughout the southeastern part of Cambrésis, initially because of the area's poor-quality soil and the tremendous efforts that the soil demanded. But by midcentury, the appeal of weaving was such that even more prosperous agricultural villages fell into the network. For despite intermittent commercial crises, demand grew immensely over the century, and production soared. Villages throughout the region proved willing to invest in the equipment and more importantly in the complex skills needed for weaving. They were not disappointed, for weaving, indeed, provided real improvements in the standard of living.

8

Trade

Cottage industry opened up new avenues for Montigny's residents. It brought an additional source of income for those households that took it on, but more importantly it presented a potential for growth that had hardly been conceivable for peasants in earlier times. Peasants had always found supplementary sources of income, be it by marketing garden produce or manufacturing small wares, doing odd jobs, lending money, hiring themselves out at harvest time, or accumulating land and lease-holds. But there were limits to these possibilities for enrichment. Only one or two families could combine luck and savvy and advance in the hierarchy. There were only so many leases to be had, so much agricultural produce to market. Rural industry changed that. The cloth trade, in particular, seemed endlessly expandable, open to all, within the reach of anyone with a bit of capital. To be sure, there were risks, but the rewards were there for all to observe. The region's merchant-weavers were the late eighteenth-century nouveaux riches. Affluence had come to the village. The next three chapters will describe this phenomenon, treating in turn the mechanics of the trade, the rise of the merchant-weavers, and the nature of their entrepreneurship.

Finishing Processes

Once the pieces of linen were woven, they had to reach a market. This meant that the weavers either took their product to a nearby town or relied on some middleman to do it for them. There was the further possibility of selling the cloth to merchants who peddled it themselves to foreign lands, creating parallel networks to the ones based in the towns. Before the cloth could be sold, however, it had to be bleached, and before it could be bleached it had to be verified and stamped. Like trade, these formalities required that the weaver go beyond the village. All the major market towns had official stamping stations, yielding, besides revenue, reports that historians have used to gauge industrial production in the eighteenth century.

There were two kinds of seals: that of the individual linen manufacturer, and the official stamp which attested that the cloth had been properly woven. In Cambrai such quality controls, administered by the urban authorities in conjunction with the guilds, had existed since the fourteenth century.[1] In July 1752 the king created royal stamping stations in Cambrai, Valenciennes, and Saint-Quentin, and he endowed them with an inspector of manufactures. All of the pieces that were sold in these towns (and theoretically every piece ever produced) underwent a thorough check before receiving the city seal. This cost one sou per piece.[2]

Crommelin, the inspector of manufactures throughout the period, vehemently opposed any freedom of production, which he associated with a deterioration in quality. He combated the 1762 edict that recognized rural production—that is, production outside of the regulated urban guild framework—and his objections brought a spate of restrictive legislation over the region's textile production. In May 1779, however, the authorities had to acknowledge this illicit production, and they lifted a number of restrictions. The new order allowed a mitigated freedom of production beyond established norms as long as the product bore a clear *plomb de la liberté,* a seal declaring its independent origins and distinguishing it from regulated products. In 1771 the merchants of Saint-Quentin had already obtained the right of marking local cloth with their own particular stamp, a privilege extended only to Cambrai and Valenciennes in 1789. The stamping stations were abolished altogether in 1791.[3]

In June 1780 and again in August 1781, at Crommelin's urgent request, letters patent once again regulated the production of fine linens in the region.[4] This meant that the length, width, number of threads, and type of weave had to conform to the strict guidelines that harked back to Colbertist legislation. The edicts applied to batistes and the finest linons, while freedom continued to prevail for coarser linons and gazes. This led to some confusion, which Crommelin tried to resolve in favor of strong legislation. The Bureau de Commerce in Paris, on the other hand, hedged toward economic Liberalism. Rural merchants from the gaze-weaving regions of southern Cambrésis would have profited from such freedom from controls were it not for the surveillance imposed by bleaching establishments and the organization of urban trade.

Both Cambrai and Saint-Quentin had bleaching works, but neither attained the reputation of Valenciennes. Valenciennes drew its renown from the expertise of its workers and from the quality of the water that rinsed the cloth after its eight ablutions in a potash solution.[5] Customers were attracted all the more easily after 1737 when the duty (*octroi*) was abolished on pieces that entered the town only for bleaching.[6] The whole region depended on Valenciennes, and merchants came from afar to have their plain cloths as well as finer batistes and linons bleached there.[7] The cloth might be left from one to three months, and the process added 3 percent to the cost of the pieces.

Bleaching was enmeshed in the regulated urban manufacturing process that rural production managed to evade up to the city gates. The pieces listed in the Cambrai bleaching registers thus carried the stamp of their individual manufacturer. The various stamps were described in the records. In one case, where the seal displayed the name of its owner *J Batiste Lamouret* of Caudry, the weaver had to pay two extra sous to cover the expense of adding the city seal.[8] Bleachers who whitewashed uninspected and unmarked cloth were liable to a fine of five hundred livres, as were the merchants who sold their products. The finishing process therefore imposed added controls on the weaver and merchant. It is thus likely that Lantier's cloth, which carried no seal, would have been caught once it went through the official channels: "The witness declared that going to the fields he indeed found a linen cloth that bore no trace of the master to which it belonged; that he took it to his own master's and that three days later he heard tell that Jean Pierre Lantier had lost it on his way to Saint-Quentin."[10] Rural merchants sometimes disregarded official regulations, but it was in their interest to follow manufacturing guidelines and secure the city's seal that vouched for the quality of the product.

Urban Brokerage

Montigny traded with the three major centers in the region: Cambrai and Valenciennes to the north and Saint-Quentin to the south. This trade involved relations with major merchant houses that distributed the cloth throughout the world. These relations, however, had long been mediated by a set of official middlemen, or brokers. Rural producers could not sell their cloth directly. They could not set up booths and hawk their product in the marketplace. All official sales had to be performed by means of intermediaries known as *courtiers* named by the municipality, who were meant to act as impartial middlemen between buyer and seller. In Valenciennes the courtier's commission was fixed at eleven sous three deniers for a cloth worth more than forty livres, and five sous for cloth selling for less.[11] Saint-Quentin had possessed eight courtiers since 1560. Thereafter, the number increased to twelve, and the office could be purchased. The monopoly remained secure until the eighteenth century when the city council attempted, with only partial success, to reassert some control.[12] These officials could only sell cloth bearing the weaver's and inspector's seals, and they received commissions from both parties. The weaver who relinquished his batiste or linon paid five to ten sous depending on the length of the piece, and the merchant disbursed one to five sous for the very same cloth. The *coupon* or segment beyond regulation length, which was duly snipped off, could be sold freely by the artisan or else remain with the broker who handled it for the price of one sou.[13] As the courtier also sold cloth, he naturally favored his own stock and neglected or acquired at rebate the pieces that he received from others; contemporaries regularly complained that the brokers took advantage of weavers who parted with their cloth for less than its value.[14]

There were also complaints about the means of payment. Brokers received cash from merchants but paid the weavers in bills of exchange and credit notes of various duration, despite the municipal ruling of 1735 that forced them to pay the producers within a fortnight unless they had obtained a special dispensation.[15] The curé of Serain complained that local bankruptcies could be traced to those urban merchants who had distributed bills of exchange that had become worthless once they defaulted. One local inhabitant, Jean Charles Taine, lost more than two thousand livres when the brokers and merchants Dachery, Picard, and Campion failed to honor their debts. So did Adrien Dron, to whom the cloth merchant Dachery and the merchant-broker Cambronne, all of Saint-Quentin, owed a similar sum.[16]

Buying and selling also took place outside official channels in taverns beyond the city gates; there, merchants met surreptitiously with rural suppliers. In July 1757, officers of the General Farms accused Jacques Delahaye of Cambrai of carrying three batistes made in Picardy on which he had not paid the export duty of ten livres per hundredweight. The pieces belonged to Ignace Taine, a merchant-manufacturer of Cambrai, who had been born in Montigny. He denied that he had imported them from France and swore he had bought them from villagers in a suburban inn. "On June 12, being on the premises of the Fleur de Lys the inn belonging to Hubert Béguin in the faubourg of St. Sepulchre, parish of St. Nicolas in Cambrai, he met there several fine linen weavers from the country from whom he bought the cloth in question and the next day sent the said Delahaye to fetch them."[17] The innkeeper corroborated this statement, vouching that on that Sunday; "[Taine] had been at his place where there were a number of merchant-weavers from the country [unknown to him] who offered the said Taine some of their unbleached cloths and after a certain amount of haggling and bargaining they agreed on a price with the said Taine who left the linens with him until the next day." The pieces were released by order of the intendant, Blair de Boisemont, on 23 June 1757.

The bankruptcy papers of Jean Philippe Taine, farmer and weaver from the village of Clary, show the way rural producers and merchants relied on a multiplicity of outlets. The inventory lists three venues: the village, the city, and the suburb.

> Three unfinished pieces of linen that were given out to be properly completed and that were sold at auction with the proceeds going to their creditors.
> One piece of linen of theirs presently in the hands of the Sieur Plouchard, broker in Valenciennes.
> Six pieces of linen deposited with Alexis Rebleq, innkeeper of the Lyon d'or in Valenciennes.[18]

Buying and selling, then, took place in various places, although rural merchants found it easier to establish solid and long-lasting links with urban wholesalers. A measure of specialization developed, with some villages relying on urban brokerage, and others attaching themselves to an alternate network where rural merchants peddled linens abroad. The split occurred even within villages. There, some country merchants dealt with the town, while others set off for foreign parts. While the towns acted as trading centers, not all traffic passed through them, to the great chagrin of the inspector of manufactures Crommelin, who wished to preserve the trade as a properly policed urban monopoly.[19]

Peddling

It is possible to analyze the role of independent rural traders,[20] thanks partly to the information provided by the passports granted to Cambrésis merchants between 1763 and 1790. The passports, issued by the local Estates, confirmed legitimate, temporary absences from the applicants' places of residence and vouched for their good conduct. Such documents were more likely to be requested routinely by merchants who plied an annual route than by occasional absentees, or so at least it appears in the two registers extant for Cambrésis.[21]

Table 31. Passports Issued by the Cambrésis
Estates, 1763–90

Occupation	Number	Percentage
Cloth merchants	1,010	58
Other merchants	171	10
Agricultural laborers	119	7
Artisans	117	7
Weavers	102	6
Militiamen	79	4
Pilgrims	33	2
Other professions	25	1
Professions unknown	55	3
Trips for personal reasons	30	2
Totals	1,741	100

Source: Archives départementales du Nord, C états 209 and
C20776.

Travel in late eighteenth-century Cambrésis, as table 31 shows, was overwhelmingly in the service of cloth merchandising. Of course, the distribution does not reflect the extent of mobility since the table shows the number of passports, not the number of individuals. Also, departures were clearly underregistered, and many travelers left the province at various times without official documents. This laxity could be traced, in part, to the laws forbidding the emigration of workers, especially those employed in manufactures.[22] Cambrésis, a Province Reputed Foreign, lay outside the boundaries of the General Farms and close to the northern border. The strictures against permanent expatriation did not apply to temporary employment and specifically exempted authorized traders cleared of any suspicion of smuggling. This would then account for the preponderance of passports issued to merchants. Yet the authorities were aware of the discrepancies in the records. The inspector of manufactures complained bitterly about both fraudulent exports and the exodus of weavers. In 1760, for example, he reported that many had gone to Belgium (the Austrian Netherlands) to look for work.[23] He could also point to those seventeen weavers from the village of Clary who were believed to have emigrated illegally to England, some taking their families with them.[24] Yet even the more readily acceptable movement south, toward France, was unevenly monitored. Notarial and parish records attest to the dispersal of family members as well as to temporary absences. To cite but one example: in the village of Montigny at least one weaver moved temporarily to Troyes in Champagne, a common destination in that period.[25] His name does not appear on the Estates' registers. Nonetheless, despite the uneven distribution, the passports, combined with other data, provide crude but valuable insights into the origins and destinations of various types of migrants.

The Estates' records reveal a remarkable concentration in the allocation of such documents. Although there were some ninety villages in the province, half of the passports were issued to four localities, while the remainder were scattered among another fifty-four. This involved both a degree of specialization—the more obvious since the same people requested passes year after year—as well as a chain reaction that encouraged workers of all types within a given locality to ask for official documents. In table 32, villages are arranged by order of total requests for five professional categories: cloth merchants, other merchants, agricultural laborers, artisans, and weavers.

The geographic concentration southeast of Cambrai shown in table 32 is not surprising. The provincial boundaries extended primarily in that direction, and much of the soil in that part was of poorer quality so that inhabitants had readily looked for supplementary incomes. The localities that sent out the fewest migrants were those with the best land (only eight villages out of twenty-one in that category received passports), and these went to artisans, weavers, or cloth merchants. Agricultural laborers, it would appear, could readily find work in the region.[26] The same applies to villages with mixed soil (half of such villages received passports). Migrant farm laborers, looking for work, begin to figure in villages with mediocre soil (eleven out of twenty-three requested passports, four specifically for farmworkers) and then, like weavers and merchants, in villages with poor and very poor soil.

Work opportunities obviously played a crucial role. At the same time, there is no apparent correlation between migration and landownership. In a village like Doignies with 590 inhabitants, where 88 percent peasant proprietors controlled 39 percent of the land, the push to leave may have been weaker than in Béthencourt, with the same mediocre soil and 610 residents, where peasants accounted for 82 percent of owners but possessed only 15 percent of the soil.[27] No passports were requested in Doignies, whereas fourteen requests were received from Béthencourt. Fontaine au Pire, on the other hand, with its forty passports (twenty

Table 32. Number of Passports According to Occupation

Village	Soil	Location	Cloth merchants	Other merchants
Troisvilles	mediocre	SE	208	20
Bertry	very bad	SE	151	10
Inchy	very bad	SE	116	39
Saint-Souplet	very bad	SE	65	10
Busigny	very bad	SE	98	3
Reumont	—	SE	87	—
Maurois	—	SE	60	—
Fontaine au Pire	bad	SE	7	13
Prémont	—	SE	17	4
Borneville	mediocre	SE	2	10
Walincourt	bad	SE	19	5
Aubencheul-au-Bois	—	SE	6	10
Avesnes-les-Aubert	mediocre	NE	19	8
Ligny	very bad	SE	11	1
Quiévy	good	E	20	—
Beaumont	bad	SE	4	14
Audencourt	bad	SE	5	12
Clary	very bad	SE	17	1
Marest	bad	SE	14	1
Saint-Hilaire	good	NE	16	—
Montigny	very bad	SE	4	—
37 others*			61	8
Other			—	1
Unknown			7	2
Totals 58			1,010	171

*Those under 1 percent.

to day laborers) and 795 inhabitants, had 91 percent peasant proprietors sharing 39 percent of the land. Similar variations can be observed
throughout the province.[28]

The significant variable was in fact geographic. People migrated from
the core of the weaving belt northeast and southeast of Cambrai. Not
surprisingly, most of the villages that requested passes for cloth merchants lay in the heart of this area of linen production, crowded along an
imaginary line connecting Valenciennes and Saint-Quentin, often skirt-
ing the major thoroughfares. Yet location along the main roads linking
Cambrai, Le Cateau, and Saint-Quentin cannot be neglected. It is there
that we find Troisvilles, Bertry, Inchy, Saint-Souplet, Busigny, Fontaine

			Totals	
Laborers	Artisans	Weavers	Number	Percent*
8	3	9	248	16
8	1	23	193	13
1	1	2	159	10
12	34	20	141	9
3	6	—	108	6
—	—	1	88	5
1	—	—	61	4
20	—	—	40	3
18	—	—	39	3
13	—	9	34	2
1	2	7	34	2
3	9	5	33	2
—	2	2	31	2
14	—	1	26	2
2	—	—	22	1
1	2	—	21	1
—	—	3	20	1
—	—	2	20	1
—	2	1	18	1
—	1	—	17	1
—	—	—	4	
14	48	5	136	
—	1	—	2	
2	4	—	15	1
119	116	102	1,518	

au Pire, Borneville, Audencourt, Aubencheul au Bois, or Prémont, recipients of two-thirds of all passports. Still, a number of trading villages such as Clary, Ligny, or Quiévy lay along those smaller channels and back roads that led from one village to the next (fig. 10).

Destinations varied depending on the occupation and the period. Some 80 percent of cloth merchants headed north, through Flanders and Brabant; another 15 percent did the same with a stopover in "France," while a mere 5 percent traveled only to France. Other merchants and agricultural laborers went primarily north (74 percent and 72 percent). This was reversed for artisans (55 percent) and weavers (62 percent) who chose France as their destination, especially after 1775.

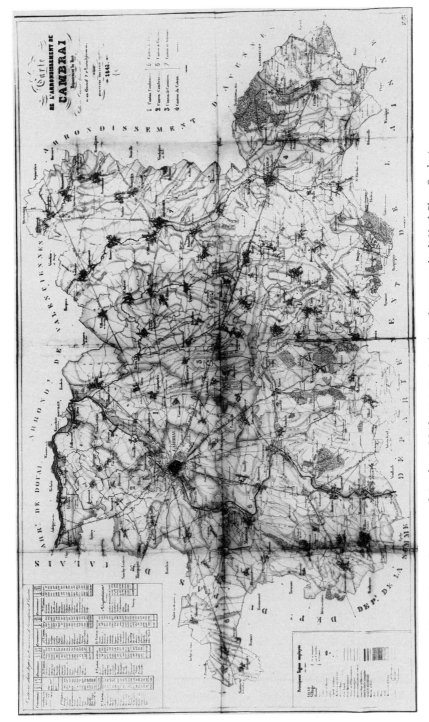

Figure 10. Map of Arrondissement of Cambrai, 1843   *Photo Populu, Archives départementales du Nord, Plans Cambrai.*

Table 33. Route Followed by Denis Cardon, Merchant from Troisvilles

Date of issue of passport	Months	Number of compagnons	Destination
4 May 1765	6	1	Flanders, Brabant, Liège, Germany (route I)
12 December 1765	6	2	Germany
24 May 1765	6	1	I
1 January 1767	8	3	Flanders, Brabant, Liège, Holland, Germany (route II)
10 October 1767	12	4	I and Prussia
20 July 1768	6	3	I
6 February 1769	6	3	I
20 May 1769	6	3	I
1 January 1770	6	4	I
19 January 1771	12	6	I
17 February 1772	12	1	I
1 January 1773	12	1	I
14 May 1774	12	1	II
29 April 1775	12	1	II
5 February 1776	12	1	I
31 January 1777	12	1	I
6 February 1778	12	3	I
1 January 1779	12	1	II
31 January 1780	12	1	II
18 January 1781	12	1	II
4 May 1782	12	1	II
16 January 1784	12	1	II
11 January 1786	12	1	II
18 July 1787	12	1	I

Linen merchants overwhelmingly favored the northern circuits. They usually left in groups of three, four, or even six, and their destinations varied little. Denis Cardon, a married weaver and merchant from Troisvilles, for example, trekked a route that ranged through Germany and Prussia (see table 33). Another, Pierre Maseret, sometimes accompanied by his cousin Jacques, "employed as his servant," set out for similar journeys (see table 34). Even though there are no available registers prior to 1763, it is clear that in the last quarter of the eighteenth century, merchants gradually extended their routes so that most were absent for a year.

The merchant-weavers who joined the trade in the 1780s—from Busigny or Quiévy, for example—differed little in their destinations, head-

Table 34.   Route of Pierre Maseret of Troisvilles

Date of issue of passport	Months	Destination
29 May 1763	3	Germany
1 January 1764	4	Germany
24 May 1764	6	unknown
15 February 1765	6	unknown
2 July 1765	8	Flanders, Brabant, Liège, Germany
28 February 1766	8	Flanders, Brabant, Liège, Germany, Prussia
5 October 1767	12	Flanders, Brabant, Liège, Germany, Prussia
12 July 1768	8	Flanders, Brabant, Liège, Prussia
21 March 1769	8	same

ing in the same traditional pattern toward Flanders, Brabant, and Liège, while some continued on to Germany or Holland.[29] A handful of merchants chose different routes. From Fontaine au Pire in 1765, 1766, and 1768, one cloth merchant set forth for Brabant, Liège, Germany, Poland, Denmark and Sweden in one year, and for Flanders, Brabant, Liège, Germany, Prussia, Poland, and Saxony on two subsequent trips. A merchant-weaver from Reumont made a circuit through France, Germany, and Switzerland (1773–79), while two brothers from Saint-Souplet went all the way to Russia to sell their cloth (1774). One or two named the provinces of Normandy or Lorraine as their destination, while Jean Baptiste Rousseau, *négociant* of the village of Saint-Souplet, set sail for America, without stating his specific destination or the reason for his voyage.

These itinerant merchants were not paupers. They owned property in their villages, and their families stood as security for their good behavior and return to the community. In one or two cases where more than a mere name was entered in the register, a note (from the village authorities of Saulzoir) attested to the good mores of Antoine Meriau, single and thirty years old, owner of a house and garden as well as a hectare of land. Similarly, when Antoine Botteau of Troisvilles received a six-month pass in February 1764, he possessed "2,000 livres of real estate"; in May 1765 Jean Paul Delhaye of Bertry left behind "his wife, children and some property"; and in February 1765 Philippe Joseph Cauchy, a bachelor, off to sell cloth in Germany, Flanders, Brabant, and Liège, had a mother who owned her house in Montigny.

There is no tally of the amount of cloth sold on these northern

ventures, but clearly it was substantial. In the 1820s, when linen production was at its ebb, merchants traveled with three hundred to four
hundred pieces.[30] Based on this figure, and with an average of thirty-six
passports issued a year, itinerant trade in the latter part of the century in
Cambrésis would have involved as many as 10,800 to 14,400 pieces, that
is, the same amount marketed by the city of Cambrai—a clear indication
of its significance.[31]

The itinerant merchants who traveled abroad did not create completely independent networks, nor did they evade all controls. Probably
about one-third of the goods they carried were contraband, to judge by
cases of seizure. Their absences and their lack of involvement in village
affairs make these merchants and their activities difficult to trace. One
can presume that, like other village merchants, they raised capital on the
strength of mortgageable property.[32] Their dependence on, or independence from, urban merchants is harder to assess. The bankruptcy of
Nicolas Daigle, merchant-weaver from Neuvilly, and of his two sons,
"linen merchants in Holland and foreign parts," points to an urban
connection. Their debts came to 8,340 livres 10 sous, earmarked toward
merchants in Valenciennes and Saint-Quentin and various inhabitants of
Cambrai, Bertry, Fontaine au Pire and Beauvais, Vaux-en-Arrouaise, and
their own village of Neuvilly.[33] Both balance sheet and debt distribution
were similar to those encountered for middlemen who took their cloth to
town. Thus, Jean Pierre Lantier, a somewhat more substantial linen
merchant from the village of Montigny, also raised his capital in Cambrai,
Valenciennes, and Saint-Quentin while owing smaller sums to a number
of rural suppliers.[34]

One can surmise from this information that itinerant merchants obtained their capital locally, rather than abroad, and that they used those
funds to purchase cloth in the countryside. They then sold it on northern
markets, but their modes of payment can only be conjectured. The
inspector of manufactures, dismissive and contemptuous, saw them as
independent though highly vulnerable:

> Cambrai's [linen] trade is still languishing: there are no wholesale mer-
> chants, only a few small ones, the rest is in the hands of manufacturers
> who get the cloth bleached and then sell it themselves throughout Ger-
> many. A few make a go of it (une espèce de fortune) but countless are
> ruined, since they have few funds to fall back on should sales be delayed.
> They are forced to undersell to meet their payments and to provide for
> their basic necessities, and this does considerable harm to this trade since
> the cloth sold in the stores then seems more expensive than that which is

peddled directly. This is not surprising since these itinerant merchants often sell at a loss.[35]

Crommelin, who thoroughly disliked this form of trade, is a prejudiced observer. The number of passports and annual caravans suggests that the situation was not as desperate as he believed. Moreover, although he stressed the German connection, rural cloth merchants also regularly made for Holland. Those links appear to have been long-standing. Linen yarn was regularly bleached in Holland and then brought back to France.[36] Dutch merchants also purchased cloth in the region. After the catastrophic bankruptcies of the late 1750s, the Cambrésis Estates had curés tally individual losses. Most weavers displayed unpaid promissory notes from merchants in Cambrai, Saint-Quentin, or Valenciennes. In the case of the village of Bertry, half of the losses, estimated at 16,271 livres, were attributed to the failure of Amsterdam merchants.[37] From the 1770s onward, Cambrésis linen merchants included Holland as a matter of course in their northern journeys.

Religion may have played a part in this choice. Some of the trade to Holland, Germany, and especially Prussia, was controlled by the province's Protestants. In 1772 they numbered three thousand, located mainly in "Quiévy, Inchy, Walincourt, Elincourt, Marest, Clary, Serain, and thereabouts," as well as in the village of Caudry (technically part of Hainaut, and therefore absent from Cambrésis registers).[38] These Protestants were renowned for the quality of their cloth production, and it was feared that obvious persecution would drive them away to the more tolerant Austrian Netherlands.[39] In 1783 the intendant received the following report from one of his subdelegates: "Quiévy and some of the neighbouring villages have indeed a number of Protestant families. Almost all are weavers who manufacture, buy, and sell their linen cloth in Saint-Quentin, Holland, or Germany."[40]

In 1772 a foreign factor who had ordered cloth in the region explained some of the mechanisms in a letter to the intendant. Delivery had been interrupted by the arrest of Caudry's leading Protestant linen merchants:

> I am a foreigner, I have come from England and am on my way back to my own country of Brandenburg very far from here. Our company had asked me to visit the manufactures of cambrics in this area which I did and, after advising our agents, I began to do business with the said Sandras and others like him, but since I have had no other dealings with them, I am free to leave the merchandise I had ordered especially since it looks like

they will not be able to finish it properly, since they are in jail. While in the area, I spoke with some of his co-religionists who take part in the same trade who assured me that there was no reason to break with them and that there were . . . three thousand Protestants in the region.[41]

Prussia was the final destination of most itinerant merchants, by which many, surreptitiously or not, may have meant Silesia, which had developed its own linen industry. French authorities were aware that French cloth arrived there unstamped, received a Silesian seal, and was then transported to England where French linens had faced very stiff import duties before being forbidden entry altogether in 1748.[42]

In fact, reviving trade with England was something of a Cambrésis obsession. London had been Cambrai's major market, and the town suffered greatly from the import prohibition.[43] Lobbying in England failed to repeal this legislation,[44] but there were attempts to create trading companies, even from tiny Cambrésis villages. When Jean Pierre Lantier of Montigny went bankrupt in 1763, he ascribed the bulk of his losses to a failed venture with two English merchants, Baralle and Halygraf.

As for the itinerant merchants who went off to Holland and Germany, their primary purpose may indeed have been clandestine trade to Britain. Any measure that would reduce the price of imported French linens was welcome at a time when these were liable to a 40 percent duty.[45] One way was to obtain the cloth directly from rural linen producers without resorting to urban merchants. Peddling abroad, then, both reduced the sale price and increased the outlets of French linens at a time when they suffered heavily from German competition. Peddling, therefore, belonged to a hazy category that included both licit and illicit activities. But, aside from the shortsighted inspector of manufactures, French authorities did not question too closely the nature of these cloth exports, which it was in their interest to encourage. Itinerant merchants formed a necessary link in the networks that connected Cambrésis with international markets.

The more usual accusation leveled against itinerant merchants was not so much that they transported unmarked cloth, but that they were involved in the illegal export of yarn. The local inspector of manufactures made a twofold accusation. The first was that the General Farms did not check the bales of cloth leaving Saint-Quentin since they were not subject to export duties. Many pieces, therefore, left France without proper manufacturing seals and, what is more, actually hid the fine-linen thread that was so valued abroad.[46] The Châtellenie of Le Cateau, for one, with its special duty status, was a major culprit sending baskets of thread hidden beneath cloth to Bavai and on to the Austrian Netherlands through the forest of Mormal. Cambrai merchants were also suspected of exporting yarn through fictitious sales to Lille, while the product was in fact on its way to Tournai, Belgium, and Holland.

In 1751 the *sous-inspecteur* Tribet attempted to uncover these illegal networks. He approached a number of merchants in Le Cateau and along the northern frontier, claiming he wished to take yarn across the border. He had no problem gaining the necessary information, but when, after much effort, he finally prompted the General Farms to make an arrest, the culprits eluded him. Moreover, instead of the expected fifty pounds of threat, he found only three and a half.[47] In fact, the Farms had argued all along that the amount of contraband trade had been exaggerated.

This accords with whatever else we know about smuggling. In 1722 three young men of the village of Montigny faced charges for breaking into two merchants' safe and stealing five hundred florins and some yarn worth another few florins.[48] The accused, ages twenty-one and twenty-two, were well-known smugglers "who usually went about armed with pistols." Though they did not mention the sale of yarn and called themselves weavers, they most likely would have peddled that thread as they did their other wares. Their route took them through Le Cateau, Bohain, Saint-Quentin, Han, Valenciennes, Douai, Tournai, Mons, and Bavai where they bought and sold cotton kerchiefs, coffee, chocolate, muslin, and one pound of cochenille dye. They had borrowed the wherewithal for those purchases from a Valenciennes weaver who kept their coats as security. They, better than the married cloth merchants who set out in groups on their yearly caravans, fit the portrait drawn by Crommelin of the reckless souls who risked their lives for a mere thirty-six livres to smuggle some seven hundred to eight hundred livres' worth of yarn."[49]

If some of the yarn produced in the region was leaving illegally, the rest was traded along the patterns established for the cloth trade. The flax spun in the region came primarily from Flanders, and the networks established to bring it to Cambrésis in fact antedated those of the rural cloth trade. The leading Montigny merchants, such as Lantier, probably began as yarn suppliers, and families continued to specialize in this area. When Jean Lefort described his activities in the early decades of the century, he claimed that he had sold flax and yarn and distributed it about. In the same period a member of the Allart family (with branches in Montigny, Clary, Troisvilles, and Le Cateau) married a Bertry "fine linen thread merchant." Subsequently, the business of selling cloth and yarn was frequently combined. In Beauvois, for example, two brothers divided the work: one sold thread, while the other purveyed local cloth to Valenciennes. In 1782 the Bourlets of Caullery sold both thread and cloth. In Cambrai, moreover, one could only sell yarn if one also manufactured cloth.[50]

Flax was peddled as well, but not on the grand scale that recalled itinerant trading. In 1722, during the trials of the three Montigny smugglers, Charles Domise of Valenciennes came forward with evidence. He declared that he was fifty years old and that he was a "merchant who carried flax to the villages." He knew the accused well because "while he was selling flax in the countryside, he had often sold it in their houses where he had seen them."[51]

Such village flax vendors continued to circulate in the late eighteenth century. In 1779 François Lesage of Cambrai demanded to be paid thirty-three livres for the flax he had delivered in Neuvilly, and in the spring of 1784, another Cambrai supplier, Prevost, pursued similar debts in Fontaine-Notre-Dame.[52] Comparable evidence sometimes surfaces for Montigny. In 1778 J. B. Broutin, merchant-weaver of Cambrai, sued Dominique Ego for the twenty florins he still owed him for the "fine linen yarn that he had sold him and delivered to his satisfaction."[53] While Jean Pierre Lantier's bankruptcy pleas revealed links with Cambrai or Le Nouvion yarn merchants, promissory notes created in the 1750s and 1760s showed him dealing with a Troisvilles merchant, Desvignes.[54]

Village merchants provided other products used in cottage industry, besides the fibers, such as the grease that served to moisten the threads. Jean Charles Marcaille, a cloth merchant from Saint-Aubert, owed 369 livres to a Cambrai tallow seller. The clothier Pierre François Colan owed 730 livres to another such Cambrai merchant.[55] At the turn of the century François Faré was a shopkeeper in Montigny, and in 1713 he was also described as the village's tallow supplier. Both his sons became weavers, and in 1737 Charles Huguet took on the duties of "storekeeper and seller of grease which suits both his trade and the needs of the community."[56] Supplying such basic raw materials, whether grease, flax, or yarn, rapidly expanded into collecting and selling the finished product.

Nevertheless, various channels and modes of marketing continued to coexist. Weavers periodically took their own pieces to urban markets or suburban inns: "since weaving is the major occupation [*commerce*] in Caudry these artisans have to go sell their product once a week in Saint-Quentin and Valenciennes."[57] While walking down the roads (and we know that they walked because of the arguments they had along the way), they might be overtaken by rural merchants on horseback—intermediaries between village producers and urban brokers—or encounter itinerant merchants carting heavy loads and smaller fry peddling pieces in a sack.

Weaving brought to the eighteenth-century countryside new forms of mercantile activity as well as new forms of work, for urban merchants by no means monopolized merchandising of the cloth that the village produced. Both government regulations and urban domination of the finishing processes could have favored urban merchants, but in late eighteenth-century Cambrésis, rural merchants in fact handled about as much cloth as their urban competitors. Such trade might involve villages in wide-ranging networks, extending regularly to Prussia, and occasionally to still more exotic locations. Although a handful of villages specialized in such commerce, it had a galvanizing effect on other forms of local trade. The next chapters will examine more closely how linen sales were handled in the village and how rural merchants managed to carve themselves an important place within the Ancien Régime's older commercial structures.

9

The Rise of the Merchant-Weavers

There had been weavers in Montigny since at least the seventeenth century. Some catered to local needs and were known as tisserands. But there were also a number of fine-linen weavers who went by the name of mulquiniers, and it is that specialized production that became associated with cottage industry. At first, the households involved in this activity— Allart, Delacourt, Henninot, Lamouret, and Pigou—still devoted most of their energies to farming, turning to weaving in their spare time. Two of those families, the Allarts and Pigous, stood apart even in this period because they already sold yarn, even if not cloth, at the turn of the century. These mercantile activities allowed them to survive the awful winter of 1709. Only a few villagers (the farmers and the clerk, Michel Allart and Grégoire Pigou, as well as Marguerite Godart, a shepherd's widow) still had grain supplies in the spring of 1709.[1] Of the two weaving families, the Allarts would merge with the Lantiers to form Montigny's biggest entrepreneurial network and one of the most important in the region. The Pigous, on the other hand, did not become as successful and were only marginally involved in the cloth trade. By the second half of the eighteenth century, villages such as Montigny, where more than half of the households were engaged in cottage industry, were producing waves of merchant-weavers, some of whom can be considered small entrepreneurs.

The first group of rural merchants to rise to prominence were rooted in the village's agrarian structure. They were either sons of laboureurs or weavers who had accumulated sufficient landed assets to raise loans. They began by delivering their own and other people's products; then, after the commercial collapse of 1760, they took on a more active role in the trade. By the 1770s and early 1780s, they were joined by weavers with fewer landed assets. Credit had become easier to obtain, and more weavers were able to launch small businesses.

Historians of rural industry have not prepared us to find such figures. They have described the weavers as fulfilling only marginal commercial or entrepreneurial functions, if any at all, because they left those tasks to the urban merchants.[2] Rural merchants figure in these discussions, but their origins remain hazy. They are sometimes dismissed as nothing more than agents of urban firms—fulfilling only a subsidiary function—or

they are fused within a rural farming elite that sought to vary investments. These views stem partly from the need to conciliate what is
perceived as a contrast in mentality between peasants (and by extension
rural artisans) and merchants. The peasants set physical subsistence as
their goal, whereas merchants did not regulate their activities to satisfy
limited needs but to expand profits.[3] Peasants remained inward-looking;
merchants responded to the outside world. Montigny and other Cambrésis villages, however, demonstrate the similarities between trader,
rural artisan, and peasant.

Origins of the Merchant-Weavers

Who were the men who entered the trade in the second half of the
eighteenth century? They were all of peasant stock, although only a
negligible percentage came from independent farming families. Younger
sons of tenant-farmers took up weaving, but they rarely became cloth
merchants. They were given a room on the farm or a small cottage, a loom
or two, and left to fend for themselves. The farm's capital was not frittered
away on improving their lot, although the big tenant-farmers sometimes
loaned money to local merchant-weavers. Laboureurs in such places as
Normandy or Germany may have invested directly in the cloth trade.[4] Big
farmers in Montigny did not. Montigny's cloth merchants were not so
much farmers who were diversifying as weavers with small patrimonies
who were able to raise sufficient funds to buy the pieces produced by
their neighbors. Urban merchants made 10 percent to 12 percent on a
piece of cloth, and such profits were attractive enough to tempt numerous weavers.[5]

As a group, Montigny's merchant-weavers came from the middle
ranks of inhabitants, being neither the richest nor the poorest in the
village. Two sets of documents allow us to trace their origins. The first
consists of an assessment of village wealth compiled in 1743, along with a
contemporary tax roll, and the second is a compendium of the victims of
the commercial crises of the early 1760s. In 1743 the Cambrésis Estates
delegated country priests to take a census of their parishioners and divide
them into three gradations of wealth.[6] Montigny's curé included forty-
two households in his count: nine in the top category, thirteen in the
second, and twenty in the third.[7] For no apparent reason, he left out
twelve families that figured on the 1744 tax roll a year later; similarly,
nine of the families on his list were not on the village tax roll. They were

Table 35. Breakdown by Profession of the 1743 Census

Occupation	Prosperous	Less prosperous	Poor
Farmer	4	1	—
Small farmer	—	—	4
Farm laborer	—	—	2
Weaver	5	8	10
Other	—	5	1
Average tax in 1744	40.5 florins	10.7 florins	8.8 florins
Excluding Crinon	27.3 florins		

Source: C suppl. 524.

not excluded for their poverty, for if five had belonged in the lowest income category, one had ranked in the first and three in the second. Despite its incompleteness, the curé's list remains significant because, unlike contemporary fiscal records, it assessed all forms of wealth rather than merely landownership.

The wealthiest members of the village were the farmers Moyse Crinon of La Trappe, the brothers Antoine and Michel Labbé, who held the lease to Cantimpré, the laboureur François Malesieux, and five weavers (Jean Baptiste Lantier, Jean Baptiste Taine, Michel Allart, Pierre Dron, and Jean Baptiste Pigou). These weavers were not among the top taxpayers, according to the 1744 tax roll, and this indicates that their inclusion among the prosperous rested on income other than land (table 35). Jean Philippe Malesieux, who occupied the fief and farm of La Bruyère and who paid higher taxes, led the second category and ranked below these weavers. In Montigny, half of the affluent group consisted of weavers, and this penetration of the upper crust by weaving families is paralleled in nearby villages (table 36).

Most curés confined themselves to noting professions and household size, including the number of children and resident servants. All of the major farmers had live-in help, sometimes described as *domestiques* and sometimes as *valets*. Such valets also appear in artisan households. In Clary a shoemaker had two apprentices, while a tailor and a potter each had one.[8] The curé of Ligny was exceptional in including the rationale for his assessments and in jotting down the nature of the residents' assets. The farmers in the top category rented and owned property. The weavers were rich in assets and land. The source of one weaver's wealth was purely commercial; he was *aisez en facultez*. Five others were prosperous landowners (*aisés en propriété*) who also employed live-in assistants to

Table 36. Breakdown by Profession of the 1743 Census in Clary, Ligny, and Troisvilles

Occupation	Prosperous	Less prosperous	Poor
Clary			
Farmer	5	5	—
Day laborer	—	—	146
Weaver	2	19	—
Beggar	—	—	24
Other	2	14	1
Unknown	—	4	—
Totals	9	42	171
Ligny			
Farmer	7	3	—
Day laborer	—	4	31
Weaver	7	27	1
Beggar	—	—	5*
Other	5	10	6
Unknown	3	1	—
Totals	22	45	43
Troisvilles			
Farmer	1	7	—
Day laborer	—	—	21
Weaver	—	13	10
Other	—	5	19
Unknown	7**	2	2
Totals	8	27	52

*Beggars with no other occupation.
**Number of live-in servants suggests these were also farmers.
Source: C20769, C21042, C21175.

work at the loom.[9] Those in the middling category all had a bit of land, and this distinguished them from the day laborers and married journeymen in the last category, who had none. For not all weavers were independent. Eight married men with families worked for other weavers and were described as *valets de mulquinier*. Three day laborers, one weaver's assistant, and a tisserand were so impoverished that although the curé stated their occupation, he added that they had been reduced to begging. While some weavers were mere wage laborers even in the first half of the eighteenth century, the majority thus owned a bit of land and worked independently. Indeed, as one of the German prototypes would have it, they sold their cloth directly to urban brokers, from whom they received redeemable promissory notes.

Yet Montigny's situation was more complex than these models would suggest, for villagers by the middle of the century had begun to involve themselves in the cloth trade. The extent of their involvement was made clear in 1761. The Seven Years War had disrupted international trade, and the result was a major commercial crisis.[10] The Cambrésis Estates, concerned about the repercussions that urban defaults were having on the countryside, asked the curés to assess the extent of the losses in their parishes, and they then dispensed the hardest-hit from paying taxes. Since this was an investigation of the losses caused by the failures of the major urban houses, the curés did not describe the domino effect of such defaults. We know which villagers suffered because of urban bankruptcies; we do not know how many local weavers were affected in turn by their insolvency.

The weavers showed their priests the unpaid promissory notes that they held from urban merchants. Rivart, Montigny's curé, jotted down the amounts, explaining that he had obtained the information as discretely as possible.[11] Eighteen local weavers sustained losses, nine of them for more than five hundred florins (table 37).

Since a piece of cloth sold in town for about sixty florins, this group was handling more than its own production; some had, in fact, become small merchants, either acting as middlemen for fellow weavers or speculating on their own. Of the village's fifty weaving households, at least eighteen traded independently, bringing their own production to market, and half of these sold more than their own pieces. In the middle of the eighteenth century, therefore, one-fifth of the village's weavers acted as middlemen, buying cloth from the remainder of the weaving population. The line between production and commerce had been easily crossed.

The list of victims in nearby villages shows a similar pattern (see table 38). There were independent weavers marketing their own cloth, dependent weavers who turned over their output to local middlemen (and who did not figure on the list), and local merchants who lost large sums. Losses could be as small as twelve and thirteen livres (in Clary) or seventeen livres (in Elincourt).[12] In the village of Serain, Marie Marguerite Devigne, a widow, was owed 160 livres by Dachery of Saint-Quentin, one of the major defaulters. She had received a bill of exchange made out to herself and her partners in nearby villages ("une lettre de change qu'elle avoit avec quelques consors des villages circonvoisins"). These

Table 37. Losses in Montigny Due to Bankruptcies, 1760–61

Name	Amount (livres)	Location of bankruptcy
Etienne Lesage	3,000	Saint-Quentin
Guillaume Boursier	1,959	Saint-Quentin
Pierre Deudon	1,700	Saint-Quentin, Cambrai
Jean Pierre Lantier	1,500	Saint-Quentin
Widow of J. Fr. Faré	1,000	Saint-Quentin
François Levesque	880	Saint-Quentin, Cambrai
Thomas Prévôt	752	Saint-Quentin
Jean Philippe Milot	513	Saint-Quentin, Cambrai
Philippe Godart	507	Saint-Quentin, Cambrai
Widow of Joseph Denoyelle	400	Saint-Quentin
Jean Louis Pigou	300	Saint-Quentin
Jean Philippe Pigou	300	Saint-Quentin
Charles Huguet	271	Cambrai
Felix Ego	200	Saint-Quentin
Nicolas Deudon	100	Saint-Quentin
Jean Louis Labbé	83.5	Saint-Quentin
Jean Philippe Souppé	75	Saint-Quentin
Charles Antoine Labbé	60	Saint-Quentin

Source: C21158.

tiny amounts might represent the balance of a larger debt or else indicate that country weavers were receiving yarn from urban wholesalers and were merely being paid for their labor.

The 1761 bankruptcies display the geography of mid-eighteenth-century trade. The villagers dealt chiefly with Saint-Quentin, and they dealt directly with large mercantile firms and brokers. The same culprits appear over and over again in all of the nearby villages: Boutillier, Cambronne, Campion, Crommelin, Darchery (or Darchies), Gautier, and Picard of Saint-Quentin. In Cambrai the defaulters were Dherique, Rubay, and Taine. The names given in Bertry for Amsterdam were Antoine Caveau (an Italian), Joseph Levie, Samuel Jerome Pinto, L. Trufaut and Co., and Diel de Neubourg from Guadeloupe. Some people suffered from the bankruptcy of a single firm, and others were the victims of several. More importantly, the distribution of debts shows that the big brokers dealt with a whole range of producers, small, middling, and large, to whom they owed anywhere from ten to ten thousand livres (table 39).

Table 38. Distribution of Losses from Bankruptcies (livres)

Village	Less than 100	100–500	500–1,000	1,000–5,000	More than 5,000
Montigny	4	6	4	4	
Bertry	3	6	5	4	
Clary	23	53	9	14	5
Elincourt	3	18	10	8	1
Ligny	1	9	4	1	
Troisvilles	1	7	1	1	
Total	35	99	33	32	6

Source: C21158.

All of the weavers in the region were affected by the defaults of the major wholesalers.[13] There were a few exceptions. In Montrécourt the losses were attributed to The Hague and Amsterdam; Holland was also partly blamed in Selvigny and Elincourt; and in Saulzoir, one individual lost 14,000 florins through bankruptcies at The Hague and London, while another in Saint-Souplet lost 1,000 florins in Frankfort, revealing, once again, the importance of northern circuits. In the case of Bertry, weavers were frequently owed money both in Holland and in France. Jean Guillaume Taine, for example, lost a total of 2,848 livres: 1,300 to Cambronne of Saint-Quentin, and in Amsterdam 545 to Trufaut, 674 to Dield de Neubourg, and 325 to Joseph Levie.[14]

According to a contemporary register, there were sixty-seven active merchant houses in Saint-Quentin between 1753 and 1763.[15] Only a few appeared to specialize in trade with the countryside. The Cambronne family spawned a number of companies such as the firm Lefebvre Cambronne or Petit and Cambronne, but the only Dachery who appeared on the list was Dachery Dhercourt, who at one point countersigned the Montigny merchant Jean Pierre Lantier's bills of exchange. Either he or a close relative had served as mayor of Saint-Quentin in 1751 and 1752.[16]

If Picard and Cambronne dominated the Montigny market in the 1750s, the losses declared in 1761 did not account for all of the ties between Montigny weavers and Saint-Quentin merchants. Jean Pierre Lantier, for example, declared that his association with Cambronne, Picard, and Crommelin had cost him 1,500 livres in 1759. At that time he also dealt with other Saint-Quentin merchants, notably Boutillier, as well as with Taine and the widow Rubay of Cambrai. In 1763 Lantier

Table 39. Sums Owed in Montigny by Bankrupt Firms

City	Firm	Amount	Creditor
Saint-Quentin	Boutillier	300 livres	J. Ph. Pigou
		300 livres	J. L. Pigou
		200 livres	Felix Ego
Saint-Quentin	Darchery, Campion	3,000 livres	Etienne Lesage
	Picard, and Cambronne	1,700 livres	Pierre Deudon
		1,500 livres	J. P. Lantier
		914 livres	G. Boursier
		800 livres	Fr. Levesque
		752 livres	Thomas Prévôt
		552 livres	G. Boursier
		461 livres	G. Boursier
		412 livres	P. Ph. Milot
		406 livres	Ph. Godart
		300 livres	Widow Denoyelle
		100 livres	Nicolas Deudon
		83 livres	J. L. Labbé
		65 livres	P. Ph. Souppé
		60 livres	Ch. Ant. Labbé
		32 livres	Guislain Boursier
Saint-Quentin	Gautier	800 livres	Widow Faré
	Gautier	100 livres	Widow Denoyelle
Cambrai	Dherique	101 livres	Ph. Godart
		101 livres	P. Ph. Milot
	Rubay	271 livres	Ch. Huguet
	Taine	80 livres	Fr. Levesque
		? livres	Pierre Deudon

Source: C états 208.

listed two creditors in Saint-Quentin, Gambier and Poitevin, while Cambronne, Boutillier, and a man named Mariage were responsible for a number of irretrievable losses.[17] Twelve years later, Lantier's network had widened, and eight of his twelve creditors figured among the recognized merchants. They were Megret-Gambier, Lefebvre-Cambronne, Lefebvre-Marolle, Blondel, Duplessis-Borneville, Lefebvre, Cambronne Senior, and Soyez. The remaining four, Vieuville, Deulin, Touchon, and Martin, may or may not have been involved in trade.

Lantier had, at the very least, indirect ties with other important Saint-Quentin merchants such as Daniel and Alexandre Cottin, who negotiated a bill of exchange bearing his name and which he failed to honor.[18]

Lantier also received several bills issued by Dachery Dhercourt.[19] (This reliance on merchant guarantors will be examined later.)

In the 1780s Druon Ruol of Montigny conducted his trade with a different set of merchants: Dauffremont and Cambronne, Douay Junior, Arette, and Dervilly, who did not appear on the earlier list of merchants. In town as in the country, the body of merchants had changed.

Effects of the Crisis

Some of the victims of the crisis had been and remained fairly well-off, but if we take Elincourt (where the curé included the victims' tax bracket) as an example, then the majority appeared to have been hit extremely hard (table 40). In Montigny twenty-two of the twenty-nine villagers who suffered losses in the early 1760s could be traced to the 1743 income groups.[20] Only one major merchant, Jean Pierre Lantier, emerged from the top group both via his father, Jean Baptiste, and his father-in-law, Michel Allart. On a much lower scale, three sons of the farmer Michel Labbé, in the same category, claimed small sums, most likely for linens they had produced themselves. Nine others were connected to households in the second category; in the case of five of these, the families had been assessed below the tax average for that bracket and in only one instance above the average. Eight weavers came from the third category. The families of four of these had paid more, and four had paid less, than the average of 8.8 florins in taxes (they may not have been actually too poor, for they were connected to widows who were generally assessed more lightly).

In short, aside from Lantier, the victims of the bankruptcies belonged to a middling group: the lower half of the second category and the upper half of the third. This placed them, as one might expect, below the major farmers and on the same level as some laboureurs or artisans such as the blacksmith or mason, but above the rest of the weavers and of the farmhands. The bankruptcies divided them into more distinct groups: producers and traders.

Although some weavers still retained their independence and continued to sell their products in town, the 1759 crisis proved a turning point. The curé of Wambaix wrote the Estates that "the said fine-linen weavers were mostly young couples who had apparently invested almost all they had in the trade."[21] Elincourt's priest gave a grim account of the repercussions of the crisis.[22]

Table 40. Bankruptcy Losses in Elincourt According to Gradations of Wealth

Losses (livres)	Prosperous	Semiprosperous	Poor	Not ranked	Total
0–100	—	—	—	3	3
100–500	1	3	11	3	18
500–1,000	2	2	4	2	10
1,000–5,000	2	1	4	1	8
More than 5,000	—	1	—	—	1
Total	5	7	19	9	40

Source: C états 208.

All these losses have meant that the master weavers stopped giving out work so that a number of workers have left the region, they have cut down their supplies of yarn, they cannot pay the farmers who have given them wheat on credit so that everyone suffers, conditions are very bad and half of my parish is reduced to begging. We are overburdened with paupers. All these hardships have brought on illnesses that have lingered for some time and since I have almost no land reserved for the poor, I can no longer provide much relief. I urge the farmers by my example and my pleas to go on giving the weavers credit, assuring them that trade will revive with the coming peace, but the farmers are getting impatient.

This difficult period transformed commercial relations in the countryside. The weavers at the bottom of the scale suffered the most, as Clary's curé told the Estates: "A number of weavers lost more than they had and are therefore reduced to begging. . . . Those who lost twelve, fifteen, or twenty to thirty crowns deserve more pity than those who lost one thousand or more because the first have lost everything while the others still have something to fall back on."[23] And, indeed, as one Montigny weaver had complained three decades earlier: "When some years . . . it took a long time to sell the linens that he produced, or there was a long wait before the brokers paid for the pieces, and if trade was sluggish, did that mean that the plaintiff should not get paid?"[24]

After the crisis, some families continued to weave, surviving on the margins, paying very low taxes. In Montigny this was the fate of such previously independent weavers as the Souppés, Sedents, Huguets, and Jean Louis Pigou, who numbered among the 1759 victims. The damage was not irreparable, however. Charles Antoine Labbé, who lost the least in 1759, retained a measure of independence. Although he died in 1779, a decade later his widow raised five hundred florins partly to settle his debts and partly to obtain raw materials: "Since her children are now old enough to work, the supplicant hopes to restore her husband's business once she has the money to buy the necessary merchandise that would allow her children to go on weaving."[25] Some careers were cut short as the men died single or childless or left no direct heirs to revive or carry on the trade, although in the case of Guillain Boursier, his mother and brother developed a fairly successful business. Some of the victims of the bankruptcies continued to weave, like Jean Michel Labbé and Jean Martin Pigou, and did fairly well, for they rose to the top quarter of Montigny taxpayers in 1787 without feeling the need to invest in commercial ventures.

Having lost their wherewithal, some men turned away from weaving. Jean Philippe Pigou became a lime burner and died in 1775, leaving little except a brood of children who were scattered in different villages. Pascal Pigou opened a tavern. Hubert Denimal became the village's churchwarden and tax collector. Jean Louis Labbé moved to Troyes, which attracted weavers in this period.

The families at the top of the curé's bankruptcy list of 1761, however, recovered and resumed their trading activities. They included Jean Pierre Lantier, Etienne Lesage, and Thomas Prévôt, a group that readily intermarried. Etienne Lesage and Dominique Ego (the son of Felix Ego, who figured among the victims) were Jean Pierre Lantier's brothers-in-law. Such bonds linked most of the village's merchants. Pierre Philippe Milot (owed 513 florins) was the father-in-law both of Thomas Prévôt (752 florins) and Jean François Godart (507 florins). Jean François Faré's widow lost 100 florins, her daughter Marie Anne (widow of Joseph Denoyelle) 400 florins. Marie Anne later married Jean Baptiste Cauchy, another Montigny merchant. Another daughter, Catherine, was the wife of Jean François Levecque (880 florins). In 1787 Joseph Faré, son of the merchant Jean Baptiste, would rank with Jean Baptiste Lantier among the 10 percent of villagers who paid more than fifteen florins in taxes. Jean Martin Levecque, who succeeded Jean François, did even better, for he numbered among the 5 percent who contributed more than twenty florins.[26]

A number of these families had already acted as intermediaries in the first half of the century. After the crisis, their intercession became crucial. The crisis taught both urban traders and rural weavers to rely on buffers. The middlemen who had begun by purveying local cloth turned to small-scale entrepreneurship, commissioning pieces and paying the weavers. They now shouldered most of the risks. This gave the town merchants greater flexibility and freed them from worry about potentially trouble-some relations with the weavers. Circumstances compelled the weavers, who were the primary victims of the crisis, to turn to rural middlemen for supplies and advances. Yet they did not become totally helpless, for they could exert greater pressure on local men than on far-away merchants. Bankruptcy records show that this was indeed the case. Rural merchants who filed for bankruptcy proved heavily in debt to urban wholesalers and financiers who advanced them funds and raw materials. They owed practically nothing to weavers in the countryside, who figured, instead, among their debtors.

When Jean Pierre Lantier went bankrupt in 1763, for instance, he owed 9,000 livres to various merchants and farmers. Weavers in sur-rounding villages owed *him* 500 livres. At his second bankruptcy in 1775, his debts to urban merchants amounted to 10,000 livres, while various weavers and spinners owed him a total of 1,500 livres.[27] The situ-ation had changed since the first half of the century: merchant-weavers in the countryside were borrowing money to pay their weavers; the weavers made less from a piece than they might have by leaving it with the brokers themselves, but they could count on immediate payments.

Landed Assets

The crisis that began in 1759 created a new pattern of trade even if its elements had already existed before. The weaving population became polarized into a group of relatively well-to-do traders and a body of weavers who worked for them, although some weavers recovered their independence. Rural merchants were no longer simple intermediaries who carried the cloth to town and waited for returns from foreign sales to trickle in before paying the weavers. They were laying out capital to purchase the weavers' pieces, which they turned over to the urban brokers. These urban merchants handed the rural merchant-weavers credit notes that eventually translated into hard cash. In the meantime, rural merchants needed money to buy supplies, to pay their work force, and to keep their concerns going.

Credit mechanisms were central to the trade, but the first generations of merchant-weavers raised their capital essentially on the strength of their landed assets. The merchant families in Montigny were also the land buyers in the village. The Lantiers, for example, made eleven purchases and three sales; the Farés, thirteen purchases and one sale; the Pigou clan, thirty-three purchases but also twenty-two sales; the Cauchys, seven purchases and two sales; the widow Boursier, eight purchases and two sales; and finally the Lesages acquired eight plots and sold one.[28] This compares well with the farmers. The Tamboise family bought thirteen plots and sold only one. The Labbés came out even with six sales and six acquisitions, while the Malesieux, economically declining farmers and weavers, sold nine times and bought only five.

The career of Jean Pierre Lantier demonstrates the importance of mortgageable assets, for it was on the basis of his father's carefully accumulated holdings that he expanded the Allart trading network, once he married into that family and launched his own business ventures. Land provided an independent source of capital that lessened the rural merchant's dependence on credit from urban merchants. Lantier was especially lucky in inheriting land, because patrimonial bequests were not liable in cases of insolvency.

Jean Pierre's father, Jean Baptiste Lantier, was raised in the village of Clary, the son of a local cobbler. Jean Baptiste became a weaver and moved to Montigny, where he married in 1719. We know little of his trading activities except that they enabled him to buy property and in 1743 count among the village's well-to-do. Beginning with his wife's share in a house and garden, and her half of a mencaudée of arable (along with his own hundred florins' worth of looms, tools, yarn, and bricks), Jean Baptiste invested steadily in land, so that by 1744 he owned fifteen mencaudées as well as four cows. In 1745 he gave his son, Jean Pierre, two small fiefs (measuring two mencaudées), another 2½ mencaudées in Montigny, the lease of a mencaudée in Clary, and 1,600 florins in cash.[29]

By 1750 Jean Pierre Lantier had increased those holdings to thirty mencaudées (ten hectares), and this made him one of the biggest resident landowners in the village. He continued to buy land, but in 1762 he parted with twenty-four mencaudées for the sum of 2,875 florins, although some of his opponents later claimed that the sale had been fictitious. Lantier had raised four thousand florins by mortgaging twenty-seven of the thirty mencaudées shortly before the sale.[30] In 1756 he had only had to provide two mencaudées as collateral for a 1,200-florin loan.[31] The earlier lender had been Luc Frémicourt, canon of Saint-Géry in Cambrai, while André Joseph Lecocq, Cambrai's treasurer of fortifications, provided the larger sum. *Rentiers,* widows, officers, and clergymen in the nearby towns of Cambrai and Le Cateau with money on their hands, or else guardians of minor children in the countryside with money to invest, and even prosperous peasants, remained a constant source of loans. They figure most prominently in the records of mortgages and annuities (at 5 percent) overseen by village authorities. Notaries acted as intermediaries in these transactions.[32]

After the sale of most of his property in 1762, Jean Pierre Lantier never again owned as much land. He farmed some of his brother-in-law's plots in the 1760s and was accused of mauvais gré.[33] In the 1770s he fought a lawsuit over the ownership of a thirty-six-mencaudée fief in the village of Marcoing and apparently succeeded in obtaining half, but at his death in 1784, he left only 15⅔ mencaudées (burdened with various mortgages and annuities) to his three children.[34] The eldest, Jean Michel, lived in Walincourt, and the second son, Jean Baptiste, took over the Montigny concerns. The family had not fallen on hard times, but its prospects seemed less bright and its dowries less well-endowed. In 1770 Jean Baptiste's marriage contract had stated that he would receive two thousand livres and three looms that never materialized and to which he relinquished all claims at the division of the inheritance in 1785. His brother Jean Michel similarly abandoned his claim to the four looms that had been promised him.[35]

Montigny had no landless merchant-weavers functioning merely on the basis of cash, expertise, credit, and a persuasive tongue. They all persistently built and rebuilt patrimonies and toward the end of the century steadily incorporated farming with weaving. Land, however, was the more significant the smaller the operation. It provided the initial capital that fueled the move into trade. A merchant of Lantier's caliber functioned with a double source of credit: commercial and landed. Both needed protection. The merchant had to salvage his property and shelter it from seizure. He also needed to safeguard his reputation. Lantier and his counterparts fought countless lawsuits to keep his reputation untarnished. This was no mean task in a period of repeated bankruptcies and accusations of shady practices.

The process can be envisaged in chronological terms. Capital accumulation in the form of land took place in the first half of the century as with the Lantiers, establishing the owners as worthy members of their communities. At a later stage, merchant-weavers bought land and very quickly put it to speculative uses. They also relied increasingly on the credit afforded by urban merchants, credit that depended on the returns of the trade rather than on the provision of collateral. The weaver who had given up hopes of independence might well forgo his plot of land. By the same token, loss of property kept him in a subservient position since money was necessary to anyone who wished to expand, and land provided the surest way of obtaining it.

Yet combining land and commerce did not always spell success. Another Montigny family, the Pigous, had allied weaving to farming from the late seventeenth century on. When Marie Poré, widow of the ménager Jacques Pigou, died in 1704, she left money and several fields to her most distant relatives and the revenue of eight mencaudées to her three fatherless grandsons along with 600 florins' worth of yarn, wheat, a cow, a loom, and other movables.[36] The Pigous apparently acted as local yarn suppliers along with the Allarts. By the time the boys married, their share had grown to 6⅓ mencaudées and 800 florins each. The eldest, Louis, inherited an additional 2½-mencaudée fief.[37] While one of the brothers emigrated to Marcoing, and another, Jean, had only daughters (who all but one left the village), Louis learned how to weave from Jean Lefort and carried on the hybrid occupation of farmer-weaver. He ranked among the village notables, a situation that his sons failed to emulate, although two of them were marginally involved in the cloth trade. The youngest may have been slightly more successful than the elder, especially once he joined forces with his brother-in-law, François Renard, one of the village's new merchant-weavers, for until then he had distinguished himself only by selling land or by borrowing money.[38]

Mortgages were established features in the countryside. There is no doubt that all strata of society found themselves strapped for funds at one time or another because of agricultural or commercial crises. The village's records of mortgages are fairly evenly spread between 1681 to 1790, except for two periods, 1761–70 which concentrated a quarter of all the village's borrowing, and 1781–90 which witnessed another concentration.[39] The first period coincides with the advent of the new rural entrepreneur who needed capital to carry on his trade and who mortgaged his land in order to obtain it. A period of easy credit followed where real estate played a lesser role. The bankruptcies of the late 1780s prompted a return to traditional forms of borrowing.

The merchant Charles Antoine Dubois regularly mortgaged his plots to raise capital for his linen trade. His experience also demonstrates the quandary that such debts imposed. Dubois was the son of a Prémont wood merchant and had been orphaned early. At eighteen he married the sixteen-year-old daughter of a Montigny weaver. At that time they owned three mencaudées in Prémont, two and a half in Montigny, a cow, and the bride's share in her father's house. They bought another half a mencaudée

in 1774, but in 1776 had to borrow four thousand livres, having spent
their entire capital on securing two large fiefs in Clary (measuring nineteen and fourteen mencaudées, or a total of eleven hectares).[40] Rather
than part with this property, they chose to mortgage it to raise the funds
necessary to pursue their "linen business" (*commerce de mulquinerie*). In
March 1779 they borrowed another twelve hundred florins and in July a
further fifteen hundred. By 1781 they were forced to sell the fourteen-
mencaudée plot. They continued to borrow regularly: four thousand
florins in 1784; six thousand florins a year later, each time providing a
part of their property as guarantee. A last loan of six hundred florins was
recorded in 1789, which further mortgaged 1¼ mencaudées.[41]

In 1786 and 1787 Dubois had to relinquish another seven mencaudées. He sold these to local residents, mostly other Montigny merchants. Although he later claimed that the proceeds had gone to repay his
6,000-florin loan, the buyers, who just learned of the mortgage, confiscated the rest of his property. They were trying to secure the repayment of
Dubois's debt and avoid seizure of the plots they had just purchased.
They were right because Dubois had not repaid the loan with the money
they had given him, and he did so only when Milot of Le Troncquoy
acquired the nineteen-mencaudée fief.[42] Dubois's behavior was violently
denounced. "Once upon a time an affluent man, come to very little
through his own fault, Dubois is right in putting the finishing touches on
his own destruction and that of his large family, by inciting unwarranted
and unseemly squabbling, and dragging into court those who for fear of
accelerating his own decline showed enough commiseration and consid-
eration not to accuse him of fraud (*stellionat*)."

Failed Transitions

While land facilitated borrowing and family ties brought support in the
form of connections, capital, and workers, chance also played a role in
the making and unmaking of merchants. For two Montigny families,
"chance" meant ill luck, for they suffered from premature deaths and
overly large households.

The Malesieux had been a family of middling and even big farmers. In
the early part of the century one branch had occupied the farm of La
Bruyère and another that of La Trappe, while a third had collected a
number of smaller leases including that of the abbey of Prémy. The next
generation turned to textiles, although one side retained the farm of La

Bruyère until the 1770s. La Trappe fell to Moyse Crinon when he married the previous tenant's widow, and the younger Malesieux either left the village or set to weaving as their major occupation. Michel Malesieux, the rightful but displaced heir of La Trappe, managed to land on his feet by obtaining the handsome dowry that came with the mother of his bastard son. The bride had been raised by her childless aunt, Catherine Clais, widow of Jacques Lefort and aunt of Jean, who thus lost his expected inheritance. It was rumored that Michel Malesieux had been bribed with 7.5 mencaudées to bring her to the altar.[43] His own portion included 1.5 mencaudées and 400 florins.[44] With his stepfather, Moyse Crinon, as mayor, Michel easily became Montigny's churchwarden.[45] He was called a ménager in 1744 when he held thirteen mencaudées and owned two cows. He died in 1746 at the age of forty-four in a period when both farming and industry were suffering a recession. His eldest son, Jean Baptiste, might have effected the transition into trading had he not died at the age of twenty-nine. He owned property in Montigny and Caullery, while his wife, Marie Anne Faré (a good match from another local trading group), brought a fourteen-mencaudée fief in Caullery and land and a house in Montigny, looms, yarn, and two hundred florins.[46] Their daughter, Marie Angélique, married Charles Antoine Dubois, who came to Montigny where he sold cloth and farmed a number of properties, eventually proving unsuccessful at both.

Though big families could potentially enhance the economic viability of the household by the contribution of extra labor, Montigny's large households did not especially thrive; in fact, they exemplified the dangers of such proliferation. Some of the difficulties experienced by the Dubois in the 1780s may have been aggravated by the need to support a growing brood. While four children had died in infancy, by 1788 the couple had to feed six others (from a newborn to a twelve year old); their eldest son was only eleven and too young to work at the loom, and three children were yet to come (two of them died in infancy).

The Malesieux' reverses can also be linked to the same phenomenon. Jean Baptiste Malesieux died leaving only one daughter, but his brother Pierre Joseph lived to sixty-five and fathered fourteen children. Ten of them survived beyond childhood, although several died in their late teens. According to the 1780s census, Pierre Joseph supported nine children.[47] The family reconstitution chart shows that at that time the household was composed of six daughters (aged twenty, eighteen, fourteen, four, and two—some earning their keep as spinners) and three boys (aged sixteen, nine, and a few months), only one of whom could be counted to work at the loom. Pierre Joseph's sisters were equally fertile. One gave birth to eight children in fourteen years, while a second (married to Michel Delbart) had seventeen in twenty-two years.[48] In 1778, eleven of those children lived under the paternal roof, not counting one married son. The girls (aged twenty-six, twenty-two, twenty-one, eleven, eight, and six) and the boys (twenty, eighteen, seventeen, ten, and eight) were quite capable of contributing to the household economy.

Such extensive households were no boon, and these families fared poorly. If land can serve as a barometer, they sold more than they acquired, an indication of their poverty.[49] They also secured loans to survive (rather than to speculate). Thus, Pierre Joseph Malesieux borrowed fifteen hundred florins in 1761, and Sebastien Delbart borrowed four hundred florins a year later.[50] They fought hard to hold on to their land. The bitter conflict that opposed Michel Delbart and his two nieces over the possession of a hedge and pear tree testifies to their exacerbated need. The two girls were "poor single women who earn their daily bread by the sweat of their brow." They had only a small house built on half a mencaudée of land and could not afford the lawsuit against their uncle "who got it into his head to tear up the hedge which separated their half mencaudée from his land."[51] As for him, he led an arduous life "burdened with twelve children that he supports by the fruits of his own labour."[52] While neighbors and sympathetic kin turned out to uphold each side, Michel Delbart was still pursuing the matter two years later.[53]

Disputes over land encroachments were common to all groups of villagers. However, the summoning of witnesses to testify whether tree branches leaned this way or that, and to attribute de facto or de jure possession of one-tenth of a hectare of land, reinforced with a wealth of detail, underlines the extent of some weavers' strained situations much better than any tax assessment. It was not within everyone's reach to become a merchant.

Political Power

The existence of a group of successful merchants and small landowners had political repercussions within Montigny. The composition of the village council shifted its locus from the older agricultural elite to the new merchant class. At the end of the seventeenth century the tenant-farmers were the undisputed leaders of the village. They not only monopolized the best land but controlled many of the village's resources by bidding for and collecting local taxes and tithes. They represented the seigneurs and served as the village's mayors. While some of the laboureurs (in a lower category) sometimes contested this hegemony, power in Montigny rested in the hands of its major farmers.

By the middle of the eighteenth century, the social composition of the village had altered. Weaving now occupied two-thirds of the households, and a group of merchant-weavers had appeared on the scene. Ordering their activities around the supply of yarn and the transport of locally produced cloth, these men also invested in land. While a number overextended themselves and went bankrupt, a tightly knit group prospered and managed to remain afloat precisely through a judicious combination of mercantile and landed assets. They soon displaced the farmer-mayors. Until the middle of the century the village had been run by farmers from the Labbé, Lefebvre, Delacourt, and Crinon families. Thereafter, merchant-weavers could be found at the helm so that in the second half of the eighteenth century the village's mayors included Jean Baptiste Faré (1758–62), Thomas Prévôt (1762–70), Pierre Tousaint Dron (1769, 1777–79), and Dominique Ego (1779–89).

Dissensions arose in midcentury because the then farmer-mayor, Robert Milot, raised the tax base, set at ten mencaudées per head in 1713, to twenty mencaudées. By this reckoning, a property measuring one hundred mencaudées would count only as five taxable units rather than ten. This measure favored the bigger landowners, mainly nonresidents, such as the mayor himself (who lived at Le Troncquoy), and correspondingly increased the burden of payments of the remainder of the population. Since villages were assigned fixed amounts of taxes, which they divided among the inhabitants, the farmers' lesser share would have to be met by greater payments from the others.

Records of land sales show that there was another mayor serving concurrently or in opposition to Milot during the 1760s.[54] The protest against this change in the tax structure, signed by the village's advocate, must have represented the council and the weaver-mayor, Thomas Prévôt, as it is unlikely that Milot would consent to plead against his own measures.[55] The fact that the guidelines to the 1787 tax roll read "ten mencaudées of land per head" indicates that the inhabitants won their suit, though it may well be that the value of such official documents was quite spurious.[56] Nonetheless, the successful replacement of the mayor in Montigny's case suggests that local grievances were appeased.

Few municipal documents survive for 1771 to 1778 when the Chapter's bailli took over many judicial functions, but several records attest to the presence of yet another Troncquoy farmer as mayor, assisted by a third.[57] But aside from this appearance by Pierre Aubert Tamboise and Louis Petit, no farmers were henceforth imposed on the community, and until the Revolution the village's major duties were split between a local merchant-weaver and the bailli in Cambrai.

The linen traders who came to the fore from the middle of the eighteenth century onward thus altered the social composition of the village. The top echelon that had once been composed exclusively of a landed group now included men who merged real estate and commercial assets and weaving with farming. In an era when cottage industry occupied a growing proportion of the population, the villagers came to see such men as their representatives and rejected the notion that village leadership rested with the farming elite.

The new leadership had emerged because of a combination of circumstances and strategies. The commercial shocks of the mid-eighteenth century encouraged weavers to turn to intermediaries who would take on some of the risks of the cloth trade: village weavers could exercise far more influence over local merchants, and happily exchanged a share of their profits for this security. The merchants established their position through careful speculation with their landed assets. Hence, both the origins and the development of this new group: they came from the village's middling households, with a reasonable portion of inherited land. This real estate provided the collateral for loans, and they continued to buy land as a necessary basis for future commercial activity.

10

Credit and the Crisis in Entrepreneurship

A number of factors combined to stimulate trade in the countryside in the second half of the eighteenth century. The crisis of the late 1750s encouraged weavers to rely on the steady wages provided by local middlemen, and these same men handled transactions with urban merchants who now depended on them for cloth supplies. Rural trading was also given a boost by the 1762 edict that liberated production in the countryside. The act officially acknowledged an existing situation, since by midcentury half of the inhabitants of rural Cambrésis wove, and many traded independently, despite regulations that had limited such activities to the towns. Nevertheless, official approval following the recent disarray of urban firms could only encourage rural enterprises. The increase in such activities, especially in the 1770s and early 1780s, also derived from the widespread use of credit in the countryside.

A huge extension of credit marks the second half of the eighteenth century and demarcates it from the first. In the earlier period, coins, even if not plentiful, circulated in the countryside. Commercial debts recorded in the early eighteenth century were cash debts entered in the merchants' registers and not yet composed of promissory notes or bills of exchange.[1] Peasants had long raised money by mortgaging their land and establishing annuities (rentes) on behalf of urban lenders. But, as the curé of Rumégies (a village northwest of Valenciennes) reported, the introduction of paper money, following John Law's reforms of the banking system in 1719–20, had allowed rural inhabitants to repay their creditors and to unburden their land.[2] The mid-1720s, therefore, found them in a more secure position.

Cash, and especially cash donations in Montigny dowries, rose steadily until the middle of the century when the average reached 700 florins. Then, from 1750 to 1775, there was a marked drop (to 135 florins), followed by a resurgence (465 florins) in a period when weavers were regularly paid for their work.[3] In the intervening period, and especially in the 1750s, urban merchants had provided rural producers with promissory notes in return for their pieces. These were then either negotiated for supplies or eventually turned into cash. The system collapsed in the late 1750s with the series of bankruptcies that rendered the notes valueless. The weaving households then turned to local merchants for cash earnings, leaving the merchants to fend with the insecurities of urban credit.

At the same time, Montigny and its neighbors shifted their orientation away from Cambrai and Valenciennes toward Saint-Quentin. This move was reflected in the shift of currency from the florin to the livre. Only 5 percent of marriage contracts mentioned the French currency prior to 1750. In the next twenty years this figure rose to 40 percent, and then from 1776 to 1790 to 76 percent. The move to the currency in which the weavers were paid, concurrent with a decline in property, denotes the importance and viability of industrial incomes in the last part of the century.

In the early eighteenth century the weaver and yarn merchant Michel Allart conducted his affairs on a monetary basis. In 1722 he and his brother had five hundred florins stolen from their safe.[4] As Jacob Allart tells the tale: "He noticed that some yarn had been stolen, worth about 4 florins, and about 540 or 550 florins that were kept in three small bags in different parts of the safe, and as far as he can recall they included a gold louis with the cross of Malta and some old crowns." It must have been common knowledge that the Allart brothers hoarded their takings, although the amount apparently surprised the thieves, who returned all but eighty florins. "Michel Allart, her husband, opened his door early one morning and found part of the coins in the very bag that had been taken, which had been placed at the entrance to their basement, and about four or five days later, Allart found another little bag, with some money in it, so that all the money that had been stolen was returned in this way except for about 80 florins which they never recovered."[5] The three youths suspected of the deed already had a bad reputation and were known in the village as "gun-carrying vagabonds, bandits, and good-for-nothings; everyone in the area feels the same and they are widely believed to be thieves." One of them had also taken a gold louis and two florins from the pocket of Jean Lenglet as he lay asleep in a barn. There, too, most of the money was later returned. On the very night of the robbery the three were seen drinking in a local tavern "where they paid their expenses in old currency whose value they did not even know." The possession and loss of money were duly noted, and expenditures, especially extravagant ones, were carefully monitored. It was therefore easy for the prosecutor to follow the trail of the culprits from their native village all the way to Flanders.

But coins could not meet the needs of the commerce that developed by 1760. Thus, from the middle of the century the rarity of capital plagued both cottager and merchant. All the Montigny weavers who branched out into trade came to rely on credit and use it extensively. Credit and the recovery of debts created major sources of conflict between big and small merchants. The lawsuits that ensued, however, permit us to understand the nature of such transactions.

Credit depended on anticipated returns from cloth sales, a process that could last up to a year. Two forms of credit were widely used: the bill of exchange and the promissory note.[6] Middlemen and urban merchants generally provided each other with bills of exchange and furnished promissory notes to their local suppliers. They also used them whenever they needed credit at short notice since it was easier to create a promissory note than a bill of exchange.

In the 1750s and early 1760s the merchant Jean Pierre Lantier gave out promissory notes to his fellow villagers, as he did to Pierre Boursier in 1756, and he received similar notes from others, like Pierre Joseph Bens of Montigny, in 1763.[7] Later, he would pay the weavers in cash and supply promissory notes only when returns proved particularly late.[8] His dealings with bigger merchants, on the other hand, involved more formal bills of exchange. These bills had to be negotiated by banking establishments and so required the intercession of major urban wholesalers who held such accounts. The backing of urban firms would also have induced greater trust in the small merchant's solvency. In 1754 Jean Pierre Lantier and his associate, Pierre Normand of Clary, thus paid their supplier, Noel Malfuson of Blancourt, with two bills of exchange, which were endorsed by a Saint-Quentin merchant.[9] A note dated 18 November 1754 promised:

> On 25 May we will make out to Monsieur Noé Malfuson bills of exchange drawn on Paris endorsed and signed by one of the twelve brokers of this city for the 850 livres of goods received from the said Sieur.
>   Signed: P. Leantier P. J. Normand.

Malfuson eventually obtained two bills:

> At Saint-Quentin, 8 July 1755 P.L.402
> In six and a half months by this bill of exchange pay into the account of Monsieur P. Picard 402 livres that you will transfer when so notified by your obedient servant
>   Signed: d'Achery d'hercourt and sons.

To Monsieur Guldiman, banker in Paris
Made out to Monsieur P. Lantier for the amount received from Monsieur
Dachery in Saint-Quentin on 8 July 1755.

Signed: Picard P. Lantier

The second bill, for 447 livres, read much the same way, except that it
had passed from Dachery to Nicolas Boutillier and then to Picard before
reaching Jean Pierre Lantier. Rural merchants who wanted to use major
credit facilities needed to establish ties with urban wholesalers.

When the Saint-Quentin money market dried up in the wake of the
1759 crisis and his Cambrai contacts, like the widow Rubay, went bankrupt, Lantier had to scramble to find new sources of credit. His long-time
opponent, the merchant Pierre François Colan of Cambrai, told a tale of
woe concerning his loans to Lantier.[10] In 1785 the Cambrai merchant
finally went bankrupt, partly undone by innumerable lawsuits for which
he still owed five thousand livres. One of these legal actions involved his
renewed attempts to recover a 500-livre bill of exchange that he claimed
to have received from Lantier in 1762. The story was complicated, with
each side accusing the other of unscrupulous behavior and marshaling an
abundance of evidence.[11] Colan had endorsed a note created by Lantier's
partner, Antoine Cannesson of Caullery, because the two men were not
sufficiently trusted by local lenders. Lantier had assured Colan that he ran
no risks since Lantier had just deposited a substantial number of linens
with a Cambrai wholesaler.[12] The promissory note itself was made out in
Cambrai on 8 April 1762, with the following understanding:

> Pay to J. P. Lantier 500 livres received from him at my residence at
> Monsieur d'herbois concierge of the quinze-vingt, rue Saint Honoré in
> Paris.
>
> Signed: Antoine Canson.

It was discounted in various stages.

24 April	to P. F. Colan	of Cambrai
5 May	to J. Leduc	of Cambrai
18 May	to S. Watier	of Cambrai
4 October	to the Widow Descamps	of Lille
10 October	to Mahieu and co.	of Lille
29 October	to Delafosse and co.	of Rouen

When the funds failed to materialize, the note wound its way back to
Colan. Both Leduc and Cannesson went bankrupt, and Colan was stuck
with the note. As for Lantier, he refused to acknowledge any respon-

sibility, and the subsequent lawsuits dragged on for twenty years. The transfer of the paper shows Cambrai's commercial links to Lille. Most of the bills that have survived for Montigny, on the other hand, were made payable either in Saint-Quentin or in Paris.

Bills of exchange also circulated within villages. In 1753 Etienne Lesage of Montigny borrowed 2,200 florins from Pierre Philippe Waxin of the village of Bévillers, for which he mortgaged his property. The capital could be refunded either in cash or with valid bills of exchange.[13] "The accused did this with the clear understanding that if he paid him with bills of exchange, he would have to accept them and without charging any interest, and since this led to a number of altercations, the plaintiff refusing such offers, the accused insisted that he would only bind himself under these conditions, even telling him that even if these bills of exchange came due within six or eight months he would still have to accept them in that state."[14] Lesage then repaid him with a single bill of exchange created by the widow Rubay and drawn on her son, a Paris banker, made out to Jean Pierre Lantier, Lesage's brother-in-law. Waxin deemed the amount too high to be easily negotiated, and the widow exchanged it for five smaller bills of 700, 300, 300, 800, and 650 livres. Unfortunately for Waxin, the bills became worthless with the bankruptcy of Mme Rubay. Picard's bankruptcy, which followed soon after, similarly perturbed Lantier's line of credit.[15] This explains some of the difficulties he experienced in raising money at that time and the deception that he had to perpetrate to secure loans. Picard's setback was only temporary, however, and in 1769 a Clary weaver owed Guillain Boursier of Montigny 275 livres, for which he gave him a promissory note payable at his "residence . . . at Monsieur Picard Senior's, linen broker in Saint-Quentin."[16]

The merchant-weaver who raised capital by mortgaging his property or by using local connections gained some freedom from urban merchants. In Montigny, land was never offered as collateral for loans from urban merchants. Annuities (that mortgaged property) were made out to lenders from official, military, or clerical milieux. Urban merchants, on the other hand, provided advances and supplies in return for credit notes that were contingent on eventual sales and that did not directly engage the borrower's assets. These became liable only when the defaulter went bankrupt and his property was put up for sale to settle his debts. This, as we have seen, did not affect patrimonial holdings, and it was often in the creditors' interest to ensure that the merchant remained partially solvent so that he could put his affairs in order and recover from his temporary misfortune. They therefore usually agreed to his request for royal *lettres de cession misérable* that attested to his honesty and protected him from imprisonment. They then settled on a schedule of repayment. The process required that all creditors agree, but in practice the authorities readily issued such letters and left the dissenting members to obtain what satisfaction they could from the courts.

Merchant-weavers also secured a measure of independence from the city by borrowing from family and neighbors. These often figured as major creditors when merchants were establishing themselves. When Lantier went bankrupt in 1763, he owed four hundred livres to his brother-in-law, Jean Baptiste Allart of Le Cateau, and nearly as much to the farmer Pierre Aubert Tamboise of Le Troncquoy. He also owed two thousand livres to Pierre Lantier of Clary. These three creditors accounted for one-third of his debts.[17] Such local and kin relations were no longer apparent in his 1775 bankruptcy. His debts then amounted to more than ten thousand livres divided among Saint-Quentin (one-third), Cambrai (one-twentieth), Esqueheries (one-quarter), Oisy (one-eighth), and Le Nouvion (one-quarter). Three merchants from Le Cateau claimed a total of 181 livres, while a resident of Cattenières was owed forty livres.[18] More impersonal business relations predominated, even if merchants attempted to humanize them, as when Lantier named one of his creditors godfather to his daughter.

In the 1780s credit had become so commonplace that it demanded no special backing and no particular assets. Gone were the days when the rural merchant had to rely on the known credit of an urban merchant to secure his loans. Gone were the days when he had to reassure his creditors with a full stockroom or ensnare them with false assurances. In 1788 the Montigny merchant Druon Ruol became embroiled in a suit over the repayment of a debt in which the mechanisms of the creation of such promissory notes were fully described:

> Bourlet [of the village of Clary] owed Ruol some money and he owed some in turn to Mr. Dervilly of Saint-Quentin. When Ruol asked to be paid, Bourlet offered to write him promissory notes since he had no money. Ruol consented as long as they would be accepted by Mr. Dervilly. The parties therefore went to see Pierre Antoine Hocquet, Montigny's village clerk, to request that he draw these up, and once they had explained their business, he agreed to write the three notes not in fact in the name or to the order of the said Ruol but rather to Mr. Dervilly for Ruol explained that since he owed him money it made sense to make the note out to him. The said Bourlet replied that this was all right but since he did not know how to write, he would just make a cross.[19]

This would have invalidated the note, so Hocquet guided Bourlet's signature to a paper that read: "At the end of next December I will pay the Sieur Dhervilly the sum of 83 livres 10 sous which I received in cash from the said Sieur, at my residence at Monsieur Arcelle, innkeeper of the Ange on the main square of Saint-Quentin, done this 28 January 1785." The note was then forwarded to the Saint-Quentin merchant, who meanwhile acknowledged another payment from Ruol and so returned Bourlet's note. At this point, Ruol sent it to cover a debt to a Cambrai wholesale merchant. When the latter claimed the sum, he discovered that no funds had been provided and summoned Bourlet to recognize his signature as proof that he had issued the note, whence the troubles started. The so-called imposture was no aberration since Bourlet had created yet another note worth six hundred livres toward the Saint-Quentin merchant Douay the Younger.[20] The whole affair ruined Ruol, however, who defaulted in 1786.[21] In 1788 he was still suffering the stings of his association with Bourlet. When he tried to get paid for some pieces by another Montigny merchant, Jean Baptiste Lesage, he was reminded that he had provided false bills of exchange and had faked signatures.[22] This situation indicates that a merchant still needed to protect his reputation, but more than that it illustrates the ease with which credit was invoked and notes were issued and circulated.

Litigation provides a window into the mechanisms of trade, but it rarely furnishes a complete picture. To begin with, it focuses on failure rather than success, although it would be a mistake to overstate the seriousness of such reverses. Bankruptcy was common, and although it expressed the insolvency of a particular merchant, more often than not this discomfiture proved to be temporary. Within a year or two of the catastrophe, the merchant had begun trading again and was once more embroiled in lawsuits. The legal evidence is partial at best, since an action in court by one party engendered a countersuit by the accused that divided the arguments into two separate bundles. We rarely find both and have to reconstruct the story from a few scraps. But while we may be unable to settle the origins of any dispute to our satisfaction, the body of litigation presents an impressive picture of the extent to which credit had penetrated the countryside. It also reveals the fragility of the system.

We can divide the merchants' concerns into two categories: the first involved the procurement of credit, and the other the attempt to bid for time. When rural merchants first entered the trade, they depended on urban brokers who provided them with negotiable bills of exchange, drawn on their Paris bankers. When such urban firms failed in the late

1750s, the merchant-weavers had to find a new set of endorsers and backers. Lantier looked for funds in Cambrai in this period and, since he had suffered some losses, formed partnerships in a number of surrounding villages with men whose reputation might still attract lenders. By the 1780s, however, promissory notes had supplanted the bill of exchange as the major form of payment from rural merchants. The litigation involving Montigny merchants of that period, such as Léonard Delacourt, Jacques Michel Renard, or Charles Antoine Dubois, dealt primarily with the provision of promissory notes.[23] And these, as we have seen, were created with the greatest of ease.

Merchants appeared under constant pressure, pressed from all sides to meet their obligations and to honor their credit notes. They stalled for time. They provided new bills to cover those that had come due.

> Madame Rubet,
> I am sending you a bill [of exchange] for 253 livres for the promissory note that has been protested if you would have the kindness to grant me a little time for the remainder as you promised, you would be doing me a great favour, I beg of you not to say anything as I have business to transact with that individual and I am afraid that [I] will be discredited, it could be in my interest [he could charge me interest?] In the hopes that you will grant me this favour, I remain, dear Madame, your humble servant,
> Leantier.[24]

Merchants procrastinated. When called upon to recognize their signatures, they waffled. They fastened on technicalities. Some bills turned out to have been made to the wrong individual, or they argued that an offer to pay had been refused and that they had reinvested the funds. They hoped that such delays would allow the five years granted by the statute of limitations on bills and notes to elapse. They were wrong, and such bills were contested even twenty years after the fact. The procedure could be extremely costly. In 1787 Druon Ruol was condemned by the courts to pay a 200-livre bill of exchange as well as 600 livres 4 sous and 6 deniers for the costs of the protest and transport of the bill and for the legal costs and expenses.[25]

In most cases the payments were evidently met, or else the system would have collapsed at its inception. Nonetheless, the insecurities surrounding payments were such that it is easy to see why some lenders took undue advantage of borrowers, especially those whose reputation no longer allowed them more reasonable sources of loans. Pierre Antoine

Hocquet was forced to resort to one such loan shark, Chrisostome Burlion of Bertry. Charles Antoine Dubois reported the event:

> A little while ago, though he can't recall exactly when, Hocquet told him of his predicament and that he needed 300 livres to meet his obligations, so that he took Hocquet to the said Burlion who gave him the sum both in goods and in cash, and consequently Hocquet made out a promissory note to the order of the said Burlion for that amount and they haggled over the interest. Burlin took advantage of the great necessity in which Hocquet found himself and charged 24 livres interest for three months, when the note became due, which comes to 32% interest a year.[26]

In fact, Hocquet proved unable to pay the original 198 livres, and the loan was extended for another two months. The lender then deemanded 250 livres instead of the 215 livres 9 sous 9 deniers that Hocquet was willing to concede.[27] By the end of the Ancien Régime, the interest, which amounted to 32 percent a year, far exceeded the 4.5 percent that rentes usually earned. Jacques Michel Renard, another Montigny merchant, recalled how the same Burlion had charged his father 18 livres interest on 150 livres loaned for four and a half months (representing 30 percent per annum).

A Rural Entrepreneur: Jean Pierre Lantier (1720–1784)

While all Montigny merchants were embroiled in lawsuits, Jean Pierre Lantier left behind a particularly impressive amount of litigation. Lantier was Montigny's leading merchant. His active career spanned forty years, from his marriage in 1745 to his death in 1784. His experiences paralleled the development of rural trade and mirrored the difficulties that it engendered. For Lantier went bankrupt several times and fought countless lawsuits. On the other hand, despite his ups and downs, he raised his family to affluence. He owned sufficient land to rank as an independent farmer; he served as the village's salt and tobacco supplier; he employed more than a hundred spinners. He moved from selling yarn to selling cloth, thereby earning the title of linen merchant, *marchand de toilettes*. Like other middlemen, Lantier raised his capital by mortgaging his property. The size of these assets differentiated him from the middlemen of the next era. His supply networks ranged farther as well, encompassing Flanders, Hainaut, and Picardy, although, after the collapse of his own export company, he traded primarily with the major firms in Saint-Quentin. Part of his funding came from the capital, and a number of his lawsuits involved the payment of overdue bills drawn on Paris. Although he did not export cloth himself after the 1750s, he operated a large network, buying pieces from surrounding villages, which he then sold in town. Despite his bankruptcies, he stayed afloat; his failings were those of the marketing role that he chose to assume, its lack of controls over production and over eventual sales. His career therefore exemplifies the trials, tribulations, and successes of the rural merchant.

Lantier's activities as middleman first come to light in the 1750s when he already handled part of the finishing and marketing of local cloth. He bought the product of Montigny weavers, such as the Boursiers. Their relations illustrate the ambiguities of brokerage and of the role of the middleman in this period. The widow Boursier and her son eventually established their own business, and in June 1773 Jean Pierre Boursier, calling himself a linen and gaze merchant, requested a six-month pass to peddle his wares in France. Two decades earlier, mother and son had turned over their cloth to Lantier on a regular basis and in one case received a promissory note for 414 livres.[28]

> In Montigny 28 May 1756   414 livres
> During the month of November I will pay to the order of Pierre Boursier the sum of 414 livres value received in merchandise from the said gentleman at my residence with M. Boutillier the Younger, merchant in Saint Quentin.
>
>   P. Leantier

Jean Pierre Boursier attempted to negotiate the note for supplies of thread at Le Nouvion where Lantier had sent him, but no one would accept the piece of paper, and he demanded money instead. The Boursiers argued that this was only fair since Lantier had been in full possession of the pieces he had sent to be bleached. Lantier, who had not managed to sell these, offered to return them. "In case the plaintiff should be so mean as to mistrust him and to prove to her that the goods have not been misappropriated since they are still in the accused's storeroom."[29] Sometimes the turnover was slow and the merchant remained stuck with a mass of unsold cloth, which he had to unload at great personal cost. Lantier thus declared a loss of more than six thousand livres in 1763.[30] The middleman could hold on to the stock but at the risk of seeing it deteriorate. Such was the fate of the pieces acquired from the Boursiers, which Lantier still held almost a year after their purchase.

The lower-scale merchant, in this case the widow Boursier, suffered from the predicament of this local entrepreneur who was himself the victim of the collapse of international sales. Hardest hit was the individual weaver who had entrusted his cloth either directly to the broker or to a local intermediary. As the squabble with the Boursier shows, Lantier had to contend with pressure from local weavers, who saw him, even in the 1750s, as the outright owner of the pieces rather than as a mere broker who would pay them when the cloth was sold. The weavers seemed eager to emphasize their dependence on Lantier if that assured them of their wages. Pride was not at stake, nor independence, for no lifelong contract chained weavers to a particular merchant or to any merchant at all.[31] All but the poorest were in a position to market their own cloth. Yet they saw the advantages of relying on local merchants, just as those merchants were happy to have a steady pool of workers. The only difficulty came when times were hard and the returns of the trade were especially slow. Then, the rural merchants might pretend that they were merely brokers. The relationship between merchant and weaver was a precarious one that functioned as long as it proved advantageous to both parties and from which either party was free to withdraw.

Besides marketing local cloth to town, Lantier had also become the village's official salt and tobacco salesman as a supplement or even temporary alternative to the linen trade, which was experiencing a slowdown. Salt and tobacco sales were rigidly controlled within three leagues of the French border for fear of contraband trade. These activities, however, led him into trouble, and he was twice hauled before the intendant on charges of fraud made by the director of the General Farms.[32] It was in the same period, the 1750s, that he established a trading company with two English merchants, de Baralle and Halygraf.[33]

> These had asked [Lantier] to join them in establishing a fine linen business and to provide them with large quantities of cloth. Lantier, who only saw in such proposals the opportunity to expand and increase his own business, did so without reserve and consequently made a number of deliveries in the city of London, but no sooner had he done so, that he began to realize that he would soon repent his hastiness, for these Englishmen were very slow in paying him. Since money was not coming in at the desired rate, his business was seriously disrupted; he was forced to make several trips to London . . . and finally he was left with a stack of merchandise which he had to sell cheap in order to meet his debts and to pay for a number of expensive lawsuits, all of which brought havoc to his affairs.

England had been the major market for Cambrésis linens until their import was forbidden in 1748. Lantier must have found informal if not illegal ways of getting his cloth across the Channel. Whatever the potential of such a venture, however, the outbreak of the Seven Years War cut it short. Nevertheless, Lantier had demonstrated his ability to mobilize a large work force and to purchase cloth on a grand scale. His reversal of fortune temporarily soured his relations with local producers, such as the Boursiers, who took him to court to obtain a payment.

Since the pieces were eventually sold at a loss of six thousand livres, and a series of bankruptcies disrupted the major markers, Lantier found himself short of funds as well as of stock. Jean Albert Collignon, once of the village of Bruille in Flanders and subsequently of Cambrai, recounted how in this period (the early 1760s), Jean Pierre Lantier and his associates duped him into advancing them 3,400 florins by giving false assurances of prosperity.[34] Lantier and his partners, including a Cannesson of the village of Caullery, showed Collignon (and others) a closet full of linens in one house, and, while the potential investors were led from house to house, someone quickly transported the same pieces from stockroom to stockroom, lulling the lenders into belief in their solvency.

Lantier hoped to consolidate his ties to Collignon by naming him godfather to his last child (the other four children had all had local godparents).[35] Lantier benefited from the association, at least financially, since he repaid Collignon only ninety-six livres of the four thousand he owed him (equivalent to the 3,400 florins he borrowed) in a notarized settlement worked out by a Clary merchant twenty years later.[36] In the intervening period, however, Collignon had repeatedly served as a hostile witness, blackening Lantier's reputation. This was a serious matter since a reputation for honorable conduct and dealings was important in securing loans. When Lantier's son, Jean Michel, believed that his integrity had been questioned, he demanded not only a public retraction and damages but that fifty notices be placarded throughout the province restoring his good name.[37]

In 1763 Lantier went bankrupt, and his creditors granted him terms of repayment. His ability to survive this ordeal could be explained in part by the unfair but widespread tactic of faked land sales and other types of fraud. Lantier was accused of hiding his best stock in the house of the Saint-Quentin merchant Boutillier, with whom he stayed when he was in the city. Lantier's opponents went so far as to claim that he had locked up the merchant in his house so that he could not testify that the merchandise was in his possession.[38] Yet Lantier's losses were real, even if partial, and he would never again rank among the village's top landowners as he had been in previous decades. His bankruptcy statement showed him struggling on two mencaudées, with a debit of 29,706 livres. His "irremediable losses," however, included ten thousand livres attributed to Guillaume Clary, who turned out to work for Lantier.[39] He nonetheless recovered and resumed his entrepreneurial activities.

Lantier's entrepreneurial role was widely recognized. When two of his creditors, Bussy and Cottard, challenged his second bankruptcy in 1775, they argued that Lantier "agreed that he had his own business and that he put out work so that there was no point in trying to minimize his successes."[40] He not only collected the finished product but gave out orders and controlled an extensive network of spinners in a dozen villages near Montigny. In 1782 Jean Jacques Poulet testified: "He knew Lantier well because he had been making cloth for him for twenty-two years . . . that in periods of hardship he had helped all the poor weavers and spinners of the region to live."[41]

In an uncertain economic climate such relations and dependency could lead to mischief. In September 1771 several Cannessons attacked Jean Michel Lantier, eldest son of the Montigny merchant, in a Caullery tavern where he had ridden after a feast day. They hit him with a log, causing an open wound.[42] One of the accused, Jean Baptiste Cannesson, a twenty-three-year-old tailor, stated that he bore Lantier no grudge. "His only grievance was that the previous summer, when times were hard, Jean Baptiste Lantier, Jean Michel's brother, and his workers had beaten him up in the village of Clary, and that he had never found out the reason for this mistreatment." While drinking bouts could easily degenerate into violence, this time the run of insults included accusing Jean Michel Lantier of being the "son of a bankrupt" (fils de banqueroutier). The roots of the conflict were not as hazy as the participants suggested. Ten years earlier, Antoine Cannesson of Caullery, a relative of these young men, had been Lantier's partner. The association had ended in disaster with complicated legal consequences, and the Cannessons clearly felt hard done by, especially since all the testimony pointed to the fact that Cannesson had been only a front for Lantier, who let him take all the blame.[43] All of Lantier's partnerships, which occasionally crop up in lawsuits, show a similar pattern. Lantier, having exhausted his good-will, found someone more trustworthy to act in his name, rarely to the associates' benefit because they soon became enmeshed in various schemes to delay payments that degenerated into years of litigation. In the end, he may have had no other choice except to rely on relatives such as his brother-in-law, Dominique Ego, and his nephew, Jean Baptiste Lesage, who became his trading partners.

In 1782 Pierre Bonneville, a weaver and publican from Clary, summed up the man: "He knows Lantier to be a man who has traded linens on a large scale, who has rendered essential services to all the producers in the witness's village, that indeed his excessive confidence in his debtors forced him twenty to thirty years ago . . . to beg mercy from his creditors . . . but that he has always continued his business and has worked in order to fulfil his commitments."[44] This reference to past achievements was echoed by a fellow villager, the Montigny "cotton merchant" Pierre Gueury, who described Lantier at the same hearing as "a man who once was an important linen merchant and who still trades, although on a smaller scale."

Not all of the testimony was as generous. The Denoyelles of Fontaine au Pire refused to acknowledge that he was an "honest man" because he had a poor reputation "among the public" and he swindled everyone by buying goods for which he did not pay.[45] A Beauvois weaver expressed the sensible sentiments that those who had profited from their association with Lantier considered him worthy, while those who had experienced reverses called him a crook. The initial testimony had the same weaver confirm that a dozen years earlier he had heard Lantier boast to someone who was voicing some doubts about declaring bankruptcy: "what's the big deal, I who stand before you have done it three times."[46] At the hearing itself, the witness gave a more nuanced account. Quite the opposite, he had heard Lantier advise someone whose affairs were in disarray: "I do not advise you to go bankrupt because it is a sad business and no one trusts you afterwards but it happened to me three times."

Repeated failures, especially his troubles in 1775, spelled retreat for Jean Pierre Lantier, who lacked the strength and financial backing to recover his leading position—particularly once a number of local contenders filled the gap created by his discomfiture. Although his son, Jean Baptiste, still counted among the higher taxpayers in the village, the Lantiers no longer led the other merchants.

Their later situation recalled that of the 1750s when the Lantiers had acted primarily as brokers. They now once again tried to reduce their commitments to the weavers. In 1788 two Caudry weavers asked to be paid for the various pieces they had given Jean Baptiste Lantier.[47] He, however, argued that rather than owing them forty-two crowns for the cloth (for which they claimed to have gotten a deposit of twenty-four florins), the sum had merely been an advance on the final sale. The pieces had gone to a Saint-Quentin merchant, and he would pay them the balance when the final returns came in. He had not himself acquired the pieces but acted purely as a middleman. The Lantiers were disengaging themselves from direct involvement and seeking refuge in mere brokerage.

Lantier never sought to consolidate his hold over the work force. He owned at least seven looms but did not seem to employ a body of assistants. When he repossessed a weaver's belongings, he quickly leased these back, including the looms. He preferred to rely on a loose system of orders, purchases, and brokerage that allowed greater maneuverability. The rural merchant who could not control the debit and export of cloth had to maintain flexible relations with the weavers so that he could adapt (usually belatedly) to circumstances: encouraging greater production when appropriate or cutting his losses by refusing to take responsibility for their output.

Jean Pierre Lantier's career shows how strong competition, uncertain and unreliable economic trends, and insufficient capital may have decreed a mixture of aggressivity and guile. Yet one is hard put to conclude that they were the touchstone of his success. While it is difficult to gauge the impact of individual character, Lantier's vision, boundless energy, and craftiness certainly played a part in stimulating this man to dream of vast commercial empires from his country cottage. One may well wonder why he chose to remain in Montigny. Ignace Taine, a fellow Montignacien, moved to Cambrai where he became a merchant and the city's cloth stamper. Did Lantier's early failure to export linens convince him that he could not break into the urban mercantile elite and that his fortune lay indeed in establishing networks in the countryside? He may well have been unable to leave, his repeated difficulties and bankruptcies tying him to Montigny, his resources further drained by countless lawsuits. Twenty dossiers (representing fifteen cases) lie among the records of the Cambrai Officialité and of the Parlement of Flanders, while others are regularly mentioned in notarial records.[48] Some of Lantier's assets may indeed have lain elsewhere, beyond the compass of the local notary and tax assessor. Yet no property outside of Montigny appeared in his will.[49] We know little of his life outside the village, and not much more of it inside, for whereas he served as salt and tobacco vendor for at least fifteen years, he never sat on the village council. His brother-in-law, Dominique Ego, and one of his associates, Thomas Prévôt, ran the village for twenty years. The Lantiers' marriage strategies symbolized their removal from the village. While Jean Baptiste the Elder had moved from Clary to marry a local girl, and his children also found local spouses among the village elite, Jean Pierre's sons chose their brides elsewhere. Jean Michel married the daughter of a Walincourt merchant, and Jean Baptiste married Rosalie Delahay from Bertry. Their sister, Celestine, married the village clerk who had come to Montigny from Reumont.

Whatever Jean Pierre Lantier's relations with his fellow villagers, ninety-four turned out in 1767 to sign an affidavit on his behalf—which cannot be dismissed as subservience. It appears rather as a display of group solidarity, one that brought out almost every head of household in this village of four hundred people. "We the undersigned, residents of the parish of Montigny-en-Cambrésis certify and will confirm anywhere that is needed that Jean Pierre Lantier, resident of the said parish, is completely trustworthy (honnête homme) and that we know nothing about him that could lead to any suspicion of wrongdoing. . . ."[50] Still, the family's economic position in the village was not wholly secure. Though the Lantiers employed people in Montigny as they did within a larger radius, they held no monopoly on labor or production. Weavers continued to work independently and to market their own cloth and create their own ties with urban brokers and wholesalers, and these sometimes expanded into competitive networks.

Other Montigny Merchants

Other Montigny linen merchants included Jacques Michel Renard, Pierre Philippe Cauchy, Charles Antoine Dubois, Dominique Ego, Jean Baptiste Pigou, Léonard Delacourt, and the clerk Pierre Antoine Hocquet, who also dabbled in the business. Some, like Lesage and Ego, were associated with Lantier; others, such as the Renards and Delacourts, participated in other networks, and their connections with Cambrai and Valenciennes suggest an involvement with northern peddlers. Others still, like Ruol, established their own ties with Saint-Quentin firms, independently of Lantier, although he eventually succumbed and had to join the Lantier-based consortium.

Ruol went bankrupt in 1786. He then owed 150 livres to a local weaver, Guislain Renard.[51] Most of his creditors, however, were located in Cambrai and Saint-Quentin, and they allowed him to repay his debts within eight years.[52] In 1788 he was selling cloth to Jean Baptiste Lesage, Jean Pierre Lantier's nephew.[53] The same Lesage was listed among the victims of another bankruptcy, that of Jacques Joseph Campain of the village of Quiévy whose losses amounted to 76,130 livres.[54] Another Montigny merchant-weaver, Jean Baptiste Renard, lost 450 livres in the same bankruptcy.

In September 1788 the same Jean Baptiste Renard filed a complaint against Philippe Daillencourt of Beauvois who impugned his good name while drinking in a Valenciennes tavern "where there were also a number of foreign merchants." Daillencourt harmed his reputation and shed discredit on his affairs by his loud and public denunciations that he was "a scoundrel . . . a rascal . . . a known thief and calling him all sorts of horrible names, even threatening to wring his neck."[55] Daillencourt had to make public amends. In 1789 Renard's daughter was impregnated and then wed by Pierre Alexandre Cocu, a cloth merchant from Monbrain south of Saint-Quentin, who would make a fortune speculating in biens nationaux.[56]

Another member of that family, Jacques Michel Renard, had cosigned a promissory note for a relative in Cambrai, François Renard, who filed for bankruptcy in 1781. He owed at least ten thousand livres in Cambrai and Orchies (in Flanders).[57] The note that Jacques Michel was jointly responsible for had been extended for a fortnight with a new note that the defendant had not signed and for which he felt he was no longer liable.[58] Unlike his younger brother, Jean Baptiste, Jacques Michel Renard did not sell cloth. Rather he combined farming with weaving and was known as a mulquinier-laboureur. Hybrid occupations were reappearing in the village, and well-to-do weavers took over leases and devoted more time to farming. Even Charles Antoine Dubois, the failed merchant-weaver, spent some of his time farming and called himself a merchant-farmer (marchand de toilettes et laboureur). Martin Levesque, son of the merchant-weaver François, had abandoned trading altogether to become one of Montigny's wealthiest laboureurs. By the 1780s such merchant-farmers figured among the top 15 percent of village taxpayers. Middlemen, seeking refuge from the vagaries of the cloth trade, had begun to look to grain production and the grain trade as a viable alternative.

Other merchants, however, continued to sell linens, and Jean Baptiste Pigou and Léonard Delacourt had dealings with the Cambrai merchants Philippe Caramiaux and Augustin Broutin, respectively, while Charles Antoine Pigou and Pierre Antoine Hocquet accumulated debts in nearby Clary and Bertry.[59] Many of these merchants were in fact newcomers to Montigny. Jean Baptiste Lantier the Elder and Thomas Prévôt had come from Clary, the Rousseaus from Bertry, the clerk Jean François Mora, whose descendants would sell cloth during the Revolution, from Brimeux. Etienne Lesage, who married Jean Pierre Lantier's widowed sister, and Jean François Levesque were born in Beauvois; the flax merchant Charles Huguet came from a village near Coutances in Normandy; Charles Antoine Dubois from Prémont; Jean Pierre Lantier's son-in-law, the clerk Pierre Antoine Hocquet, from Reumont; the Cauchys from Fontaine-au-Pire; the laboureur Claude Cardon from Cattenières; the Gueurys from Inchy; the list goes on.

Only a few had come with their families. The others found local brides and settled in the village. On the whole, they married well. Jean Baptiste Lantier may only have set his sights on the daughter of the weaver Pierre Delacourt, but his son married into the Allart clan of prosperous traders, and his daughter married a member of the local Malesieux family of laboureurs. Widowed young, she remarried with the merchant-weaver Etienne Lesage and, when he died, with Dominique Ego, who became mayor of the village. The clerk Pierre Antoine Hocquet joined this group with his marriage to Jean Pierre Lantier's daughter in 1786.

By the 1780s a group of merchant-weavers had emerged to challenge the Lantiers, although none would manage to re-create as large a business. Their comparative rise was mirrored in taxation records. They owned more land for one thing. This phenomenon was already evident in the 1777 *capitation* (head tax); Jean Pierre Lantier paid twice the average contribution, but Marie Anne Leclercq (the widow Boursier), Thomas Prévôt, Jean Baptiste Faré, and Charles Antoine Dubois surpassed him.[60] Not all of them were successful: Druon Ruol and Charles Dubois failed before the end of the decade—although the first would rebound during the Revolution.

In 1796 six merchants appeared on the roll of forced revolutionary contributions from the village's elite.[61] They were Dominique Ego, Philippe Cauchy, Jean Baptiste Rousseau, Louis and Ignace Denimal, and Pierre Antoine Hocquet. The only evidence of their occupation comes from the title of cloth merchants that they consistently put down in the registers of the état civil. These entries cannot always be trusted, however. Pierre Ignace Denimal, who appeared as a négociant (wholesaler) in 1793, was called a mere mulquinier several months later.[62] In Thermidor II he was still a weaver, but a négociant once more in 1796, although he once again resumed his old occupation of weaver.[63] Both of his sons became négociants in Valenciennes, a title that seems more significant within the urban context.

The 1796 list demonstrates a shift in the body of merchants marked by the appearance of new names such as the Denimals or Rousseaus and later, the Moras. The volatility of the cloth trade and the hardships of the last years of the Ancien Régime account for this turnover.

Competition and the Free Market Economy

The complex, unregulated pattern that prevailed in the countryside allowed weavers to rise and prosper in an era of easy credit, but even in the best of cases, competition could not be stretched ad infinitum. Some were bound to lose. Individualism ruled. Although merchants formed companies, little of the corporate feeling noted in craft and agricultural milieux seemed to penetrate this group. There is no evidence of weavers and merchants rushing to each other's aid in times of trouble (as did the farmers) and no overt manifestation of confraternity among country middlemen. Textile interests may have been forcefully defended by close-knit groups of urban merchants congregated in chambers of commerce, but at the lower levels, competition was so rife that it was every man for himself. Bankruptcy could be resolved by extending terms of payment, yet this speaks less of humanitarian concern or even of solidarity than of practical considerations. What emerged among those who traded regularly and frequented urban markets could take the form of mutual recognition and potential trust and respect, but not of formal coalition. Removed from the mutual support that farmers or urban guild members could count on, the merchant-weaver could rely only on his wits.

The very nature of the occupation induced an independence that contrasted with the solidarities of old. There still remained the steady employers: farmers who remained united (even if they often quarreled) and careful of their clienteles of farm laborers and local seasonal labor, for such arrangements suited them for the greater part of the century. Even in periods of recession, they had to contend with communal rights. Merchant-weavers functioned outside the realm of traditional obligations and acquired prerogatives, although it was obviously in their interest to nurture some bonds and secure a regular work force. Their aim, however, remained to provide work when they could and to reduce such commitments in times of crisis. They could only improve their own position at the expense of others: independent men whom they rendered dependent on their services, or dependent weavers whom they seduced away from others.

The merchant-weavers of the late eighteenth century were experiencing the full effects of the free market economy. Their status and their

trading activities were not controlled, even if they met with some constraints when they reached the town. In the countryside, production and
trade were unregulated. Merchants could bind the weavers through
advances and assurances of employment, but these could be provided
just as easily by competitors, and fears that workers would be lured away
(*débauchés*) haunted employers. They had no means of protecting themselves. They could only hope to secure the trust and loyalty of the
weavers or of their fellow merchants even as they repeatedly broke them
themselves. In the towns, guild regulations created contractual obligations that could be evaded in the countryside. This had been one of the
attractions of rural putting out. But it nurtured often intolerable levels of
uncertainty, all the more so in the 1780s when easy credit brought in a
string of new competitors. The result was to drive some merchants away
from the trade and into farming. It also brought a demand for regulation
that would be echoed by the barrage of legislation that protected large-
scale producers in the nineteenth century at the same time that it reduced
the workers' independence.

The pyramid of credit toppled repeatedly: in the 1760s, the 1770s,
and again in the late 1780s. War and the consequent decline in exports in
the late 1750s had led to overstocking and underselling by merchants.
Poor flax crops had simultaneously raised the price of yarn so that the
weavers were caught between the high price of raw materials and the low
returns for their labor. By 1760, as mentioned, the situation reached crisis
proportions.

While the end of hostilities improved the economic climate, Cambrai
continued to suffer from the prohibition of French linens in England, and
other towns had to contend with the competition of itinerant merchants.
In 1770, for example, Crommelin attributed the latest run of bankruptcies and the drop of trade to their activities.[64] A period of prosperity, based on the popularity of linens, followed, broken only in the late
1780s when similar overstocking recurred. This overproduction had
been spurred by unreasonable expectations from the free trade treaty that
France signed with England in 1786, when local producers presumed a
huge increase in the sale of linens. What happened instead was that the
French market was flooded with cheap English cottons. Wholesalers
were stuck with huge stocks of unsold cloth, which they disposed of at a
loss. These reduced takings and losses brought on a spate of bankruptcies
in 1788 and 1789.

If rural industry did not establish new bonds, it did not extinguish old
ties. The weaver as peasant still recognized age-old loyalties: he fought for

land, for his communal rights, and the community as a whole still represented such collective agrarian interests. Industrial production, however, remained a private concern that the community did not regulate. In 1760 the Estates charged the curés to evaluate the damage caused by the crisis. It was a matter of charitable concern rather than one of state policy.

The prerevolutionary industrial crisis, however, brought about calls for government intervention. Such sentiments were voiced by municipalities which up to that point had restricted their interventions to agrarian concerns. A statement in December 1790 by the authorities of Fontaine-au-Pire is most revealing:

> The production of linens and gazes . . . is the sole business in our village and it has been greatly disrupted by the all too frequent bankruptcies that have ruined the majority of manufacturers. We have ceaselessly asked, *as we did already in the cahiers de doléances* that this be remedied by a number of precautions that could be taken limiting the extent of the business that each individual should be entitled to undertake, and by making examples of bankrupts and all those who become insolvent. [my emphasis][65]

The prerevolutionary crisis elicited this appeal to limit competition. The local *cahier,* registering popular grievances, had called for the same measures.[66] Montigny's solution to its economic woes combined old and new measures.

> . . . Some experts from Valenciennes in Hainaut were brought in by the former seigneur and marquis of Walincourt to dig on his land and they claimed to have discovered coal deposits. We believe that it would be useful for the canton to establish one or several coal pits on the said territory for the profit of the state. . . .
>
> The work that is most profitable for the canton is the production of linens and the spinning of flax as well as its cultivation and we ask that the government provide subsidies to support these given that the bankruptcies that have multiplied in recent times have weakened this production considerably and have rendered many weavers incapable of pursuing their activities so that they have had to fire their workers.[67]

Mid-eighteenth-century Montigny saw the development of a full-blown credit system. Linen merchants ceased to depend on stocks of hard cash, and even ceased to rely on land as collateral for their loans. In the heady atmosphere of the 1770s and early 1780s, they raised capital simply on the basis of expectations and on their larger reputations.

The widespread use of credit notes, created, bartered, or discounted with the greatest of ease in even tiny villages like Montigny, had permitted a flurry of activity. Yet, if the time had seemed ripe for new merchant-weavers to prosper, the individual share of the pie would have to be smaller than the one afforded Lantier in earlier decades when entry into the trade demanded sounder assets and a more established reputation. Where some might succeed, others would be unable to overcome the uncertainties, the slow returns, the lack of control over output and foreign sales. Competition and overproduction eventually burst the bubble of credit and ended the boom. The prosperity of the early 1780s turned into the prerevolutionary crisis. Some merchants survived, others went bankrupt and returned to weaving, others turned away from the trade and invested in land.

11

Revolution in the Village

The Revolution came to the village as to the rest of France in the midst of economic hardships. The harvest had failed, commercial bankruptcies had multiplied, industrial work was scarce. The rural community looked forward to changes, and its responses to the Revolution were at first positive and even enthusiastic. Then, the fiscal burdens increased, the requisitions of men and supplies became continual, the villages' priests were taken from them; the peasants' acts grew suspect—the border was so close and fear of treason rampant—and they grew tired and disillusioned. The story is not new, its every stage amply described by the great historian of the region, Georges Lefebvre.

For Lefebvre, the peasants had become politicized in the last phases of the Old Regime. They resented the seigneurs and the fiscal burdens they imposed, all the more so since the seigneurs, desperate for income, had become more diligent in collecting dues and had reestablished some that had fallen into disuse. There had been similar conflicts between Montigny and the Chapter over a number of communal properties. Lefebvre also argued that the peasants' resentment of the regime stemmed from their desperate desire for land. He ascribed the agrarian crisis to a combination of Malthusian and political factors: population growth had led to increased fragmentation of property; a series of vexatious taxes and dues reduced what modest living peasants could eke out from their meager and insufficient parcels of land. Conditions worsened as prices and rents rose. From precarious at best, the situation of the peasantry became hopeless, and many turned to begging. Gloomy prospects deepened resentments and led to the rural revolts of 1789 and the peasants' determination to get land during the Revolution.

They managed to do so, with varying degrees of success. Lefebvre concluded that in the Nord the peasantry acquired more biens nationaux than the bourgeoisie, although, in fact, the data are inconclusive. He also estimated that one-third of the thirty thousand peasant buyers were new owners.[1] Altogether peasants gained more in the southern half of the department than in the north, partly because there were more ecclesiastical properties for sale but essentially because of their resolve to get land. Communities united to bid for available properties and to keep away outside buyers. The south, therefore, became a model of peasant activism contrasted to a more sluggish and quiescent north. Nonetheless, the Revolution did not resolve the agrarian crisis, as far as Lefebvre was concerned. As such, it disappointed peasant hopes. The Revolution was successful, however, in eliminating the tithes and seigneurial dues that had so constrained the peasantry. At that level, therefore, it won their allegiance. All in all, the balance sheet was more negative than positive. The abolition of feudalism and the purchase of biens nationaux rallied the peasantry to the new bourgeois order, but the revolutionary regime's fiscal pressures as well as its economic, religious, and military measures alienated them in the end.

The account of the eighteenth century I have been proposing shows that Lefebvre overstated the peasants' desire for land. He dismissed rural industry as merely the agency of further pauperization, and read what he saw as the peasant program during the Revolution back into the *longue durée*. The example of Montigny shows that the peasants had actually found alternative, viable forms of income in cottage industry. The pre-revolutionary crisis created an obsession with land, among all strata of the peasantry, that had become dormant in the period of industrial prosperity. The peasants had willingly abandoned farming and turned to weaving and trading. In the 1780s the need to create landed assets and the insecurities of commercial enterprise encouraged merchant-weavers to invest in land and take farming seriously once again. The Revolution offered them a golden opportunity to continue this process. For the poorer weaving peasants, the industrial crisis and their sudden under-employment reminded them of the advantages of a plot of land. When nationalized property came up for sale, they formed village-wide consortia that attempted to win each of them a parcel. On the whole, however, the small peasant was not successful in his search for land. The real winners were the village's merchant elite.

Other aspects of the Revolution pushed in the same directions. The region had to face the disarray and collapse of its commercial networks. Although much of the process is obscured by war, emigration, and the absence of notarial records, by the Napoleonic period a new system had been put into place that depended heavily on the towns and left middle-men little maneuverability. There was no place in the new organization for independent rural entrepreneurship, and this too made land an attractive alternative.[2]

The Revolution also had political repercussions. The village community had always been alert to rifts among its members. A prolonged lawsuit with Caudry brought out the different interests of farmers and peasants and the realization that village councils could pursue policies inimical to the rest of the villagers. The village had also witnessed conflicts between weavers and local merchants, among farmers, between priest and parish. The Revolution turned these dissensions into formal political alignments. The village began by rejecting its Old Regime rulers and voting in a new council. As the Revolution became more radical, so did its choice of local representatives. Whether the changes were spurred from within or imposed from without, they solidified into parties and programs, dividing patriots from traitors, "citizens" from "aristocrats," and as suspicion mounted, one inhabitant from the other and one village from the next. What had begun as a celebration of unity disintegrated into a confusion of interests and finally gave way to retreat and depoliticization.

The Course of Events

The Revolution would dramatically underline the extent of the village's awareness of, and responsiveness to, outside events.[3] This was not a new phenomenon, and at some points during the Old Regime, Montigny and Caudry had been able to manipulate the legal system. Echoes of the Enlightenment can be found in the names given to children in the 1780s. There was a general move away from saints' names to such female names as Amélie, Clotilde, Caroline, Désirée, Delphine, Julie, Rose, Sophie, and Victoire that would prevail in the next century, and for boys, less variety but a departure from the Pierres, Josephs, and Jean Baptistes to Constant, Clément, Amable, and Benoît. There was some interest in the ancients with such names as Appoline, Sylvine, Justine, or Auguste, but none as striking as that of Jules César, given to the infant son of the local cotton merchant Jean Pierre Gueury in January 1788.

We know little of the early phases of the Revolution in the village, except for an eagerness to play at soldiering as 110 local citizens joined the newly created regiments of national guard. The Revolution had divided the male population into active and passive citizens based on their fiscal contributions, but three-quarters of Montigny's households passed muster and were entitled both to participate in the national guard and to vote. In December 1789 the villagers elected a new municipal council.[4] The new administration consisted of merchant-farmers, such as Pierre Ignace Boursier, and merchants and weavers, such as Jean Baptiste Gave, Philippe Cauchy, and Charles Antoine Labbé.[5] This was a straightforward rejection of the Ego-Hocquet-Lantier network that had ruled the village in the past decade, bringing to power members of the other trading nexus. Half of the council was replaced annually, but it was not until 1793 that some of the old guard reappeared. Dominique Ego and Pierre Antoine Hocquet were included in a new council consisting of a younger group of weavers and the mayor, Alexandre Cocu, a négociant who speculated in biens nationaux and who had married the daughter of a local linen merchant, Jacques Michel Renard. This group remained in charge until December 1794 when the authorities deemed both Cocu and Ego unfit (because they never attended meetings) and recommended that Charles Antoine Labbé become the new mayor.[6]

In 1792 the municipal council, then led by the same Labbé, had tried to resign, "given that it was daily disrupted by threats and other unpleasantness."[7] The district authorities rejected this plea, declaring instead that "all the residents of the said locality would be advised to respect their elected officials and to obey existing laws."[8] One of the council's outspoken opponents had been the clerk and schoolmaster Pierre Antoine Hocquet. A month earlier, he had declared in the local pub "that half of the council were no better than scoundrels and thieves and other such nonsense."[9] The purchase of biens nationaux may have been behind such denunciations as different groups in the village competed for land, some led by the council and another faction by Hocquet. Religious tensions were also coming to the fore. Labbé and the council had attempted to purge Hocquet and the two female teachers in the village for refusing to swear the oath to the Constitution demanded of clerics and civil servants.[10] Hocquet may have capitulated, since he served on municipal councils for the next five years. The curé himself emigrated, and Montigny was assigned a constitutional priest who served a number of adjoining communities. Hocquet, although suspected of reactionary sympathies, continued to serve as the village's *agent national* (the official liaison between district authorities and local council), showing an ambiguity in the village's ideological orientation that the government would repeatedly deplore.

The first councils were composed of the farmer-weavers who had risen to prominence in the last decade of the Old Regime. They gave way to poorer weavers in the more radical phases of the Year II, when Jean Baptiste Hutin, Louis François, and François Olivier joined their ranks.[11] The latter became assistant mayor and was described as being illiterate. One may well wonder at the popularity of these councils. In Crèvecoeur, "citizen Jacques Deveaux had the audacity to insult the council, saying that it was composed of ne'er-do-wells, which deprives them of the good name that they so much need among the public."[12]

The municipal elections of 1795 made Jacques Borain the new *agent national,* assisted by Jacques Labbé.[13] The first was a thirty-three-year-old weaver, the second, a twenty-seven-year-old defrocked priest, the son of a local farmer. In 1796 the municipal officers included the same Labbé, and the weavers François Mora (aged thirty-three), Jean Baptiste Hutin (thirty), Louis François (forty), Hocquet, and the farmer and former mayor Pierre Ignace Boursier (sixty-four). Several of these men figured in a report to the minister of the interior assessing local authorities in the canton.[14]

> *Agent:* Labbé, poorly educated, regretting the old days, elected in Germinal, eliminated in fructidor of the Year V.
> *Agent:* Piere Joseph François, patriot, poorly educated, named by the central authorities in accordance with the Fructidor decrees.[15]
> *Assistant:* J.-B. Hutin, somewhat educated, good republican, elected in Germinal, eliminated in Fructidor V.

Local administrators in the canton were accused of reactionary sympathies, of harboring émigrés and priests, of abetting deserters, and sanctioning such forbidden acts as the ringing of church bells for religious ceremonies.[16] The more radical municipal council of Walincourt (the cantonal seat) was unpopular, perhaps for sending men to the front rather than for its other political stances. A local soldier, who was home on leave, refused to drink to the health of the council. "He would not raise his glass to the municipality because he didn't give a damn about them and sent them all to hell."[17] In April 1798 the representatives of the village of Ligny were denounced as "the least reputable section, full of *chouans* and fanatics, but they unfortunately have a strong voice since they can count on the support of four other sections in this canton, including the villages of Montigny and Clary. The first has become famous for harboring émigrés, and the second for its uprisings of the third to the sixth of Thermidor of the Year IV and for its fanaticism . . . since the inhabitants still sing the Christmas mass. . . ."[18]

In the shuffle that ensued, the government named what it hoped would be more loyal representatives, and Benoit Delhaye (a thirty-five-year-old weaver) and Pascal Pigou (a weaver and clerk, aged twenty-seven) became Montigny's *agent* and *adjoint,* respectively. In 1798 these positions were held by Jean François Mora and Jacques Michel Stievenard, two weavers with "doubtful republican sentiments."[19] In February 1799, renewed suspicion of local administrators brought further changes, and Pierre François and Pascal Pigou obtained those same posts.[20] In September and October 1799 the area's republican loyalties were still being questioned when the Napoleonic coup cut short such inquiries. We have no way of telling how these externally imposed changes were received in the village and to what extent they affected its life. Some evidence of ideological opposition between pro-Revolutionary and counter-Revolutionary groups occasionally surfaces. We know that some local administrations were slow to respond to the war efforts, while others were at least more careful to toe the line. We also know that the villagers grew suspicious of their farmers and denounced at least one, Joseph Petit, to the district authorities. The records of the justices of the peace as well as the registers of the district authorities give good indications of popular sentiments in this region. They reveal in particular the confusion brought about by war and invasion.

If some of the villagers abetted "reaction," primarily out of religious zeal, others readily showed a revolutionary fervor. In 1794 Montigny offered the district its church ornaments—which an earlier administration had knowingly safeguarded by declaring that there were none—and "a cartful of hay to feed the horses of the brave defenders of the Republic."[21] With the Austrians at their gate, "two citizens from the village of Montigny reported that they had pushed the enemy back and requested a detachment of fifty cavalrymen that they offered to feed at their own cost."[22] Yet the community was not united in supporting the republican side, and a number of people fled or emigrated, including the three major farmers: Milot, Petit, and Tamboise, along with a weaver, Mora, and the local *desservant,* the juring priest, Roy. War and pillage, as opposing armies swarmed through the region, and levies of men and of monies, had rendered the farmers' situation difficult. Yet when they retreated, it was toward enemy lines. "Jacques François Milot, farmer at Le Troncquoy, in the canton of Walincourt, near Cambrai, explains that after having groaned for several months under the cruel treatment of the enemies who invaded his village, and lacking the strength to withstand their excesses any longer, he took his family to the town of Le Cateau and then to Valenciennes, both of which had been invaded so that he could not make his way to the interior."[23] Milot's land and equipment were seized and put up for sale, but he managed to convince the authorities of his good faith and was back in the village in November 1794 (Frimaire III).[24] Since his farm had been nationalized, he had to lease it from the government until his name was removed from the list of suspects several years later. The widow Tamboise also left the village for a brief period but returned to Le Troncquoy, which she continued to farm until her death in 1821. One of her daughters was arrested on 2 Thermidor II, accused of emigration. She was released two weeks later.[25] Joseph Petit, the third Troncquoy farmer, took the greatest gamble. He joined the national guard and became a secretary in Dumouriez's army. When the general switched camps, Petit followed suit.[26] He remained suspect many years after he returned to the village[27] and was not granted an amnesty until July 1802. It can only be surmised that relations with neighbors who viewed him as a traitor remained quite strained, and the Petit family left the village soon after.[28] One local inhabitant actually became a victim of the Terror, conducted under the aegis of the Parisian representative Joseph Lebon. The Chapter's old gamekeeper was guillotined for keeping his old uniform. He was seventy-six.[29]

Worsening economic conditions and increasing governmental exactions fueled a general discontent and uncertainty that could only be exacerbated once the region became a battlefield. "The same delegation declares that the young men of the village of Montigny who were part of the first requisition have still not gone to the cantonal headquarters, because the enemy has threatened to burn the village if they did."[30] The presence of enemy troops gave a new twist to local antagonisms as in the village of Caullery: "Vitou is a traitor to the homeland, an ally of Cobourg . . . who has declared that he gave his watch, a silk stocking, and other objects to the ferocious Austrians. He also had the audacity to go to Cambrai to get the enemy money and we believe that he is a scoundrel since, as we will show, he even urged several members of this village to give their money to the enemy."[31] The accused explained that the community had asked him to take some requisitioned carts to Solemnes "because the enemy was holding Auguste Mairesse hostage there," and he was freed from any accusation of wrongdoing.

On 7 May 1794 a battle between the French and the army of the prince of Saxe-Cobourg took place in Caudry on the spot known as La Ramette. Montigny claimed losses totaling 72,460 livres 12 sous "caused by the pillage of the tyrants coalesced against our Republic."[32] They received 4,000 livres as compensation.[33]

Some municipal councils were accused of collaborating with the enemy, and of wreaking vengeance on the patriots.[34] Others were denounced for cowardice: "When public clamours announced the arrival of the Austrians . . . they abandoned their stations to protect their belongings" and so allowed the cavalry to make off with the village's cattle.[35] War pitted one villager against another as in Esnes where a widow blamed a surgeon for her recent loss: "now you're happy, you miserable man, you led the enemies to my husband, if I had a gun, I would kill you."[36] It also heightened the climate of violence. A drunkard and his son knifed a woman, shouting: "Let's kill, let's kill, after all, there's a war on!" (tuons, tuons, morbleu, il est la guerre).[37]

The farmers, who had been the victims of endless levies, hoarded grain in hopes of greater profits and defied the government-imposed maxima on prices.

> Today, this eleventh of Frimaire, the guard arrested two individuals . . . who were carting flour to Clary and Walincourt, areas with which the enemy has daily contacts. We called out to them to tell us where they had gotten the flour, and they told us that they had bought it from Simon Le Roy, a farmer and miller in Banteux, for the price of 18 livres a men-caud. . . .
>
> The general council of this commune denounces Simon Le Roy as a hoarder and as a man who would bring famine and chaos to the Republic (la famine et la zizanie) . . . and orders that he be taken to the local house of arrest to suffer the penalties sanctioned by the law.[38]

The farmers bore the brunt of local antagonism in a climate of general deprivation and unrest.

> Citizen Marie Madelaine Marlier, widow of Thomas Desenne testified that on the 21st of this month at about four o'clock in the evening, citizen Pierre Manfrois, who was in the barn while she was measuring the grain she owed her harvesters, told her that she wouldn't need any bags, that the grain there would be enough for him and the others, and when she told him that she needed some for her workers the said Manfrois said that even if I'm guillotined for this, I need some, meaning that he would have struck her and that in order to avoid a worse fate she found herself forced to give him part of what she owed her workers.[39]

In Ventôse of the Year II, a Lesdain farmer was called a "scoundrel and an aristocrat," but he retorted that "no aristocrat would have given up going to mass or would have given over his horses and carts to serve the Republic."[40] Such new threats rolled easily off the tongue as the villagers learned to associate opulence with counterrevolutionary leanings. Thus in the same month, yet another inhabitant of Lesdain was called a "scoundrel who deserved to be guillotined."[41]

Such radical outbursts would be short-lived. While the weaver councils of the Years II and III denounced the farmers with greater and lesser success, their opponents were returning to power, where they would stay for more than a century. In Montigny, the list of mayors chosen by the prefecture from the Consulate until the 1920s was dominated by the major farmers, led by the Milots and Tamboises. Jacques François Milot acted as the village's mayor between 1802 and 1810, when his son succeeded him. A conservative and hierarchical state machine replaced not only the more radical experimentation of the Revolution, but also the Ancien Régime structure in which conflicts between royal and seigneurial authorities meant that local complaints often got a sympathetic hearing. It also reinstated the major landowners to a powerful position, one they had held in the early eighteenth century before the farmer-mayors had been replaced by the merchant-weavers. This stemmed partly from the ideological bias of the Restoration, which counted on the support of landowners, but also expressed the retreat of local merchants. The Ancien Régime traders had either left Montigny or joined the farming elite, principally by purchasing nationalized property.

The Sale of Biens Nationaux

While war and deprivation wreaked havoc in the region, pitting citizen against citizen, the sale of biens nationaux appeared to generate widespread enthusiasm and communal cooperation. Yet the process could prove just as divisive, as one group of local purchasers vied against another. Moreover, not all of the peasants were able to acquire or to hold on to their shares of land. Before assessing their gains, however, it will be useful to review the process of purchase in this village and others.

Overall, the clerical property seized by the Constituent Assembly and auctioned off to the population as a way of resolving the state's financial crisis represented about 10 percent of French soil.[42] In Cambrésis the proportion was much higher, since ecclesiastics had owned 40 percent of the land. Between 1791 and 1800, 191.1 hectares were sold in Montigny, the bulk, 159.2 hectares, consisting of clerical lands, and the balance, seized émigré properties. The local peasantry managed to acquire 60 percent of the plots. The remainder went to nonresidents, some of them urban rentiers who had owned very little property in these southeastern villages prior to the Revolution.[43] They farmed out the properties to local residents. In Caudry 811.2 hectares became available, representing three-quarters of its territory, and 93 percent passed to the peasantry.

Table 41.   Land Purchased by Peasants During the Revolution

Village	Number of hectares sold	Hectares of clerical land	Village area (%)	Land sold/bought (%)	Village area (%)
Montigny	191.1	159.2	27	60	38*
Audencourt	45.4	37.9	17	51	10
Bertry	442.5	342.8	40	39	20
Caudry	811.2	806.0	75	93	71
Caullery	152.2	151.5	61	100	61
Clary	600.2	565.6	57	83	50
Ligny	113.1	103.6	12	87	11
Troisvilles	346.7	141.4	17	72	30

*This corrects Lefebvre's figure of 20 percent.
Source: Lefebvre, *Paysans du Nord*, appendices IV and XVII.

Montigny offered proportionally less land for sale than most of its immediate neighbors. The purchase by the local population of 60 percent of
biens nationaux surpassed, however, the departmental average of 52
percent, but was lower than that for Cambrésis, which rose above 80
percent (table 41).

Analysis of the sale of biens nationaux forms the heart of Georges
Lefebvre's study of the peasants of the Nord.[44] He perused every available
document and, luckily, deposited his notes in the departmental archives.
Since some of the records he consulted were destroyed during World
War I, his jottings are invaluable to the modern researcher.[45] The notes
show that Montigny followed the pattern discerned by Lefebvre for the
region: the inhabitants coalesced to request groups of parcels; foreign
invasion then interrupted the sales, and recognized speculators acquired
the leftover plots during the Directorate. These latter-day buyers of
Montigny property included such well-known figures as Claro and Vardon from Douai and Lille.[46]

The villagers formed a number of associations to bid for local plots.
These coalitions were typical of Cambrésis, partly because the peasants
seemed determined to gain access to land but also, most likely, because
they were used to collective action and to the claims on property devolv-
ing from mauvais gré.[47] As early as December 1790 a group of weavers,
small farmers, and the wholesale merchant Pierre Eloi Cocu, then resident in the village, requested 88¾ mencaudées.[48] Most of the bidders sat
on the village council, and there is no explanation as to why they

restricted themselves to so few tenancies. In this first period of sales, lots were auctioned by leaseholds, although bids on parts were entertained as long as the offers surpassed the amount proposed for the entire unit. In this case, the consortium requested just that section of La Trappe farmed by the widow Mairesse, an outsider from Caullery, as well as the thirty mencaudées attached to the Chapter's mill (again farmed by a nonresident from Clary) and smaller lots including the curé's portion. Although the application was completed in due form and mentioned the leases that formed the basis of the price evaluation, it was replaced by a second, more comprehensive bid in April 1791. This time the association was led by Jean Baptiste Lantier, Hilarion Denoyelle (member of the council), and once again the merchant Pierre Eloi Cocu. This second submission included a flat estimate of fifty livres per mencaudée (rather than submitting the relevant documents), and this may have been considered preposterously low and therefore rejected out of hand as illegal "monopoly," for that bid too was unsuccessful.[49] In the 1780s a mencaudée had been worth an average of six hundred livres.

A more fruitful attempt followed in 1792 when Pierre Antoine Hocquet, Dominique Ego, Jean Baptiste Delbart, and Alexandre Cocu purchased 102 mencaudées belonging to the abbey of Cantimpré, for 13,970 livres (or 175 livres a mencaudée—that is, very near the average of 180 livres for which biens nationaux sold in the district).[50] We do not know how much of that property went to its farmer, Jean Baptiste Labbé, who did not bid independently for the property, unlike the other branch of Labbé farmers who purchased their portion of the estate. In 1793 François Labbé bought the 18 mencaudées of abbatial property that he farmed for 3,141 livres 12 sous, that is, for the same unit price of 175 livres.[51] The Labbés did not emigrate and suffered heavy losses during the invasion. Both sides of the family would continue to farm during and after the Revolution.

The same consortium had also hoped to buy the Chapter's 155.5 mencaudées and the eighteen of the All Saints Chapel, but in fact it only secured the Cantimpré property, the priest's portion (belonging to the abbey of Honnecourt), and the Guillemains' thirty mencaudées.[52] Once again we find no farmers taking part in the bid. The farmers of Le Troncquoy confined themselves to the farms that had belonged to the abbey of Anchin. In May 1791 its 174 hectares were auctioned off, and the farmers acquired two-thirds.[53] They showed no interest in La Trappe, probably because it was not a compact estate and consisted instead of dispersed fields. They may have put pressure on the villagers or the authorities to desist from bidding on the Chapter's farm, but we have no direct knowledge of such acts.

The Montigny consortium also bid for parcels in Clary, and here an actual account of the auction exists.[54] Parcel Nos. 17 and 18, measuring 1 and 1.5 mencaudées, respectively, were available either individually or jointly. Since no one wanted them separately, the auction proceeded on both parcels. They had been adjudicated provisionally at 120 livres to the Lambert Claisse association of Clary, a group that had requested and purchased vast tracts of land in that village. The final bidding went as follows:

Pierre Antoine Hocquet (Montigny):	265 livres
Jean Jacques Poulet (Clary):	280 livres
Pierre Antoine Hocquet (Montigny):	300 livres

Hocquet and his Montigny associates obtained the plots for that sum. They provided a 12 percent deposit of 36 livres. That same day the Claisse group acquired a lot consisting of about 4 mencaudées (also in Clary), that no one contested, for 750 livres. Then another 1.25 mencaudées passed to the Hocquet group.[55]

For Lefebvre's notes it appears that two associations were functioning simultaneously in Montigny. They purchased plots that they divided among a number of shareholders, some of whom then resold their shares. Thus, between December 1792 and May 1793 Jean Baptiste Lantier bought 4 small shares for 25 livres and another for 30 livres; the Cocus purchased 6 shares (all of about 1 mencaudée) for 40 to 300 livres; the Wibails from Preux-au-Bois got 7 mencaudées, some for 22 and others for 40 livres; and the last buyer, another nonresident, Pierre Malesieux, paid more dearly—between 200 and 560 livres—for his 13 in what was then, however, debased currency.[56] Not all villagers, then, were either able or interested in holding on to their parcels. Some of the local grievances against the village council in this period may have related to the sale and resale of biens nationaux, and it may be no coincidence that the consortium headed by Hocquet, Ego, and Cocu regained power in this period.

Once the Austrians had been repulsed, land sales resumed, and on 12 Thermidor III (July 1795) the community, represented by Antoine Mora, Charles Antoine Labbé, and Toussaint Charlet, once again bid for the Chapter's farm. Jean Baptiste Hutin (another member of the council) entered a similar application a week later.[57] The district authorities

Table 42. Bids for Biens Nationaux in Montigny

		Properties (in mencaudées)					
Bid	Date	Chapter	Anchin	Cantimpré	Honnecourt	Guillemains	All Saints Chapel
I.	Dec. 1790	70.54		6.25	9.00		3.0
II.	Apr. 1791	154.25	12.25	11.00	32.75	30.0	16.5
III.	Aug. 1792 and Dec. 1792	155.50					18.0
IV.	July 1795	129.00					
V.	July 1795	200.00					

Source: 1Q95, 124-6.

considered the latter a "good citizen," and he still held on to that reputation in 1797 when he was deemed a "good republican."[58] Nevertheless, both his bid and that of the village council failed (table 42).

Part of the Chapter's farm of La Trappe was eventually bought by Pierre Eloi Cocu in 1796. He had left Montigny for Valenciennes, and, although he called himself a wholesale merchant, his main activity was trading in biens nationaux.[59] By then, sales took place in Douai near Lille, which explains why so many parcels fell into the hands of speculators. In 1797 Jacques François Milot, the Ancien Régime farmer, was described as the farm's previous occupier, and only subsequent sales at the end of the decade reveal the extent to which the Chapter's old property had been dismembered.[60] Milot had apparently continued to farm the land until his emigration. In July 1793 he tried to defer the "rent payments he owes the Republic since he counts among its creditors."[61] Given that he owned part of Le Troncquoy—hence his advances to the state—the lease must have concerned the Chapter's old farm. He may actually have intended to purchase those plots and thus blocked municipal bids, but there is no indication to that effect.

After he decamped, the property was subdivided. Some of the new owners represented the new breed of farmers, like the merchant and former mayor Pierre Ignace Boursier or the former cartwright François Wibail. Another beneficiary, Jean Baptiste Labbé, had previously leased the bulk of the Cantimpré farm, purchased by the municipality (and subdivided), and had relocated to what was considered more fertile ground.

Religious scruples may have played a part in delaying the sale of local parish property, for the 41.5 mencaudées attracted only an outside buyer,

Delbeque Castel of Lille, who obtained them for 80,000 livres in the summer of 1798.[62] The farm of La Bruyère, measuring 82 mencaudées, was sold in the same period to Cocu, for 34,600 livres.[63]

Except for the farm of La Bruyère and five mencaudées owned by one Marianne Denimal, who fled in the Year II, no other émigré property was put up for sale in Montigny. Although the three farmers of Le Troncquoy emigrated and the government seized their land, they returned in time to claim it. In fact, had Lefebvre realized that Le Troncquoy, which he listed separately, belonged to Montigny, he would have concluded that local inhabitants obtained 38 percent of the village's surface.

The peasants acquired land in three ways. The community purchased blocks, which it then redistributed among various "shareholders." The villagers also bought a number of parcels directly and obtained others secondhand either from fellow residents or from speculators. The latter did not hoard their bounty.[64] Their purpose was, of course, to resell it at a profit. We know the way in which some Lille and Douai buyers disposed of Montigny property. Claeyssens sold 1.5 hectares that had belonged to the Chapter to Auguste Ledoux of Le Cateau in 1807. Vardon and Vasseur bought Montigny's church on behalf of Etienne Taine of Ligny in 1799, and the same partners sold four mencaudées that had once belonged to the Chapel of All Saints to another speculator, Claude Pavy of Vaux-en-Arrouaise.[65] A speculator, who had once resided in Montigny (Pierre Eloi Cocu), resold Montigny's windmill to Pierre Joseph Carez of Valenciennes.[66] When he obtained the seigneurie of La Bruyère in the fall of 1798, he declared that he had bought half on behalf of a certain Delacharbonnay.[67] In 1797 he had acquired eleven hectares that had belonged to the Chapter, which he passed on to a group of Cambrai merchants with whom he was associated.[68] That same conglomerate returned La Bruyère to its original owner, Adrien Mairesse, and may well have sold other plots to Montigny residents.[69]

In 1806 the speculator Claro went bankrupt, and the eleven hectares that he owned in Montigny became liable to forced auction. The prefect intervened because the ownership of the plots was contested.[70] Cocu had purchased a number, but another individual by the name of Renaud had acquired some of the same properties in 1800, although that second sale had been invalidated a year later.[71] The eventual fate of the village's largest leasehold therefore remains somewhat uncertain. It eventually may have fallen into the hands of Desrochers, a rentier from Douai who then moved to Paris, and who, according to the village's land register of 1854, owned nearly twenty-four hectares in Montigny.[72]

The village representatives bought at least 132 mencaudées. These had belonged to the abbeys of Cantimpré and to the Guillemains of Notre-Dame of Walincourt. It is not known how the plots were redistributed, but the region offered two models, one of equal and the other of unequal partitioning. The contract that the notary Leducq drew for a Bertry society in December 1791 involved a number of unequal shares.[73] These ranged from 1 to 150 mencaudées and made up a total of 450.5 mencaudées. The names of nine of the fifty-two associates who were allowed to bid were listed separately, and a special note was attached stating that the one woman, Elisabeth Labalette, had clearly understood this restriction! In Saint-Hilaire, however, a similar society stipulated that all participants, including the major farmer, would receive an equal share priced according to the quality of the soil.[74]

Excluding Le Troncquoy, the peasants acquired 29 percent of Montigny's surface. At the end of the Old Regime, these same peasants had owned between 30 percent and 40 percent of the soil. The Revolution nearly doubled that amount. Since all of the farms except for Le Troncquoy were dismembered, the benefit to the small farmers was impressive. For there is no doubt that they benefited the most from the redistribution of land. They not only purchased parcels but also farmed the biens nationaux owned by nonresidents. Of course, weavers also leased some of the plots and some clearly gained from the sudden availability of land.[75] While some resold their shares, others mentioned them in dowries that once again included land. A Clary weaver thus declared that he owned one and one-half mencaudées of nationalized property worth five hundred florins when he married in Fructidor II.[76]

The purchase of biens nationaux changed the configuration of the arable. In Montigny the Old Regime pattern of three to four sizable farms and countless tiny plots gave way to a leveling, which left only one estate, Le Troncquoy, more or less intact. The same process was observed throughout the province.[77] The evidence of peasant associations and the modalities of land sales would point that way. Nationalized property sold for a fraction of its value, and the terms of purchase were exceedingly generous. Furthermore, the paper currency used in the payments became so devalued that the buyers profited even more.[78] The government estimated that the poor peasantry could afford a maximum of 500 livres per hectare, and, if some plots sold for less, that is about what the village of Montigny spent on its communal purchase.[79] The 175 livres per mencaudée required a deposit of 14.5 livres, hardly a tremendous sum, even if it had to be made available on the spot.

The fact that the peasants were able to pay tells us something about their condition. While land hunger explains the rush of requests, the prerevolutionary and revolutionary crises had presumably depleted peasant resources. An abundant harvest in 1790 eased some of the pressure, but grain prices were once again rising in 1792 and 1793, alarming food buyers all the more because the industrial recession was in full swing.[80] Yet the rural population of southeastern Cambrésis bought massively— the villages of Caudry or Clary got practically every available plot—and quickly acquitted the full amount. The reappearance of such means might mitigate the catastrophic overtones with which historians have surrounded the prerevolutionary situation. It would at least presume a partial recovery. There is also reason to think that the abolition of tithes and feudal dues, as well as widespread tax evasion, liberated funds that were then invested in land.[81]

Companies were established to supply loans to buyers.[82] Local merchants may have performed a similar function in the villages, and this might explain why men such as Cocu were so prominent in the Montigny associations. Yet whatever the means at hand and whatever the political climate (which at one point facilitated the acquisition of small plots), the peasantry benefited unevenly from communal purchases. The poor, moreover, resold their shares to merchants and farmers. Even Lefebvre, who believed that communal acquisitions established a new society of small landowners, wavered on the fate of the indigent, whom he sometimes described as winners, and at other times as losers in the purchase of biens nationaux. When Lefebvre talks of peasant purchases, he usually refers to "rural dwellers," without specifying income brackets. We are not told how much a poor peasant would have received as opposed to a middling or rich one, although 60 percent of peasant buyers are said to have acquired less than one hectare and another 20 percent between one and five hectares.[83]

Lefebvre often proves hard to pin down. He treats the peasantry sometimes as a block and sometimes as a series of subgroups. These shifting definitions involve a methodological problem since Lefebvre meant to tote up "peasant" as opposed to "bourgeois" gains in the Revolution. Although he placed the major tenant-farmers in a special category—the rural bourgeoisie—in the prerevolutionary period, he included them among the peasantry when writing about peasant purchases of biens nationaux. "If the rural bourgeoisie profited more than *the rest of the peasantry* from the changes in property-holding, the others did, in some sense, get their revenge with the fragmentation of farmsteads."[84] The rural bourgeoisie, however, vanishes when he comes to describe the actual sales: farmers mix with the small tenantry, middling leaseholders, and day laborers in opposition to urban investors.[85] The rural bourgeois have merged with the peasantry to swell that group's achievement vis-à-vis the middle classes. What is more, in order to argue that the peasants acquired twice as much land as the bourgeoisie, Lefebvre disregarded bourgeois purchases of nobiliar property since there was no real "class" transfer: the privileged of old had become part of the "new" bourgeoisie."[86]

In Montigny itself the evidence points less to the "democracy of small landowners" that Lefebvre liked to envisage than to the pattern observed by another historian, Marcel Marion, for the Gironde. There, "the richest peasants benefitted most. The Revolution did not create new landowners as much as increase the amount owned by small proprietors."[87] Indeed, one of the most striking results of the Revolution was the "pastoralization" of the majority of local merchants. François Crouzet coined the term for Bordeaux merchants, but this applies to the Cambrésis plain as well. Some local traders continued their activities during the Revolution, such as the Renards and Denimals, who eventually moved to Valenciennes to sell cloth, or the Moras who acted briefly as linen merchants. Others, who had traded but recently, bought land and became farmers.

In 1796 the revolutionary authorities exacted yet another contribution, a forced donation from the top quarter of taxpayers.[88] Montigny's contingent included eighteen weavers, ten farmers (now called *cultivateurs*), two merchants, four wholesale merchants (négociants), three spinners (widows of merchants), a brewer, and a guard (table 43). The document listed each contributor's estimated capital in preinflationary terms (1790) and indicated his or her current assessment for the two major taxes: on movables and land (*mobilière* and *foncière*). The document may not be fully trustworthy since people such as Jean Baptiste Lantier ranked fairly low despite heavy investments in land. The nomenclature may have been slightly fanciful as well. Whereas Montigny listed four wholesale merchants, Ligny's contributors consisted of seven farmers and eighteen wholesalers, while Clary, with three times the population, reported no wholesale merchants at all.[89] Nevertheless, we can draw a number of conclusions. Several Old Regime merchants (Boursier, Levecque) abandoned trading early in order to farm the plots they had recently purchased. Others continued their activities a while longer (such as the Cauchys or Egos) and a new group of merchants (Denimal, Rousseau) emerged in this period. The size of their property tax, however, indicates that they too had invested in land.

Table 43. Assessments of the Top Thirty-nine Montigny Taxpayers (in livres, sous, deniers)

Name	Occupation	Estimated capital	Taxes	
			Mobilière	*Foncière*
François Milot	farmer	100,000	2.03.00	478.02.04
Widow Tamboise	farmer	50,000	2.03.00	318.03.08
P. A. Bisiaux	farmer	10,000	2.01.07	64.12.11
Ph. Cauchy	wholesaler	10,000	5.04.11	11.13.11
L. Denimal	wholesaler	6,500	2.02.04	1.14.07
J. B. Gave	weaver	4,100	1.18.10	16.03.08
P. A. Tamboise	farmer	4,000	2.06.00	6.07.01
J. B. Rousseau	wholesaler	4,000	4.18.10	11.13.08
P. I. Boursier	farmer	3,050	7.16.02	24.05.03
Ch. Ant. Lenglet	brewer	2,500	2.03.00	12.01.04
P. I. Denimal	wholesaler	2,500	4.17.06	11.07.10
Widow Dron	spinner	2,200	1.18.10	19.10.03
Fr. Wibail	farmer	2,000	1.17.06	16.09.00
Widow Prévôt	spinner	1,600	1.18.10	12.01.01
M. Levecque	farmer	1,600	1.19.07	16.11.03
J. B. Labbé	farmer	1,500	2.03.00	86.02.03
J. B. Lantier	weaver	800	5.05.08	18.09.00
P. J. Delacourt	farmer	600	1.17.06	11.13.04
Fr. Pigou	weaver	500	1.18.10	2.02.05
D. Ego	linen merchant	400	1.17.06	10.08.05
P. Cauchy	weaver	350	1.18.00	7.10.06
J. B. Delbar, Jr.	weaver	350	1.17.06	0.05.04
P. J. Pigou	weaver	300	1.17.06	2.06.01
Fr. Denoyelle	weaver	300	2.03.00	2.03.07
P. François	weaver	300	1.18.02	1.08.06
B. Delhaye	weaver	250	5.05.10	0.08.08
J. B. Delacourt	weaver	250	1.18.10	3.01.10
J. M. Pigou	weaver	250	1.18.02	8.11.07
Widow Delacourt	spinner	200	2.03.00	2.15.04
M. Labbé	weaver	150	1.17.06	8.15.08
J. M. Rousseau	weaver	140	1.17.06	14.05.00
L. Lefebvre	farmer	120	1.19.07	5.18.09
P. A. Hocquet	merchant	120	5.05.10	6.04.10
H. Depré	weaver	80	1.18.10	3.02.01
P. Pigou	weaver	60	5.05.10	4.01.01
J. B. Denoyelle	weaver	50	2.01.07	1.03.00
S. Gallieque	weaver	50	1.19.03	2.10.00
J. Jh. Malesieux	forest guard	50	12.02.06	8.04.09

Source: L1794.

The "pastoralization" process was drawn out, and the Wibails bought the last of the village's biens nationaux in 1821.[90] Some of the merchant-weavers, as mentioned, switched occupations early. Others, including the Gaves, Lantiers, and Rousseaux, who would rank among the village's most prominent farmers in the nineteenth century, continued to trade during the Revolution.[91] This may have reflected the new opportunities, licit and illicit, offered by the outbreak of hostilities. It also indicates the persistence of textile production despite the confusion and the restructuring of old networks that occurred over the decade. Still, a principal result of the Revolution in Montigny was to encourage villagers to return to agriculture by making land available to them. The Montigny that emerged from the Revolution, then, was closer in some ways to the subsistence farming village of 1700 than to the commercial village of 1780.

An Industry in Decline

The prerevolutionary bankruptcies had disrupted textile production in the region and once more perturbed credit and commercial relations. The Revolution brought further uncertainties. The onset of war interrupted foreign sales, and the local luxury market declined as priests and notables emigrated and as cheap cottons became more fashionable than either fine linens or silks. To be sure, many villagers continued to declare that they were weavers and apparently managed to make a living at it. Some were even able to buy land with their savings or earnings. Some merchants also continued in the textile trade. In 1791 the Revolutionary government carried out its first survey of industrial production, and, despite earlier complaints regarding the effects of the recent commercial collapse, the villages described a still vigorous textile sector.[92]

By 1794, however, the situation appeared catastrophic. Village after village told the government that industrial activity was nearly at a standstill.[93] Since the survey meant to assess the maximum on local wages and to requisition clothing for the army, it is not surprising that the response was overwhelmingly negative. Production continued to drop as the number of operating looms fell by one-third between 1789 and 1800.[94] Although this was blamed on the decline in production, the Revolutionary levies also reduced local manpower. Yet many of Montigny's residents continued to weave. The communal registers sometimes called them fine-linen weavers, or mulquiniers, and at other times they were called loom owners or linen loom workers (*ouvriers fabricants à métier* or *mulquiniers fabricants à métier*), but we cannot tell if this reflected a new level of dependency or different types of cloth production. There was no sudden rise in the number of day laborers that would suggest a recourse to agrarian occupations, although it is true that these were now limited to a few remaining large farms. Peaks in mortality in this period attest to a series of hardships. The highest occurred in 1793–94, followed by another in 1819, although a slight rise was noticeable in 1802 as well. The government tried to assist the needy, especially those who had suffered from enemy invasions, but its contributions fell far short of actual losses.[95]

In addition, the disruption of credit and unstable or counterfeit paper currency created an atmosphere of mistrust, perhaps all the more so among people already accustomed to such methods of payment. As *assignats* lost their value, people insisted on being paid in cash. Marriage contracts mentioned "2,400 livres in coin," "3,000 livres in hard cash," and the spread of counterfeit paper notes in the countryside angered the population.[96] "On the first of Pluviôse he went to see Mairesse to return a counterfeit assignat that the latter had given him but Mairesse went wild and tried to hit him with a shovel."[97] In Walincourt, a spinner asked to be paid in cash, not assignats, and in that same village in October 1793 thread was being paid for in both currencies.[98]

Even if the industry had not collapsed completely, payments had become more difficult. The squabbles recorded and mediated by the justices of the peace between 1791 and 1794 recall many earlier complaints of deferred payments for cloth and yarn.[99] In March 1791 a weaver from Villers-Outréaux complained that he had not been paid for the pieces he had delivered to an Elincourt weaver the summer before.[100] Similar complaints were voiced in Montigny. In the summer of 1791 Jean Baptiste Lantier owed Jean Baptiste Ramette and François Oudart fifty-four and 108 livres for pieces of cloth.[101] In September 1794 a merchant had to return two pieces of cloth to a weaver because he was unable to sell them.[102] Commercial losses forced another weaver to surrender his house to his brother-in-law.[103] In some places the cloth was ruined "because of the number of times it had to be hidden from enemy pillage."[104]

Local middlemen still provided yarn that they obtained both locally and from more distant purveyors. One got his supply in Floyon, in the eastern district of Avesnes, while others bought theirs in Cambrai.[105] Foreign trade had not ceased altogether. In the spring of 1790 a cloth merchant from the nearby village of Inchy, home of many of the region's itinerant linen merchants, was away traveling "in foreign lands on business."[106] War interrupted regular circuits, and some merchants relocated abroad while retaining local contacts. In 1796 Jean Jacques Bricout, "merchant from Fontaine-au-Pire . . . now residing in Rotterdam in Holland," came to sell some property to his brother, "a linen merchant from the village of Estourmel," also in Cambrésis.[107] Other rural merchants departed for nearby towns. The Denimals of Montigny eventually were so successful that they moved to Valenciennes where they became linen brokers (*courtiers de toilettes*), and one of the Lantiers similarly relocated to Cambrai.[108] The town, the locus of new political and economic agencies, of speculation and deals, became the center of renewed activity, attracting profiteers and successful countrymen. It offered the sort of opportunities that were once realized in the countryside.

While the Old Regime linen merchants probably continued to sell cloth, they also were quick to invest in two new lucrative outlets: nationalized property and provisioning the various armies in the region. The only real operator connected to Montigny, the merchant and speculator in biens nationaux, Pierre Eloi Cocu, must have combined both activities. In 1794 the cloth merchant Druon Ruol acted as "merchant on behalf of the Armée du Nord."[109] Ruol continued to buy up local produce and in the spring of 1795 complained about the tardy delivery of "200 bundles of hay."[110] Another Montignacien, André Logé, had worked as a purchasing agent (*marchand commissionnaire*) in 1791, although it is not clear on whose behalf and what this activity entailed.[111] As the French currency devalued, agricultural exports increased.[112] When in 1796 Valenciennes paid its forced contribution, its affluent elite was regarded as a bevy of "speculators and hoaders who had profited from the Revolution."[113] They not only displayed an "unabashed and ostentatious luxury," but they used their positions to line their own pockets, as that *garde magasin des vivres* who had an estimated capital of half a million livres "who had made huge profits from a lucrative post that allowed him to steal with impunity." Yet another had amassed riches by selling fodder to the English. It is more than likely, then, that rural Cambrésiens shared in this profitable traffic. In the same period the wholesaler Jean Baptiste Lantier lost 6,000 livres, 4,343 of these for primary products. Only one person in the village lost more, the farmer Jean Baptiste Labbé.[114] Some of these losses may have represented provisions for the army. On the other hand, descriptions of Lantier's occupations continued to alternate between those of merchant and weaver. His brother, Jean Michel, who had once sold cloth in Walincourt would end up a linen broker in Cambrai, so that Jean Baptiste might have continued to sell cloth.[115] Whatever his activities, however, his sons would abandon commerce and become full-fledged farmers, although they too eventually left the village.

The marketing of rural cloth was no longer the road to riches. The Revolution had reestablished urban dominance in this area, leaving ambitious weavers with the option of moving to town or transferring their allegiance to the land. In the middle of the nineteenth century the most heavily assessed local inhabitants included, in descending order, the farmer and manufacturer Pierre Cauchy and the various farming dynasties, some of which had emerged during the Revolution: the Gaves, Levecques, Wibails, Tamboises, and Rousseaus, as well as the Godarts, Gallieques, Sedants, and Leforts who appeared on some tax rolls as cultivateurs and sometimes as tisserands.[116]

The Aftermath

By 1850 the industrial picture in Cambrésis had radically changed. The region had moved away from its exclusive attention to linens to include the production of cottons, woolens, and even silks (table 44). Cotton was spun mechanically, but most wool thread was still produced by hand. Fine-linen yard had proven difficult to mechanize because it was so fine and brittle, and although this had originally inflated linen prices, widespread competition had forced them down. These textile industries remained dispersed, and the merchants continued to intervene in the spinning, weaving, and finishing stages.[117] Yet relations had changed, and the contrast between putters-out and work force was captured in the vernacular. The new factory terminology for employers, overseers, and workers (patrons, contremaîtres, and ouvriers) applied to the countryside as did the term piecework (façon). The workers' grievances revealed their dependence on urban merchants. In 1848 the weavers, complaining that manufacturers weighed and measured the cloth to their advantage, demanded a change in the system of piece rates.[118] The custom of subcontracting may have involved intermediaries, but they had lost their entrepreneurial functions and were merely agents of big urban firms.[119]

In 1856 one lone fine-linen weaver survived in Montigny.[120] All of the others were known as tisserands. The number of female spinners, on the other hand, indicated that they still produced either fine-linen yarn or wool, neither of which had been mechanized. In the 1830s official reports still praised the quality of Montigny linens.[121] Twenty years later,

Table 44. Nature of Textile Production in
Montigny and Surrounding Villages
in 1833

Village	Industry
Audencourt	cotton
Bertry	cotton and silk
Caudry	cotton and tulle
Caullery	cotton and muslin
Clary	cotton
Ligny	cotton and linen
Montigny	cotton and linen
Troisvilles	silk, wool, and linen

Source: *Annuaire statistique du département du Nord*, 1833.

fine linens had just about disappeared. The decline of the industry had
begun with the Revolution. During the Empire, cotton and wool had
come to supplement this traditional branch, but cottons suffered from
the dismantling of Napoleon's Continental System. In the 1820s, however, cotton tulle production was introduced in Caudry and became a
phenomenal success. The village prospered and drew its neighbors,
including Montigny, into its nexus, giving work to the inhabitants of the
region. It rapidly transformed into a boomtown.

Caudry bought its first steam engine in 1852 but continued to procure
its thread from England since it proved impossible to duplicate such a
sturdy product in the region. The fact that the cotton industry no
longer relied on local spinners meant that the weavers could be employed
more steadily, and this in turn lessened their bonds to the land. Unlike
their forebears a century earlier, most mid-nineteenth-century Montigny
weavers owned nothing more than a house and garden. This nonetheless
favorably impressed observers in 1848: "The houses of rural workers
come with little gardens where they grow produce which provides them
with some private resources, besides which its cultivation exercises their
bodies and invigorates their tired limbs."[122]

In 1854, the year the village's land register was compiled, 58 percent
of the 539 hectares in the village belonged to nonresidents (8.4 percent of
these by Tamboise descendants who had moved to Cambrai but who let
family members till their share). If we disregard absentee owners living in
nearby villages, 40 percent remained in the hands of outsiders, urban
rentiers who like the eighteenth century's clerical owners rented out the

Table 45. Landownership in Montigny in 1854

Profession	Hectares	Resident	Nonresident
Farmers	129.29	87.47	41.82
Owners and *rentiers*	237.09	21.41	215.68
Day laborers	24.29	19.55	4.74
Weavers	85.86	64.57	21.29
Spinners	18.22	13.30	4.92
Artisans, others	44.76	20.17	24.59
Totals	539.51	226.47	313.04

Source: cadastre, J857/10.

properties to local farmers. The latter therefore farmed larger properties than the figures in table 45 indicate. Since a new, specialized body of small and middling farmers had emerged in the village, weavers did not participate in such rentals as they had in the Old Regime. The proportion of local owners had dwindled since the Revolution, with the departure of a number of purchasers of biens nationaux. Yet, as mentioned, local owners sometimes kept their properties and leased them to Montigny farmers. On the other hand, they also sold land to town dwellers, a group that had rarely invested in the area in the Old Regime. Taken as a group, Montigny farmers, then, still owned more of the village's surface than they had before the Revolution. As in the Old Regime, they also rented much of the remainder. Individual peasant-weavers, on the other hand, clearly fared worst.

Cottage workers continued their seasonal work on the farms, especially during the beet harvest, and, since they had no fixed contracts, alternated between the two occupations. They moved from the loom to the land and back, to the dissatisfaction of their employers, who deplored such laxity.[123] Tables 46 and 47 show how the local population divided the land they owned in the village.

By the middle of the nineteenth century, weavers who once could pretend to some affluence had become truly impoverished. On the average, they now possessed only half a hectare or, in Ancien Régime terms, 1⅓ mencaudées. The average of the 86 smallest plots came to even less: one-quarter of a mencaudée. Even the larger plots averaged no more than 2 hectares, or 5.5 mencaudées. In contrast, late eighteenth-century weavers had occupied about 3.5 mencaudées,[124] and many successful ones had accumulated more than that. The decline in landownership had already been evident in the prerevolutionary period when couples mar-

Table 46. Land Owned by Montigny Inhabitants

Profession	Entries (in cadastre)	Entries (%)	Land (%)	Average plot (hectares)	Average plot (mencaudées)
Farmers	16	6.7	38.6	5.47	15.4
Owners, rentiers	7	3.0	9.5	3.06	8.6
Day laborers	30	12.6	8.6	0.65	1.8
Weavers	141	59.0	28.5	0.46	1.3
Spinners	24	10.0	5.9	0.55	1.5
Artisans, others	21	8.8	8.9	0.96	2.7

ried with little or no property, but massive pauperization only occurred in the nineteenth century when the weavers lost their independence and their production barely earned them a living.

Production in the middle of the nineteenth century remained dispersed among rural cottages except for a few tulle workshops. "There are no factories in this canton; wool and silk workers only deal with their overseers. A few cotton manufacturers put out work."[125] The linen sector was in shambles because mechanically spun yarn had lowered the quality of the final product, which had led to a reduction in wages. Hand loom weavers who once had earned two to two and one-half francs a day were now receiving only one franc a day. "This explains . . . why parents are turning their children away from a trade that now brings them merely 25 to 30 centimes a day, when all around new industries are cropping up that can furnish them with a wage of 50 to 75 centimes."[126] Nowhere was the situation as appalling as in the canton of Clary, which included Montigny.[127] While in other areas, children were apprenticed between the ages of eleven and fifteen, here their training started as young as nine

Table 47. Distribution of Land in Relation to Average Size of Plots

Profession	Number of entries (in cadastre)	Less than average	Half the average	More than average	Twice the average
Farmers	16	4	8	3	1
Day laborers	30	3	20	4	3
Weavers	141	21	86	13	21
Spinners	24	8	10	2	4
Artisans	21	4	11	2	4

or ten and continued for three to four years. Silk and wool were only worked nine months of the year, but other cloths were produced year-round, fifteen hours a day. The working day was as long in the canton of Marcoing, but it lasted twelve hours elsewhere. Agricultural workers were employed eight months of the year, at the rate of one franc a day, and they were fed on the farm. Weavers often earned less than the minimum needed to keep a family. "In order to avoid impossible levels of deprivation, the worker needs to earn at least 1.25 francs a day, 300 days of the year, if he is single. He must have twice as much with the help of his wife in order to support two children." Despite such difficult conditions, hand loom weaving survived in Montigny, where weavers still worked their looms by hand as late as 1908. "All day long and often into the wee hours they pulled the rope while the feet moved the pedals," wrote the curé, "life was hard!"[128] Mechanical looms finally made their appearance in 1925, and a curtain factory, which would eventually employ one hundred workers, opened in 1924. Yet even then cottage industry survived until the 1960s, a flickering reminder of a tricentenary activity.[129]

Conclusion

The later eighteenth century in Cambrésis, this book has argued, was a period of prosperity and quick profits as well as quick losses. Industry had spread to the countryside under the aegis of urban merchants who sought out rural producers without necessarily wishing to exercise too much direct control over their production. This allowed weavers to produce cloth more or less independently and then to sell it either to the urban brokers or to turn, for convenience sake, to local intermediaries. The emergence of rural middlemen who performed independent entrepreneurial and managerial functions demarcates the eighteenth century from previous eras. They rose to the fore in midcentury at a time when urban merchants and rural weavers were recovering from a major commercial crisis. The weavers grew wary of the uncertainties associated with independent marketing and were ready to sell their product to rural middlemen. Urban merchants were happy to abandon direct links with the weavers and rely instead on a smaller number of steady suppliers. The middlemen profited when the market expanded, especially if they could keep competitors at bay, but they also took on all of the risks.

Rural industry of a similar scope had already existed in parts of Europe in the late Middle Ages and in the sixteenth century. This production, however, had been controlled from the town.[1] Cities remained the unchallenged centers of industrial and commercial networks. If the system generated middlemen, their successes were crowned with a move to town where they joined the mercantile elite. In the eighteenth century such men ran their businesses from their villages, and their achievements depended on their presence in the countryside where they had direct links with the work force. Such prosperous merchants stimulated urban trading activities, but they also generated income in the villages and profits that they reinvested in the countryside. While part of peasant earnings wound their way into the pockets of urban brokers, a portion accrued to local merchants, who bought land in the village and continued to promote local production. Credit loosened and expanded so that it became easy for country dwellers to enter the cloth trade.

While such trading activities offered opportunities for enrichment, they also involved a whole range of uncertainties. Rural merchants held no monopoly over either trade or production. They could try to bind

their work force through advances and loans, and sometimes by employing workers directly in their own homes, but they could not vanquish all
their opponents. New merchants rose in the village who were willing to
offer attractive terms to the weavers or who had other claims over them,
even if only of kinship. At the other end of the spectrum, except for those
merchants who peddled the cloth themselves across northern Europe,
rural merchants had no control over exports, which remained in the
hands of urban firms. These outfits were themselves dependent on the
vagaries of foreign sales. When international trade lagged or collapsed,
when returns were slow and credit overextended, the urban merchants
retrenched, stopped buying cloth, and failed to honor their debts. The
middlemen suffered from this curtailment in purchasing and were unable
to repay their own loans, which had gone to pay their workers and to buy
raw materials. Middlemen were especially vulnerable because it took so
long for market conditions to become apparent. They often did not stop
buying cloth until it was too late. Although the lack of regulation and of
contractual bonds gave the system a theoretical elasticity, rural merchant-
weavers in fact rarely benefited from such flexibility. When they proved
unable to take any more orders, or when they defaulted, they alienated
their workers and their fellow villagers. The weavers who depended on
them were forced to search for alternate arrangements and new sources of
employment, and, given the number of competitors, the search would
prove fruitful. By the last quarter of the eighteenth century, the province was overrun by rural linen merchants who vied for the weavers'
production.

Unregulated, competitive capitalism dominated the late eighteenth-
century countryside. Easy credit conditions allowed people to enter the
trade and to survive for a while until loans were called in, overproduction
created a glut in the market, and the boom came to an end. This
experience of the free market economy taught entrepreneurs the value of
greater control over the work force. It showed them the dangers of
unfettered competition, and when they moved to the town, during and
after the Revolution, they eagerly coalesced in employers' associations,
fixing wages or prices, even as they denied workers the right to combine.[2]
Others disengaged themselves from trade and found new vocations in
farming.

Agricultural prosperity underlay this expansion, and a second concern of this book has been to demonstrate its improvement over the
eighteenth century. Better husbandry and greater investments on the part
of farmers who had benefited from an extended period of low rents

promoted these changes. In Cambrésis the disappearance of independent small farmers in the middle of the century left most of the grain production to the large farms, which benefited from rising demand and growing specialization. The village had been barely able to feed its two hundred inhabitants in 1700; in the 1780s it fed six hundred. By the late 1770s and 1780s the independent farmer emerged once more as merchant-weavers rediscovered the advantages of farming. They had always relied on real estate to back part of their loans and had therefore invested in land. From the 1770s onward, mortgages declined as the major source of loans, and merchants used commercial credit instead. At the same time, agricultural produce was rising in value and appeared a desirable as well as fairly secure investment. Merchant purchases of land and their involvement in farming increased during the Revolution, when vast tracts of nationalized property suddenly became available. The merchant-weavers bought land and settled down to farm both their own properties and those of absentee landowners.

These economic changes brought complex changes to the village's social and political organization. At the end of Louis XIV's reign, the village resembled the subsistence village of social theory. Population had so fallen that the survivors shared more land. There were a few major farmers (the censiers who leased local estates), a sizable proportion of independent farmers, and a group of subsistence farmers, along with a few weavers, merchants, and other artisans such as the blacksmith. The proportion of weavers rose dramatically in the next decades, and by the 1750s they composed two-thirds of households. The weavers were a heterogeneous group: some were quite prosperous and were already involved in the cloth trade; others worked independently. This regular income allowed them to survive as well if not better than before, although a few remained dependent journeymen who barely managed to eke out a livelihood. By midcentury, the middling farmer had just about vanished; the subsistence farmer was nowhere in sight. Both had turned to weaving. Agriculture was relegated to the big farmers who hired a number of full-time workers and a throng of seasonal laborers. In the next decades this structure grew even more fluid as weavers rose from all ranks to participate in the province's cloth trade. Montigny's political life reflected these changes; by the 1770s the once-dominant large farmers had to share power in the village with merchant-weavers.

The Revolution decisively altered this situation. In the early 1800s production fell under urban control and reduced the weavers' independence, even if they continued for a while to make a satisfactory living. Weaving ceased to provide the sort of opportunities it had in the eighteenth century, and the weavers, except in unusual circumstances, no longer ranked among the local elite. They then appeared not as weavers but as local manufacturers, *fabricants*. After the Revolution, the villages were divided once more into a pyramid of farmers of all ranks, and they were ruled by an oligarchy composed of the richest among them. The weavers had become impoverished and figured among the poorer members of the community. The Revolution reinvigorated the towns, which attracted the successful and the ambitious. The village had ceased to be a locus of commercial and industrial experimentation.

Montigny's experiences suggest important facts about peasant economic calculations and responses to opportunities and about how peasant economic practices intersected with other areas of life. Tradition and routine did not bind the peasantry to repeat old patterns or to deny and reject outside stimuli. Quite the contrary, Montigny's peasants proved quick in using the opportunities and challenges that came their way. Yet this did not completely overhaul their way of life. They retained whatever older forms of organization they found suitable, such as the practices of mauvais gré. They continued to function within an agrarian setting and to view themselves as members of a rural community. They did not cease to be peasants. In fact, rural entrepreneurs like Jean Pierre Lantier were able to rise because of their manipulation of a whole range of communal practices: counting at times on village solidarities while at others resorting to an individualism that rejected such bonds; relying on the security that membership in the village provided in the forms of real estate and rentals in order to speculate and plunge into the world of commercial credit. Old and new forms of organization joined in Cambrésis's industrial villages.

Notes

Introduction

1. George Eliot, *Silas Marner* (Penguin Books, 1967), pp. 51–52.
2. Robert Redfield, *Peasant Society and Culture* (Chicago, 1956), pp. 64–65.
3. Oslo, 1931. Translated as *French Rural History: An Essay on Its Basic Characteristics* (Berkeley, 1966).
4. Since he believed that French agrarian structures could be traced to neolithic tribal organization, he placed less emphasis on the contrast between Germanic and Latin roots.
5. Ibid., p. 241.
6. Ibid., p. 242.
7. Jean Meuvret, *Le Problème des subsistances à l'époque de Louis XIV,* 6 vols. (Paris, 1977–88). See also George Grantham, "Jean Meuvret and the Subsistence Problem in Early Modern France," *Journal of Economic History* 49 (1989): 184–200.
8. Emmanuel Le Roy Ladurie, *The French Peasantry, 1450–1660* (Berkeley, 1987; orig. French ed., 1977), p. 9.
9. Pierre Goubert, *The Ancien Régime: French Society, 1600–1750* (New York, 1974; orig. French ed., 1969), p. 109.
10. Ibid., p. 113.
11. See, for example, Georges Lefebvre, *Les Paysans du Nord pendant la Révolution français* (Paris, 1972, orig. ed., 1924); Pierre de Saint-Jacob, *Les Paysans de la Bourgogne du Nord au dernier siècle de l'Ancien Régime* (Dijon, 1960); Jean Jacquart, *La Crise en Ile-de-France, 1550–1670* (Paris, 1974).
12. Lefebvre, *Les Paysans du Nord.*
13. Ibid.; also Florence Gauthier, *La Voie paysanne dans la Révolution française, l'exemple picard* (Paris, 1977).
14. P. M. Jones, *The Peasantry in the French Revolution* (Cambridge, 1988). For a critique of Lefebvre's approach, see Liana Vardi, "Peasants and the French Revolution: A Re-examination of Lefebvre's *Les Paysans du Nord,*" paper presented at Bicentennial of the French Revolution conference, Washington, D.C., May 1989.
15. See Lefebvre and Goubert cited above.
16. M. M. Postan, *The Medieval Economy and Society* (Harmondsworth, 1972), pp. 124, 147.
17. Pierre Goubert in E. Labrousse et al., *Histoire économique et sociale de la France,* II (Paris, 1970), 147.
18. Rodney Hilton, *Bond Men Made Free* (London, 1973), p. 37.

19. Alan Macfarlane, *The Origins of English Individualism* (Cambridge, 1978).
20. In fact, that is what recent studies of the French countryside continue to demonstrate; see Gay Gullickson, *Spinners and Weavers of Auffay* (Cambridge, 1986). Michael Sonenscher likewise has shown the inadequacy of rigid definitions for urban trades. *Work and Wages: Natural Law, Politics and the Eighteenth-Century French Trades* (Cambridge, 1989).
21. Eric Wolf, *Peasants* (Englewood Cliffs, N.J., 1966), p. 46.
22. Ibid., pp. 4, 13.
23. Goubert, *Ancien Régime,* p. 109.
24. Theodor Shanin ed., *Peasants and Peasant Societies* (Oxford, 1987), p. 4.
25. A. V. Chayanov, *The Theory of Peasant Economy,* ed. Daniel Thorner, Basile Kerblay, and R. E. F. Smith (Homewood, Ill., 1966; orig. Russian ed., 1925).
26. Shanin, *Peasants* (Harmondsworth, 1971, 1987), pp. 14–15, 3–4.
27. On the other hand, when Wolf allies anthropological and historical research, as in his book, *Europe and the People Without History* (Berkeley, 1988), he adopts more nuanced and more complex perspectives.
28. Karl Polanyi, *The Great Transformation* (London, 1946); George Dalton and Raymond Firth, eds., *Themes in Economic Anthropology* (London, 1967); Richard Hodges, *Primitive and Peasant Markets* (Oxford, 1988).
29. See Lynn Hunt, ed., *The New Cultural History* (Berkeley and Los Angeles, 1989).
30. Marshall Sahlins, *Historical Metaphors and Mythical Realities* (Ann Arbor, Mich., 1981); *Islands of History* (Chicago, 1985).
31. Clifford Geertz, *The Interpretation of Cultures* (New York, 1973). Although new ethnographers have recently questioned some of these elements (see, for example, Vincent Crapanzano, "Hermes' Dilemma: The Masking of Subversion in Ethnographic Description," in James Clifford and George E. Marcus, *Writing Culture: The Poetics and Politics of Ethnography* [Berkeley and Los Angeles, 1986], pp. 51–76), the influence of cultural anthropology is evident in recent studies of peasant mentalities. Robert Darnton, "Peasants Tell Tales: The Meaning of Mother Goose," in *The Great Cat Massacre and Other Episodes in French Cultural History* (New York, 1984), pp. 9–72; Carlo Ginzburg, *The Cheese and the Worms* (Baltimore, 1980), and Keith P. Luria, *Territories of Grace: Cultural Change in the Seventeenth-Century Diocese of Grenoble* (Berkeley and Los Angeles, 1991).
32. The view that rural industry was a specific stage of economic development was given its impetus by Franklin Mendels in "Proto-Industrialization, the First Phase of the Industrialization Process," *Journal of Economic History* 32 (1972: 241–61. For elaborations and discussions, see Maxine Berg, Pat Hudson, and Michael Sonenscher, *Manufacture in Town and Country Before the Factory* (Cambridge, 1983), and Peter Kriedte, Hans Medick, and Jürgen Schlumbohm, *Industrialization Before Industrialization* (Cambridge, 1981). For the most sophisticated view on the linkages between urban and rural

economies in the eighteenth century, see Jan De Vries, *European Urbanization, 1500–1800* (Cambridge, Mass., 1984).

33. On the diversification of rich, big farmers who invest in industry, see Jonathan Dewald, *Pont-St. Pierre, 1398–1789: Lordship, Community, and Capitalism in Early Modern France* (Berkeley and Los Angeles, 1987), and Kriedte in *Industrialization Before Industrialization*. On peasants' exclusion from entrepreneurial roles, see, e.g., Philippe Guignet, *Mines, manufactures et ouvriers du Valenciennois au XVIIIe siècle: Contribution à l'histoire du travail dans l'ancienne France* (New York, 1977), pp. 32, 47, 208–16.

34. See, for one, Franklin Mendels, "Industrialization and Population Pressure in Eighteenth-Century Flanders," unpublished Ph.D. diss., University of Wisconsin, 1970, pp. 20–22.

35. Hans Medick in Kriedte et al., *Industrialization Before Industrialization*, pp. 67, 68ff. Similar objections to Medick are raised by Berg, Hudson, and Sonenscher, *Manufacture in Town and Country*.

36. Franklin Mendels, "Niveau des salaires et âge au mariage en Flandre, XVIIe–XVIIIe siècles," *Annales, économies, sociétés, civilisations* (1984): 939–56; David Levine, *Family Formation in an Age of Nascent Capitalism* (New York, 1977). See also Guignet, *Mines, manufactures,* for similar emphases.

37. See the critique of the moral economy of the peasantry offered by Samuel Popkin, *The Rational Peasant: The Political Economy of Rural Society in Vietnam* (Berkeley and Los Angeles, 1979).

38. Paul Bois, *Paysans de l'Ouest* (Paris, 1971), p. 206; Medick, *Industrialization,* p. 69.

39. Myron P. Gutmann, *Toward the Modern Economy: Early Industry in Europe, 1500–1800* (New York, 1988), p. 149, although note that he criticizes the distinction between peasant and proletarian.

40. Medick, *Industrialization,* pp. 69, 70.

41. Jerome Blum, *The End of the Old Order in Rural Europe* (Princeton, N.J., 1978), p. 176.

42. Medick, *Industrialization,* p. 69.

43. The nobility thus can be seen as profiting from capitalist developments in the eighteenth century. Guy Chaussinand-Nogaret, *La Noblesse au XVIIIe siècle: De la féodalité aux lumières* (Paris, 1976).

44. Their experience as middlemen explains why a number adapted to easily to urban shopkeeping in the nineteenth century. I am indebted to Christopher Johnson for making that connection.

45. Recent work on gender relations within the proto-industrial household addresses some of these issues. See Tessie Liu's work on the Choletais (Cornell University Press, forthcoming). In *Spinners and Weavers,* Gullickson shows the connections between agricultural and artisanal activities in a village where women performed most of the proto-industrial work. Given Gullickson's focus on gender involvement in agriculture and textile produc-

tion, other aspects of the village economy (e.g., the role of the tanning industry or the origins of landlessness) remain unclear, and we only get a partial sense of how things worked.

1 The Human Context

1. Twenty kilometers from Cambrai and ten from Le Cateau.
2. See Liana Vardi, "Peasants and the Law: A Village Appeals to the French Royal Council, 1768–91," *Social History* 13 (1988): 295–313, for details on this case.
3. Jean Le Carpentier, *Histoire généalogique des Pais-Bas ou Histoire de Cambray et du Cambrésis*, 3 vols., I (Leiden, 1664), 291.
4. Ibid., II, 7.
5. Arthur Young, *Travels in France During the Years 1787–1788–1789,* ed. with introduction by Jeffry Kaplow (New York, 1969), pp. 261–64.
6. Charles Burney, *Music, Men, and Manners in France and Italy, 1770* (London, 1974), p. 3. Consider this appraisal of Saint-Omer: "[I] was forced to put up at a miserable house in the suburbs, where I could get nothing to eat after my sea-sickness and total depletion, but stinking maquerel; a sallad with stink-ing oil; and an omelet made of stinking eggs."
7. Young, *Travels in France,* p. 79.
8. Burney, *Music, Men, and Manners,* p. 7.
9. Archives départementales du Nord, M641/5, Year IX and Year X, Cambrai and Le Cateau. (Unless otherwise indicated, all documents are located in the Archives du Nord.)
10. M264/2. "Conseil d'hygiène publique et de salubrité. Séance du 9 mai 1859. Canton de Clary." In 1820 the nearby canton of Marcoing was described in very similar terms. Garbage, miasma, overcrowding, and lack of fresh air turned "most of those people who were forced to live there such as spinners, the elderly, and weavers . . . pale and sickly." Cited in "Résumé des Enquêtes ouvertes dans l'arrondissement de Cambrai sur l'Organisation du Travail Industriel et Agricole," Cambrai, 12 June 1849, p. 3, M547.
11. M641/5, Year IX and Year X, Cambrai and Le Cateau, and C. Douchez, "Notice historique sur Beauvois," *Mémoires de la Société d'Emulation de Cambrai* 32 (1872), 283–553, who lists peas, beans, carrots, leek and cabbage, and fruit of uneven quality, pp. 264, 375.
12. M641/5, Cambrai, 28 Prairial IX. Clothing was made of rough hemp and linen. Women, however, also wore woolen skirts, black shawls, and head-gear.
13. Ibid.
14. *Annuaire statistique du département du Nord pour l'an XI de la République,*

Rédigé par l'invitation du citoyen Dieudonné par S. Bottin, son secrétaire particulier (Douai, 1802–3), p. 7.

15. Douchez, "Notice," pp. 363–64; see also E1555, "registre aux plaids" of the village of Ligny.

16. Pierre Bougard, "Dénombrement de la population du Cambrésis en 1778," in *Hommage à Marcel Reinhard* (Paris, 1973), 77.

17. C20869.

18. C supplement 524 [hereinafter C suppl.] counts inhabitants or households in 1709, 1716, 1743, 1780. Other sources for Montigny's population include C20869 (1778); A. Lottin et al., *La Désunion du couple sous l'Ancien Régime: l'exemple du Nord* (Lille, 1975), p. 19; Christophe Dieudonné, *Statistique du département du Nord,* 3 vols. III (Douai, 1804), tables.

19. L1341; L1343, 11 Vendémiaire IV.

20. The increase was especially marked in 1813. See also chapter 5 below.

21. A reconstitution of the population through parish records and a petition signed by the majority of heads of households showed that some one hundred families resided in Montigny in 1759 and totaled 405 inhabitants when all known dependents are included.

22. See appendixes A and B.

23. This corresponds to the findings of Gay Gullickson for the village of Auffay [*Spinners and Weavers of Auffay* p. 138] and diverges from the model presented by Mendels, "Industrialization and Population Pressure," pp. 141–51, and adopted by Medick, for example, in Kriedte et al., *Industrialization,* p. 54.

24. See the similar findings of Edward Shorter, *The Making of the Modern Family* (New York, 1975), Louise Tilly and Joan Scott, *Women, Work and Family* (New York, 1978), and Gullickson, *Spinners and Weavers.*

25. The children of one Montigny weaver, Felix Ego, provide such an example. Eight of those born in the 1730s and 1740s survived beyond childhood. One male died at twenty-five, two daughters and another son, Dominique, married in the village. A third daughter followed her husband to Clary, while three other sons settled in nearby Walincourt, Troisvilles, and Cattenières.

26. L1794, forced contribution of the Year IV.

27. 3G888, 14 March 1770. "[Marie Catherine Lantier] has a son who has successfully completed his humanities and logic, and decided to enter the priesthood." He needed a thousand livre "dotte" as well as an annual pension of at least twenty-five écus. This required that his mother sell over ten mencaudées of land (in Gattigny, Ligny, and Montigny) valued at 3,063 florins.

28. The classic statements of this view remain Georges Lefebvre, *Les Paysans du Nord pendant la Révolution française* and Ernest Labrousse, *La Crise de l'économie française à la fin de l'Ancien Régime et au début de la Révolution*

(Paris, 1944). For a more recent version, see Robert M. Schwartz, *Policing the Poor in Eighteenth-Century France* (Chapel Hill, N.C., 1988).

29. 4G2447 (1588), 4G6557 (1590), 4G6575 (1614), 4G6604 (1641), 4G6633 (1675). Account books of the Prévôtés du Cambrésis.

30. See 3G888–890. "Embrefs" of the village of Montigny.

31. For example, the notary Pierre Leducq [hereinafter Leducq] 21 October 1719, where the bride owned a house and garden by "droit de maîneté."

32. Officialité 8682 [hereinafter Off.], November 1707.

33. VIII B le série 11340, 7 February 1722.

34. Ibid., 9 February 1722.

35. Off. 1293, 1704.

36. Such examples can be found in François Mairesse, Bertry notary, as early as 10 December 1674 or Etienne Gave, also a notary from Bertry, 26 May 1692; and Leducq, 6 November 1712, and 1 July 1713, where yards are partitioned and new housing promised.

37. Etienne Gave, Bertry notary, 23 November 1690, "for lodgings."

38. Leducq, 19 May 1719. In this case on St. John the Baptist Day, 1720.

39. Leducq, 10 November 1728 and 26 November 1730.

40. Leducq, 12 November 1764: marriage contract of the weaver Henry François Lemaire and Marie Josèphe Oblin. The couple received rooms number 1 and 2, garden number 3, lot number 4, and access to the well (number 5).

41. Ibid., 11 May 1767. Marriage contract, Bertry.

42. These were usually reserved as a debased survival of the *droit de maîneté*. E. M. Meijers, *Le Droit coutumier de Cambrai*, II (Haarlem, 1955), lxi: "the youngest is entitled to his parents' house and to three pieces of furniture." Etienne Gave, Bertry notary, 23 November 1690, conserves a representative list of pots, pans, and bedding.

43. Off. 7953, Ligny, June 1724.

44. Marguerite Allart, wife of Nicolas Bantigny, aged fifty.

45. Anne Jeanne Mannessiez, no age given.

46. VIIIB le série 11340, testimony of 9 February 1772. Marie Hennotté, an unmarried spinner, aged sixty-three, from Montigny.

47. Whether out of love for her children or fear of her husband, one Caullery woman stayed up to await the return of her two sons from the tavern, and thus witnessed a brawl. She wanted to prevent her husband waking up and getting angry that the boys were so late. 4G2146, April 1772. Anne Jeanne Ramette, wife of Noël Carlier, *mulquinier*.

48. 1H507, 3 December 1734. Two Tronquoy farmers, Philippe Crinon and Pierre Joseph Ledieu "beat each other up and pulled each other by the hair when Pierre Heloire, Crinon's ploughman, came upon them and hit Ledieu over the head with his whip. . . ."

49. L13412, 10 October 1791. When one father from Villers Outréaux complained that another's son "had been so bold as to hit his son over the head

with his whip handle," the other retorted "that it was Quievreux's son who had begun by insulting and beating his son, who, finding himself so ill-treated had been forced to retaliate."

50. L13329, 7 July 1791.

51. L13413, sextidi, 2e décade, Ventôse II. Also VIIIB 1e série 27622, 14 July 1768: when the merchant Ferdinand Milot of Clary was arrested and about to be taken to Saint-Quentin, he shouted for help. "Antoine Leriche, a journeyman mason from the said Clary, alerted by his shouts, told the bailiff that neither he nor his men would be able to take away the said Milot, and that he did not give a fuck about the verdict of the judges and aldermen or about the pareatio issued by the court's chancellery; that he then jumped like a madman on the said bailiff and his men, repeating that he would rather lose his life than let them take the said Milot to jail, and began screaming for help; that the wife of Pierre Cadet arrived, and also began to shout "stop, thief, murderer, assassin!" and threw herself on the said bailiff and men, and at that very moment three or four other persons whom the bailiff does not know arrived armed with sticks and they threw themselves on the said bailiff and his men, swearing and blaspheming, and wrenched the said Milot away from them."

52. VIIIB 1e série 11340, 9 February 1722. Antoine Labbé, aged thirty, unmarried son of the tenant-farmer François Labbé.

53. Ibid., and 4G2146.

54. Off. 8682, 1707: Last year Agnes Tasson . . . came to spin at her house and . . . some young men would wander in for an hour or so." Also VIIIB 1e série 11340 and VIIIB 1e série 8020, 1730: "Last month, on the 25th, on the evening Lucien Labbé died and was to be buried in his yard during the night, he got the urge to have a look at this burial as did Adrien Grier, Jean Baptiste Hego, Jean Baptiste Prevost, Gilbert Galliez, François Denoyelles, and Jean Michel Bardou . . . he noticed that Blaise Carlier was looking them over to see who they were . . . and told them they were real fools for having come there." [All were aged between twenty and twenty-five.]

55. 3G886, 1714. The actual case has been lost.

56. VIIIB 1e série 11340, 13 February 1722. Michel Lenglet, farmer and inn-keeper of the village of Selvigny, aged sixty-four.

57. Off. 13012, 1714–16.

58. Off. 14879, 1740–41.

59. VIIIB 1e série 13918, 1778. Caroline Dugimont, Widow Mora vs. Pierre Antoine Hoquet. She won her case. 5G177, "Sentences civiles," 8 February 1782.

60. C5791, 8 February 1783. There were three thousand Protestants in this region, distributed in Quiévy, Inchy, Walincourt, Elincourt, Clary, and Serain. C6974 (1774). The appeal of Protestantism would be massive among the weavers in the nineteenth century when a wave of evangelicalism swept the

region. Montigny itself fell under the sway of an English Catholic sect, the Irvingites, and to this day possesses one of the three chapels extant in France. That new converts were being made in the eighteenth century is proven not merely by the fears and accusations proferred by local priests, but by the modification in religious practice. Protestants who had attended services in such places as Saint-Quentin or married in Tournai, realized that such trips were too expensive for the growing number of poor adepts and so resorted more and more to itinerant ministers.

61. The three young men accused of theft in 1722 had not appeared at vespers "although it is the custom to go." VIIIB 1e série 11340, 9 February 1722; Jacques Lefort, weaver, aged seventy. 4G2145, 13 March 1757: Marie Claire Hutin, widow Pigou, spinner, aged thirty, from Montigny. "Last year, on All Saints Day she came back from church and as she wished to say a short prayer she went out into the garden because the house where she lives is full of children."

62. 5G519, 1716–17. He also kicked Crinon several times in the stomach and side.

63. Ibid.

2   The Institutional Setting

1. Montigny had belonged since the tenth century to the Chapter of the Cambrai cathedral, founded along with other cathedral chapters by order of the monarch Louis the Pious in 817. Louis Trénard et al., *Histoire de Cambrai* (Lille, 1982), p. 18, and Abel Duthoit, *Montigny-en-Cambrésis, sa géographie, son histoire, sa généalogie* (Cambrai, 1965), p. 4.

2. The principal tenant-farmer lodged the chapter's representatives when they came to collect seigneurial dues at the annual *siège de rente*. Payments in kind, whether wheat or oats, however, had to be deposited each fall in the chapter's granaries in Cambrai.

3. Trénard et al., *Histoire de Cambrai*, p. 151.

4. Ibid., pp. 122, 134.

5. C20579.

6. Trénard et al., *Histoire de Cambrai*, p. 151.

7. Henri Platelle, "Cambrai et le Cambrésis au XVe siècle," *Revue du Nord* 58 (July–September, 1976), p. 360.

8. Duthoit, *Montigny-en-Cambrésis*, p. 52.

9. C20725.

10. Pierre Pierrard, *Histoire des diocèses de Cambrai et de Lille* (Paris, 1978), p. 182.

11. C20579 (n.d., late seventeenth century).

12. Ibid.
13. C Suppl. 524. See chapter 6 below.
14. 3G886 for a list of criminal suits.
15. As it did for the rest of the province. Sylvie Delloye, "Problèmes matrimoniaux dans le ressort de l'officialité de Cambrai, 1670–1762, Vol. I. Introduction générale: Les fiançailles." (Mémoire de maîtrise, Lille, 1971), p. 121. It may be that more records have survived for that particular court, but the bulk of the cases brought before it remains nonetheless impressive.
16. In 1742–43 he was paid the equivalent of four mencauds of wheat (4G6699); in 1748–49 eight mencauds (4G6705); in 1775–76 ten mencauds (4G6732); in 1778–79 twelve mencauds (4G6735). Guns at six florins and two florins eight patars appear in the accounts of 1748–49 and 1757–58 (4G6714) and one florin for a bayonet in 1760–61 (4G6717).
17. See chapter 4 below.
18. Lefebvre, *Paysans du Nord,* p. 318; Jean Pierre Gutton, *La Sociabilité villageoise dans l'ancienne France* (Paris, 1979), and Maurice Bordes, *L'Administration provinciale et municipale en France au XVIIIe siècle* (Paris, 1972); both use Lefebvre as their source for the region. The councilmen were known as *mayeur et gens de loy.*
19. Gutton, *La Sociabilité villageoise,* p. 71. For an analysis of this process in Burgundy, see Hilton Root, *Peasants and King in Burgundy: Agrarian Foundations of French Absolutism* (Berkeley and Los Angeles, 1987).
20. The notarized minutes survive in a few instances as in the dispute with the Chapter where the eventual agreement was signed by the inhabitants before the notary Leducq on 4 March, 12 March, and 16 March 1764.
21. C états 288, (1750. "Rolle fait par les mayeur et gens de loy du village de Montigny de toutes les declarations que les proprietaires, usufruitiers, et locataires qu'ils ont fournis pour satisfaire à l'édit du Roy du mois de may 1749 concernant le vingtième et de l'ordonnance de Monsieur Lintendant du premier decembre de la meme année."
22. C suppl. 524.
23. Ibid.
24. Ibid.
25. VIIIB 1e série 13918 (1778). "We the undersigned, mayor and councilmen of the village of Montigny en Cambrésis hereby certify . . . that Caroline Dugimont . . . does not own any plot in her own right or movables of any sort, except for an old shack. . . ."
26. E 1555, the seigneurial court records for the neighboring village of Ligny mention an agreement between the village's cow herder and that community (17 November 1765). He watched over both cows and pigs. On 27 December 1785 the mayor and councilmen of that village distributed the "blés d'aumône des pauvres dudit lieu," the paupers' corn.

27. 4G4266 and C 15186, 17 April 1784. The increase in the number of parishioners made the enlargement a necessity. There are stories of villagers standing outside during services for lack of room.

28. E 1555. (December 1785).

29. C17213, petition of 16 May 1787 by the assembled villagers of the Intendant; 213 signatories.

30. For details, see Vardi, "Peasants and the Law."

31. See Lefebvre, for example. Gutton makes the same point in *La Sociabilité villageoise*.

32. The average contribution per household rose by only 10.5 percent over the course of the eighteenth century.

33. Because peasants in Montigny held their land from ecclesiastical institutions, they did not pay a percentage of the sale price but a fixed amount that lasted the lifespan of a designated individual. The standard formula referring to this "homme vivant et mourant" appears on all the Chapter's registers. In reality, the custom had fallen into disuse, and the same rate of forty sous was quoted half a century apart.

34. See chapter 6 below.

35. 4G6720 (1763–64) eighth entry: two florins.

36. For a recent view on the weight of seigneurial exaction, see Dewald, *Pont-St. Pierre*, chap. 6.

37. 4G2348 (22 September 1769).

38. Off. 11515 (1705–6) provides a good example.

39. Off. 13012 (1714–15) testimony of 27 July 1715.

40. 7H154, 30 September 1747, included a report addressed by Montigny's priest, Lagrue, to the abbey of Honnecourt, detailing his sources of revenue.

41. This happened in Caudry, for example. See chapter 4 below.

42. 7H155, 28 July 1730. The abbey's correspondence rings a harsh note, though in fact too little evidence survives to build a thorough case. The archives of the abbey of Honnecourt were destroyed during the peasant uprisings of 1789, indicating the level of affection aroused by their owners. Lefebvre, *Paysans du Nord*, pp. 356, 363.

43. As mentioned before, his wages amounted to 350 florins (425 livres). The minimum elsewhere was fixed at 300 livres between 1686 to 1768 and raised to 500 and then 700 livres at the end of the Old Regime. Gutton, *La Sociabilité villageoise*, p. 189.

44. 7H154, 12 August 1743. He charged twenty sous for weddings, nine sous for funerals, but special masses could cost as much as thirty sous.

45. C états 288. For the weavers' estimated income, see chapter 8 below.

46. Deregnaucourt argues that the shift occurred in the seventeenth century when the moralizing efforts of the Counter-Reformation reached Cambrésis villages. J.-M. Baheux and G. Deregnaucourt, "Affaires de moeurs laïques et ecclésiastiques et mentalités populaires au XVIIe siècle 1594–1706, d'après

les archives de l'officialité métropolitaine de Cambrai" (Mémoire de maîtrise, Lille, 1972).

47. Lefebvre, *Paysans du Nord,* pp. 170–71, 186.

48. C suppl. 524, 13 March 1787. We find the *personnelle, moulinage, mencaudée, contrôle, extraordinaire* and *supplément, aide extraordinaire, capitation des deux vingtièmes et des quatre sols pour livre* as well as the *capitation* itself.

49. The village's tax records appear in one bundle, C suppl. 524, except for the 1750 vingtième which figures in C états 288 and C suppl. 429. Four assess property: in 1684, 1686, 1708, and 1750; records of the *capitation* are equally scarce and are available for only 1701, 1713, 1720, 1725, and 1777.

50. This is equivalent to twenty livres, which, divided by four or five persons per household, yields the ratio proposed by Lefebvre for a later period.

51. Peter Mathias and Patrick O'Brien, "Taxation in Britain and France, 1715–1810. A Comparison of the Social and Economic Incidence of Taxes Collected for the Central Governments," *Journal of European Economic History* 5 (Winter 1976): 601–50, shows that although in absolute terms per capita taxation in France doubled during the eighteenth century from nine to nineteen livres, its share of income remained stable, oscillating around 12 percent and peaking during the midcentury wars.

52. C16957. The dixième for Montigny (totals only): rounded off to the nearest florin: 1734, 119 florins; 1741, 196 florins; 1745, 245 florins; 1748, 332 florins.

53. For a persuasive account of these changes, see Myron P. Gutmann, *War and Rural Life in the Early Modern Low Countries* (Princeton, N.J., 1980).

54. C suppl. 524, 17 October 1646.

55. C suppl. 524 thus has a good sampling. 4 May 1692: "7 a 8 jeunes hommes qui sont presentement au service de portant les armes pour sa majesté tres crestinne [sic]"; 12 March 1729: "Declaration faite par le mayeur et gens de loy de Montigny et de Bruyère des jeunes hommes a mariez depuis laige de 18 ans jusqu'a 40 que nous avons jugé estre de tailles et capable pour le service"; 6 April 1726: "garçons en estats de servir dans la mellice"; 2 December 1742: "10 jeunes hommes a mariee de taille de 5 pieds et 1 pouce en nestats de servir le Roy"; 9 February 1753 also involved local duty: "Depuis que la garde a ette remis entre Colery et Montigny quelle ces fay actuellement des huit en huit jours dans chacun de notre communauté et que ladite garde a eté montez a Montigny le 4 fevrier 1753."

56. The "Etat des soldats provinciaux composant les six levées, servant à la décharge des paroisses du Cambrésis dans le bataillon provincial du Haynaut" lists none from Montigny, though there are several from nearby Clary and Ligny. C15576 (1777–88) and C1589.

57. Lefebvre, *Paysans du Nord,* p. 7, claims there was no *corvée.* C15572, 3 November 1774 and C16697, 8 November 1788, requisitions for quarried stones and sacks of wheat.

58. C suppl. 524, 20 June 1744.
59. C suppl. 524.
60. C Registre 493, 9 December 1747 and 29 February 1748.
61. C suppl. 524. "ils n'entendent payer." For a thorough discussion of tax evasions, see James B. Collins, *Fiscal Limits of Absolutism: Direct Taxation in Early Seventeenth-Century France* (Berkeley and Los Angeles, 1988).
62. C suppl. 524, 1685.
63. Ibid., Cambrai, 26 January 1754.
64. C Registre 635, 3 June 1775.
65. This was the case in the Auvergne, for one. See A. D. Puy de Dôme 4C138 plea of the village of Saint-Jean Desollières in 1788.
66. Lefebvre, *Paysans du Nord,* p. 183.
67. C15868, 8 September 1746.
68. C suppl. 524. There is no record of who took over in 1769 or if Lantier continued to serve in that capacity despite his run-ins with the Farms.
69. Pierre Bonnassieux, *Conseil de Commerce et Bureau de Commerce, Inventaire analytique des procès-verbaux* (Geneva, 1979), pp. 265–66.
70. C16883, 22 April 1755. The ordinance, of 1680, allowed the General Farms a right of control.
71. C suppl. 524, 27 March 1755. A year later the same Lenglet was sentenced to a fine of six livres following a similar incident. C19203, 23 October 1756.
72. C suppl. 524, 15 February 1782 and 4 June 1783.
73. C suppl. 524.
74. *Histoire de la France rurale,* II, 430–31.

3   Landholding

1. For a fuller discussion of these various views, see the introduction to this book.
2. This proposition was reiterated by Mendels in "Niveau des salaires." See also Mendels, "Industrialization and Population Pressure"; Pierre Deyon, "L'Enjeu des discussions autour du concept de "Proto-industrialisation," *Revue du Nord* 61 (1979): 9–15.
3. The argument that the proletariat emerged in the countryside before it moved to the cities appears, for example, in Charles Tilly, "Flows of Capital and Forms of Industry in Europe," *Theory and Society* 12 (1983): 123–42.
4. 4G6557 (1590); 4G6661 (1705).
5. These figures all come from Montigny's tax records and correspondence with the Cambrésis estates located in C supplement 524.
6. Lefebvre, *Les Paysans du Nord,* pp. 12–13.
7. Ibid., p. 13.
8. C états 288 (1750–56).

9. Lefebvre, *Paysans du Nord*, p. 15.
10. Size of Montigny's territory (1593–1787) in mencaudées

Year	Amount
1593	789
1672	980
1683	973
1684	984.25
1686	959.50
1708	943
1728	785
1734	886
1734	1,141
1744	1,039
1746	1,015
1750	973.50
1752	919
1754	1,002.25
1755	900
1787	927

Source: C18610, C18494, C suppl. 524, C états 288, C16957, 7H122, C5444, C15428.

11. According to Lefebvre, 191.1 hectares (539 mencaudées) of Montigny's soil changed hands during the Revolution, mostly as *biens de première origine,* that is, ecclesiastical holdings. (*Paysans du Nord,* pp. 972, 981). In 1728, as demonstrated in table 9, ecclesiastics, religious foundations, and priests possessed 58 percent of the arable, while in 1750 and 1754 they controlled 45 and 46 percent, respectively. (C suppl. 524 and C états 288). This last figure translates to a total of 450 mencaudées, as in Lefebvre's calculations, once the fief of La Bruyère, in the hands of a lay seigneur, is discounted.
12. Surviving documents belonging to the various religious institutions have yielded further evidence. Whereas in its description of tithable property in Montigny, the abbey of Honnecourt assigned 150 mencaudées to the abbey of Cantimpré, the latter's own registers (*terrier*) show 126.5 mencaudées, leased to four individuals with perhaps an extra 1.25 mencaudées. The Chapter records similar discrepancies. In 1670 it claimed ownership of 162.75 mencaudées. Later leases varied. That of 1735 covered 165.23 mencaudées; that of 1746, only 146.5. When the domain was split between two farmers in 1765, the first (Robert Milot) took more than two-thirds (103.5 mencaudées), and the second (Henri Mairesse) the remaining 60. The property was professionally surveyed in 1775 when it was declared to cover nearly 180 mencaudées (7H122, 7H155, 37H229, 4G3297). The abbey of Prémy has left a description of 39 mencaudées, which it held in

Montigny, and there is also a record of the lease of 26 mencaudées belonging to the abbey of Notre Dame de Walincourt (the Guillemains) (65H13, 50H93).

13. The discrepancies noted in table 8 result from sloppy or uneven bookkeeping and do not reflect major shifts in landownership. This also applies to the sixty-five mencaudées or so of yards, gardens, and plots leased by the parish. Fourteen and a half of those were held in long-term leases, but the remainder (*biens d'église et de cure*) were bid for publicly at nine-year intervals, as were the fifteen mencaudées, donated by the Chapter, whose revenue was untaxed and distributed among the poor of the parish each fall.

14. C Bureau des finances, fiefs No. 3554. At the time of the sale it was said to contain 179 mencaudées, part of which lay in the territory of nearby Ligny. This same property had earlier figured on tax documents under the name of Madame de Baralle.

15. Lefebvre, *Paysans du Nord*, pp. 41–42.

16. See appendix A at end of this chapter.

17. It should be noted that the apparent decline of sales in the 1780s in Montigny can be attributed to lacunae in the records. For much of the decade, because of dissensions in the village, administrative matters were divided between the bailli in Cambrai and the local council. Transactions may have been registered more sporadically, and some registers may have been lost. Sales did not fall off either in Ligny or in Cattenières.

18. I refer here, in particular, to the elusive de Baralle family, about which very little information survives.

19. Emile Zola, *Earth* (Penguin Books, 1980), p. 38.

20. See chapter 4 below for a full discussion of this phenomenon.

21. Since the latter figure includes twenty-four mencaudées belonging to Jean Pierre Lantier, a merchant-weaver who went bankrupt in this period, it may be inflated. He sold them to a Cambrai resident who then resold them to someone in Clary. There were rumors that the sale had been fictitious, meant to salvage Lantier's property from his creditors, but the matter was never properly elucidated.

22. See below, chapter 9, for the use of landed assets in commercial ventures. For a similar discussion of the land market, see David Sabean, *Property, Production, and Family in Neckerhausen, 1700–1870* (Cambridge, 1990), pp. 355–70, and Dewald, *Pont-St. Pierre*, chap. 2.

23. 3G887–90.

4 Tenancy

1. Antoine Boursier, Clary notary, 1768.

2. Off. 19984.

3. Off. 12848.
4. C suppl. 429 and 2E26/540.
5. Etienne Gave, Bertry notary, 16 December 1681.
6. Off. 11515.
7. Pierre Leducq, Prémont notary, 1 January 1720.
8. He also leased the eighteen mencaudées of the Chapel of All Saints in 1750. C suppl. 429.
9. Leducq, 24 June 1749, and C suppl. 429.
10. J857/5, Montigny parish register, 29 November 1789. Louis Petit, like Robert Milot, became a farmer of Le Troncquoy by marriage.
11. 1Q904.
12. Antoine Boursier, Clary notary, 4 July 1677.
13. Leducq, 19 November 1733 and 1 January 1772.
14. Leducq, 9 January 1787.
15. Leducq, 5 November 1718.
16. C suppl. 524.
17. C suppl. 524 (leased in 1749) and 37H229.
18. VIIIB 1e série 11150.
19. 4G508. It was most probably their farm that was burned down in the 1690s.
20. 1H208.
21. 1H669.
22. Off. 3686, 4G6675, 1H669, 4G2848.
23. 1H669, Off. 1261. Father Abel Duthoit, Montigny's historian, however, dates the arrival of the Tamboises at Le Troncquoy to the Wars of Religion when a wounded Scottish officer, "Mac-Tambo-See," was carried to the farms where he recovered and eventually married one of the farmers' daughters.
24. The Milots led the village during World War I and sold their share of Le Troncquoy to the Tamboises. Duthoit, *Montigny-en-Cambrésis,* p. 58.
25. C suppl. 524. Half of the population paid less than six florins in taxes; three-quarters of the leasors paid more. The statement is somewhat circular, since the more one leased, the more one paid in taxes.
26. See below, chapter 9, the discussion of the merchant Jean Pierre Lantier.
27. Hugues Neveux, *Vie et déclin d'une structure économique: Les grains du Cambrésis fin du XIVe-début du XVIIe siècles* (Paris, 1980), p. 266.
28. C20299, "Bans politiques," Cambrai, 1722, Nos. LIX–LXIV.
29. C3987, "Extrait des Registres du Conseil d'Etat," 25 November 1724.
30. Dejardin, Cambrai notary, attestation, 8 August 1784.
31. A. de Calonne, *La Vie agricole sous l'Ancien Régime dans le Nord de la France* (2nd rev. ed., Paris, 1885), p. 71.
32. 4G2161.
33. Dejardin, Cambrai notary, 31 March 1786.
34. Leducq, Prémont notary, 4 June 1774.

35. VIIIB 1e série 19524. "The following day, 6 July, several people came to see the witness [Jean Bracq] at around 1 P.M. [among them were Philippe Leclercq and Joseph Ledieu, both farmers of Le Troncquoy], who, once they had asked the witness if he had taken the tithe in his name or in that of the community and that he had answered that it was for himself only and that they were well aware of it, they all started to call the witness names and to revile him, telling him that without him they would have gotten the tithe for fourteen *muids* of wheat a year instead of eighteen which is what the witness must provide, whereupon the witness having responded that it was none of their business and that he took the loss upon himself and that they would not have to pay for him, they all started to shout at him . . . and on leaving, told him that they would give him only until that same evening to agree to return the tithe to the community."
36. VIIIB 1e série 22804.
37. Ibid., "il estoit de cela comme ceux qui represnnent des terres sur autre et qu'on se coupe la gorge les uns aux autres."
38. Dejardin, Cambrai notary, 8 August 1784.
39. Off. 18732.
40. Ibid.
41. Off. 13073.
42. Another traditional institution, the guild system, could be manipulated in similar ways. See Sonenscher, *Work and Wages;* Gail Bossenga, *The Politics of Privilege: Old Regime and Revolution in Lille* (Cambridge, 1991), and "Protecting Merchants: Guilds and Commercial Capitalism in Eighteenth-Century France," *French Historical Studies* 15 (1988): 693–703; as well as Liana Vardi, "The Abolition of the Guilds During the French Revolution," *French Historical Studies* 15 (1988): 704–17.
43. Etienne Gave, notary, lease of 25 April 1689 to a Montigny laboureur.
44. Leducq, 28 March 1768. Eighteen-year lease. Since the payment was annual in this case, and the terrain divided into three rotations, the rent was actually higher.
45. C suppl. 406, C21182, *vingtièmes* (1755).
46. Leducq, leases of 19 May 1738, 16 February 1739, 12 May 1749, 31 December 1753, 16 July 1762, 27 May 1777, 13 April 1778, 12 June 1788, and 30 December 1789.
47. Pierre de Saint-Jacob argued for a strong alliance between courts and landowners in Northern Burgundy, as well. For England, especially in the sixteenth century, see the summary in Keith Wrightson, *English Society, 1580–1680* (London, 1982), pp. 130–32. Rents then became more modulated. Peter J. Bowden, *Economic Change: Wages, Profits and Rents, 1500–1750* (Cambridge, 1990).
48. See Vardi, "Peasants and the Law"; Dewald, *Pont-St. Pierre,* p. 150; Root, *Peasants and King in Burgundy,* chap. 5.

49. 1H669.
50. 4G6656 to 4G6744, 4G2448.
51. De Calonne, *La Vie agricole,* pp. 75–76.
52. Labrousse et al., *Histoire économique et sociale de la France,* II, p. 379; also Ernest Labrousse, *Esquisse du mouvement des prix et des revenus en France au XVIIIe siècle,* 2 vols. (Paris, 1933), where the rise between the 1730s and the 1780s is said to be 82 percent.
53. Wilhelm Abel, *Agricultural Fluctuations in Europe from the Thirteenth to the Twentieth Centuries* (London, 1986), p. 214.
54. See, for example, J. D. Chambers and G. E. Mingay, *The Agricultural Revolution, 1750–1880* (London, 1966).
55. The fact that the wheat from each village was sold separately and made for a separate entry means that we can gauge specifically the value of the Montigny crop.
56. Although the first payment was not due until October 1784, I included the 1783 figure in the table to convey the parties' expectations when they signed the contract.
57. The sum seems extraordinary. Georges Lefebvre contends that in this area the gratuity, or entry fines, represented between one half and a full year's rent. The lease that went into effect in 1784 set it at 465 florins 15 patars, and indeed that amount approximated the value of the previous annual payments. The actual amount paid out in kind, however, came to nearly three times as much. Although Lefebvre, again, argued that a similar increase in the village of Crèvecoeur was meant to be divided by three, according to crop rotation, so that in fact only one-third of the stated rent had to be paid each year, this only applied to very small plots. Should it have been the case, then the Chapter's farmer would have owned 80 rather than 240 mencauds. If we take that amount and combine it with one-ninth of the entry fees (or gratuity), the result immediately comes into line with the previous leases.

Estimated Rents for the Farm of La Trappe, 1783–87

Year	240 mencauds + entry fees (florins)	80 mencauds − entry fees (florins)	80 mencauds + entry fees
1783	880.17	276.08	328.03
1784	1,491.15	480	531.15
1785	1,323.15	424	475.15
1786	1,020.00	340	391.15
1787	1,347.15	432	483.15

The account books kept by the Prévôtés du Cambrésis report, however, an annual income of 39 mencauds 12 pintes of wheat as their share, which, prorated, approximates the full 240 mencauds, or original amount. The rent indeed doubled and then immediately trebled.

58. See, for example, Fernand Braudel, *Capitalism and Material Life* (New York, 1973), p. 79, and the discussion in chapter 5 below.
59. Neveux, *Vie et déclin,* p. 137. Lefebvre deemed it one-third. *Paysans du Nord,* p. 268.
60. Saint-Jacob, *Les Paysans de la Bourgogne,* p. 42.
61. Jean Jacquart in *Histoire de la France rurale,* vol. 2 (Paris, 1975), p. 243. Pierre Goubert gives the same figure.
62. For more details, see Vardi, "Peasants and the Law."
63. See appendix B in this chapter.
64. Le Troncquoy measured 550 mencaudées. Half, 275 mencaudées, owed 208 mencauds of wheat, and one-quarter, or 137 mencaudées, 104 mencauds. La Trappe covered about 150 mencaudées. The Cantimpré farm of 102 mencaudées with its 80 mencauds of wheat in rent remains in the same range.
65. C18610. We find similar requisitions in the 1700s, 1770s, etc.

5   Agriculture

1. For an example of this view, see Emmanuel Le Roy Ladurie, ed., *Histoire de la France rurale,* vol. 2 (Paris, 1975), part 3.
2. See, for example, Robert Forster, "Obstacles to Agricultural Growth in Eighteenth-Century France," *American Historical Review* 75 (October 1970): 1600–1615. For other interpretations, see T. H. Aston and C. H. E. Philpin, eds., *The Brenner Debate: Agrarian Class Structure and Economic Development in Pre-Industrial Europe* (Cambridge, 1985); Jack Goldstone, "Regional Ecology and Agrarian Change in England and France, 1500–1700," paper presented at the All-U.C. Conference in Economic History, Los Angeles, 22–24 May 1987. James Goldsmith presents a more positive overview in "The Agrarian History of Pre-Industrial France: Where Do We Go From Here?" *Journal of European Economic History* 13 (1984): 175–99.
3. For a more recent example, see G. E. Mingay, ed., *The Agrarian History of England and Wales,* vol. 6, *1750–1850* (Cambridge, 1989). Also Maxine Berg, *The Age of Manufactures, 1700–1820* (Oxford, 1985); P. K. O'Brien and C. Keyder, *Economic Growth in Britain and France, 1780–1914* (London, 1976).
4. Neveux, *Vie et déclin.*
5. Michel Morineau, *Les Faux-semblants d'un démarrage économique: Agriculture et démographie en France au XVIIIe siècle* (Paris, 1971). Technically speaking, Morineau analyzed two Hainaut villages dependent on the Cambrai Cathedral. They were located very close to Cambrésis with comparable terrains

and agrarian regimes. Neveux, whose vision differs from that of Morineau, has made too much of the contrast between the regions.

6. C15428.

7. C18494 (1750) elaborates on Montigny: "located 3 leagues from Cambrai with a mixture of mediocre and very bad soil; both soils are worth the set rates and produce wheat, secondary grains (*menus grains*), clover and a little rapeseed. The inhabitants are industrious, some are weavers, and very few can be considered comfortable."

8. C états 288.

9. L6596.

10. *Annuaire statistique du département du Nord* (Lille, 1829), p. 21.

11. *Annuaire statistique du département du Nord* (Lille, 1833), p. 15.

12. Bruyelle, *Dictionnaire topographique de l'arrondissement de Cambrai* (Cambrai, 1860), pp. 225–26.

13. Jules Gosselet, "Constitution géologique du Cambrésis," part 3, *Mémoires de la Société d'Emulation de Cambrai* 31, 1 (1869): 403.

14. Duthoit, *Montigny-en-Cambrésis,* p. 14, cites a 1932 report. "The soil consists of thick, clayey, alluvial deposits, unevenly spread over a sublayer of chalk. They may be four to six meters deep. They rest on sandy strips and tertiary clay."

15. C états 288. That corresponds to the breakdown of 1750 where 515 mencaudées of arable (60 percent) had poor soil, and the remainder (347 mencaudées) were of average quality.

16. Ibid., pp. 14, 31–32.

17. C états 288 (1750).

18. See the following section.

19. Neveux contends that the maslin contained little or no rye, but the eighteenth-century documents I encountered mention it specifically.

20. Dieudonné, *Statistique,* I, 375.

21. C suppl. 524. 23 July 1709. In August 1751 peasants were fined for gleaning in fields covered with wheat and barley (1H539, Le Troncquoy, seigneurial court). Marriage contracts talk of carrot or bean crops and mention a variety of fruit trees.

22. L6632.

23. L6596.

24. L6632. The cantonal authorities complained that "the lack of cultivation in the northeast of the canton has meant that many fields were not sown in the fall. Mice also caused considerable damage so that we estimate that we will need 2500 quintaux of spring crop as well as barley in order to sow all the land. The bad weather and mice destroyed the fall fodder and clover, so that we will also need 4500 of beans and vetch."

25. M651/24. The shift indicates improvements in agricultural methods since the mixture of rye and wheat had served to support the less resistant wheat

stalks. B. H. Slicher van Bath, *The Agrarian History of Western Europe: A.D. 500–1850* (London, 1963), p. 263.

26. *Annuaire statistique,* 1833, p. 78.
27. Slicher Van Bath, *Agrarian History of Western Europe* p. 263.
28. Albert Demangeon, *La Picardie et les régions voisines, Artois-Cambrésis-Beauvaisis* (orig. publ., 1905; Paris, 1973), pp. 238–39.
29. The following figures all come from Montigny's tax folder, C suppl. 524.
30. Ibid., 23 July and 28 August 1709.
31. In 1752 the arable extended to 825 mencaudées, so that its sections would have measured 275 mencaudées each. In June 1795 they covered 290 mencaudées, but this did not mean a real increase since Montigny now encompassed the farms of Le Troncquoy. In fact, it meant a reduction brought about by the emigration of tenant-farmers, the lack of ploughs, teams, and manpower, as well as by poor harvests. L6640.
32. M651/24. The 572 hectares represented the arable, excluding houses and gardens. If we convert the village's surface back to mencaudées and subtract the 550 covered by Le Troncquoy in order to restore the original area, we are left with 900 mencaudées, showing that the arable had not extended beyond its eighteenth-century confines.
33. 7H154 (1775).
34. In 1684 and 1686 the arable extended to 984¼ mencaudées and 952½ mencaudées, respectively, in each case divided into three sections, "en trois roies" (C suppl. 524).
35. C suppl. 524, 26 July 1686.
36. C20299. The printed set of *Bans Politiques,* dating from about 1700, were used by the Chapter to regulate the harvest and police the countryside.
37. Jean Meuvret argued that such divisions of the arable into three discrete units were the norm, and that they suited all but the poorest inhabitants who did not have enough plots to scatter. He also believed that the system was sufficiently flexible to allow for variation and that people were at least theoretically able to opt out of communal arrangements so that a little land remained outside the rotations, although, in the seventeenth century, at least, it did not amount to much of the cultivated surface. *Le Problème des subsistances,* I, chap. 1.
38. 1Q1050.
39. Leducq, 28 March 1768, *bail amphitéotique,* for eighteen years. The 18 mencaudées were located in Clary, the others in Bertry.
40. Leducq, 10 January 1781 and 13 August 1764. The property was located in Clary.
41. Leducq, 10 March 1777.
42. L6651.
43. C19257, 3 February 1776, inquest held in Montigny related to the lease of

its pastures, described the pasturing of sheep in pens (*parcs*) set in various parts (*quartiers*) of the territory.

44. Jean Meuvret makes the same argument but believes that the intermingling was limited. *Le Problème des subsistances*, III, 20. Only one village argued that the sheep ruined the soil; the rest were concerned with their eating their crops.

45. L6651-2, November–December 1790. The last point was made most forcefully by the villages of Walincourt and Lesdain.

46. For a rational reading of scattering, see Donald N. McCloskey, "The Persistence of English Common Fields," in William N. Parker and Eric L. Jones, eds., *European Peasants and Their Markets* (Princeton, N.J., 1975), pp. 73–119.

47. Exchanges of land and purchases of adjoining plots do occasionally appear in notarial records.

48. *Plan figuratif des Plusieurs Chemins au terroire de montigny aves Les pieces des terre y aboutissante Renseigné par Lettres alphabetique.*

49. 4G3297, "declaration des terres appartenantes à l'Aumosne Prevostée de Cambrésis et à l'office des vicaires de l'Eglise de Cambray, à Montigny," 22 July 1670. Chapter lease of 12 December 1765. 37H229, abbey of Cantimpré leases of 24 February and 11 March 1772. C Bureau des Finances/fiefs No. 3554, purchase of La Bruyère, 3 September 1768.

50. See McCloskey, "Persistence of English Common Fields."

51. Demangeon, *La Picardie*, p. 211.

52. Dieudonné, *Statistique*, I, 361–65.

53. Sir E. John Russell, *The World of the Soil* (London, 1961), p. 214.

54. Dieudonné, *Statistique*, I, 364, 376.

55. Demangeon, *La Picardie*, chap. 5.

56. "Whichever way one looks in the countryside come spring, one sees groups of weeders (*sarcleurs*), crawling on their knees, looking with the most scrupulous attention for weeds that need pulling out." Dieudonné, *Statistique*, I, 376. On the importance of weeding see also Meuvret, *Le Problème des subsistances*, I, 119–20.

57. Charles Crinon's lease of La Trappe in 1757, for example, made him "bien dument fumer et amender lesdites terres," presumably with manure, though marl and ashes were also used. 4G3297, 15 July 1757.

58. Lefebvre, *Paysans du Nord*, p. 210. Dieudonné, *Statistique*, I, 420.

59. 5G519, 31 March 1716. Another villager, Jean Philippe Pigou, worked as a weaver until 1762, after which he became a *chaufourier*, producing lime.

60. Leducq, 10 March 1777.

61. Neveux, *Vie et déclin*, p. 137; de Calonne, *La Vie agricole*, p. 107; Young, *Travels in France*, p. 262; 5G330, 10 April 1782.

62. C suppl. 524, 26 May 1709.

63. Dieudonné, *Statistique,* I, 382–83.
64. 1H507, 26 November 1734. A quarrel between two farmers at Le Troncquoy took place in a barn where one was spending the day "measuring the grain that his threshers had threshed that day." Leducq, 8 February 1782: an inventory listed 1,500 sheafs of wheat that had not yet been threshed.
65. C20299. *Bans politiques.*
66. Dieudonné. *Statistique,* I, p. 352.
67. Etienne Gave, Bertry notary, 13 November 1690; Off. 4000, 20 July 1761.
68. Off. 19984 and VIIIB 1e série 8918.
69. Leducq, 6 May 1777. Marriage contract from the village of Bertry: "une étille de mulquinier et une faux servant à la moisson."
70. Off. 11515.
71. Off. 13012.
72. Off. 12848, 2 October 1750.
73. 4G2161.
74. VIIIB 1e série 11150, 6 April 1680: "Because of the great, lengthy wars that have gone on forever, they and their predecessors suffered periodically from serious ravages both in their horses and crops, so that they fell into the most dire straits." One of them added that their misery could also be traced "to some evil spells [*maléfices*] since almost every day a horse would die leaving them nothing to plough with."
75. Antoine Boursier, Clary notary, marriage contract between Valentin Taisne of Wambaix and Michelle Leduc, widow of Nicolas Legibo, of Montigny, 29 June 1678, and settlement between Calixte Gabet of Montigny and his daughter Anne Gabet and her husband, Michel Malezieux, 25 July 1678.
76. C suppl. 524 (Montigny); C20969, C états 270 (Clary); C suppl. 474 (Bertry); C21043 (Ligny).
77. Leducq, 19 November 1733.
78. Leducq, marriage contract 29 October 1728, and C suppl. 524, 1744 tax roll.
79. Leducq, 6 October 1736.
80. C suppl. 474.
81. C21043.
82. L1794, "Contribution patriotique" of the Year IV (1796). Postmortem inventory, Leducq, 8 February 1782.
83. C suppl. 524, 13 September 1745.
84. Dejardin, Cambrai notary, 30 June 1781. Inventories of the goods belonging to Catherine Jeanne Defontaine, widow of Jean Baptiste Warlet, farmer at Cantaing.
85. 1Q1050, No. 7, 18 Messidor VI (1798).
86. M651/24.
87. Off. 18930, 2 May 1786.
88. 5G350, 30 September 1790.

89. See Steven L. Kaplan, *Provisioning Paris: Merchants and Millers in the Grain and Flour Trade During the Eighteenth Century* (Ithaca, N.Y., 1984), Charles Tilly, *The Contentious French* (Cambridge, Mass., 1985).

90. L1462, March 1797.

91. L6598.

92. Saint-Jacob, *Paysans de la Bourgogne,* p. 151.

93. Pierre Goubert in E. Labrousse et al., *Histoire économique et sociale de la France,* II (Paris, 1970), 444. and Jean Jacquart in E. Le Roy Ladurie, ed., *Histoire de la France rurale,* II (Paris, 1975), 238.

94. Braudel, *Capitalism and Material Life,* p. 79; Goubert in *Histoire économique et sociale,* II, 443.

95. Neveux, *Vie et déclin,* p. 240.

96. Lefebvre, *Paysans du Nord,* p. 207.

97. L6598 (1792) and C15428 (April 1750).

98. M651/24, *Statistique de la France,* 1836.

99. C suppl. 524.

100. Marriage contracts at times assigned wheat allowances to those parents who ceded the greater part of their belongings to the new couple. In 1746 Etienne Lenglet, a subsistence farmer, and his wife received three mencauds a year that would be reduced to two should one of them die. By the mid-1780s, Dominique Ego and his wife, more prosperous weavers, were to get fourteen mencauds. 3G888, 5 May 1746 and Leducq, 17 November 1784. Some historians have suggested that prohibitive amounts were set to stimulate filial piety so that such figures are completely meaningless. Yves Castan, *Honnêteté et relations sociales en Languedoc (1715–1780)* (Paris, 1974), p. 229. See also the evidence in David G. Troyansky, *Old Age in the Old Regime: Image and Experience in Eighteenth-Century France* (Ithaca, N.Y., 1989), chap. 6. Pierre Goubert estimated that a family of five or six needed 19.5 hectolitres of grain. A mencaud measured .55 hectolitres so that the stated amount would come to forty mencauds, or 6.66 per person, a figure that exceeds Montigny's average yield. *Cent mille provinciaux au XVIIe siècle: Beauvais et le Beauvaisis de 1600 à 1730* (Paris, 1968), p. 127.

101. David Sabean makes similar observations. *Property, Production and Family,* pp. 21–22, and 51ff.

6   Rural Transformations

1. Boursier, 29 October 1678, and 29 June 1678. Leduc's spouse came from Wambaix and contributed 200 florins in cash.

2. Jean Charles Aimé or Haymé in the 1740s and Jean Louis Lefebvre in the 1770s—at which time they married in the village.

3. L6651, Crèvecoeur.

4. One revolutionary survey asked whether they should continue to do so, and received a variety of answers, some positive, stating that it gave shepherds a stake in the well-being of the flock, but more were negative, concerned with limiting the damages that sheep inflicted on the crops. L6651-2, November and December 1790.

5. C suppl. 524. *Capitation.*

6. 1701 capitation: Ligny, C21043; Clary C20969; Troisvilles C21175.

7. C21175.

8. C suppl. 524, July 1689, and C20711; Leducq, 1 January 1732; C suppl., July 1744 (Jean Baptiste Lamouret); C suppl. 429, 1754–56; Leducq, 12 May 1749, 31 December 1753, and 16 July 1762 (leases).

9. Off. 12848, 2 October 1750.

10. Leducq, 25 February 1786.

11. Leducq, 25 November 1718. Jean Druon, Bertry notary, 31 December 1688. François Mairesse, Bertry notary, 8 February 1692. Leducq, 26 January 1727, 29 October 1728.

12. Leducq, 9 January 1787.

13. Leducq, 12 February 1720.

14. C suppl. 524, 22 January 1746.

15. The same was true of the ownership of asses and donkeys, which in the seventeenth century had allowed the marketing of local produce in provincial markets. Thus, Jacques Lefort owned one or two cows and several small horses and asses with which he carted local wood to town. In the late seventeenth century three households owned three donkeys each. They were not used for farm work and, for the most part, were replaced in the eighteenth century by horses (which could also pull the plough). Local merchants, like Jean Pierre Lantier, rode on horseback. In the eighteenth century, donkeys ceased to figure either in dowries or on tax rolls. The small-scale trading in which they had played such a role had been overshadowed by larger trading ventures.

16. C suppl. 524.

17. Ibid.

18. Pierre de Saint-Jacob noted a similar effect in northern Burgundy in the 1780s, where cattle disease pushed laboureurs already in a precarious position out of farming. *Paysans de la Bourgogne,* p. 537.

19. C. Douchez, "Notice historique sur Beauvois," p. 349.

20. J857/3.

21. Leducq, 2 February 1742 and 4 June 1743; 6 November 1712, 18 January 1728, 22 November 1728, 16 February 1730, 3 February 1733.

22. C suppl. 524; Leducq, 28 October 1728, 6 February 1738: Isidore Delacourt received 2½ mencaudées, 17 mencauds of wheat and one loom. C 20969, C suppl. 524, C états 269–70 (tax records).

23. 3G889, 18 April 1785. He and his wife also owned property in Caullery. Jacques Michel Renard, one of his contemporaries, also appeared in one document as a "cloth merchant and *laboureur*."
24. Off. 4000, 20 July 1761.
25. Jean-Pierre Jessenne, *Pouvoir au village et Révolution: Artois, 1760–1848* (Lille, 1987), who argues for the continuities in structures and organization does not examine possible changes in membership.
26. C20969, 18 July 1762.
27. 4G2145, February–March 1757.
28. 4G7778-9.
29. Olwen H. Hufton, *The Poor of Eighteenth-Century France, 1750–1789* (Oxford, 1974).
30. L11967, Tribunal criminel du département du Nord, Year VI (1798).

7 Weaving

1. Emile Coornaert, *Un Centre industriel d'autrefois, la draperie-sayetterie d'Hondschoote (XIVe–XVIIIe siècles)* (Paris, 1930).
2. Philippe Guignet, *Mines, manufactures et ouvriers du Valenciennois au XVIIIe siècle: Contributions à l'histoire du travail dans l'ancienne France* (New York, 1977), p. 494: in town, workers received ten, twelve, or twenty livres depending on the fineness of the cloth; in the countryside, wages ranged between eight and eighteen livres.
3. Neveux, *Vie et déclin*, dates its introduction to the early seventeenth century. Fine linen weavers appear as witnesses to lawsuits later in the century, in Robert Muchembled et al., *Prophètes et sorciers dans les Pays-Bas XVIe–XVIIIe siècles* (Paris, 1978), p. 202.
4. For a full discussion of this process, see Guignet, *Mines, manufactures*.
5. Gay Gullickson has argued that soil fertility did not determine the spread of industry in the Pays de Caux. She is right to correct Franklin Mendels's argument that only areas of subsistence farming attracted rural industry. Nonetheless, the pattern in Cambrésis shows that soil fertility did play a role, although at the regional rather than individual village level. *Spinners and Weavers of Auffay*, chap. 3.
6. C15428, 1750.
7. L7622, and L6724, 1791 tax rolls, "contribution foncière."
8. Dieudonné, *Statistique*, II, 278–80.
9. L6722 and 6724.
10. These figures were obtained by comparing Dieudonné's data on looms with that on population size [vol. III, tables]. As 22 to 25 percent of the inhabitants owned looms, this yielded a proportion of one loom per household

(containing approximately four persons). The number of households corresponded to the number of houses also cited by the prefect and so seemed a valid approximation.

11. L6651-2. Two hundred fourteen male and female spinners in the village of Lesdain.

12. Aubencheul-au-Bac, a village with very poor soil outside the weaving belt, provides a perfect example (L6722). In 1790 most of the inhabitants still worked on the land: 7 percent as farmers, 21 percent as ménagers, and 34 percent as farm laborers. There were also 12 percent publicans, a few artisans, and one lone linen weaver. Inchy, by comparison, a village with similar soil but in the weaving region, had only 3 percent farmers and 7 percent farm laborers, whereas 58 percent were linen weavers, 11 percent spinners, and 7 percent merchants (L6723).

13. *Paysans du Nord*, pp. 896–99.

14. Guignet, *Mines, manufactures*, pp. 216–18.

15. C21715, C suppl. 727 (1701), C suppl. 730 (1704), C états 739 (1754), C états 269 (1776).

16. C20969, Clary (1701); C21043, Ligny (1701 and 1743). The examples appear in the papers of Antoine Boursier, Clary notary.

17. C suppl. 474.

18. Guignet, *Mines, manufactures*, pp. 170–71.

19. L6651-2. Not all villages responded and not all answered the questions in detail.

20. Dieudonné, *Statistique*, II, 287; Lefebvre, *Paysans du Nord*, p. 289. One author estimated that the average worker produced twenty-four pieces annually with a hiatus for the harvest. Archives nationales F12 658B, "Observations sur la manufacture des toiles dites Baptistes et Linons dont le commerce se fait par les villes de Saint-Quentin et de Valenciennes," 1788. He apparently arrived at this figure, which seems disproportionately high, by dividing an approximate number of cloths sold in the major centers by an estimated number of looms. It bears no relation to any other evidence I have encountered and can be dismissed as hypothetical.

21. The more specific answers range from eight pieces in Caullery to ten per loom in Saint-Aubert and to twelve per weaver in Saint-Souplet—in other words, five to eight months' worth of work. The data are not always consistent. Dieudonné's figures for the number of looms in villages in 1790 fit awkwardly with the number of workers. In Caullery, Esnes, Fontaine au Pire, Ligny, Montigny, Saint-Aubert, and Selvigny, the ratio of looms to weavers is two to one. Some villages like Lesdain or Haucourt, however, had three looms per worker, and in Saint-Souplet the ratio jumps to five to one. Similar discrepancies appear if we reverse the process and assess production by loom rather than by weaver.

Cloth Production Per Loom

Village	Workers	Pieces	Looms	Average per loom
Crèvecoeur	20	240	110	2
Esnes	70	850	132	6.5
Fontaine au Pire	128	1,152	176	6.5
Haucourt	21	250	65	4
Lesdain	—	52	[60]	—
Ligny	152	1,138	254	4.5
Montigny	60	440	124	3.5
Saint-Aubert	—	—	—	10
Selvigny	55	825	114	7

From twelve pieces per worker, Crèvecoeur falls to two per loom. This example again shows the difficulty in determining precisely the amount of time spent weaving and in distinguishing clearly between those who worked regularly and those who did so only occasionally. To complicate matters, the villages' declarations to the government do not always correspond with the evidence found in the tax rolls. Crèvecoeur's twenty weavers exceed the five who figure on the 1790 tax return. Esnes as well recorded forty-one weavers on its tax roll and declared seventy in the 1790 survey. For Montigny, the gap between the number of weavers listed in 1787 and those declared in 1790 represents a drop of one-third. All we can do, then, is rely on the time span indicated by the weavers themselves and posit that they worked half of the year.

22. Leducq, 16 April 1784, Walincourt: a widowed mother left her son "two fine linen looms with the relevant utensils, one on which he works and the other which is in the house of her worker, in Walincourt."

23. C21043, 16 December 1743.

24. Leducq, 1 July 1713, and 26 November 1730.

25. Leducq, 8 February 1771 and 13 November 1786, for example. The last contract arranged for the groom to share the cellar and *ourdoir* and to receive the loom on which he habitually worked.

26. All of the following details on weaving and spinning come from Dieudonné's *Statistique,* vol. 2. Leducq, 8 November 1770, and J. B. Cardon, Cambrai notary, 5 November 1770 for the value of the looms.

27. This was a specialty of the Puche family who moved into the village at that time.

28. Off. 10707.

29. C5720, Opposition of the Estates and Cambrai magistrates to the edict of 4 July 1752 regulating the linen industry. "This trade needs apprentices, because one cannot produce without them, the inhabitants of the country-

side have had no other masters than their fathers, who train each succeeding generation. . . ."

30. C suppl. 524.

31. Dieudonné, *Statistique,* II, 287.

32. C21043, 16 December 1743.

33. Ibid., three weavers had two children; one had three children; two had four children; one had five children and one other had six.

34. Serge Grafteaux, *Mémé Santerre* (Paris, 1975).

35. Off. 15613, October 1773.

36. The recurrence of names makes identifications sometimes hazardous. Honoré Faré, weaver (fourteen and a half) [21 December 1765]; Celestin Joseph François, weaver (fourteen) [2 November 1788]; Jean Joseph Rousseau, weaver (fifteen) [30 November 1790]; Marie Claire Rousseau, spinner (eight) godmother to her brother [21 May 1790].

37. Jean Baptiste Aimé, ouvrier (twelve) [12 March 1765]. The ten-year-old Jean Joseph Rousseau is called a weaver's son on 29 April 1786, but a pupil two years later [6 April 1788], as was the case of his eight-year-old brother [21 May 1790]. Other schoolchildren appear in this period in the Denimal, Mora, and Lantier families. They included both boys and girls.

38. J857, 7 March 1766.

39. Dieudonné, *Statistique,* II, 287.

40. Ibid., II, 290–91. Lefebvre estimated the wages as fifteen to twenty livres, *Paysans du Nord,* p. 289; and Guignet as eight to eighteen livres, *Mines, manufactures.* These estimates provide the only information extant on individual earnings.

41. One livre equaled four-fifths of a florin.

42. 5G338, 26 May 1787.

43. L1505, 17 January 1791.

44. According to Dieudonné, they began at the age of five or six. *Statistique,* II, 229.

45. In Saint-Quentin a quart measured 240 and not 200 threads. Guignet, *Mines, manufactures,* p. 36. See this work as well for a detailed description of the types of cloth and their method of manufacture.

46. C16017, 7 July 1781. Crommelin, the inspector of manufactures, provided a different range than that given by Dieudonné. Batistes, he said, ranged from seven to twenty-seven, narrow linons from five to twenty-one, and wide ones from five to twenty-four.

47. VIIIB 1e série 9532, accounts of the Cantimpré bleaching works in Cambrai, owned by the Frémicourt family. The common cloth brought by a Ligny weaver for bleaching measured between 22½ and 43½ to as many as 79 ells. One Cambrai ell was equivalent to 0.729 meters.

48. André Dolez, *La Mulquinerie à Cambrai des origines à 1789* (Lille, 1932), p. 10.

49. A. N. F12 658B, 29 November 1785. The gaze, a light transparent cloth used mostly for kerchiefs, was invented in 1765. Charles Picard, *Saint-Quentin, de son commerce et de ses industries,* 2 vols., I (Saint-Quentin, 1865), 193.

50. C18516, Crommelin reports, 1780s.

51. Dieudonné, *Statistique,* II, 219.

52. L6651-2.

53. A.N. F12 658B.

54. Mendels, "Industrialization and Population Pressure," pp. 23–24, 201.

55. L6651, 1791.

56. VIIIB 1e série 8420, October and November 1782. Witnesses actually attributed him 100 or 125 *étils* or *étilles pour recueillir les fillets,* which might have referred to the warping mechanism and therefore involved even more spinners.

57. In 1766 Marie Josèphe Beauvois of the village of Marcoing sued the estate of her late husband, the Prémont wood merchant Antoine Dubois, and her stepson, Charles Antoine Dubois, who had moved to Montigny (Off. 12952). She demanded the money she had earned spinning flax during her married life. These earnings had been earmarked for her own use in her marriage contract, but she had, in fact, spent them on household necessities. Her opponents brought forth witnesses who argued that she had rarely sat at her wheel "so that she barely produced two portées a week, if that much, since there were times when she didn't spin at all because she didn't care for that sort of work." What is more, her output was shoddy and barely worth seventeen patars the quart. The widow responded by claiming "that she *could have* [my emphasis] spun two quarts a week" and of the finest quality, worth 30 patars and even 33 patars a quart, but that she was ready to estimate her income at 52 patars for two quarts. She lost her case, but it is interesting to note how readily neighbors judged each other's work.

58. 3U145/34, testimony of 16 Germinal XI. Men also appeared: a master weaver aged fifty-three and his thirty-year-old worker, who shared the same cellar.

59. L1505, 17 January 1791.

60. Off. 8682, 7 November 1707.

61. IXB276/149, December 1725.

62. Off. 10707, and 5G169, "Sentences civiles," 13 November 1732. The issue was settled in the aunt's favor.

63. See Guignet, *Mines, manufactures,* for a full portrait of Crommelin. A cloth merchant himself, whose small company went bankrupt, he forever mistrusted and resented unfettered rural production.

64. C5271, Crommelin reports.

65. Comparative table communicated by Philippe Guignet.

66. See Hufton, *The Poor of Eighteenth-Century France;* and Schwartz, *Policing the Poor.*

67. See the discussion of wages above.
68. I obtained these averages by dividing the number of villagers by the number of houses listed in Dieudonné's tables, at the end of vol. III, *Statistique*.

8   Trade

1. Dolez, *La Mulquinerie à Cambrai*, p. 84, and Picard, *Saint-Quentin*.
2. Dolez, *La Mulquinerie à Cambrai*, pp. 90–91.
3. Ibid., pp. 3–5.
4. Guignet, *Mines, manufactures*, p. 93.
5. Ibid., pp. 180–85.
6. Ibid., p. 187.
7. A Clary linen manufacturer, Jacques Boursier, owed 528 livres to a Valenciennes bleacher in 1789. In October 1788 Jean Charles Marcaille from Saint-Aubert acknowledged a debt of 240 livres to the bleacher Houlieux also of Valenciennes. When Jean Baptiste Taine, merchant as well as royal cloth stamper of Cambrai, went bankrupt in 1787, he owed more than 2,500 florins to the Sieur Brabant for the same service, and that same establishment had tried to recover 235 livres from Ignace Taine, his predecessor, thirty years earlier. Jean Pierre Lantier of Montigny, although he traded mainly with Saint-Quentin, consigned twenty-three pieces with Ignace Taine which the latter sent to Valenciennes for bleaching. (Off. 4611, 5G340, Off. 19713, Off. 9115, VIIIB, 1e série 25050.)
8. VIIIB 1e série 9574, 25 May 1767.
9. Picard, *Saint-Quentin*, p. 192 and pp. 348–53, article XIX of the "Arrêt du Conseil d'Etat" of 12 September 1729 regulating linen production.
10. 4G2145, 25 March 1757.
11. Cited by Dolez, *La Mulquinerie à Cambrai*, p. 114, note 6.
12. Picard, *Saint-Quentin*, pp. 163–69.
13. "Arrêt du Conseil d'Etat fixant les droits de courtage dus aux courtiers de Saint-Quentin," 4 August 1750, in ibid., pp. 404–8.
14. Such was the claim of the weavers from the villages of Hapres and Haussy in Hainaut to whom Valenciennes officials had offered "advances" at one-quarter of the value of their cloth in 1750. Guignet, *Mines, manufactures*, p. 209.
15. Picard, *Saint-Quentin*, pp. 166–67.
16. C états 208, Serain, February 1761.
17. C17785.
18. Off. 4000, inventory of 20 July 1761.
19. C5271, 10 January 1770.
20. For England, see, for example, Margaret Spufford, *The Great Reclothing of Rural England: Petty Chapmen and Their Wares in the Seventeenth Century*

(London, 1984); Joan Thirsk, *Economic Policy and Projects: The Development of a Consumer Society in Early Modern England* (Oxford, 1978). For nineteenth-century France: C. Robert Muller and A. Allix, *Les Colporteurs de l'Oisans* (Grenoble, 1979; orig. ed., 1925), and in a more popular vein Claire Krafft Pourrat, *Le Colporteur et la mercière* (Paris, 1982).

21. C états 209 (1763–76) and C 20776 (1776–90).
22. A.N. F12 644, edicts of 14 July 1682, 31 May 1685, renewed 1785.
23. C5270, report of 16 May 1760.
24. C états 270, 1770.
25. Leducq, Cambrai notary, lease, 25 July 1777. Jean Louis Labbé, born in Montigny in 1719, died there in 1793, married twice in the village.
26. This was also the case of a village with very poor soil, Aubencheul au Bac, located nearby. It had not attracted cottage industry and its poorer inhabitants survived by hiring themselves out as day laborers.
27. Population figures for 1790 from Dieudonné, *Statistique*, III, tables; figures on peasant landownership from Lefebvre, *Paysans du Nord,* tables.
28. To cite a few more examples: in Bertry (193 passports), population: 1,294, peasants making up 90 percent of landowners controlling 35 percent of the land; in Inchy (159 passports), population: 775, with percentages of 76 and 9, respectively; in Viesly (3 passports), population: 1,751, 93.5 percent and 47 percent; Saint-Soupplet (141 passports), population: 1531, peasants making up 85 percent of landowners with 17 percent of the land; Paillencourt (no passports), population: 1,141, peasants representing 70.5 percent of landowners for 17 percent of the land.
29. Between 1763 and 1776, only eleven cloth merchants headed for France; thirty-three did so between 1776 and 1790. Forty-six merchants included France on their way north in the first period; ninety-three in the second.
30. Brayer, *Statistique du département de l'Aisne,* p. 285.
31. We know little about this itinerant trade partly, as the inspector of manufactures suggested, because some of it was contraband. In fact, the borders were more carefully watched than Crommelin admitted. Ignace Taine, a cloth merchant from Cambrai, lost eight thousand livres through two seizures of merchandise which he was importing from Holland as well as another six hundred because, as he described, "while passing through the Menin stamping station, his cloth was seized and confiscated, on the pretense that he had failed to declare its exact length and that he had to plead his case in Courtrai where he finally reached some agreement" (Off. 9112).

In January 1769 Philippe Delhaye of Bertry requested permission to travel to Magdeburg in Prussia to pick up a case containing eighteen bundles of fine linens, stamped P, L, J, which had been deposited there when his brother, an itinerant merchant, had died. All his cloth therefore bore some sort of a seal (C états 209). Even the peddlar from Maurois—in an altogether different category from the cloth merchants described above—carried mostly stamped cloth when he was arrested by the Farms' brigade on the road to Maubeuge one October morning (C19600). The seal of Cateau-Cambrésis appeared on four pieces, another eight and a half had a manufacturer's stamp, while five more had no seal and were impounded. By this account, one-third of the lot was unregistered, and so perhaps a maximum of one-third of the cloth woven in the countryside was dispatched illegally and failed to appear in official evaluations.

32. Ibid.
33. 4G2155, 4 April 1786, bailliage court of the Chapter of Cambrai.
34. Off. 298 (bankruptcy, 1763), VIIIB 1e série 25050, 1782 (bankruptcy of 1775).
35. C 5270, report of 5 January 1771.
36. See, for example, A.N. F12 646, discussions concerning a trade treaty between France and the Spanish Netherlands, 1703. The actual export of linen thread had been prohibited for fear of undermining French manufactures.
37. C états 208, including the listing by the curé of Bertry, dated 10 February 1761.
38. C 6974.
39. Ibid., Versailles, 16 May 1757, letter from the controller-general asking the intendant to urge the archbishop to be gentle with local Protestants: "I would beg you to explain to the archbishop of Cambrai how harmful it would be for the welfare and trade of the province if these manufacturers were forced to emigrate."
40. Ibid., letter of 28 January 1783.
41. Ibid., 1772.
42. A.N. F12 660, report from London, 9 May 1751. Similar accusations had already been prevalent at the turn of the century (A.N. F12 646). See also N. B. Harte, "The Rise of Protection and the English Linen Trade, 1690–1790," in *Textile History and Economic History: Essays in Honour of Miss Julia de Lacy Mann,* ed. N. B. Harte and K. G. Ponting (Manchester, 1973), pp. 74–112.
43. C 5270, Crommelin continually alludes to this in his reports.
44. A.N. F12 660.
45. Harte, "Protection and the English Linen Trade," sec. II.
46. A.N. F12 658B, 1785, and F12 660 for 1751.
47. A.N. F12 660, in this case, mailed by coach.
48. VIIIB 1e série 11340, Parlement of Flanders.
49. A.N. F12 658B. Guignet, who examined a number of the complaints regarding the illegal export of yarn, believes that they arose when the textile trade as a whole was in trouble. He also supports the intendant Taboureau's contention that the spinners preferred to sell their yarn to smugglers who paid them more than to local or urban merchants (*Mines, manufactures,* pp. 134–38).

50. Off. 10707; Leducq, 3 February 1733; 5G342, 344 (1788–89); 5G328, 5 June 1782; C5721, 1772.
51. VIIIB 1e série 11340, 10 March 1722.
52. 5G324, 17 April 1779, and 5G326, 26 April 1784.
53. 4G2163, 21 January 1778.
54. Off. 10633.
55. 5G340, 22 October 1788; Off. 19365, 10 January 1785.
56. C suppl. 524 for all of the information on the storekeepers.
57. C6974, 11 May 1777.

9 The Rise of the Merchant-Weavers

1. C suppl. 524, 25 May 1709.
2. See, for example, Kriedte et al., *Industrialization Before Industrialization*. This is also the conclusion of William Reddy, although within a different perspective that allows far greater control over production to the individual weaver. *The Rise of Market Culture: The Textile Trade and French Society, 1750–1900* (Cambridge, 1984), pp. 4–11, 24–34.
3. Ibid., pp. 64, 101.
4. See Kriedte, *Industrialization Before Industrialization*, and Dewald, *Pont-St. Pierre*.
5. Guignet, *Mines, manufactures*, p. 38; Charles Picard, *Saint-Quentin*, p. 549.
6. The list is included among the various villages' surviving Ancien Régime tax records.
7. C suppl. 524, December 1743.
8. C20969, 18 October 1743.
9. C21043, 16 December 1743. One entry read "avec trois domestiques pour travailler a son estille," meaning *stil*, or profession, which was that of a weaver. The same went for another weaver who employed four such men.
10. England was similarly affected in 1758–59. Julian Hoppit, *Risk and Failure in English Business, 1700–1800* (Cambridge, 1987), p. 98.
11. C états 208, 7 February 1761. "Jay tachés de faire les choses le plus secretement es le mieux qu'il ma esté possible."
12. Both florins and livres were used interchangeably by curés.
13. C21158 and C états 208.
14. C états 208, 10 February 1761.
15. Picard, *Saint-Quentin*, lists them on pp. 448–50.
16. Ibid., p. 467.
17. Off. 298.
18. Off. 15534, 1755.
19. Ibid., p. 1755.
20. Besides the list of actual losses and the tax waivers provided by the Estates in

1761–62 (C21158 and C états 208), there is another list of tax reductions for 1764–65 (C20416). The latter ranged from 4 florins 14 patars (Hubert Denimal) to 35 florins 17 patars 3 doubles (Jean Pierre Lantier).

21. C états 208, 9 February 1761.
22. Ibid., 14 February 1761.
23. C21158, 11 December 1761.
24. Off. 10707, Lefort, 1730.
25. 3G890, 14 February 1789.
26. We know little about the activities of the group of merchant-weavers, consisting of the Farés, Gaves, Cauchys, and Levesques, partly because their litigation has not survived. They appear to have formed an alternate trading network to the one that revolved around Lantier and his relatives. They may well have turned to northern trade, as the career of two of their members indicates. In February 1765 Philippe Cauchy received a nine-month pass to sell cloth in Flanders, Brabant, Liège, and Germany, and Antoine Joseph Cauchy obtained a similar passport in 1768. Although Philippe appeared periodically as godfather in parish registers, either as a weaver or linen merchant, he may have been absent too often to leave much of a trace in local records. We can only surmise that he continued to operate within the Faré-Cauchy-Levesque alliances amplified by the participation of his own brothers-in-law, Léonard Delacourt, another merchant, and Jean Baptiste Delbart, a weaver.
27. Off. 298 (1763), Off. 3285 (1775).
28. 3G887–890. Of course, one could amass tiny amounts and sell them at one stroke as happened to Jean Pierre Lantier, but the trend in land accumulation is nonetheless clear and reflected in leaseholds.
29. When his daughter, Marie Catherine, married two years later, she received the usufruct of 5 mencaudées, the family homestead, 800 florins, two looms, a cow, and a set of household goods. (Leducq, 3 February 1719, 16 January 1745, 18 July 1747, and C suppl. 524.)
30. C états 288 (1750) and 3G890 (19 June 1762).
31. 3G889, 24 July 1756.
32. Charles Antoine Dubois, one of Montigny's principal borrowers, received 6,000 florins from a cavalry officer in Cambrai, 4,000 from a barrister at the Paris Parlement, secretary of the Cambrésis Estates, 4,000 livres from a spinster in Le Cateau, 1,500 florins both from a priest in Cambrai and from one of the farmers of Le Troncquoy, 1,200 florins from a widow in Cambrai, and 600 florins from a resident of that same city (3G890 [1776–89]). The money obtained in this way could then be put to a variety of uses, some of them clearly commercial, as Charles Antoine Dubois declared in 1776 when he borrowed 4,000 livres on the strength of thirty-three mencaudées so that he could continue trading.
33. Off. 13073 (1768); see also chapter 4 above.

34. Cardon, Cambrai notary, 19 October 1770, settlement of dispute; Leducq, 10 October 1785, division of inheritance.
35. Leducq, 10 August 1785.
36. 2E26/540.
37. Leducq, 21 October 1719.
38. Off. 3908, Off. 16446 (1783); Leducq, 18 January 1771 and 25 June 1774; 3G890 18 January 1779 and 26 June 1789.
39. 4G1681, 3G887–890.
40. It is not clear whether they purchased both since the fourteen-mencaudée fief would have come to Marie Angélique through her mother.
41. Leducq, 8 January 1771, 25 June 1774; 3G890 (1776); Leducq, 10 January 1781; 3G890 12 January 1784, 11 August 1789.
42. 4G2156, 17 May 1788.
43. Off. 10707.
44. Leducq, 16 February 1730.
45. 5G545, 1735–36.
46. Leducq, 22 August 1751.
47. C suppl. 524.
48. The Delbarts, descended from the shepherd Jean Delbart, were a fecund lot.
49. 3G887–90.
50. 3G890, 18 April 1761 and 1 December 1762.
51. Off. 15452, 2 and 10 June 1776.
52. Off. 9030, 12 June 1776.
53. Off. 9085, 25 June 1778.
54. 3G887–890.
55. C suppl. 524.
56. This proved to be the case of Caudry's tax rolls, which had been faked by the village council. See Vardi, "Peasants and the Law."
57. C19205, 18 December 1774; C suppl. 524, 26 February 1774; 3G890, 5 February 1776 to 23 April 1776.

10 Credit and the Crisis in Entrepreneurship

1. In 1702, for example, Jean Baptiste Lobry, Montigny's blacksmith, owed 175 florins 19 patars to Marie Le Roux of Cambrai for various iron deliveries, as entered in her registers, and he similarly owed money to other suppliers. In December 1704 he was forced to declare bankruptcy and this, combined with other misdemeanors, condemned him to the galleys (Off. 1717 and Off. 17323).
2. Henri Platelle, ed., *Journal d'un curé de campagne au XVIIe siècle* (Paris, 1965), p. 185.
3. See above, in chap. 7, "Production" section.

4. VIIIB 1e série 11340.

5. Ibid., testimony of Marie Anne Herbert, 12 March 1722.

6. On these, see Raymond de Roover, *L'Evolution de la lettre de change, XIVe–XVIIIe siècles* (Paris, 1953), and Charles Carrière, Marcel Courdurié, Michel Gutsatz, René Squarzoni, *Banque et capitalisme commercial: La lettre de change au XVIIIe siècle* (Marseilles, 1976). Also Pierre Deyon, *Amiens, capitale provinciale: Etude sur la société urbaine au XVIIe siècle* (Paris, 1967), pp. 99–110; T. J. A. Le Goff, *Vannes and Its Region: A Study of Town and Country in Eighteenth-Century France* (Oxford, 1981), pp. 83–84, and Jean Pierre Hirsch, "La France révolutionnaire, comme berceau de la libre entreprise," paper presented at the Bicentennial of the French Revolution Conference, Washington D.C., May 1989.

7. Off. 15938 and Off. 18098.

8. One rural merchant began paying his workers with promissory notes and bills of exchange when his affairs took a turn for the worse. Jacques Joseph Campin of Quiévy went bankrupt in April 1788 with a debit of 76,180 livres. 5G345, 15 April 1788, and 5G347, 19 June 1789.

9. Off. 15534.

10. Off. 19365, 10 January 1785.

11. VIIIB 1e série 25050.

12. Colan subsequently seized the pieces.

13. Off. 5556, Off. 14139, 1757–58.

14. Off. 5556, 21 May 1757.

15. Off. 14139, and C21158.

16. Off. 7164.

17. Off. 298.

18. 5G327.

19. 5G346, 16 February 1788.

20. 5G340, 20 October 1786.

21. 5G340, 26 September 1786.

22. 5G340, 22 July 1788 and 6 August 1788.

23. Off. 6208 (1778), Off. 12180 and Off. 16446 (1783), Off. 9643 (1787).

24. Off. 20876, 1758. "Madame Rubet, je vous anvoi 1 lettre de 253 livres pour le billet proteste si vous aurie la bonte de me donne un peut de temps pour le Restant comme vous mavie promi veus me feré un grand plaisir je vous pris an grasse de nant Rien dirre comme jai afairre a se monsieur jeai peur qu'il soit decredité sela me poudroit faire interet an esperant que vous marcordere cette grasse je suius chadamme vostre humble serviteur, Leantier."

25. 5G179, Registre aux sentences, 22 January 1787.

26. Off. 6986 (1788).

27. 5G346, 16 February 1788.

28. Off. 15938. "A Montigny le 28 may 1756, p.l.414 livres. Os courant novambre prochain je pairai a Lordre de pierre boursie la somme de 414 livres

valeur reçu en merchandise dudit sieur a mon domicille che monsieur boutillie le jeune, marchand a Saint Quentin. P. Leantier."

29. Ibid.

30. 5G327, 19 April 1775, "cession miserable."

31. Reddy also notes this flexibility which he attributes to the lack of an entrepreneurial system. *Rise of Market Culture,* p. 23.

32. C16883 (1757) and C7084 (1759).

33. Off. 298, 1763. Unfortunately this is all we know about the venture. The attempt to link this Baralle with the noble owner of La Bruyère did not yield any results.

34. VIIIB 1e série 25050.

35. J857/2, 6 April 1759.

36. VIIIB 1e série 8420.

37. 5G331, 13 April 1783.

38. VIIIB 1e série 23799 (1767); VIIIB 1e série 25050 (1782).

39. Off. 15879, 30 July 1766. This sum most probably concerned salt and tobacco which Lantier sold in the village (a profitable sideline) and for which he was prosecuted for fraud. VIIIB 1e série 23799 (1767); C16883 (April 1757, October 1759); C7084 (November 1759).

40. Off. 5099, 4 July 1776.

41. VIIIB 1e série 25050.

42. 4G2146 (1771–72).

43. VIIIB 1e série 25050 (1770).

44. VIIIB 1e série 8420, 2 November 1782. Another merchant-weaver from Caullery, Jean Baptiste Leduc (aged fifty) testified that "he provided numerous services to many small merchants."

45. VIIIB 1e série 25050.

46. Ibid.

47. 5G340, Jean Baptiste and Anselme Moity, see above.

48. Such as the disputed ownership of a 36-mencaudée fief in Marcoing. Cardon, Cambrai notary, 19 October 1777.

49. Leducq, 10 August 1785.

50. VIIIB 1e série 23799, 3 January 1767.

51. 5G339, 29 January1786.

52. 5G339, September–October 1786.

53. 5G340, July–August 1788.

54. 5G345, 15 April 1788.

55. 5G340, 19 September 1788.

56. See chapter 12 below.

57. Off. 12180, 4 October 1781.

58. Off. 12180, 1783.

59. Off. 16446, (19 March 1783); Off. 6208 (26 August 1788); Off. 9643; Off. 5986; Off. 7844.

60. C suppl. 524. 126 entries. The average contribution was 1.4 florins, median: 0.8 florins; fourteen villagers paid over 3 florins. In 1787 Jean Baptiste Gave, Pierre Toussaint Dron, Dominique Ego, Martin Leveque, Jean Baptiste Lesage, and Pierre Ignace Denimal paid more taxes than Lantier (17 florins 12 patars, 19 florins 9 patars, 20 florins 2 patars, 20 florins 11 patars, 21 florins 15 patars, and 22 florins 9 patars, respectively).
61. L1794 (1796).
62. J857/5 10 February and 7 May 1793.
63. L6912, L1794, J857/5 (9 November 1800, and 3 February 1803).
64. C5271, 10 January 1770. He made a similar complaint a year later.
65. L6651, 15 December 1790.
66. The cahiers of this region have not survived.
67. L6980, 11 September 1790, Pierre Ignace Boursier, mayor.

11   Revolution in the Village

1. Lefebvre, *Paysans du Nord,* p. 500.
2. See below, "The Aftermath."
3. Some have emphasized the peasants' distress at outside intervention into local affairs brought about by the Revolution. T. J. A. Le Goff and D. M. G. Sutherland, "The Revolution and the Rural Community in Eighteenth-Century Brittany," *Past and Present* 62 (1974): 96–119.
4. L6757, 10 December 1790.
5. L6980 (11 September 1790), L6757 (25 August and 12 December 1790, 6 March and 2 November 1792); L6896 (2 December 1790); L6933 (6 February 1791).
6. L6551, Frimaire III.
7. L6364, 4 April 1792.
8. Ibid.
9. L12465, verdict of 29 March 1792. Unfortunately, the testimony has not survived.
10. Duthoit, *Montigny-en-Cambrésis,* p. 170, citing documents of 5 February and 13 February 1792.
11. L6551, 27 Frimaire III (17 December 1794).
12. L13413, March 1794.
13. Duthoit, *Montigny-en-Cambrésis,* pp. 184–86, on the councils of 1795–96.
14. Ibid., pp. 189–90, September 1797.
15. This was another weaver, aged forty-nine, and brother of Louis François.
16. L120, Vendémiaire VI (October 1798).
17. L13413, 11 Floréal III (April–May 1795) "Qu'il s'en foutoit et emmerdoit tous les membres qui la composaient."
18. Cited by Duthoit, *Montigny-en-Cambrésis,* p. 193.

19. Ibid., p. 192.
20. Ibid., pp. 199, 202–3.
21. On 19 October 1792 an earlier council had denied that Montigny had anything to offer. L6949. L6367, 17 Pluviôse II (February 1794).
22. Ibid., 25 Frimaire II (December 1793).
23. L1202, 9 Nivôse VIII.
24. L1104, 9 Pluviôse IV (January 1796), "Tableau des émigrés rentrés."
25. L6368, and Duthoit, *Montigny-en-Cambrésis,* p. 179.
26. Duthoit, *Montigny-en-Cambrésis,* pp. 173, 176. L6367, 2 Nivôse II (January 1794); "The son of the said Petit had been caught fleeing . . . with a box containing a number of documents." L6367, 22 Nivôse II: "A delegation from the Popular Society was called in, and they handed the authorities a copy of the letter written by the émigré Petit of le Troncquoy in which he tells his son who was arrested yesterday to take some things to Valenciennes [then in enemy hands]."
27. L1205, 19 Germinal IV (April 1796). The cantonal authorities asked that he be provisionally struck off the list of émigrés, although he was still on it in January 1798. M131/51 No. 592. The subprefect was told to place Joseph Petit "under the mayor's surveillance" until some decision had been reached concerning his status (September 1800).
28. M131/51 No. 2503, 10 Messidor XI. See also Duthoit, *Montigny-en-Cambrésis,* p. 55. They were gone by 1810 when a new family came to inhabit that part of Le Troncquoy.
29. Duthoit, *Montigny-en-Cambrésis,* p. 179, on 7 Prairial II (26 May 1794).
30. L6367, 19 Pluviôse II (February 1794).
31. L13415, 1 Germinal IV (March 1795).
32. L6859, 26 Vendémiaire III (October 1794).
33. L6861, 26 Ventôse III (March 1795).
34. L11246, Neuvilly, n.d.; L11242, Landas, 9 Prairial III.
35. L13413, Crèvecoeur, Ventôse II.
36. Ibid., 11 November 1793.
37. Ibid., Villers-Outréaux, Brumaire II.
38. Ibid., 11 Frimaire 1793 (December 1793).
39. L13415, 25 Frimaire III (December 1794).
40. L13413.
41. L13414, 27 Ventôse II.
42. Michel Vovelle, *La Chute de la monarchie (1787–1792)* (Paris, 1972), p. 192.
43. Lefebvre, *Paysans du Nord,* p. 972, table 3-12.
44. I more fully discussed the problems with Lefebvre's calculations in "Peasants and the French Revolution: A Re-examination of Lefebvre's *Les Paysans du Nord,*" Bicentennial of the French Revolution conference, Washington, D.C., May 1989.
45. Montigny's bundle of notes are contained in J477/44.

46. For a description of these speculators, see Lefebvre, *Paysans du Nord*, pp. 477, 487.
47. On the peasants' apprenticeship of collective action, see Vardi, "Peasants and the Law," and Root, *Peasants and King in Burgundy*.
48. 1Q125.
49. Lefebvre offers the hypothesis that the flight to Varennes in June terrified the population, which feared émigré reprisals and put a temporary end to sales.
50. 1Q124, request of 17 August 1792, sale of 11 March 1793. In the district of Cambrai a hectare of land went for an average of 541 livres (or 180 livres per mencaudée)—that is, less than its official valuation and representing one-quarter of its real value. Lefebvre, *Paysans du Nord*, p. 460.
51. 1Q124, 4 March 1793, application of 24 April 1791 in 1Q95.
52. Ibid., 24 December 1792 and 17 May 1793. J477/44.
53. Lefebvre, *Paysans du Nord*, p. 451.
54. 1Q159, 2 October 1792.
55. Ibid. The fact that Hocquet was not buying for himself is clear by his declaration that he was a *command*, or agent.
56. J477/44.
57. 1Q126, 19 Thermidor III.
58. L6551 and Duthoit, *Montigny-en-Cambrésis*, p. 190.
59. 1Q867, No. 4819, 10 hectares, 2,000 livres deposit on 15 messidor IV, sold in Douai for 4,796 livres in 24 Ventôse V.
60. 1Q126, 28 Pluviôse IX; 1Q944, No. 160, 16 Floréal VII (11 hectares); 1Q951 No. 1474, 18 Vendémiaire VIII (11 hectares); 1Q951 No. 1475, 18 Vendémiaire VIII (6 hectares).
61. L6366.
62. 1Q932, No. 2368, sold in Douai, valued at 4,820 livres (prerevolutionary currency). Lefebvre argues that communities were reluctant to take over parish plots.
63. 1Q904, No. 405, 24 Vendémiaire VI.
64. Lefebvre claims that Claro, for example, kept nothing. *Paysans du Nord*, p. 496.
65. J477/44. Other resales involved one hectare purchased by three villagers in 1800 from Lebague. Dassonville had bought the priest's house for Constant Fontaine in Montigny. Finally, Vardon's widow sold to the Montigny farmer, Jean Martin Levecque, a small yard that had once belonged to the Chapter.
66. Ibid., in Pluviôse V, for 1,500 livres cash.
67. 1Q904, No. 405, 24 Vendémiaire VI.
68. 1Q867, No. 4819, and J477/44.
69. J477/44, 21 Vendémiaire XII.
70. J477/44.
71. 1Q1216.

72. The village's *cadastre* of that year. His family paid the highest property tax in the village in 1853 (0416/73) and the second highest in 1881 (0416/77).

73. Leducq, 19 December 1791.

74. Levavasseur, Cambrai notary, 22 January 1793.

75. J477/44, 1Q159, 932, 944, 948, 951, 978, 1216. They were Aimé, Godart, Delacourt, Lefebvre, Ramette, Renard, and Rousseau, to name but a few.

76. Levavasseur, Cambrai notary, 3 June 1793 and 21 June 1793, one men-caudée each in Caudry; 25 March 1794 one in Clary sold by a soldier who had received it for volunteering. J477/44, 22 January 1793, in Montigny as well a share was given to a military replacement.

77. Lefebvre, *Paysans du Nord*, p. 545–46.

78. Ibid., pp. 460–61, and Marcel Marion, *La Vente des biens nationaux pendant la Révolution* (Geneva, 1974, orig. pub., Paris, 1908), pp. 103–5. Unlike Lefebvre, Marion believes that the peasantry benefited from the fall in value of the *assignats*. Lefebvre contends that they paid too quickly to take full advantage of the devaluation, although he concedes that land in Cambrésis sold for only one-sixth of its value.

79. Marion, *La Vente des biens nationaux,* p. 202.

80. Lefebvre, *Paysans du Nord*, pp. 615, 734.

81. Marion, *La Vente des biens nationaux,* p. 88. The peasants of Ligny refused to pay the tithe in 1789 and 1790, L12412 (12 October 1791).

82. Ibid., p. 88.

83. Lefebvre, *Paysans du Nord*, p. 448.

84. Ibid., p. 543, my emphasis.

85. Ibid., pp. 427–28.

86. Ibid., p. 506.

87. Marion, *La Vente des biens nationaux,* p. 201. Such sentiments are shared by most historians. See Maurice Agulhon in E. Juillard, ed., *Histoire de la France rurale,* III (Paris, 1976), 47; Albert Soboul in Soboul et al., *Histoire écono-mique et sociale de la France,* III, part 1 (Paris, 1976), 23; Vovelle, *La chute de la monarchie,* p. 193. P. M. Jones, *The Peasantry in the French Revolution* (Cambridge, 1988), pp. 156–58, supports Lefebvre's view on Cambrésis peasant purchases and cites alternative models for other regions.

88. L1794, 17 Nivôse IV (1796).

89. L1794.

90. J477/44.

91. Constant Lantier, called a cultivateur from 1812 on; Alexandre Rousseau, assistant mayor and farmer as of 1820; Jean Baptiste Gave, farmer after 1819. J857/6.

92. L6551.

93. L6651.

94. Dieudonné, *Statistique,* II, 278–82. The negative impact of the Revolution is described in Philippe Guignet, "Adaptations, mutations et survivances

proto-industrielles dans le textile du Cambrésis et du Valenciennois du
XVIIIe siècle au début du XXe siècle," *Revue du Nord* 61 (1979): 36–37; and
by Lefebvre, *Paysans du Nord,* pp. 734–35.

95. L6859, L6858, L6861. Some 5,500 livres were reimbursed for losses of
    more than 72,000 livres.
96. Levavasseur, Cambrai notary, 12 Pluviôse IV.
97. L13415, 1 Ventôse III, in Caullery.
98. L13412, 10 October 1791 and L13413, 10 October 1793.
99. L13412, 9 August 1791, Clary: a debt of 119 livres for yarn delivered
    between January and June 1790; 18 August 1791, Clary: goods worth 51
    livres 75 sous.
100. L13412, he was owed 222 livres.
101. L13412, 16 August 1791.
102. L13411, 28 Fructidor II, Serain and Elincourt.
103. Levavasseur, Cambrai notary, 12 September 1792, in Carnières.
104. L13411, 25 Brumaire III, Villers-Outréaux.
105. L13412, 19 April 1791. The yarn merchant Joseph Chartriaux was pursued
    for a debt of 692 livres 17 sous; Levavasseur, inventory of 22–23 Prairial II:
    three Caudry residents owed the merchant-weaver Antoinette Payen 10,
    360, and 755 livres, respectively, for yarn.
106. Levavasseur, 29 April 1790.
107. Levavasseur, 11 Vendémiaire IV.
108. J857/6. Unfortunately, we know nothing about their activities.
109. The relevant document could not be located.
110. L13411, 1 Floréal III.
111. J857/5. That is how he was referred to in the parish register.
112. Lefebvre, *Paysans du Nord,* pp. 608–9, late 1791–early 1792.
113. L1793, 19 Frimaire IV.
114. L6859. His losses of nearly 10,000 livres, however, did not compare with the
    37,294 loss sustained by Milot and 27,174 livres by Joseph Petit, both
    farmers at Le Troncquoy. L3221.
115. J857/6, profession given at Jean Baptiste Lantier's funeral on 1 May 1808.
116. 0416/64 and 0416/72 and 73.
117. *Annuaire statistique du département du Nord* (Lille, 1833), pp. 346–51.
118. Ibid., pp. 160–62. These grievances are similar to those noted by Reddy, *Rise
    of Market Culture.*
119. "Résumé des enquêtes ouvertes dans l'arrondissement de Cambrai sur l'or-
    ganisation du travail industriel et agricole," *Mémoires de la Société d'Emula-
    tion de Cambrai* 22 (1849): 149–81. The original is found in M547 (12 June
    1849). "Subcontracting is especially common in the cantons of Clary and of
    Le Cateau. The workers ask their employers to subcontract work to them
    which they then give out to others and on which they make at least 10% per
    meter and often even more," p. 163.

120. J857/10 cadastre.

121. *Annuaire statistique du département du Nord,* 1833, p. 78.

122. "Résumé des enquêtes," p. 179.

123. Ibid., p. 159.

124. Based on the 1787 tax roll.

125. "Résumé des enquêtes," p. 179.

126. Ibid., pp. 165–66.

127. The following discussion summarizes the tables annexed to the report, pp. 176–81.

128. Duthoit, *Montigny-en-Cambrésis,* p. 80.

129. Ibid., p. 82.

Conclusion

1. For a recent description of the process, see Jacques Bottin, "Structures et mutations d'un espace protoindustriel à la fin du XVIe siècle," *Annales, economies, sociétés, civilisations* (1988), pp. 975–95.

2. See Reddy, *Rise of Market Culture,* and Michael D. Sibalis, "Corporations After the Corporations: The Debate on Restoring the Guilds Under Napoleon I and the Restoration," *French Historical Studies* 15 (1988): 718–30.

Bibliography

I. Primary Sources

Archival sources

Archives départementales du Nord

Series B

VIIIB 1e série: 3336, 4373, 4579, 6096, 7001, 8020, 8420, 8918, 9145, 9385, 9434, 9438, 9442, 9443, 9448, 9485, 9500, 9519, 9532, 9547, 9553, 9574, 9582, 9638, 10317, 10617, 11006, 11150, 11340, 12435, 13451, 13918, 13984, 14013, 14040, 14283, 14800, 14876, 14947, 16099, 16643, 18548, 19524, 19568, 20662, 21893, 22052, 22098, 22804, 23178, 23799, 25050, 25075, 25177, 26799, 27622, 28031, 29016, 29233, 28447, 29900, 30442.
VIIIB 1e série: 631 (folio 224), 678 (folio 5), 680 (folio 509), 684 (folio 438), 788 (folio 185).
IXB 276/128, 276/149, 276/172.

Series C

Intendance, Flandres: 3987, 5269, 5444, 5791, 6586, 6974, 7085, 9155, 10243, 10306, 11243.
Intendance, Cambrésis: 14162, 14785, 14908, 15186, 15478, 15572, 15753, 15757, 15840, 15868, 16008, 16012, 16113, 16532, 16576, 16637, 16651, 16673, 16706, 16856, 16883, 16916, 16957, 17213, 17217, 17438, 17503, 17623, 17642, 17785, 18161, 18172, 18368, 18392, 18492, 18496, 18508, 18609, 18610, 18971, 19203–5, 19257, 19576–77, 19600, 19602, 19683, 19706–7, 20059, 20250, 20279, 20299, 20411–12, 20576, 20579, 20776, 20847, 20869, 20969, 21042–43, 21158, 21170, 21175, 21182, 21220.
C Intendance Cambrésis, Registres: 493, 632, 635.
C Intendance, Bureau des finances, fiefs: 3554.
C Intendance Cambrésis, supplément: 406, 429, 474, 492, 500, 503, 524.
C états: 9, 111, 208–10, 269, 270, 288, 727, 730, 736, 739.

Series E

1555, 1894, 2276/2, 2565/35, 2465/45.
2E26/540

Cambrésis notaries now classified in Series 2E/26:
   Bancelin, 1777–81
   Baret, 1760, 1771, 1774–78
   Boursier, Jean and Antoine, 1677–1704
   Cardon, 1765–93
   Caudron, 1745–92
   Dejardin, 1767–91
   Gave, Etienne, 1671–95
   Leducq, Pierre, 1702–55
   Leducq, Charles-Antoine, 1759–91
   Leroy, 1787–91
   Levavasseur, 1788–95
   Magniez, 1783–88
   Mairesse, François, 1671–96
   Regnart, Paul, 1631–45
   Watier, 1773–87

Series G

3G: 633, 775, 793–99, 863–75, 886–90, 1238, 1869, 2085, 2762, 2853–54.
4G: 322, 508, 1681, 2059, 2075, 2113, 2124, 2135–66, 2218, 2268, 2275, 2324, 2343–45, 2435, 2442, 2447–48, 2833, 2844, 2847–49, 2860, 3036, 3297–3307, 3756, 4064, 4265–66, 4550, 6047, 6366–67, 6557, 6575, 6603, 6651–744, 6826, 7340–48, 7778.
5G: 1, 45, 125, 132, 165–67, 169, 170, 172–73, 176–77, 179, 199, 202, 215, 272, 324–50, 355, 443, 504, 517, 519, 545, 571.

Series H

1H: 144, 208, 289, 497, 507, 539, 574, 668–69, 671.
1H supplement: 9.
7H: 2, 11, 122, 154–55, 194.
7H supplement: 1, 5.
8H: 147, 382–83, 388, 681.
37H: 152, 193, 229.
50H 93.
65H 13.

Series J

477/44, 857/1–11.

Series L

106 (fol. 102), 107 (fol. 7), 111 (fol. 39), 115 (fol. 23), 120 (fol. 129–30), 143 (fol. 39), 627, 1104, 1183, 1188/55, 1189/3, 1202/14, 1204/27, 1341–42,

1462, 1505, 1645, 1699, 1793–94, 1831, 1840, 1858, 2496, 2679, 3221, 3279, 3433, 3577, 3731, 4263, 5062, 5241, 5384, 5387, 5428, 6358–59, 6389, 6398–99, 6450, 6457, 6544, 6551, 6591, 6593–98, 6600, 6606–69, 6613, 6615–57, 6629, 6633, 6636–45, 6647, 6650, 6652, 6656, 6682, 6698, 6715, 6721–24, 6729–30, 6757, 6787, 6844, 6856, 6858–60, 6865–66, 6888, 6896, 6912, 6933, 6949, 6978–82, 10338, 11246, 11967, 12378–79, 12465, 12887–93, 13168, 13329, 13408–15.

Series M

M2/4, M65/20, M95/6, M98/8, M99/433, M140/19, M222/155, M226/150, M226/785, M262/1–3, M278/4, M305/16, M3–5/25, M316/1, M417/ 1590, M417/1721, M473/7, M528/2, M547/1, M581/166, M581/188, M641/9, M641/20, M642/2, M651/24, M653/18, M653/38.

Series O

416/11, 65, 67–86.

Series Q

95, 121, 123–26, 158–59, 167, 174, 778, 781–82, 797, 801–2, 806, 848, 867, 872, 884, 903–4, 917, 932, 944, 948, 951, 956–57, 965, 978, 1050–51, 1216, 1409, 1412.

Series T

253/13.

Series U

3U 145/10, 30–40. 7U 57.

Series Z

4838–40.

Cumulus

18548.

Officialité

298, 509, 542, 832, 845, 986, 1017, 1261, 1293, 1511, 1576, 1650, 1882, 2065, 2151, 2169, 2725, 2756, 2823, 2906, 3024–25, 3261, 3285, 3335, 3403, 3463, 3686, 3759, 3908, 3939, 4000, 4342, 4427, 4557, 4611, 4826, 5077, 5099, 5110, 5533, 5556, 5913, 5886, 6031, 6180, 6208, 6356, 6525, 6740, 7140, 7164, 7254, 7260, 7596, 7717, 7837, 7844, 7869, 7953–54, 8215, 8605, 8682, 8785, 8787, 9029–30, 9085, 9113, 9174, 9455, 9643, 10399, 10633, 10707,

10945, 11077, 11096, 11300, 11331, 11369, 11515, 11794, 11983, 12180,
12322, 12848, 12905, 12952, 13012, 13073, 14009, 14139, 14238, 14502,
14613, 14735, 14769, 14879, 14976, 15452, 15534, 15707, 15879, 15938,
16028, 16203, 16446, 16459, 16794, 17377, 17508, 17860, 18098, 18112,
18174, 18374, 18460, 18670, 18732, 18808, 18817, 18930, 19219, 19365,
19566, 19600, 19632, 19713, 19984, 20193, 20429, 20688, 20709, 20714,
20876, 21006, 21024, 21484, 22149, 22567, 22593.

Archives nationales

E1433, E1658B, F12 646, F12 658B, F12 660, H1 1485, V6 1147, V6 1150, V6
1152–53.

II. Primary Printed Sources

Annuaires statistiques du département du Nord, 1802–3 to 1833.

Bonnassieux, Pierre. *Conseil de Commerce et Bureau de Commerce, Inventaire analytique des procès-verbaux.* Geneva, 1979.

Brayer, J. B. L. *Statistique du département de l'Aisne.* 2 vols. Laon, 1824–25.

Bruyelle. *Dictionnaire topographique de l'arrondissement de Cambrai.* Cambrai, 1860.

Dieudonné, Christophe. *Statistique du département du Nord.* 3 vols. Douai, 1804.

Gosselet, Jules. "Constitution géologique du Cambrésis." Part 3, Canton de Clary. *Mémoires de la Société d'Emulation de Cambrai* 31, 1 (1869): 387–406.

Le Carpentier, Jean. *Histoire généalogique des Pais Bas ou histoire de Cambrai et du Cambrésis.* 3 vols. Leiden, 1664.

"Statistique religieuse, administrative, militaire, agricole, industrielle et commerciale de Cambrai à la fin du XVIIIe siècle." *Mémoires de la Société d'Emulation de Cambrai* 25 (1856): 245–53.

Wilbert, Alex. "Résumé des enquêtes ouvertes dans l'arrondissement de Cambrai sur l'organisation du travail industriel et agricole." *Mémoires de la Société d'Emulation de Cambrai* 22 (1849): 147–74.

III. Secondary Sources

"Les Anciennes mesures de Cambrai et du Cambrésis." *Mémoires de la Société d'Emulation de Cambrai* 60 (1906): 33–53.

Abel, Wilhelm. *Agricultural Fluctuations in Europe from the Thirteenth to the Twentieth Centuries.* London, 1986. 3rd rev. ed., orig. pub. Hamburg and Berlin, 1966 and 1978.

Aminzade, Ronald. "Reinterpreting Capitalist Industrialization: A Study of Nine-teenth-Century France." *Social History* 9 (1984): 329–50.

Antoine, Michel. *Le Conseil du roi sous le règne de Louis XV.* Paris and Geneva, 1970.

Aston, T. H., and C. H. E. Philpin, eds. *The Brenner Debate: Agrarian Class Structure and Economic Development in Pre-Industrial Europe.* Cambridge, 1985.

Aymard, Maurice. "Autoconsommation et marchés: Chayanov, Labrousse ou Le Roy Ladurie?" *Annales, économies, sociétés, civilisations* (1983): 1392–1409.

Baheux, Jean Marie, and Gilles Deraugneaucourt. "Affaires de moeurs laïques et ecclésiastiques et mentalités populaires au XVIIe siècle d'après les archives de l'officialité métropolitaine de Cambrai." Mémoire de maîtrise, Lille, 1972.

Bajart, Léonce. *L'Industrie des tulles et dentelles en France, son établissement dans le Cambrésis, l'essor de Caudry.* Lille, 1953.

Bennassar, Bartolomé, and Joseph Goy. "Contributions à l'histoire de la consommation alimentaire du XIVe au XIXe siècle." *Annales, Economies, Sociétés, Civilisations* (1975): 402–32.

Berg, Maxine, Pat Hudson, and Michael Sonenscher. *Manufacture in Town and Country Before the Factory.* Cambridge, 1983.

———, *The Age of Manufactures, 1700–1820.* London, 1985.

Berkner, Lutz K. "The Stem Family and the Developmental Cycle of the Peasant Household: An Eighteenth-Century Austrian Example." *American Historical Review* 77 (1972): 398–418.

Bloch, Marc. *French Rural History: An Essay on Its Basic Characteristics.* Berkeley and Los Angeles, 1966. Orig. pub. Oslo, 1931.

Blum, Jerome. *The End of the Old Order in Rural Europe.* Princeton, N.J., 1978.

Bois, Paul. *Paysans de l'Ouest.* Paris, 1971.

Bordes, Maurice. *L'Administration provinciale et municipale en France au XVIIIe siècle.* Paris, 1972.

Bosher, J. F. *The Single Duty Project.* London, 1964.

Bossenga, Gail. *The Politics of Privilege: Old Regime and Revolution in Lille.* Cambridge, 1991.

———. "Protecting Merchants: Guilds and Commercial Capitalism in Eighteenth-Century France." *French Historical Studies* 15 (1988): 693–703.

Bossy, John, ed. *Disputes and Settlements: Law and Human Relations in the West.* Cambridge, 1983.

Bottin, Jacques. "Structures et mutations d'un espace protoindustriel à la fin du XVIe siècle." *Annales, économies, sociétés, civilisations* (1988): 975–95.

Bougard, Pierre." Dénombrement de la population du Cambrésis en 1778," in *Hommage à Marcel Reinhard: Sur la population français au XVIIIe et au XIXe siècles.* Paris, 1973. Pp. 71–89.

Bowden, Peter J. *Economic Change: Wages, Profits, and Rents, 1500–1750.* Cambridge, 1990.

Braudel, Fernand. *Capitalism and Material Life*. New York, 1973.

———. *L'Identité de la France*. 3 vols. Paris, 1986.

Bretzner, Victor. *Histoire de Masnières*. Cambrai, n.d.

Brewer, John, and John Styles, eds. *An Ungovernable People: The English and Their Laws in the Seventeenth and Eighteenth Centuries*. New Brunswick, N.J., 1980.

Bricout, Roger. "Le Développement de l'industrie des tulles, dentelles et broderies à Caudry et dans sa région au début du XIXe siècle à 1960." D.E.S., Lille, 1964.

Burney, Charles. *Music, Men, and Manners in France and Italy, 1770*. London, 1974.

Calonne, A. de. *La Vie agricole sous l'Ancien Régime dans le Nord de la France*. 2nd rev. ed. Paris, 1885.

Carrière, Charles, Marcel Courdurié, Michel Gutsatz, and René Squarzoni. *Banque et capitalisme commercial: La lettre de change au XVIIIe siècle*. Marseilles, 1976.

Caspard, Pierre. "La Fabrique au village." *Le Mouvement social* (1976): 14–37.

Castan, Nicole. *Les Criminels du Languedoc: Les exigences d'ordre et les voies du ressentiment dans une société pré-révolutionnaire (1750–1790)*. Toulouse, 1980.

———. *Justice et répression en Languedoc à l'époque des Lumières*. Paris, 1980.

———. and Yves Castan. *Vivre ensemble: Ordre et désordre en Languedoc (XVIIe–XVIIIe siècles)*. Paris, 1981.

Castan, Yves. *Honnêteté et relations sociales en Languedoc (1715–1718)*. Paris, 1974.

Chambers, J. D., and G. E. Mingay. *The Agricultural Revolution, 1750–1880*. London, 1966.

Châtelain, Abel. *Les Migrants temporaires en France*. 2 vols. Lille, 1976.

Chaussinand-Nogaret, Guy. *La Noblesse au XVIIIe siècle: De la féodalité aux lumières*. Paris, 1976.

Chayanov, A. V. *The Theory of Peasant Economy*, ed. Danier Thorner, Basile Kerblay, R. E. F. Smith. Homewood, Ill., 1966. Orig. Russian ed., 1925.

Clère, Jean-Jacques. *Les Paysans de la Haute-Marne et la Révolution française*. Paris, 1988.

Clifford, James, and George E. Marcus. *Writing Culture: The Poetics and Politics of Ethnography*. Berkeley and Los Angeles, 1986.

Cobb, Richard. *Paris and Its Provinces, 1791–1802*. London, 1975.

Coleman, D. C. "Proto-industrialization: A Concept Too Many." *Economic History Review* 36 (1983): 435–48.

Collins, James B. *Fiscal Limits of Absolutism: Direct Taxation in Early Seventeenth-Century France*. Berkeley and Los Angeles, 1988.

Coornaert, Emile. *Un Centre industriel d'autrefois, la draperie-sayetterie d'Hondschoote (XIVe–XVIIIe siècles)*. Paris, 1930.

Crouzet, François. "England and France in the Eighteenth Century: A Comparative Analysis of Two Economic Growths," in R. M. Hartwell, *The Causes of the Industrial Revolution in England*. London, 1967. Pp. 139–74.

Dailliez, G. "Les Etats généraux de Cambrai et du Cambrésis." *Mémoires de la Société d'Emulation de Cambrai* 61 (1907): 213–26.

Dalton, George, and Raymond Firth, eds. *Themes in Economic Anthropology.* London, 1967.

Darnton, Robert. *The Great Cat Massacre and Other Episodes in French Cultural History.* New York, 1984.

Delattre, Marc. "Le Régime seigneurial, la délinquance, les mentalités paysannes dans la châtellennie du Cateau-Cambrésis au XVIIIe siècle." Mémoire de maîtrise, Lille, 1970.

Delloye, Sylvie. "Problèmes matrimoniaux dans le ressort de l'officialité de Cambrai, 1670–1762. Vol. 1, Introduction générale, Les fiançailles." Mémoire de maîtrise, Lille, 1971.

Demangeon, Albert. *La Picardie et les régions voisines, Artois-Cambrésis-Beauvaisis.* Paris, 1973. Orig. publ. 1905.

Derouet, Bernard. "Une Démographie sociale différentielle: Clés pour un système autorégulateur des populations rurales d'ancien régime." *Annales, Economies, Sociétés, Civilisations* (1980): 3–41.

De Vries, Jan. *European Urbanization, 1500–1800.* Cambridge, Mass., 1984.

Dewald, Jonathan. *Pont-St.-Pierre, 1398–1789: Lordship, Community, and Capitalism in Early Modern France.* Berkeley and Los Angeles, 1987.

Deyon, Pierre. *Amiens, capitale provinciale: Etude sur la société urbaine au XVIIe siècle.* Paris, 1967.

———, ed. "Aux Origines de la Révolution industrielle," 2e fascicule No. spécial. *Revue du Nord* 63 (1981).

———, ed. "Aux Origines de la Révolution industrielle," 2nd fascicule No. spécial. *Revue du Nord* 63 (1981).

———. "La Diffusion rurale des industries textiles en Flandre française à la fin de l'ancien régime et au début du XIXe siècle." Paper presented at Wilmington, Del., December 1977.

Deyon, Solange, and Alain Lottin. *Les Casseurs de l'été 1566: L'iconoclasme dans le Nord de la France.* Paris, 1981.

Dolez, André. *La Mulquinerie à Cambrai des origines à 1789.* Lille, 1932.

Dornic, François. *L'Industrie textile dans le Maine et ses débouchés internationaux (1650–1815).* Le Mans, 1955.

Duchez, C. "Notice historique sur Beauvois." *Mémoires de la Société d'Emulation de Cambrai* 32 (1873): 283–553.

Dumas, Georges. "Emotions populaires en 1789–1790 dans le Laonnais et la Thiérache." *101e Congrès des Sociétés savantes.* Lille, 1976. Histoire moderne, vol. 2, 95–110.

Durieux, A. "Les Chants populaires du Cambrésis." *Mémoires de la Société d'Emulation de Cambrai* 41 (1885): xix–xl.

———. "La Disette à Cambrai en 1789 d'après des documents inédits." *Mémoires de la Société d'Emulation de Cambrai* 30 (1868): 147–219.

——. "Les Drapiers cambrésiens." *Mémoires de la Société d'Emulation de Cambrai* 41 (1885): 255–73.

——. "Les Etats provinciaux du Cambrésis." *Mémoires de la Société d'Emulation de Cambrai* 41 (1885): 131–245.

Duthoit, Abel, abbé. *Montigny-en-Cambrésis, sa géographie, son histoire, sa généalogie.* Cambrai, 1965.

Engrand, Charles. "Mendier sa vie au XVIIIe siècle: de la résignation à la révolte (Amiens, 1764–1789)." *Revue du Nord* 66 (1984): 515–29.

Fairchilds, Cissie C. *Poverty and Charity in Aix-en-Provence, 1640–1789.* Baltimore, 1976.

Flandrin, Jean-Louis. *Familles, parenté, maison, sexualité dans l'ancienne société.* 2nd ed. Paris, 1984.

Forster, Robert. "Obstacles to Agricultural Growth in Eighteenth-Century France." *American Historical Review* 75 (October 1970): 1600–1615.

Gamblin, A. "Le Contact Cambrésis-Thiérache." *Revue du Nord* 41 (1959): 33–48.

Gatrell, V. A. C., Bruce Lenman, and Geoffrey Parker, *Crime and the Law: The Social History of Crime in Western Europe Since 1500.* London, 1980.

Gauthier, Florence. "Formes d'évolution du système agraire communautaire en Picardie (fin XVIIIe-début XIXe siècle)." *Annales historiques de la Révolution française* (1980): 181–204.

——. *La Voie paysanne dans la Révolution française, l'exemple picard.* Paris, 1977.

Geertz, Clifford. *The Interpretation of Cultures.* New York, 1973.

Ginzburg, Carlo. *The Cheese and the Worms.* Baltimore, 1980.

Girard d'Albissin, Nelly. *Genèse de la frontière franco-belge.* Paris, 1970.

Godon, Suzanne. "Histoire religieuse du district de Cambrai de 1789 au 9 Thermidor an II." D.E.S., Lille, 1947.

Goldsmith, James L. "The Agrarian History of Pre-Industrial France: Where Do We Go From Here?" *Journal of European Economic History* 13 (1984): 175–99.

Goldstone, Jack. "Regional Ecology and Agrarian Change in England and France, 1500–1700." Paper presented at All-U.C. Conference in Economic History, Los Angeles, 22–24 May 1987.

Goody, Jack, Joan Thirsk, and C. P. Thompson. *Family and Inheritance: Rural Society in Western Europe, 1200–1800.* Cambridge, 1976.

Goubert, Pierre. *The Ancien Régime: French Society, 1600–1750.* New York, 1974. Orig. French ed., Paris, 1969.

——. *Cent mille provinciaux au XVIIe siècle: Beauvais et le Beauvaisis de 1600 à 1730.* Paris, 1968.

——. *The French Peasantry in the Seventeenth Century.* Cambridge, 1986. Orig. pub. Paris, 1982.

Goubert, Pierre, and Daniel Roche. *Les Français et l'ancien régime.* 2 vols. Paris, 1984.

Grafteaux, Serge. *Mémé Santerre*. Paris, 1975.

Grantham, George W. "Agricultural Supply During the Industrial Revolution: French Evidence and European Implications." *Journal of Economic History* 49 (1989): 43–72.

———. "The Diffusion of the New Husbandry in Northern France, 1815–1840." *Journal of Economic History* 38 (1978): 311–37.

———. "Jean Meuvret and the Subsistence Problem in Early Modern France." *Journal of Economic History* 49 (1989): 184–200.

Guignet, Philippe. "Adaptations, mutations et survivances proto-industrielles dans le textile du Cambrésis et du Valenciennois du XVIIIe siècle et au début du XXe siècle." *Revue du Nord* 61 (1979): 27–59.

———. *Mines, manufactures et ouvriers du Valenciennois au XVIIIe siècle: Contributions à l'histoire du travail dans l'ancienne France*. New York, 1977.

Gullickson, Gay. "Agricultural and Cottage Industry: Redefining the Causes of Proto-Industrialization." *Journal of Economic History* 41 (1983): 831–50.

———. *Spinners and Weavers of Auffay*. Cambridge, 1986.

Guttmann, Myron P. *Toward the Modern Economy in Europe, 1500–1800*. New York, 1988.

———. *War and Rural Life in the Early Modern Low Countries*. Princeton, N.J., 1980.

Gutton, Jean Pierre. *Domestiques et serviteurs dans la France de l'ancien régime*. Paris, 1981.

———. *La Sociabilité villageoise dans l'ancienne France*. Paris, 1979.

———. *La Société et les pauvres: l'exemple de la généralité de Lyon, 1534–1789*. Paris, 1971.

Harte, N. B., and K. G. Ponting, eds. *Textile History and Economic History: Essays in Honour of Miss Julia de Lacy Mann*. Manchester, 1973.

Hennequin, Gilles. "La Vie matérielle de l'abbaye de Cantimpré (Cambrai) vers le milieu du XVIIIe siècle." D.E.S., Lille, 1956.

Herbert, Géry. *Le Folklore du Cambrésis: Coutumes et traditions populaires*. Amiens, 1978.

Hilaire, Yves Marie. *Une Chrétienté au XIXe siècle? La Vie religieuse des populations du diocèse d'Arras (1840–1914)*. 2 vols. Lille, 1977.

Hilton, Rodney. *Bond Men Made Free*. London, 1973.

Hincker, François. *Les Français devant l'impôt sous l'ancien régime*. Paris, 1971.

Hirsch, Jean Pierre. "La France révolutionnaire, comme berceau de la libre entreprise." Paper presented at Bicentennial of French Revolution conference, Washington, D.C., May 1989.

Hodges, Richard. *Primitive and Peasant Markets*. (Oxford, 1988).

Hoffmann, Philip T. "Taxes and Agrarian Life in Early Modern France: Land Sales, 1550–1730." *Journal of Economic History* 46 (1986): 37–55.

———. "Institutions and Agriculture in Old-Regime France." Paper presented at All-U.C. Conference in Economic History, Los Angeles, 22–24 May 1987.

Holderness, B. A. "Credit in English Rural Society before the Nineteenth Century with Special Reference to the Period 1650–1720." *Agricultural History Review* (1976): 97–109.

Honorez, André. "Le Diocèse de Cambrai pendant l'épiscopat de Fénelon." D.E.S., Lille, 1961.

Hoppit, Julian. *Risk and Failure in English Business, 1700–1800.* Cambridge, 1987.

Hufton, Olwen H. "Le Paysan et la loi en France au XVIIIe siècle." *Annales, économies, sociétés, civilisations* (1983): 679–701.

———. *The Poor of Eighteenth-Century France, 1750–1789.* Oxford, 1974.

———. "Social Conflict and the Grain Supply in Eighteenth-Century France." *Journal of Interdisciplinary History* 14 (1983): 303–31.

Hunt, David. "Peasant Politics in the French Revolution." *Social History* 9 (1984): 277–99.

Hunt, Lynn, ed. *The New Cultural History.* Berkeley and Los Angeles, 1989.

Jacquart, Jean. *La Crise rurale en Ile-de-France, 1550–1670.* Paris, 1974.

Jeannin, Pierre. "La Proto-industrialisation: développement ou impasse?" *Annales, economies, sociétés, civilisations.* (1980): 52–65.

Jessenne, Jean-Pierre. "Le Pouvoir des fermiers dans les villages d'Artois 1770–1848." *Annales, économies, sociétés, civilisations* (1983): 702–34.

———. *Pouvoir au village et Révolution: Artois, 1760–1848.* Lille, 1987.

Jones, P. M. "Parish, Seigneurie, and the Community of Inhabitants in Southern Central France During the Eighteenth and Nineteenth Centuries." *Past and Present* (1981): 74–108.

———. *The Peasantry in the French Revolution.* Cambridge, 1988.

———. *Politics and Rural Society: The Southern Massif Central, c. 1750–1880.* Cambridge, 1985.

Juillard, Etienne, ed. *Histoire de la France rurale.* Vol. 3. Paris, 1976.

Kagan, Richard L. *Lawsuits and Litigants in Castile, 1500–1700.* Chapel Hill, N.C., 1981.

Kaplan, Steven L. *Provisioning Paris: Merchants and Millers in the Grain and Flour Trade During the Eighteenth Century.* Ithaca, N.Y., 1984.

Krafft Pourrat, Claire. *Le Colporteur et la mercière.* Paris, 1982.

Kriedte, Peter, Hans Medick, and Jürgen Schlumbohm. *Industrialization Before Industrialization.* Cambridge, 1981. Orig. German ed., 1977.

Labrousse, Ernest. *Esquisse du mouvement des prix et des revenus en France au XVIIIe siècle.* 2 vols. Paris, 1933.

———, et al. *Histoire économique et sociale de la France.* Vol. 2. Paris, 1970.

Laslett, Peter. "Le Brassage de la population en France et en Angleterre aux XVIIe et XVIIIe siècles: Comparaison préliminaire de villages français et anglais." *Annales de démographie historique* (1968): 99–109.

Lecuppe, Françoise. "Les Suspects dans le district de Cambrai de 1789 au 9 Thermidor an II." D.E.S., Lille 1954.

Lefebvre, George. *Les Paysans du Nord pendant la Révolution française*. Paris, 1972. Orig. ed., 1924.

———. *Questions agraires au temps de la terreur*. 2nd ed. La Roche sur Yon, 1954.

Legrand Louis. *Sénac de Meilhan et l'intendance du Hainaut et du Cambrésis sous Louis XVI*. Valenciennes, 1868.

Le Goff, T. J. A. *Vannes and Its Region: A Study of Town and Country in Eighteenth-Century France*. Oxford, 1981.

Le Goff, T. J. A., and D. M. G. Sutherland. "The Revolution and the Rural Community in Eighteenth-Century Brittany." *Past and Present* 62 (1974): 96–119.

Le Roy Ladurie, Emmanuel. *The French Peasantry, 1450–1660*. Berkeley, 1987. Orig. French ed., 1977.

———, ed. *Histoire de la France rurale*. Vol. 2. Paris, 1975.

———. "Révoltes et contestations paysannes en France de 1675 à 1788," *Annales, économies, sociétés, civilisations*. (1974): 6–22.

Levine, David. *Family Formation in an Age of Nascent Capitalism*. New York, 1977.

———. "Industrialization and the Proletarian Family in England." *Past and Present* (1985): 168–203.

———. "The Peasant Family and the "Cottage Economy": The Political Economy of English Population History." Paper presented at All-U.C. Conference in Economic History, Los Angeles, 22–24 May 1987.

Lottin, Alain, et al. *La Désunion du couple sous l'Ancien Régime: L'Exemple du Nord*. Lille, 1975.

———. *Les Grandes batailles du Nord*. (Paris, 1984).

Luria, Keith P. *Territories of Grace: Cultural Change in the Seventeenth-Century Diocese of Grenoble*. Berkeley and Los Angeles, 1991.

McCay, Bonnie, J., and James M. Acheson. *The Question of the Commons: The Culture and Ecology of Communal Resources*. Tucson, 1987.

McCloskey, Donald N. "The Persistence of English Common Fields," in William N. Parker and Eric L. Jones, eds., *European Peasants and Their Markets*. Princeton, N.J., 1975. Pp. 73–119.

Macfarlane, Alan. *The Origins of English Individualism*. Cambridge, 1978.

McPhee, Peter. "On Rural Politics in Nineteenth-Century France: The Example of Rodès, 1789–1851." *Comparative Studies in Society and History* 23 (1981): 248–77.

Marion, Marcel. *La Vente des biens nationaux pendant la Révolution*. Geneva, 1974. Orig. pub., Paris, 1908.

Mathias, Peter, and Patrick O'Brien. "Taxation in Britain and France, 1715–1810: A Comparison of the Social and Economic Incidence of Taxes Collected for the Central Governments." *Journal of European Economic History* 5 (1976): 601–50.

Medick, Hans. "The Proto-Industrial Family Economy: The Structural Function of Household and Family during the Transition from Peasant Society to Industrial Capitalism." *Social History* 1 (1976): 291–315.

Meijers, E. M. *Le Droit coutumier de Cambrai.* Vol. 2. Haarlem, 1955.

Mendels, Franklin. "Agriculture and Peasant Industry in Eighteenth-Century Flanders," in William N. Parker and Eric L. Jones, *European Peasants and Their Markets.* Princeton, N.J., 1975. Pp. 179–204.

———. "Industrialization and Population Pressure in Eighteenth-Century Flanders." Unpublished Ph.D. diss., University of Wisconsin, 1970.

———. "Niveau des salaires et âge au mariage en Flandre, XVIIe–XVIIIe siècles." *Annales, économies, sociétés, civilisations* (1984): 939–56.

———. "Proto-Industrialization, the First Phase of the Industrialization Process." *Journal of Economic History* 32 (1972): 241–61.

Meuvret, Jean. *Etudes d'histoire économique.* Paris, 1972.

———. *Le Problème des subsistances à l'époque de Louis XIV.* 6 vols. Paris, 1977–88.

Mingay, G. E., ed. *The Agrarian History of England and Wales.* Vol. 6, 1750–1850. Cambridge, 1989.

Mintz, Sidney W. "A Note on the Definition of Peasantries." *Journal of Peasant Studies* 1 (1973): 90–106.

Morineau, Michel. "Cambrésis et Hainaut: des frères ennemis?" *Revue historique* (1977): 323–43.

———. "La Dîme et l'enjeu." *Annales historiques de la Révolution française* (1980): 161–80.

———. *Les Faux-semblants d'un démarrage économique: Agriculture et démographie en France au XVIIIe siècle.* Paris, 1971.

Muchembled, Robert. *L'Invention de l'homme moderne.* Paris, 1988.

Muchembled, Robert, et al. *Prophètes et sorciers dans les Pays-Bas XIVe–XVIIIe siècles.* Paris, 1978.

Muller, C. Robert, and A. Allix. *Les Colporteurs de l'Oisans.* Grenoble, 1979.

Neveux, Hughes. "L'alimentation du XIVe au XVIIIe siècle: Essai de mise au point." *Revue d'histoire économique et sociale* (1973): 336–79.

———. "La Production céréalière dans une région frontalière: le Cambrésis du XVe au XVIIIe siècle: Bilan provisioire," in J. Goy and E. Le Roy Ladurie, *Les Fluctuations du produit de la dîme.* Paris, 1972. Pp. 58–66.

———. *Vie et déclin d'une structure économique: Les grains du Cambrésis fin du XIVe–début du XVIIe siècle.* Paris, 1980.

Nicolas, Jean, ed. *Mouvements populaires et conscience sociale, XVIe–XIXe siècles.* Paris, 1985.

Norberg, Kathryn. *Rich and Poor in Grenoble, 1600–1814.* Berkeley and Los Angeles, 1985.

O'Brien, P. K., and C. Keyder. *Economic Growth in Britain and France, 1780–1914.* London, 1976.

Parker, Harold T. *The Bureau of Commerce in 1781 and Its Policies with Respect to French Industry.* Durham, N.C., 1979.

Picard, Charles. *Saint-Quentin, de son commerce et de ses industries.* 2 vols. Saint-Quentin, 1865.

Pierrard, Pierre. *Histoire des diocèses de Cambrai et de Lille.* Paris, 1978.

Platelle, Henri. "Cambrai et le Cambrésis au XVe siècle." *Revue du Nord* 58 (July–September, 1976): 349–81.

———. *Journal d'un curé de campagne au XVIIe siècle.* Présentation, édition et notes par Henri Platelle. Paris, 1965.

Poitrineau, Abel. *Remues d'hommes: Essai sur les migrations montagnardes en France au XVIIe et au XVIIIe siècles.* Paris, 1983.

Polanyi, Karl. *The Great Transformation.* London, 1946.

Popkin, Samuel L. *The Rational Peasant: The Political Economy of Rural Society in Vietnam.* Berkeley and Los Angeles, 1979.

Postan, M. M. *The Medieval Economy and Society.* Harmondsworth, 1972.

Poussou, Jean-Pierre. "Les Mouvements migratoires en France et à partir de la France de la fin du XVe au début du XIXe siècle: approches pour une synthèse." *Annales de démographie historique* (1970): 11–78.

Price, Roger. *The Modernization of Rural France: Communications Networks and Agricultural Market Structures in Nineteenth-Century France.* New York, 1983.

Reddy, William. *The Rise of Market Culture: The Textile Trade and French Society, 1750–1900.* Cambridge, 1984.

Redfield, Robert. *Peasant Society and Culture.* Chicago, 1956.

La Révolution française et le monde rural. Actes du Colloque tenu en Sorbonne, 23–25 October 1987. Paris, 1989.

Root, Hilton L. "Challenging the Seigneurie: Community and Contention on the Eve of the French Revolution." *Journal of Modern History* 57 (1985): 652–81.

———. *Peasants and King in Burgundy: Agrarian Foundations of French Absolutism.* Berkeley and Los Angeles, 1987.

Roover, Raymond de. *L'Evolution de la lettre de change, XIVe–XVIIIe siècles.* Paris, 1953.

Russell, Sir John E. *The World of the Soil.* London, 1961.

Sabean, David W. *Property, Production, and Family in Neckerhausen, 1700–1870.* Cambridge, 1990.

Sahlins, Marshall. *Historical Metaphors and Mythical Realities.* Ann Arbor, Mich., 1981.

———. *Islands of History.* Chicago, 1985.

Saint-Jacob, Pierre de. *Les Paysans de la Bourgogne du Nord au dernier siècle de l'Ancien Régime.* Dijon, 1960.

Schlumbohm, Jürgen. "Rationalité économique et rationalité sociale des producteurs protoindustriels: L'exemple des tisserands ruraux sur le marché des toiles d'Osnabruck au début du XIXe siècle." Paper presented at meeting of Learned Societies, Montreal. 1985.

————. "Propriété foncière et production des toiles dans les campagnes environ-nant Osnabruck et Bielefield au début du XIXe siècle," in *Actes du Colloque de Tourcoing, 17–18 February 1983*. Pp. 51–74.

Schumacher, Jean Louis. "Le bas clergé dans le diocèse de Cambrai à la veille de la Révolution." D.E.S., Lille, 1968.

Schwartz, Robert M. *Policing the Poor in Eighteenth-Century France*. Chapel Hill, N.C., 1988.

Scott, James C. *The Moral Economy of the Peasant*. New Haven, Conn., 1976.

Segalen, Martine. *Mari et femme dans la société paysanne*. Paris, 1980.

Sewell, William S. *Work and Revolution in France, the Language of Labor from the Old Regime to 1848*. Cambridge, 1980.

Shanin, Theodor, ed. *Peasants and Peasant Societies*. Harmondsworth, 1971; Oxford, 1987.

Sharpe, John. "The People and the Law," in Barry Reay, ed., *Popular Culture in Seventeenth-Century England*. New York, 1985.

Sheppard, Thomas. *Lourmarin in the Eighteenth Century: A Study of a French Village*. Baltimore, 1971.

Shorter, Edward. *The Making of the Modern Family*. New York, 1975.

Sibalis, Michael D. "Corporations After the Corporations: The Debate on Restoring the Guilds under Napoleon I and the Restoration." *French Historical Studies* 15 (1988): 718–30.

Sigaut, François. "Pour une cartographie des assolements en France au début du XIXe siècle." *Annales, économies, sociétés, civilisations* (1976): 631–43.

Sivery, Gérard. *Structures agraires et vie rurale dans la Hainaut à la fin du Moyen Age*. 2 vols. Lille, 1973.

Slack, Paul. *Poverty and Policy in Tudor and Stuart England*. London and New York, 1988.

Slicher van Bath, B. H. *The Agrarian History of Western Europe, A.D. 500–1850*. London, 1963.

Soboul, Albert, ed. *Contributions à l'histoire paysanne de la Révolution française*. Paris, 1977.

————. et al. *Histoire économique et sociale de la France*. Vol. 3. Paris, 1976.

————. "Le Village à la fin de l'Ancien Régime," in *Le Village en France et en URSS des origines à nos jours*. Vol. 2. Toulousse, 1975. Pp. 225–64.

Sonenscher, Michael. *Work and Wages: Natural Law, Politics and the Eighteenth-Century French Trades*. Cambridge, 1989.

Spagnoli, Paul. "Industrialization, Proletarianization, and Marriage, A Reconsideration." *Journal of Family History* 8 (1981): 230–47.

Spufford, Margaret. *The Great Reclothing of Rural England: Petty Chapmen and Their Wares in the Seventeenth Century*. London, 1984.

Tarlé, E. *L'Industrie rurale en France à la fin de l'Ancien Régime*. Paris, 1910.

Taylor, William. *Drinking, Homicide, and Rebellion in Colonial Mexican Villages*. Stanford, Calif., 1979.

Terrier, Didier. "Mulquiniers et gaziers, les deux phases de la proto-industrie textile dans la région de Saint-Quentin, 1730–1850." *Revue du Nord* 65 (1983): 535–53.

Thompson, E. P. "The Moral Economy of the English Crowd in the Eighteenth Century." *Past and Present* (1971).

Thomson, T. K. J. *Clermont-de-Lodève, 1663–1789: Fluctuations in the Prosperity of a Languedocian Cloth-Making Town.* Cambridge, 1982.

Thelliez, C., abbé. "De l'Etat civil de Ligny-en-Cambrésis." *Mémoires de la Société d'Emulation de Cambrai.* 62 (1936): 128–42.

———. *Histoire de Caullery.* Caullery, 1962.

Thirsk, Joan. *Economic Policy and Projects: The Development of a Consumer Society in Early Modern England.* Oxford, 1978.

Tilly, Charles. *The Contentious French.* Cambridge, Mass., 1985.

———. "Flows of Capital and Forms of Industry in Europe." *Theory and Society* 12 (1983): 123–42.

Tilly, Louise, and Joan Scott. *Women, Work and Family.* New York, 1978.

Tits-Dieuade, Marie Jeanne. "L'Evolution des techniques agraires en Flandre et en Brabant, XIVe–XVIe siècle." *Annales, économies, sociétés, civilisations* (1981): 362–81.

Trénard, Louis, et al. *Histoire de Cambrai.* Lille, 1982.

Troyansky, David G. *Old Age in the Old Regime: Image and Experience in Eighteenth-Century France.* Ithaca, N.Y., 1989.

Vardi, Liana. "The Abolition of the Guilds During the French Revolution." *French Historical Studies* 15 (1988): 704–17.

———. "Peasants and the French Revolution: A Re-examination of Lefebvre's *Les Paysans du Nord*." Paper presented at Bicentennial of the French Revolution conference. Washington, D.C., May 1989.

———. "Peasants and the Law: A Village Appeals to the French Royal Council, 1768–91." *Social History* 13 (1988): 295–313.

Vovelle, Michel. *La chute de la monarchie (1787–1792).* Paris, 1972.

Weber, Eugene. *Peasants into Frenchmen: The Modernization of Rural France, 1870–1914.* Stanford, Calif., 1976.

Weller, Robert P., and Scott E. Guggenheim, eds. *Power and Protest in the Countryside.* Durham, N.C., 1982.

Williams, Dale Edwards. "Morals, Markets and the English Crowd in 1766." *Past and Present* (1984): 56–73.

Wodarczyck-Delmotte, Marie Claude, and Armelle Essique. "La Situation sociale des curés dépendant du chapitre cathédral de Cambrai au XVIIe et XVIIIe siècles." Mémoire de maîtrise, Lille, 1978.

Wolf, Eric. *Europe and the People Without History.* Berkeley, 1988.

———. *Peasants.* Englewood Cliffs, N.J., 1966.

Wrightson, Keith. *English Society, 1580–1680.* London, 1982.

Wrightson, Keith, and David Levine. *Poverty and Piety in an English Village: Terling, 1525–1700*. New York, 1979.

Yver, Jean. *Egalité entre héritiers et exclusion des enfants dotés: Essai de géographie coutumière*. Paris, 1966.

Young, Arthur. *Travels in France and Italy During the Years 1787–1788–1789*. Ed. with introduction by Jeffry Kaplow. New York, 1969.

Index

About the Author
Liana Vardi is Assistant Professor of History
at McMaster University in Hamilton, Ontario.

Library of Congress Cataloging-in-Publication Data

Vardi, Liana.
The land and the loom : peasants and profit in northern France, 1680–1800 / Liana
Vardi.
p.   cm.
Includes bibliographical references and index.
ISBN 0-8223-1284-0
1. Peasantry—France—Montigny-en-Cambrésis—History.   2. Montigny-en-
Cambrésis (France)—Industries, Rural—History.   3. Peasantry—France—Cambrésis—
History.   4. Cambrésis (France)—Industries, Rural—History.   I. Title.
HD1536.F8V37   1993
305.5′633′094428—dc20   92-23231
                                                                              CIP